URI ODETTE

Vol. 2

Julietta Suzuki

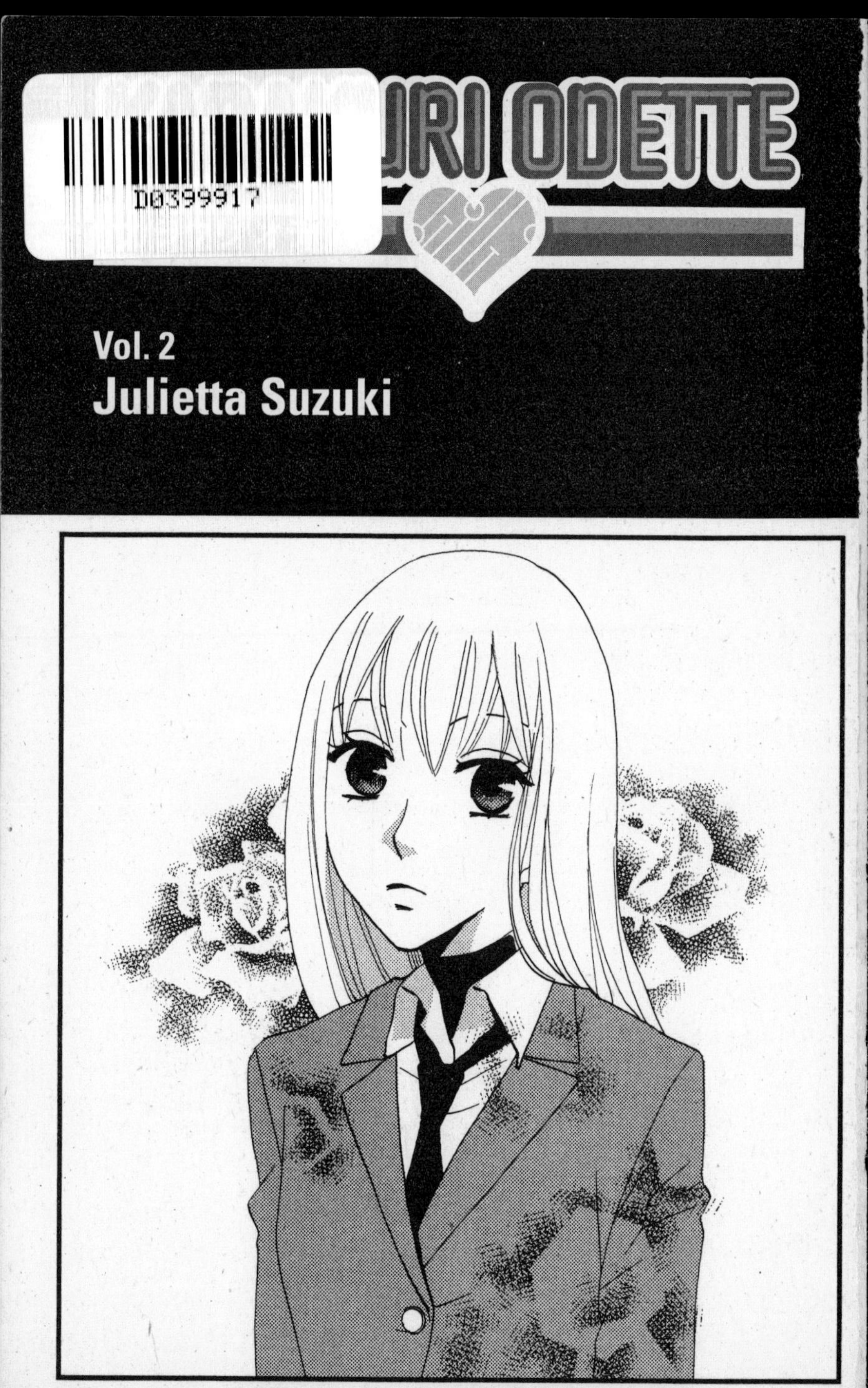

Karakuri Odette Volume 2
Created by Julietta Suzuki

Translation - Aimi Tokutake
English Adaptation - Peter Ahlstrom
Retouch and Lettering - Star Print Brokers
Production Artist - Rui Kyo
Graphic Designer - Al-Insan Lashley

Editor - Lillian Diaz-Przybyl
Print Production Manager - Lucas Rivera
Managing Editor - Vy Nguyen
Senior Designer - Louis Csontos
Art Director - Al-Insan Lashley
Director of Sales and Manufacturing - Allyson De Simone
Associate Publisher - Marco F. Pavia
President and C.O.O. - John Parker
C.E.O. and Chief Creative Officer - Stu Levy

A **TOKYOPOP** Manga

TOKYOPOP and 🐸 are trademarks or registered trademarks of TOKYOPOP Inc.

TOKYOPOP Inc.
5900 Wilshire Blvd. Suite 2000
Los Angeles, CA 90036

E-mail: info@TOKYOPOP.com
Come visit us online at www.TOKYOPOP.com

ISBN: 978-1-4278-1408-1

First TOKYOPOP printing: February 2010
10 9 8 7 6 5 4 3 2 1
Printed in the USA

KARAKURI ODETTE

カラクリ オデット

Vol. 2

by Julietta Suzuki

HAMBURG // LONDON // LOS ANGELES // TOKYO

Contents

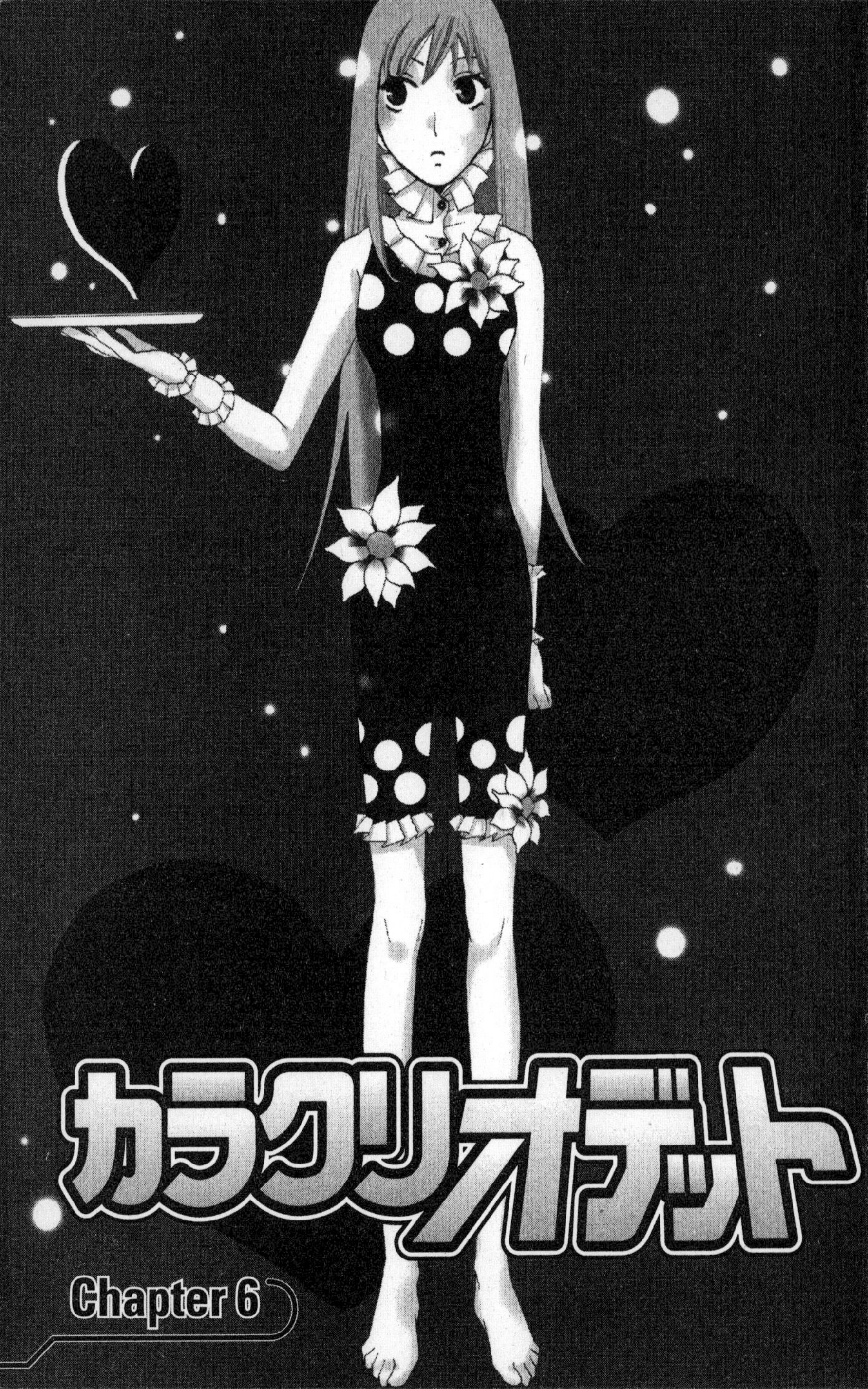
カラクリオデット
Chapter 6

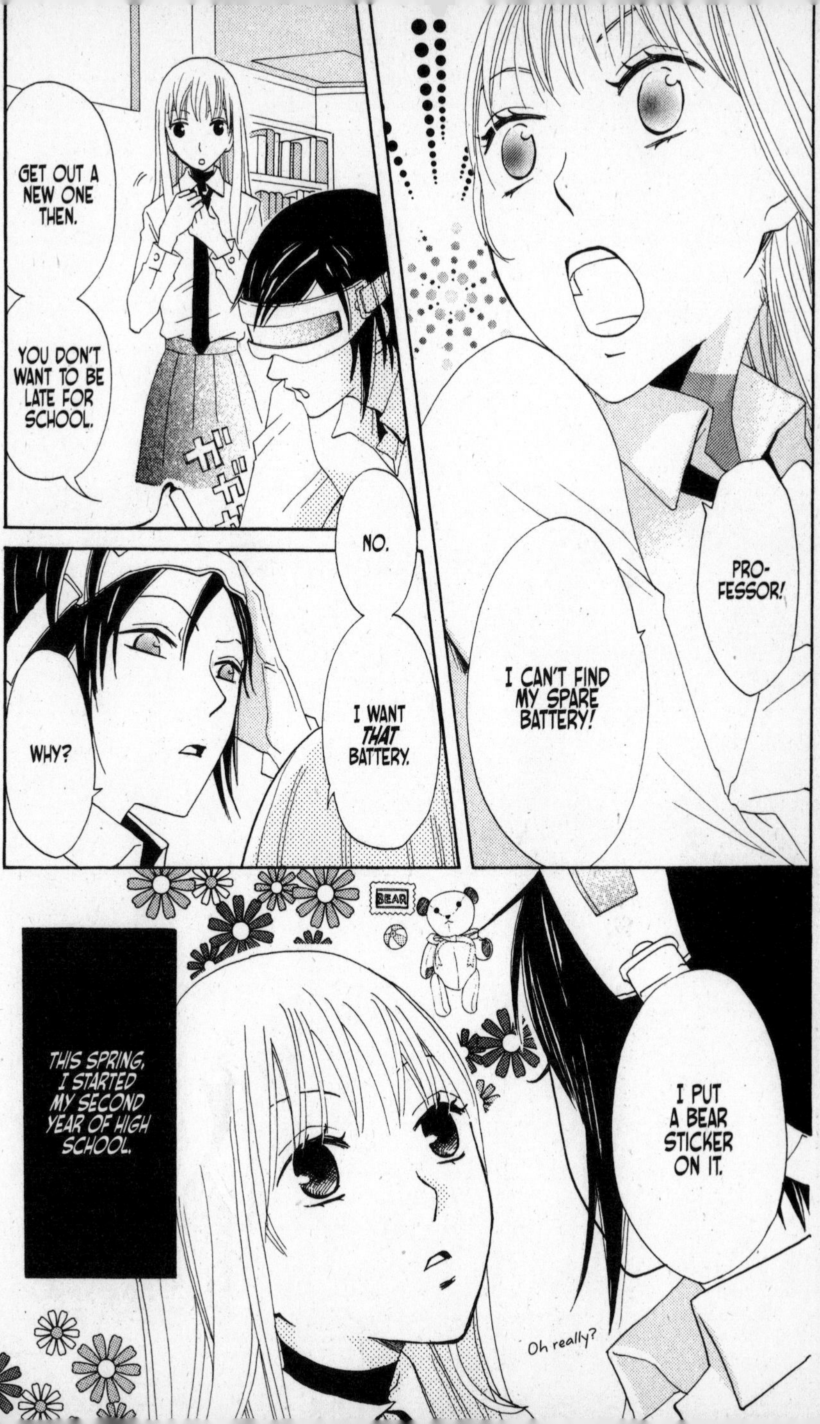
PRO-FESSOR!
I CAN'T FIND MY SPARE BATTERY!
GET OUT A NEW ONE THEN.
YOU DON'T WANT TO BE LATE FOR SCHOOL.
NO.
I WANT *THAT* BATTERY.
WHY?
I PUT A BEAR STICKER ON IT.
BEAR
Oh really?
THIS SPRING, I STARTED MY SECOND YEAR OF HIGH SCHOOL.

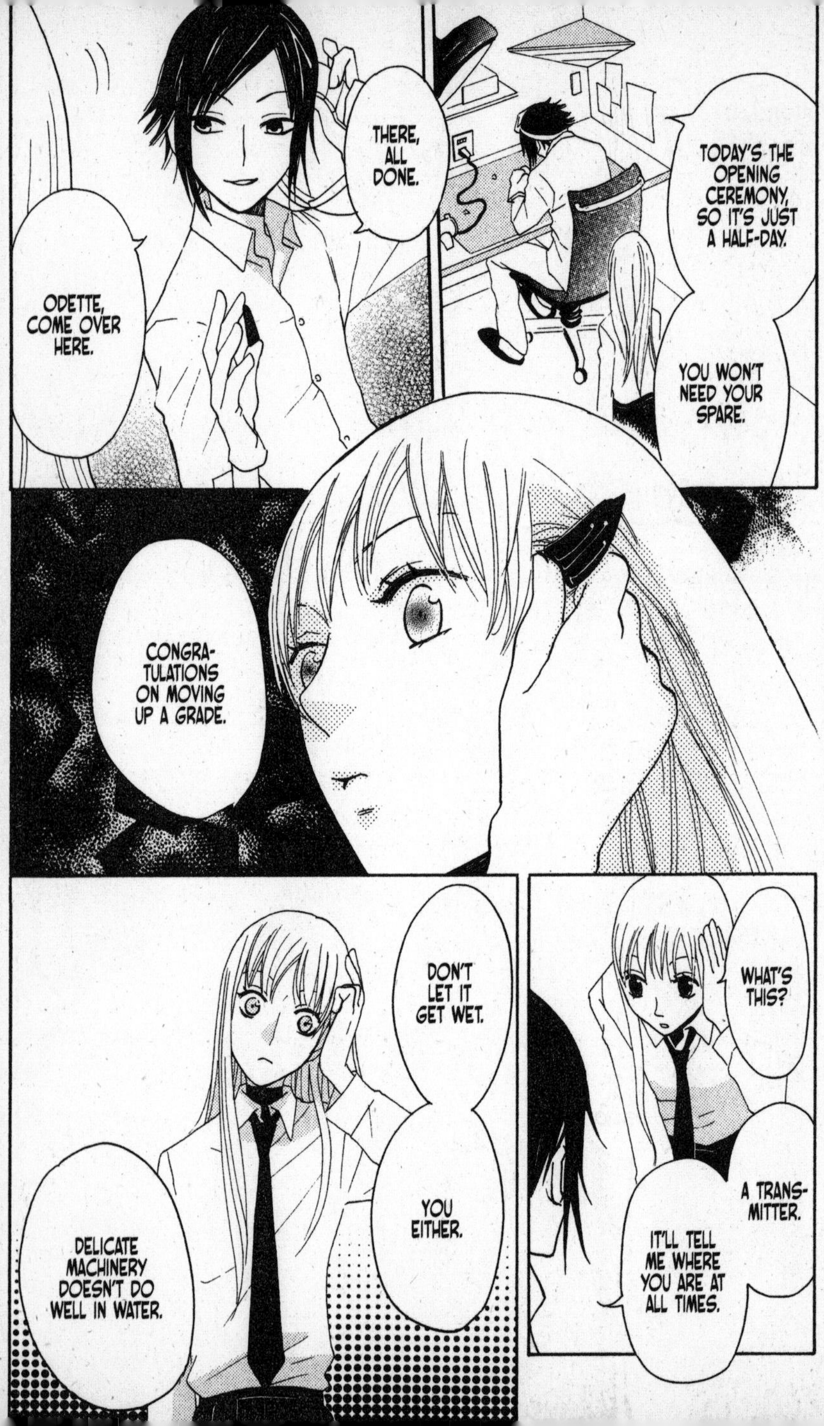
TODAY'S THE OPENING CEREMONY, SO IT'S JUST A HALF-DAY.
YOU WON'T NEED YOUR SPARE.
THERE, ALL DONE.
ODETTE, COME OVER HERE.
CONGRA-TULATIONS ON MOVING UP A GRADE.
WHAT'S THIS?
A TRANS-MITTER.
IT'LL TELL ME WHERE YOU ARE AT ALL TIMES.
DON'T LET IT GET WET.
YOU EITHER.
DELICATE MACHINERY DOESN'T DO WELL IN WATER.

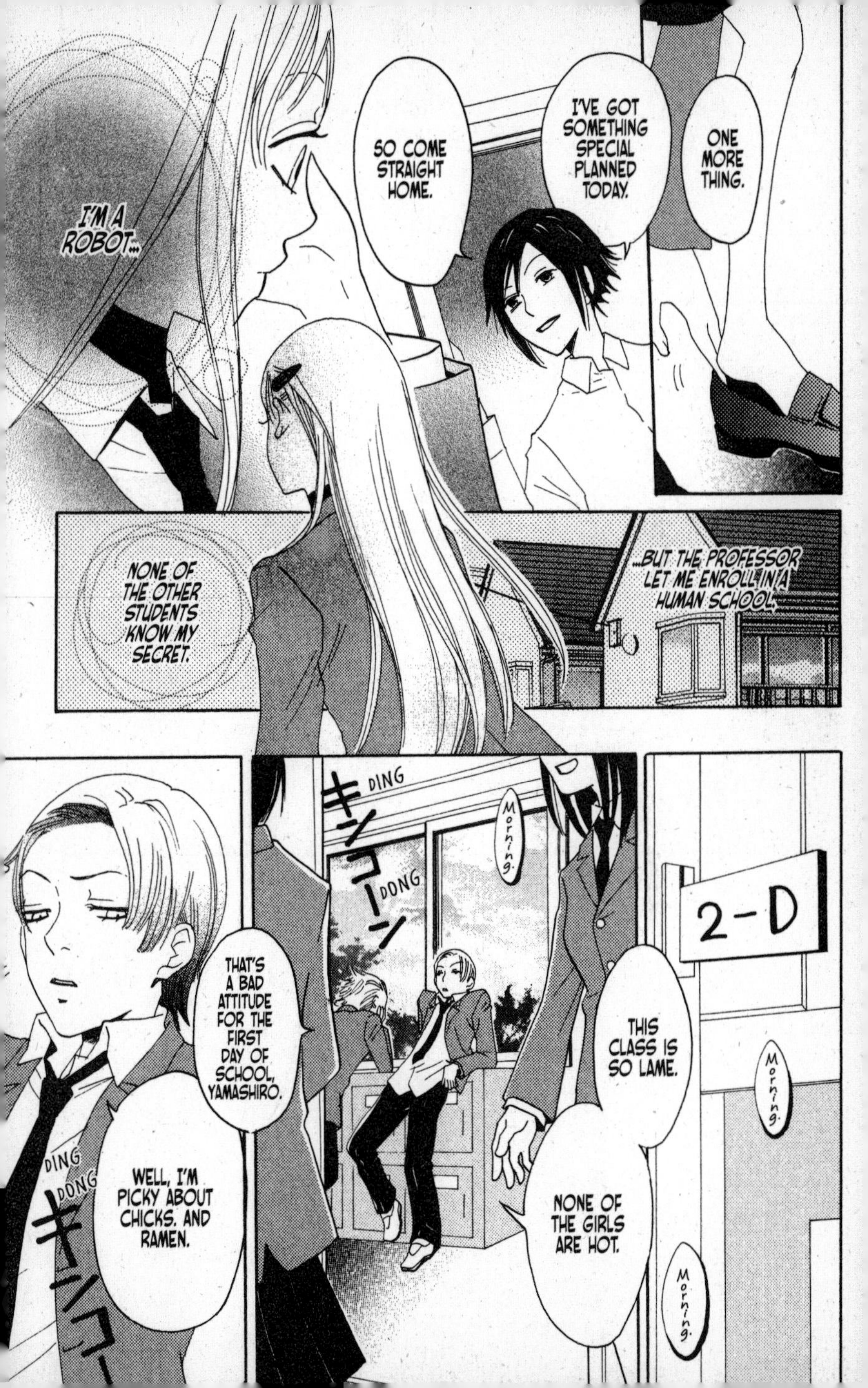
ONE MORE THING.
I'VE GOT SOMETHING SPECIAL PLANNED TODAY.
SO COME STRAIGHT HOME.
I'M A ROBOT...
...BUT THE PROFESSOR LET ME ENROLL IN A HUMAN SCHOOL.
NONE OF THE OTHER STUDENTS KNOW MY SECRET.
2-D
Morning.
Morning.
THIS CLASS IS SO LAME.
NONE OF THE GIRLS ARE HOT.
DING
DONG
Morning.
THAT'S A BAD ATTITUDE FOR THE FIRST DAY OF SCHOOL, YAMASHIRO.
WELL, I'M PICKY ABOUT CHICKS. AND RAMEN.
DING
DONG

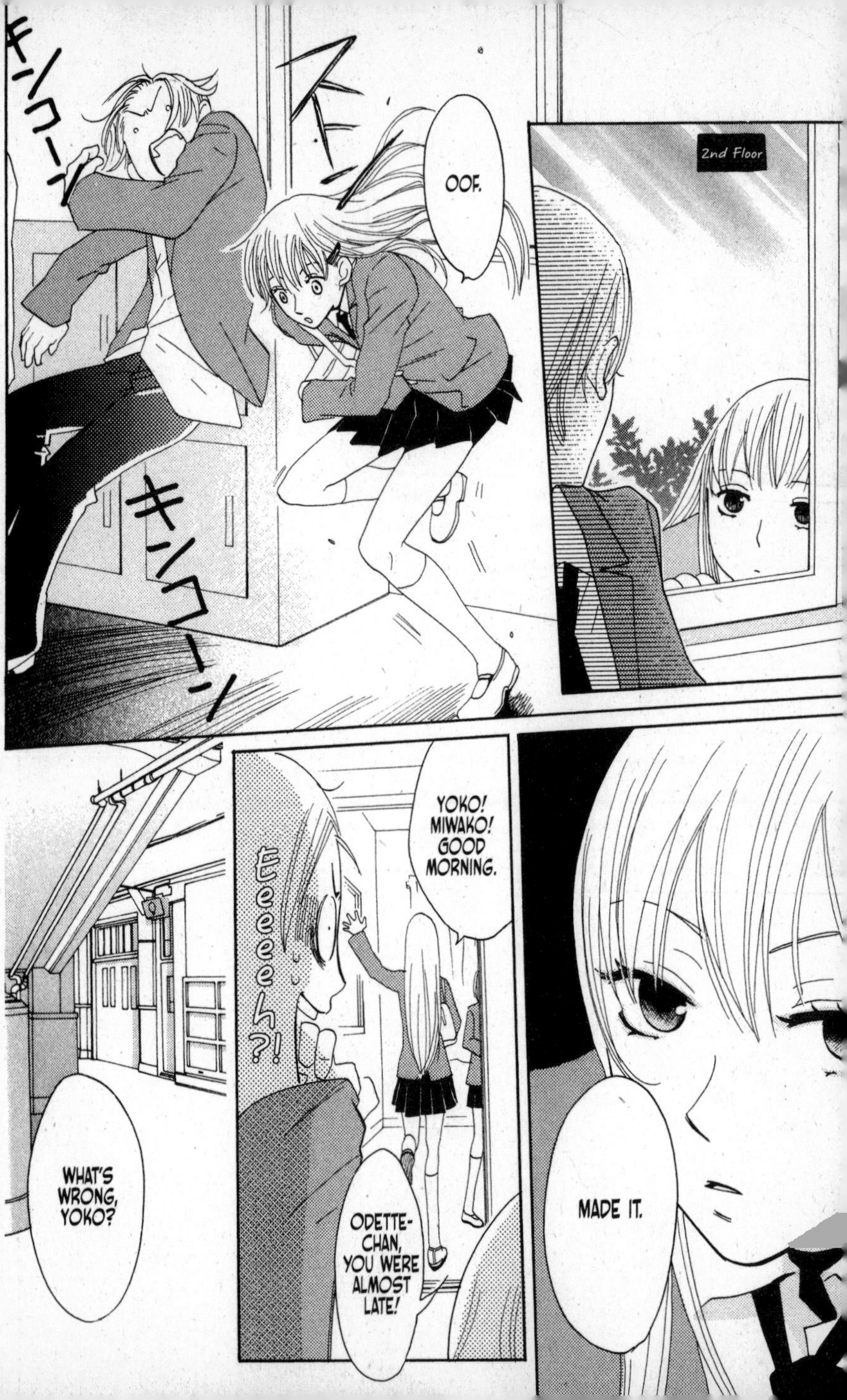
2nd Floor
OOF.
キンコーン
キンコーン
MADE IT.
YOKO! MIWAKO! GOOD MORNING.
Eeeeeh?!
ODETTE-CHAN, YOU WERE ALMOST LATE!
WHAT'S WRONG, YOKO?

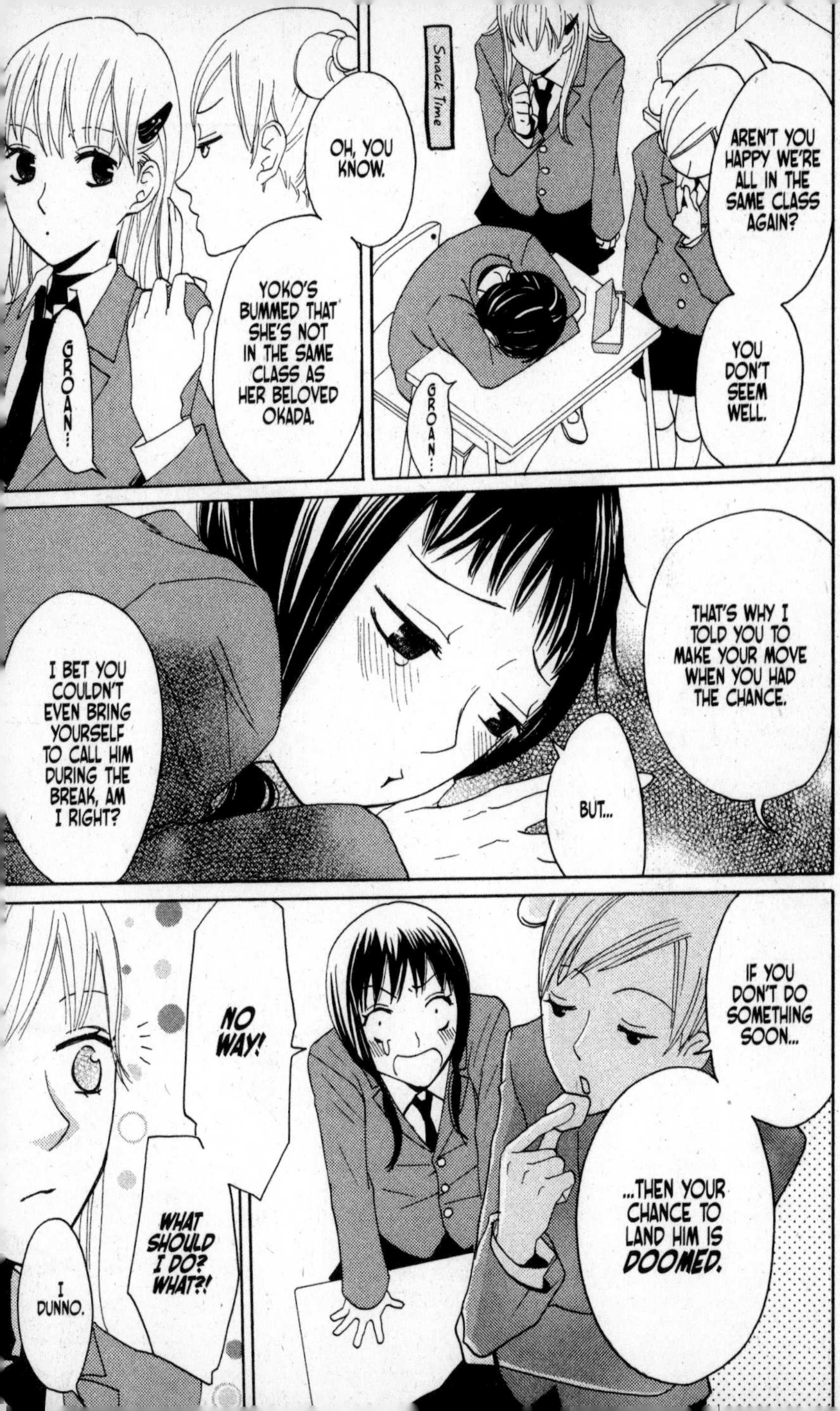
Snack Time
AREN'T YOU HAPPY WE'RE ALL IN THE SAME CLASS AGAIN?
YOU DON'T SEEM WELL.
GROAN...
OH, YOU KNOW.
YOKO'S BUMMED THAT SHE'S NOT IN THE SAME CLASS AS HER BELOVED OKADA.
GROAN...
THAT'S WHY I TOLD YOU TO MAKE YOUR MOVE WHEN YOU HAD THE CHANCE.
BUT...
I BET YOU COULDN'T EVEN BRING YOURSELF TO CALL HIM DURING THE BREAK, AM I RIGHT?
IF YOU DON'T DO SOMETHING SOON...
...THEN YOUR CHANCE TO LAND HIM IS DOOMED.
NO WAY!
WHAT SHOULD I DO? WHAT?!
I DUNNO.

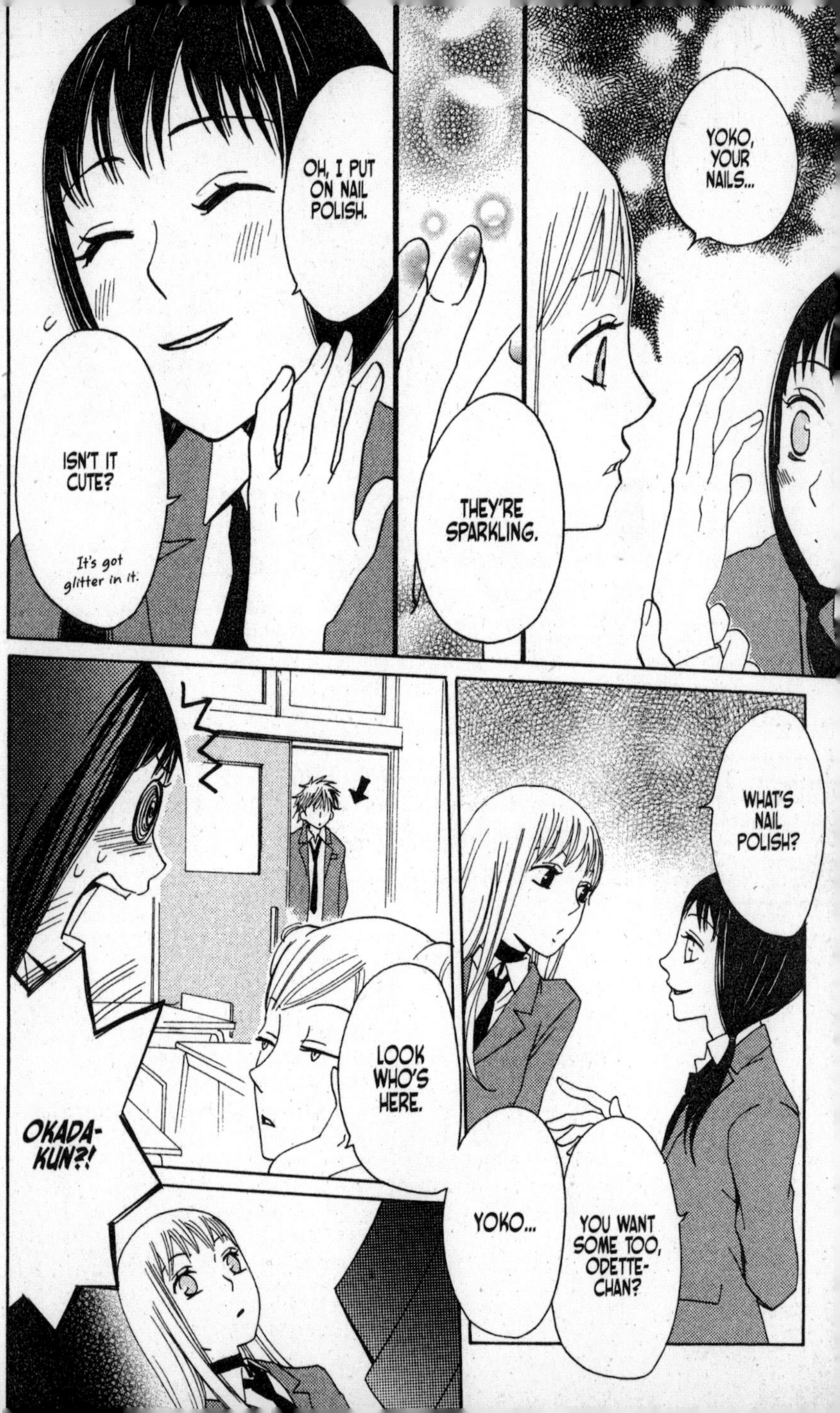
YOKO, YOUR NAILS...
THEY'RE SPARKLING.
OH, I PUT ON NAIL POLISH.
ISN'T IT CUTE?
It's got glitter in it.
WHAT'S NAIL POLISH?
YOU WANT SOME TOO, ODETTE-CHAN?
YOKO...
LOOK WHO'S HERE.
OKADA-KUN?!

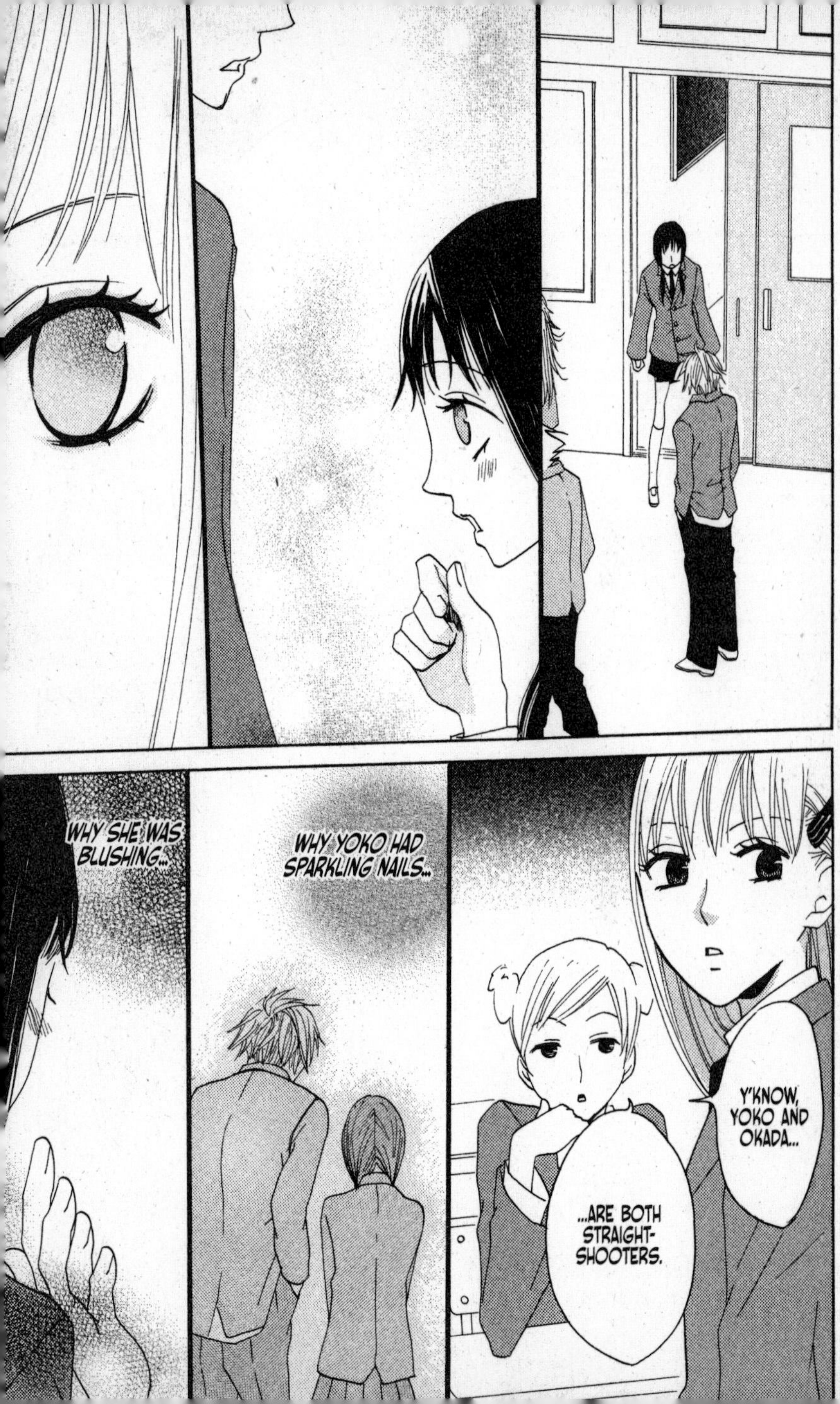
Y'KNOW, YOKO AND OKADA...
...ARE BOTH STRAIGHT-SHOOTERS.
WHY YOKO HAD SPARKLING NAILS...
WHY SHE WAS BLUSHING...

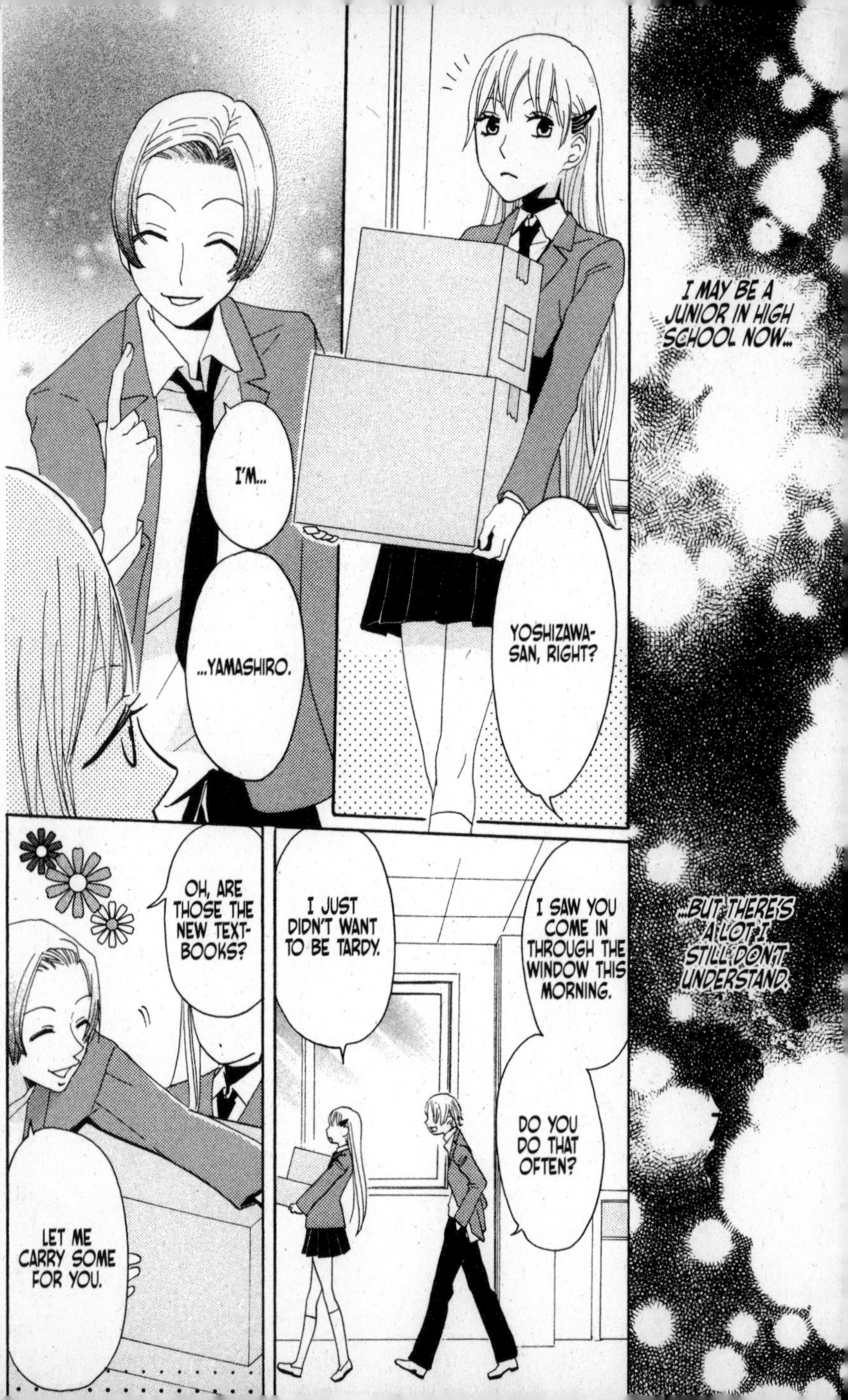
I MAY BE A JUNIOR IN HIGH SCHOOL NOW...
...BUT THERE'S A LOT I STILL DON'T UNDERSTAND.
YOSHIZAWA-SAN, RIGHT?
I'M...
...YAMASHIRO.
I SAW YOU COME IN THROUGH THE WINDOW THIS MORNING.
DO YOU DO THAT OFTEN?
I JUST DIDN'T WANT TO BE TARDY.
OH, ARE THOSE THE NEW TEXT-BOOKS?
LET ME CARRY SOME FOR YOU.

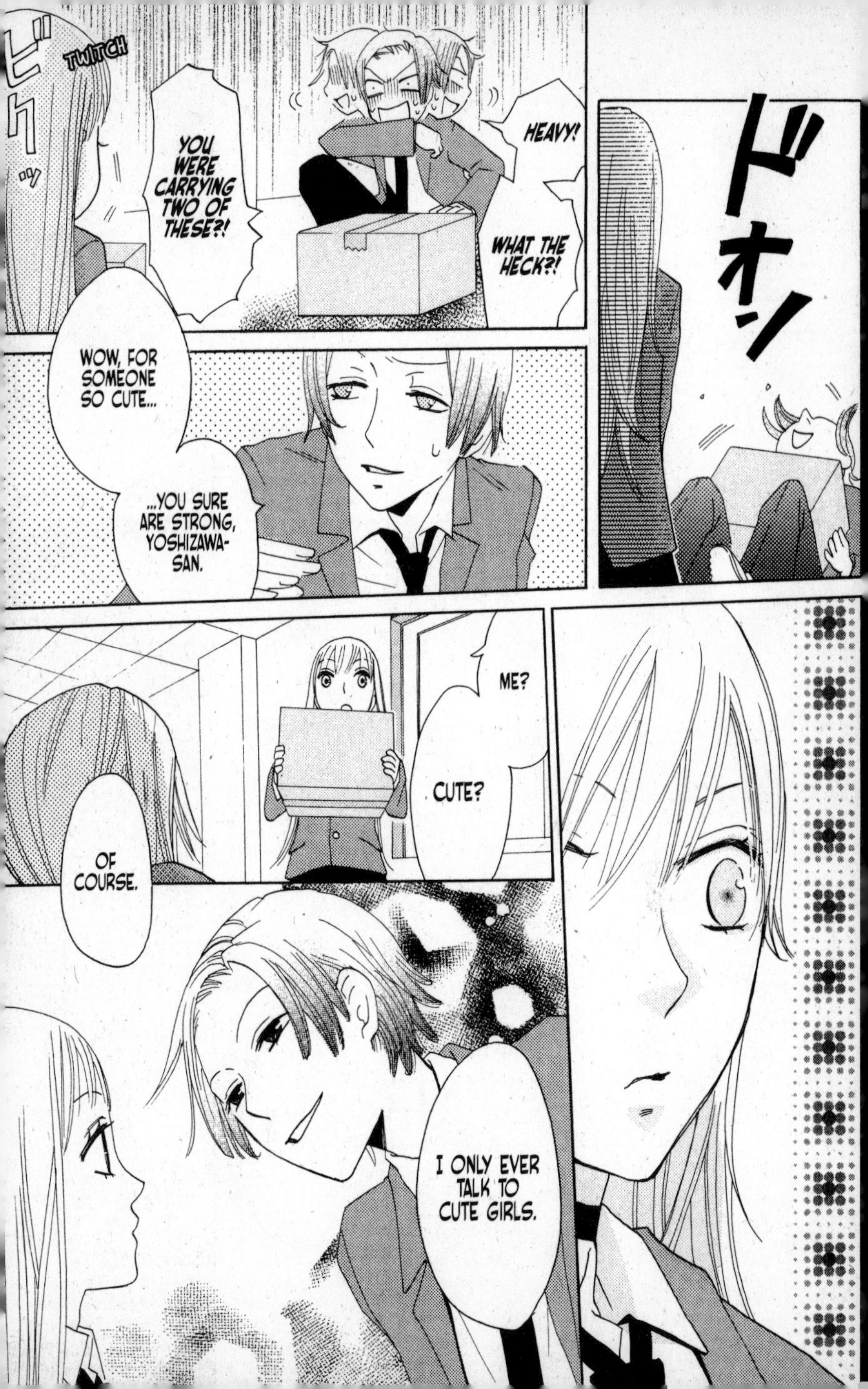
ドオッ
HEAVY!
WHAT THE HECK?!
YOU WERE CARRYING TWO OF THESE?!
TWITCH
ビクッ
WOW, FOR SOMEONE SO CUTE...
...YOU SURE ARE STRONG, YOSHIZAWA-SAN.
ME?
CUTE?
OF COURSE.
I ONLY EVER TALK TO CUTE GIRLS.

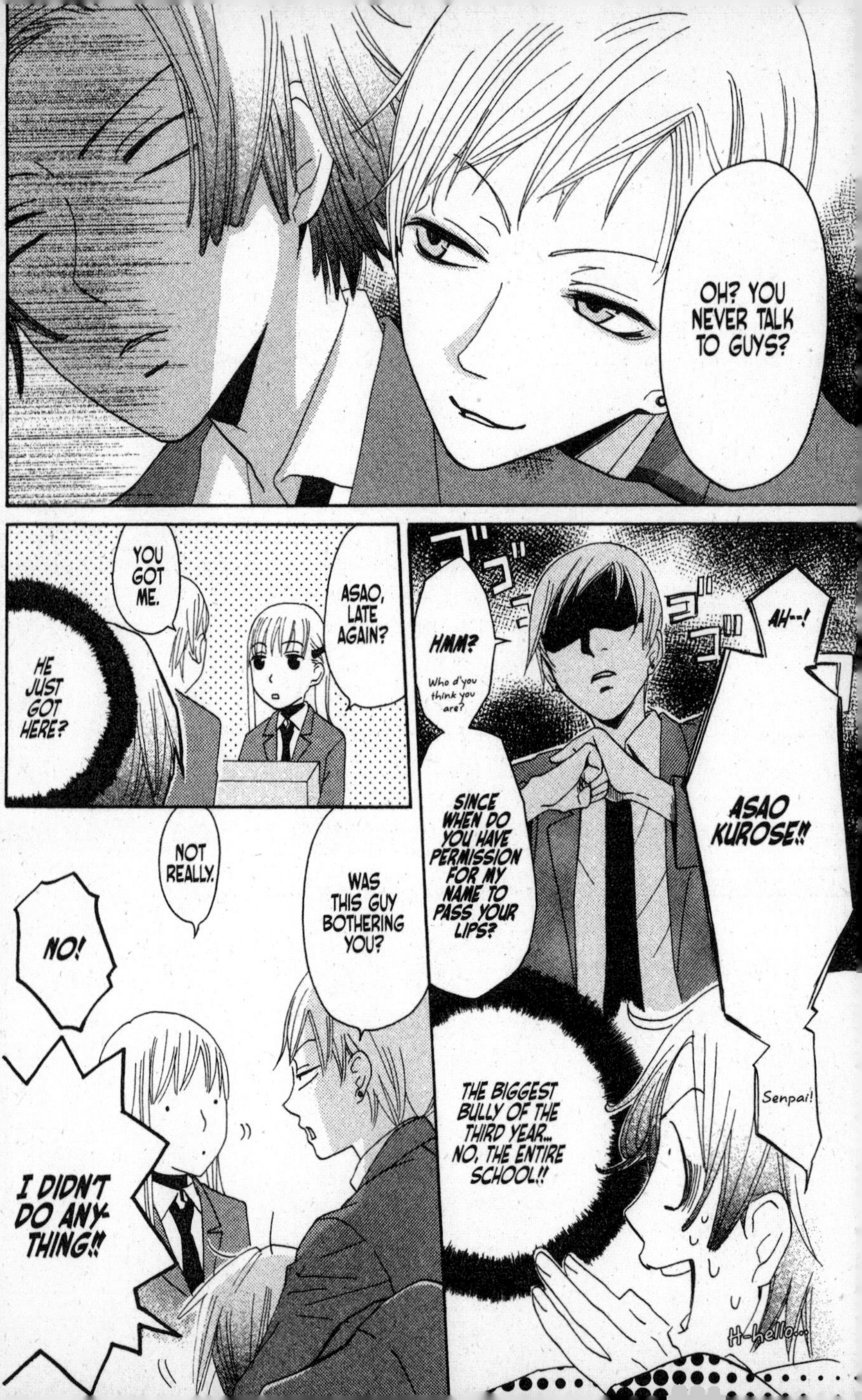
OH? YOU NEVER TALK TO GUYS?
AH--!
ASAO KUROSE!!
HMM?
Who d'you think you are?
SINCE WHEN DO YOU HAVE PERMISSION FOR MY NAME TO PASS YOUR LIPS?
Senpai!
THE BIGGEST BULLY OF THE THIRD YEAR... NO, THE ENTIRE SCHOOL!!
H-hello...
ASAO, LATE AGAIN?
YOU GOT ME.
HE JUST GOT HERE?
WAS THIS GUY BOTHERING YOU?
NOT REALLY.
NO!
I DIDN'T DO ANY-THING!!

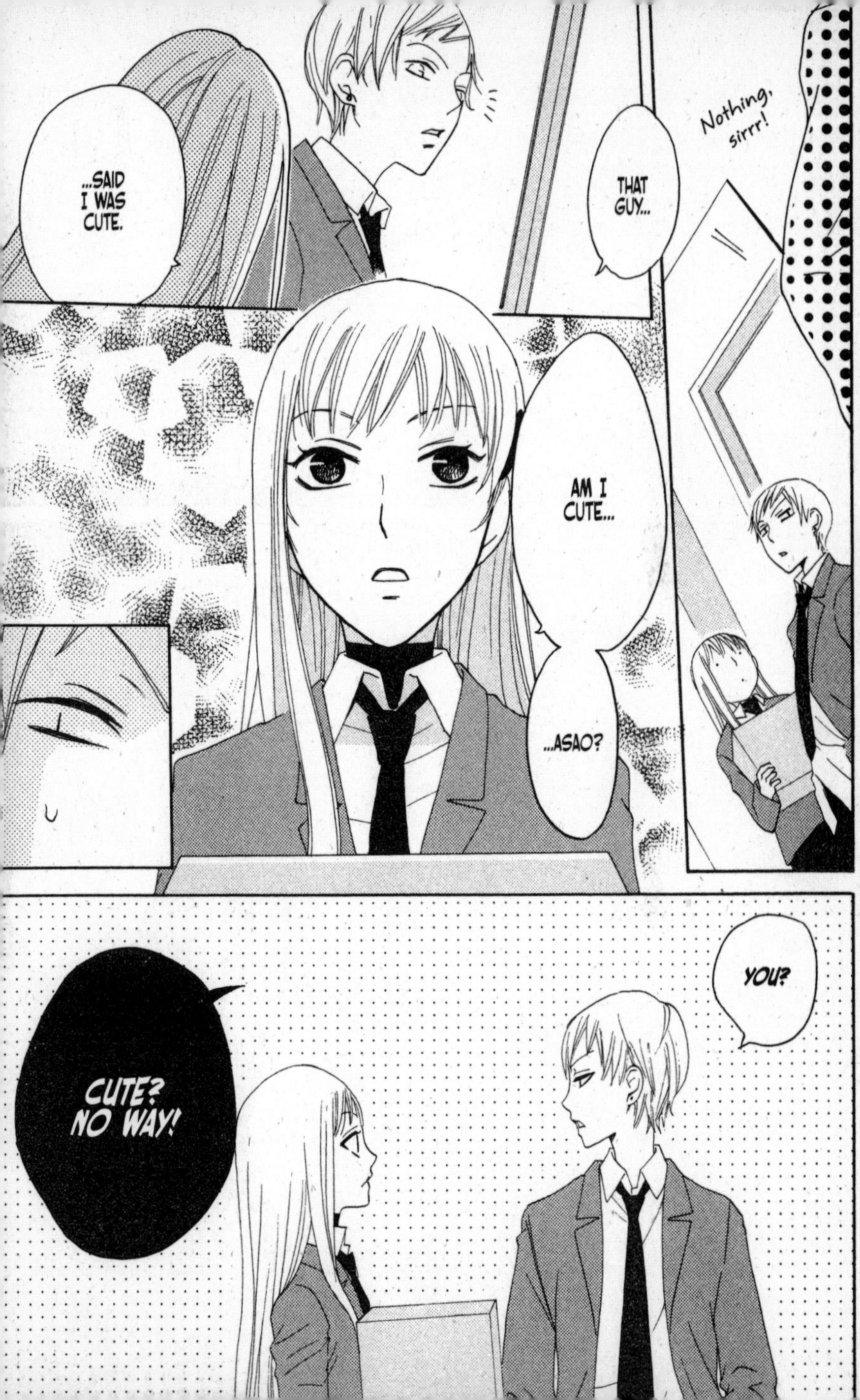
Nothing, sirrr!
THAT GUY...
...SAID I WAS CUTE.
AM I CUTE...
...ASAO?
YOU?
CUTE? NO WAY!

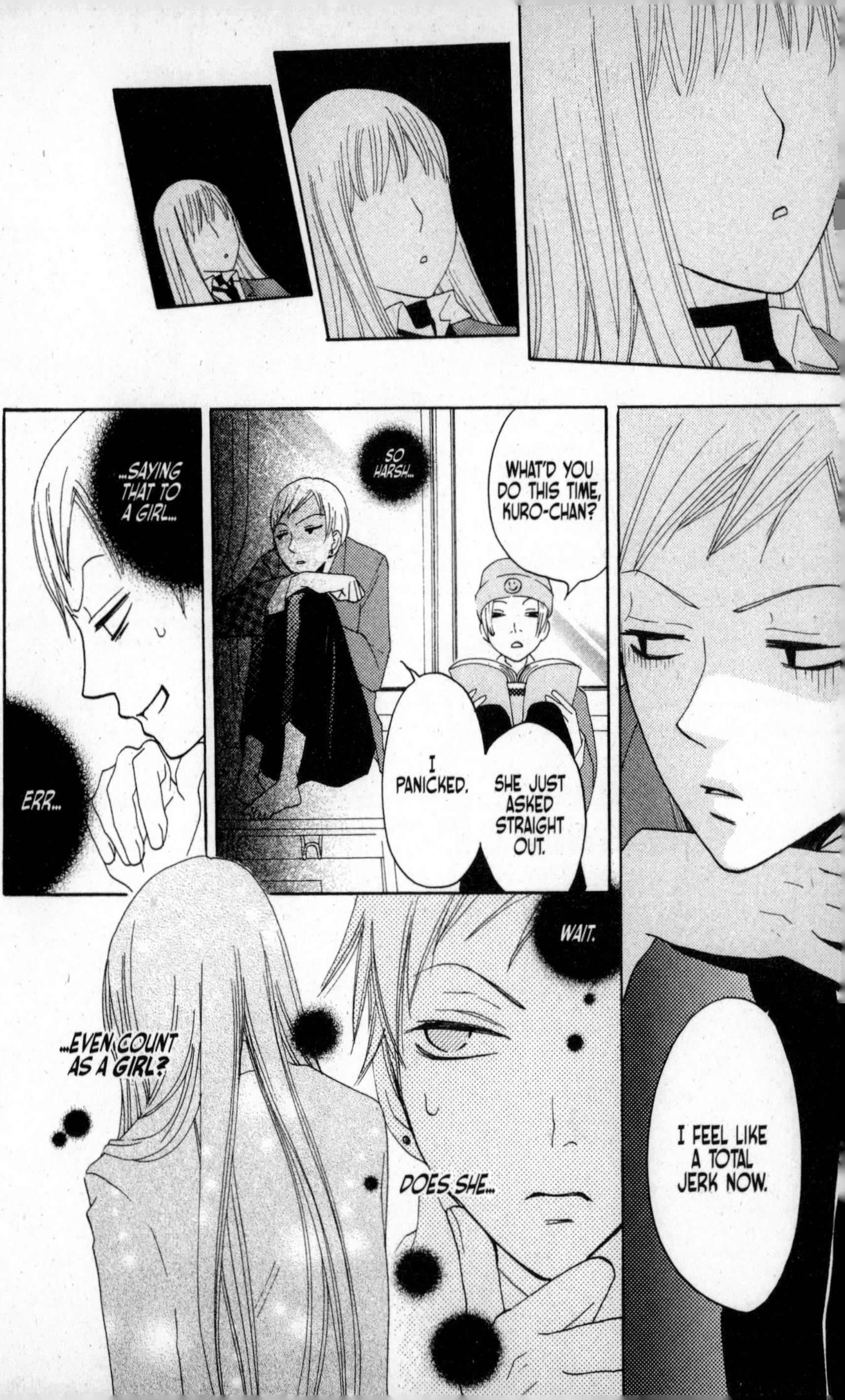
I FEEL LIKE A TOTAL JERK NOW.
WHAT'D YOU DO THIS TIME, KURO-CHAN?
SHE JUST ASKED STRAIGHT OUT.
I PANICKED.
SO HARSH...
...SAYING THAT TO A GIRL...
ERR...
WAIT.
DOES SHE...
...EVEN COUNT AS A GIRL?

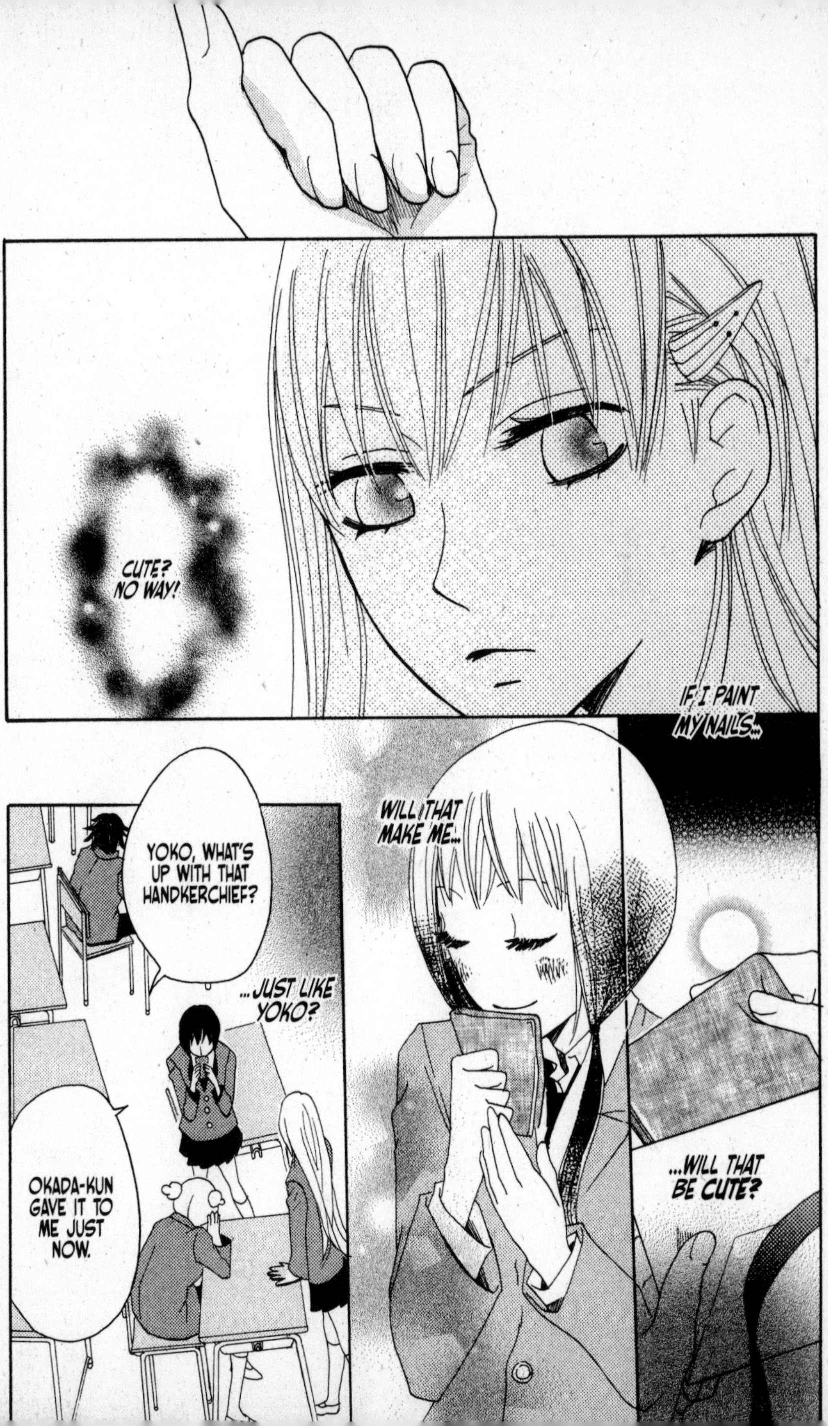
CUTE? NO WAY!
IF I PAINT MY NAILS...
...WILL THAT BE CUTE?
WILL THAT MAKE ME...
...JUST LIKE YOKO?
YOKO, WHAT'S UP WITH THAT HANDKERCHIEF?
OKADA-KUN GAVE IT TO ME JUST NOW.

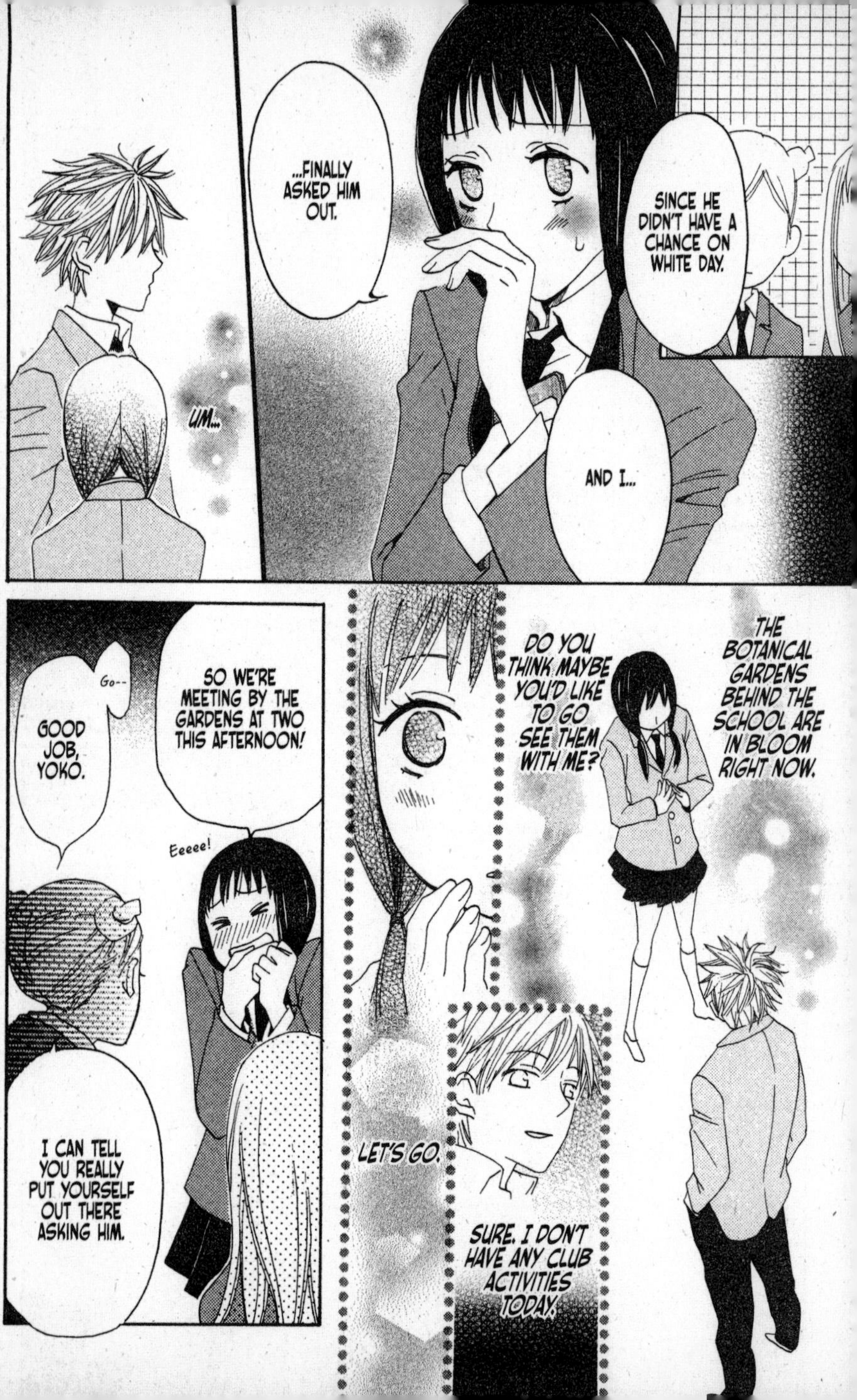
SINCE HE DIDN'T HAVE A CHANCE ON WHITE DAY.
AND I...
...FINALLY ASKED HIM OUT.
UM...
THE BOTANICAL GARDENS BEHIND THE SCHOOL ARE IN BLOOM RIGHT NOW.
DO YOU THINK MAYBE YOU'D LIKE TO GO SEE THEM WITH ME?
SURE. I DON'T HAVE ANY CLUB ACTIVITIES TODAY.
LET'S GO.
SO WE'RE MEETING BY THE GARDENS AT TWO THIS AFTERNOON!
Eeeee!
Go--
GOOD JOB, YOKO.
I CAN TELL YOU REALLY PUT YOURSELF OUT THERE ASKING HIM.

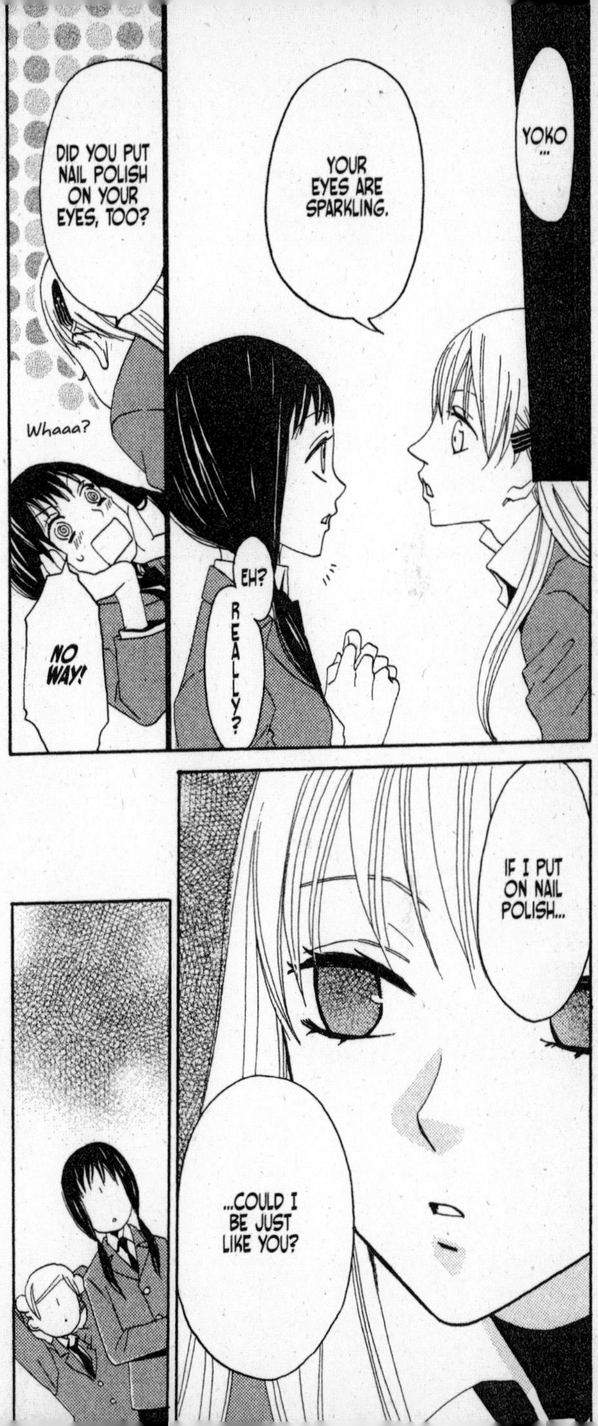
YOKO ...
YOUR EYES ARE SPARKLING.
EH? REALLY?
DID YOU PUT NAIL POLISH ON YOUR EYES, TOO?
Whaaa?
NO WAY!
IF I PUT ON NAIL POLISH...
...COULD I BE JUST LIKE YOU?

Hello! Thanks for checking out Karakuri Odette volume two! I'll be so happy if you like it.

There are six of these sidebars, so I'm going to use them to introduce the characters who appear in volume two.

Well then, enjoy!

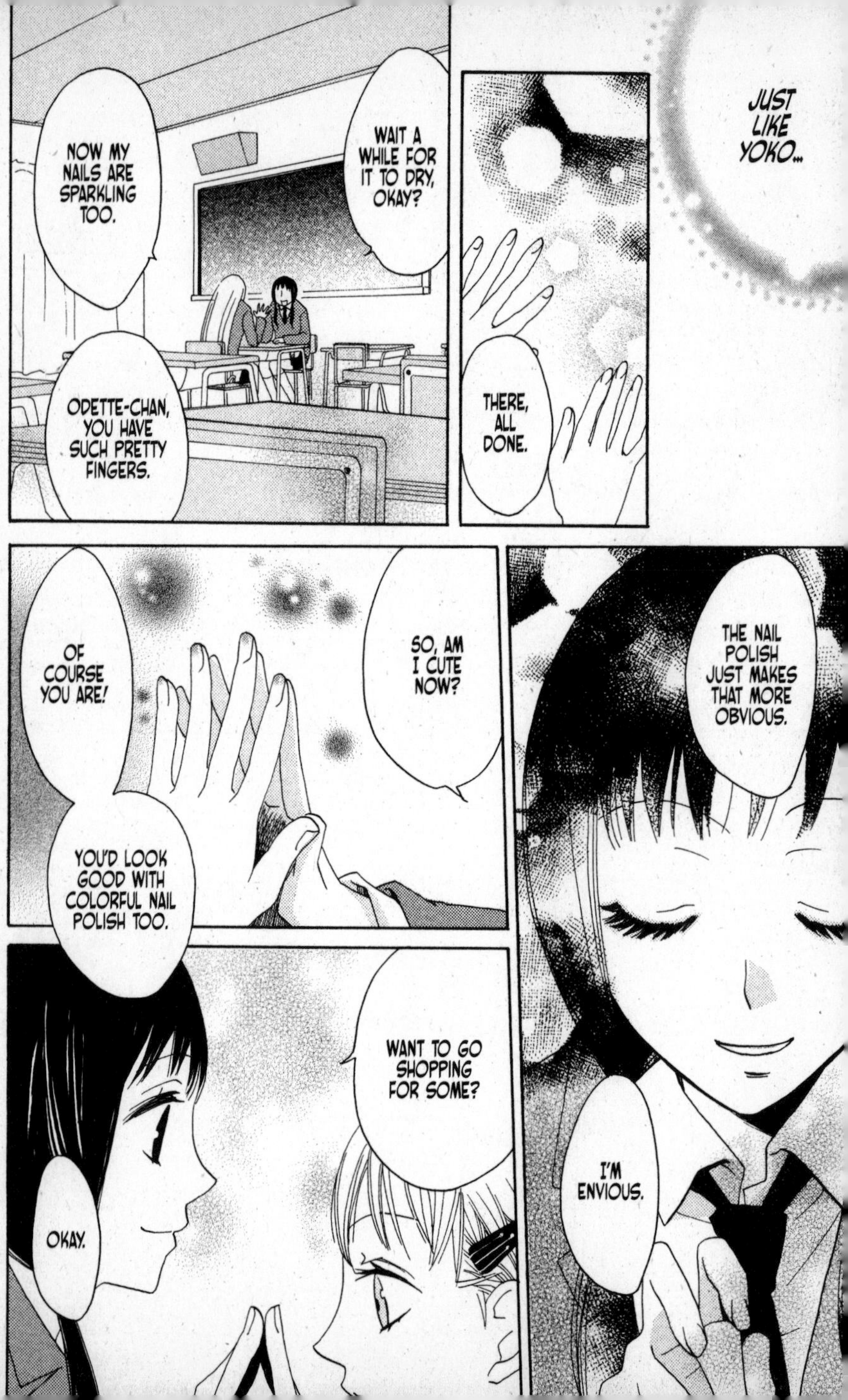
JUST LIKE YOKO...
THERE, ALL DONE.
WAIT A WHILE FOR IT TO DRY, OKAY?
NOW MY NAILS ARE SPARKLING TOO.
ODETTE-CHAN, YOU HAVE SUCH PRETTY FINGERS.
THE NAIL POLISH JUST MAKES THAT MORE OBVIOUS.
I'M ENVIOUS.
SO, AM I CUTE NOW?
OF COURSE YOU ARE!
YOU'D LOOK GOOD WITH COLORFUL NAIL POLISH TOO.
WANT TO GO SHOPPING FOR SOME?
OKAY.

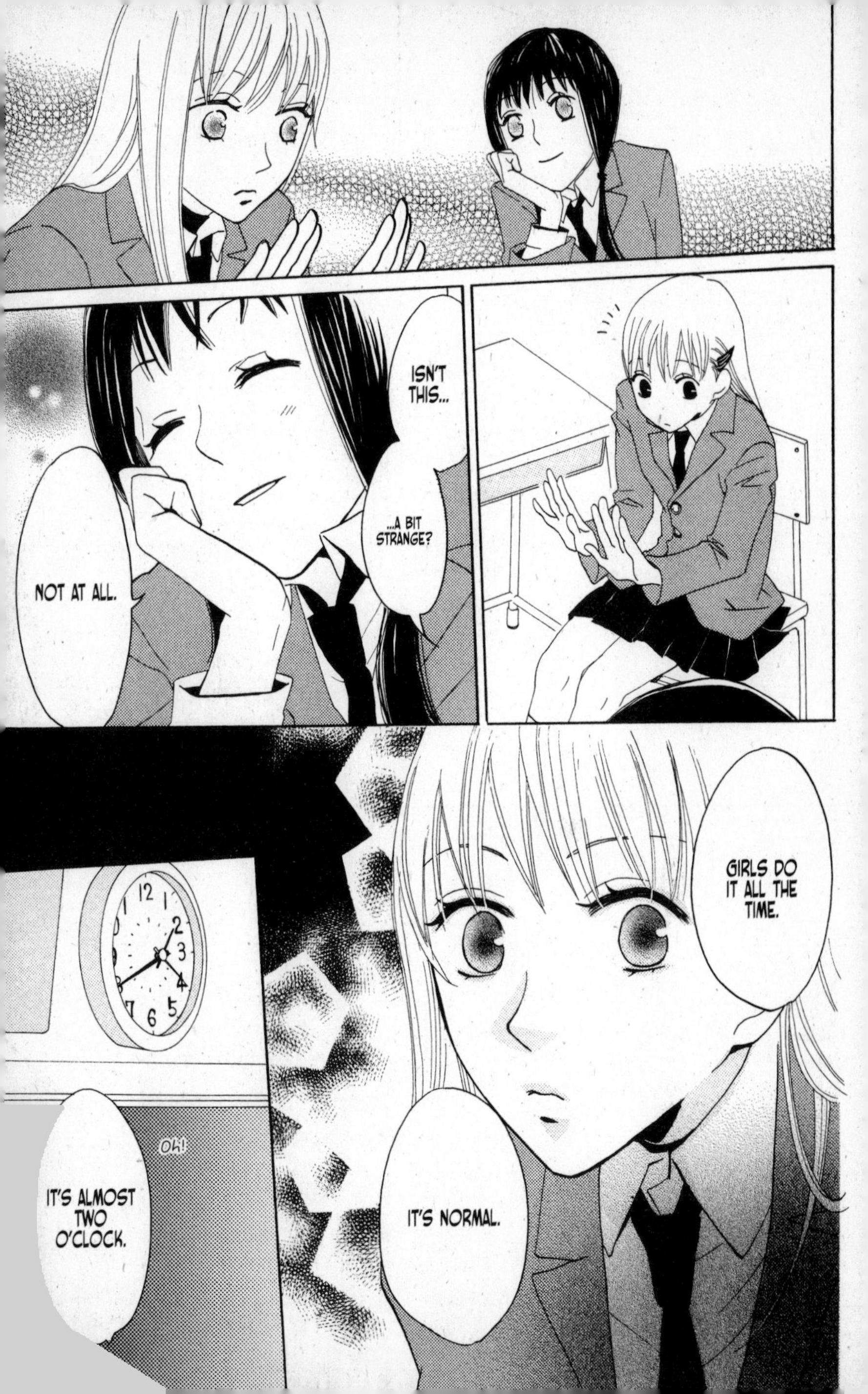
ISN'T THIS...
...A BIT STRANGE?
NOT AT ALL.
GIRLS DO IT ALL THE TIME.
IT'S NORMAL.
OH!
IT'S ALMOST TWO O'CLOCK.

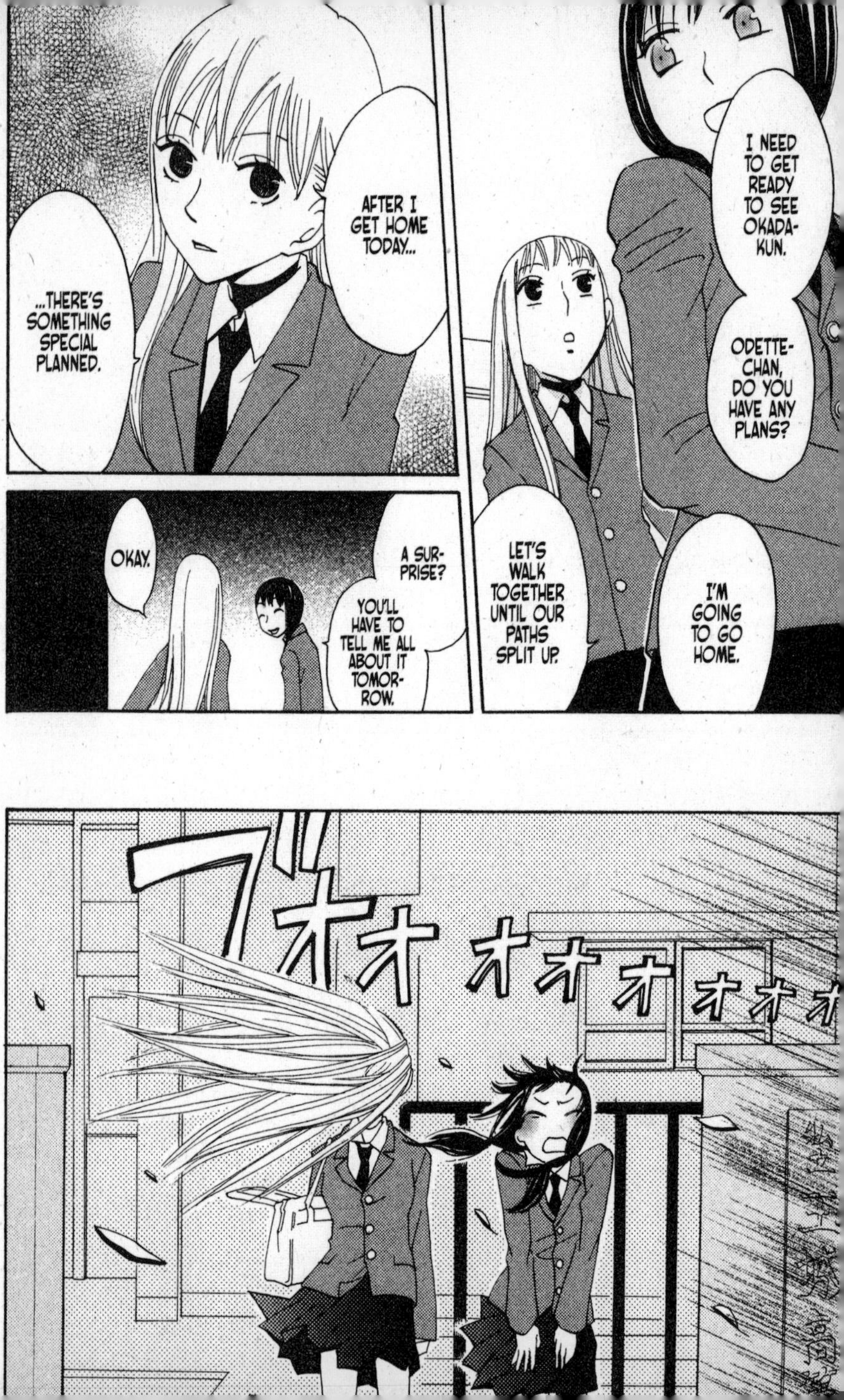
I NEED TO GET READY TO SEE OKADA-KUN.
ODETTE-CHAN, DO YOU HAVE ANY PLANS?
I'M GOING TO GO HOME.
LET'S WALK TOGETHER UNTIL OUR PATHS SPLIT UP.
AFTER I GET HOME TODAY...
...THERE'S SOMETHING SPECIAL PLANNED.
A SUR-PRISE?
YOU'LL HAVE TO TELL ME ALL ABOUT IT TOMOR-ROW.
OKAY.
ブオオオオオオオオ

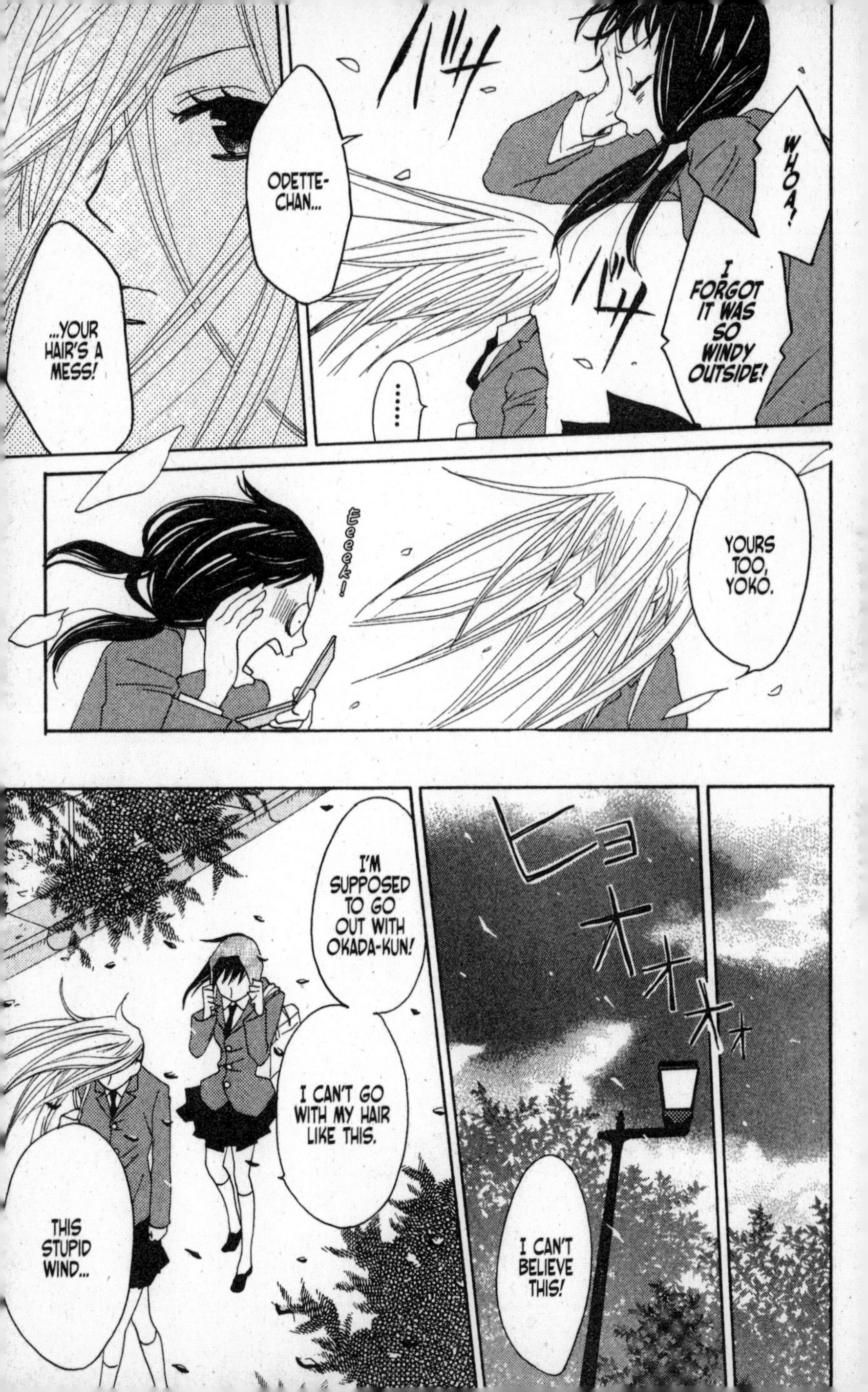
バサ
WHOA!
バサ
I FORGOT IT WAS SO WINDY OUTSIDE!
ODETTE-CHAN...
......
...YOUR HAIR'S A MESS!
YOURS TOO, YOKO.
Eeeeek!
ヒョオオオオ
I CAN'T BELIEVE THIS!
I'M SUPPOSED TO GO OUT WITH OKADA-KUN!
I CAN'T GO WITH MY HAIR LIKE THIS.
THIS STUPID WIND...

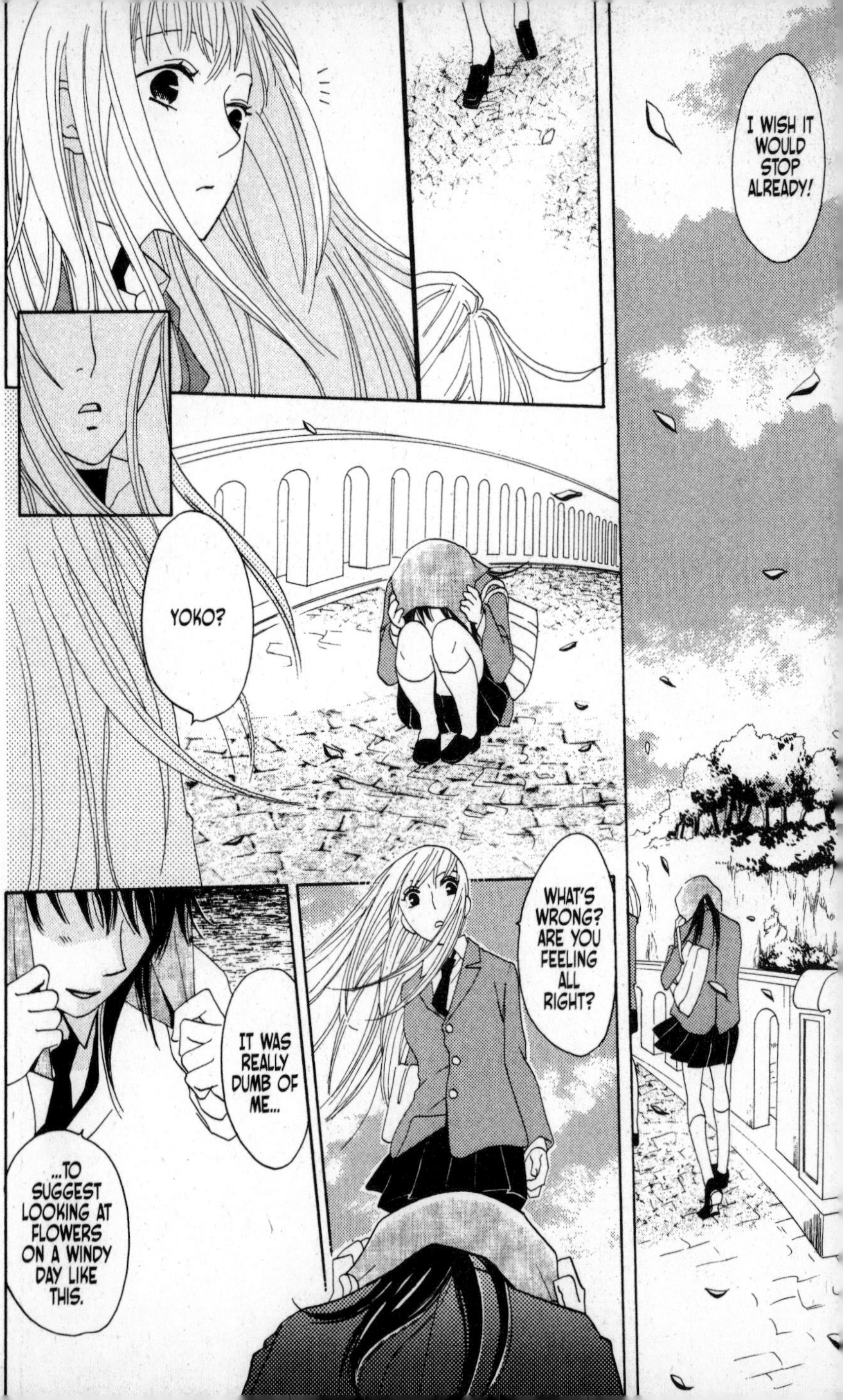

I WISH IT WOULD STOP ALREADY!
YOKO?
WHAT'S WRONG? ARE YOU FEELING ALL RIGHT?
IT WAS REALLY DUMB OF ME...
...TO SUGGEST LOOKING AT FLOWERS ON A WINDY DAY LIKE THIS.

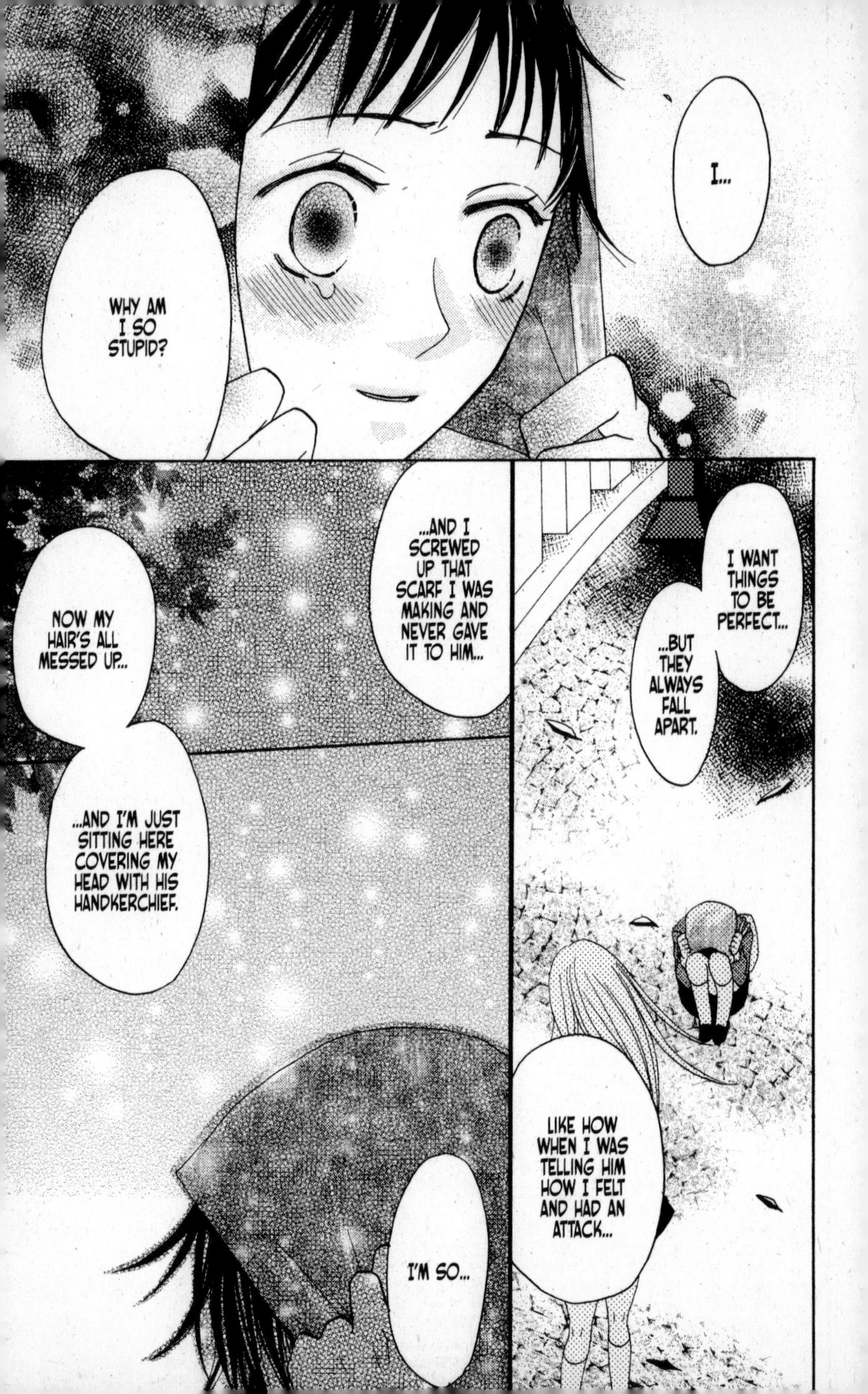
I...
WHY AM I SO STUPID?
I WANT THINGS TO BE PERFECT...
...BUT THEY ALWAYS FALL APART.
LIKE HOW WHEN I WAS TELLING HIM HOW I FELT AND HAD AN ATTACK...
...AND I SCREWED UP THAT SCARF I WAS MAKING AND NEVER GAVE IT TO HIM...
NOW MY HAIR'S ALL MESSED UP...
...AND I'M JUST SITTING HERE COVERING MY HEAD WITH HIS HANDKERCHIEF.
I'M SO...

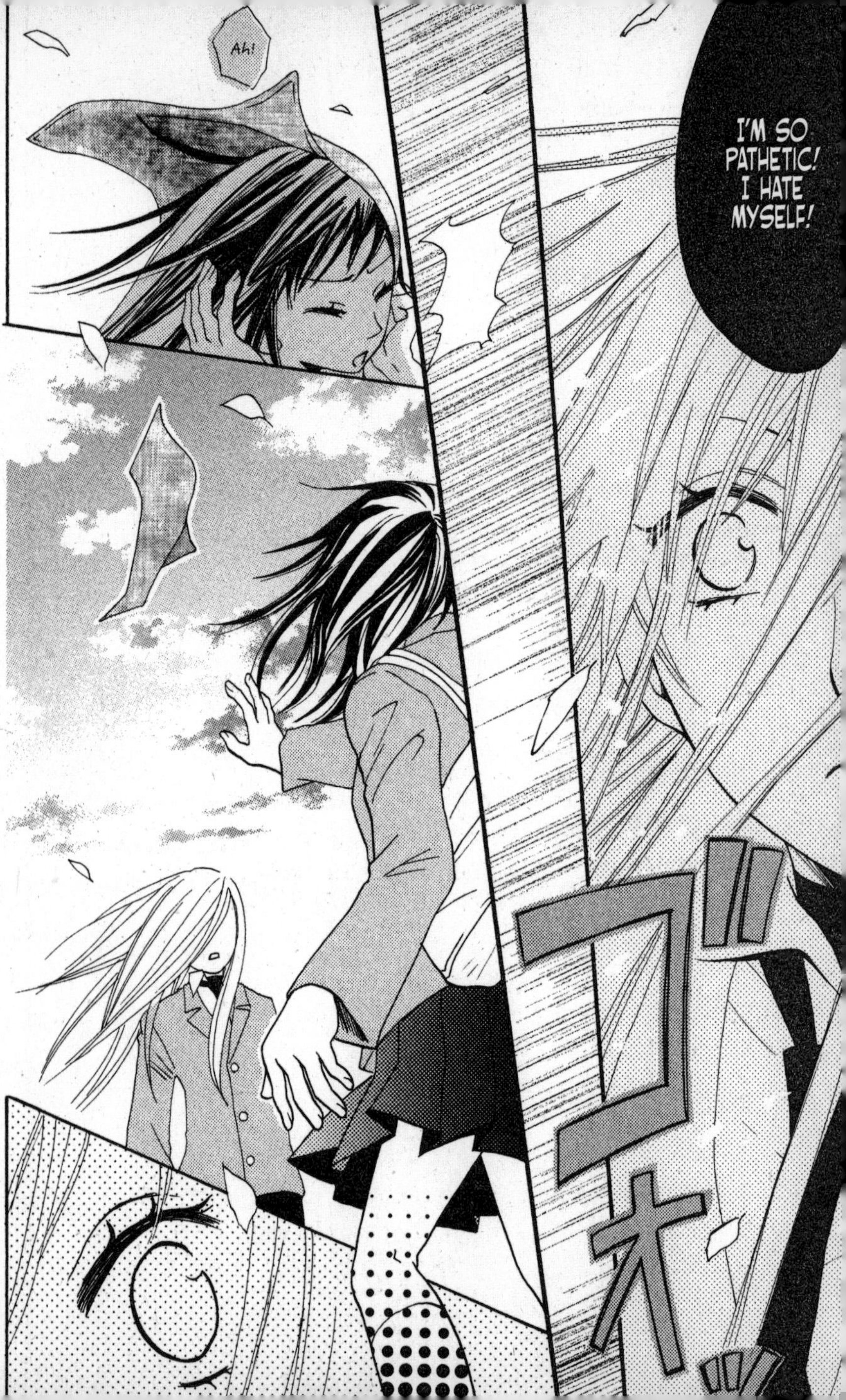
I'M SO PATHETIC! I HATE MYSELF!
ゴォ
Ah!

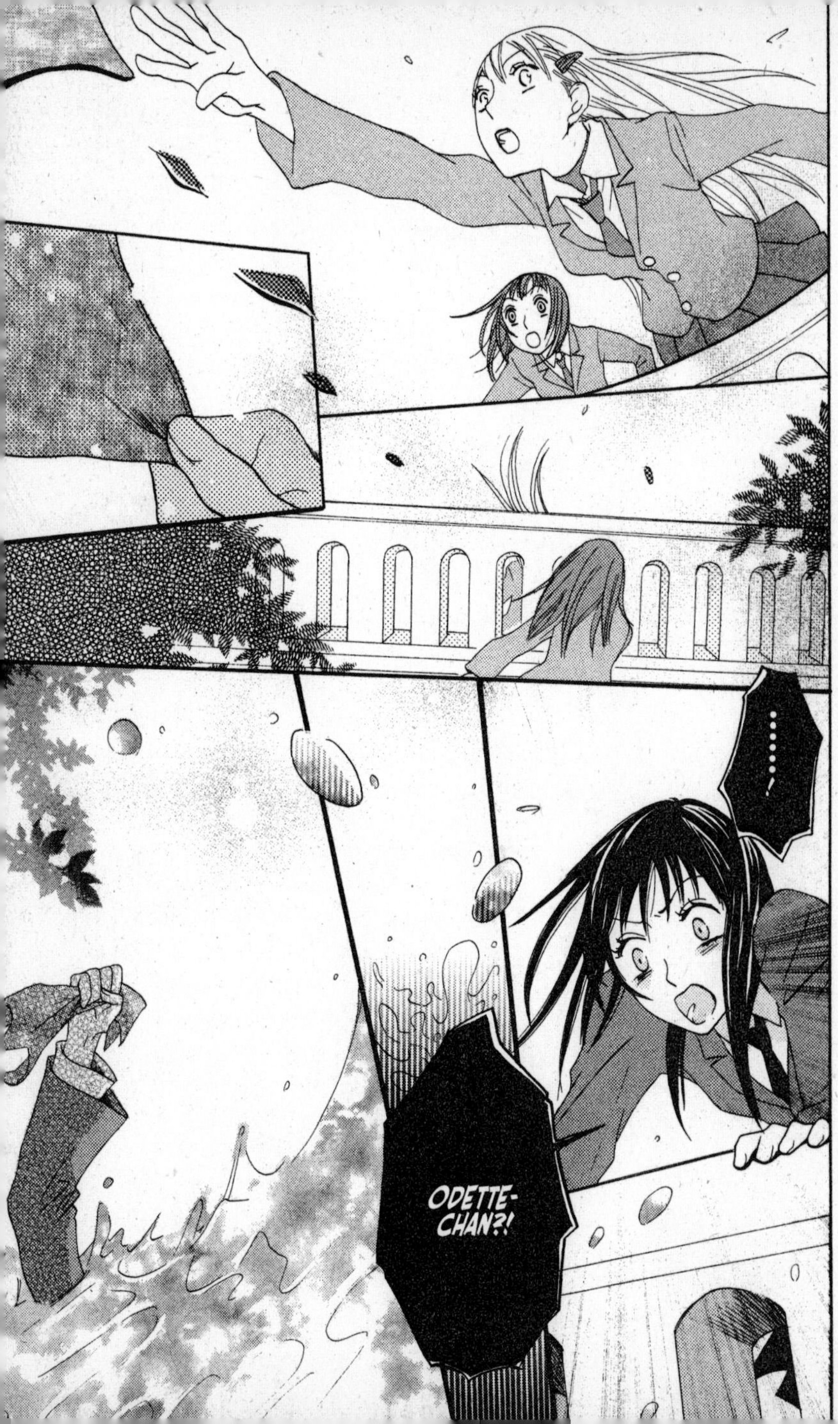
......!
ODETTE-CHAN?!

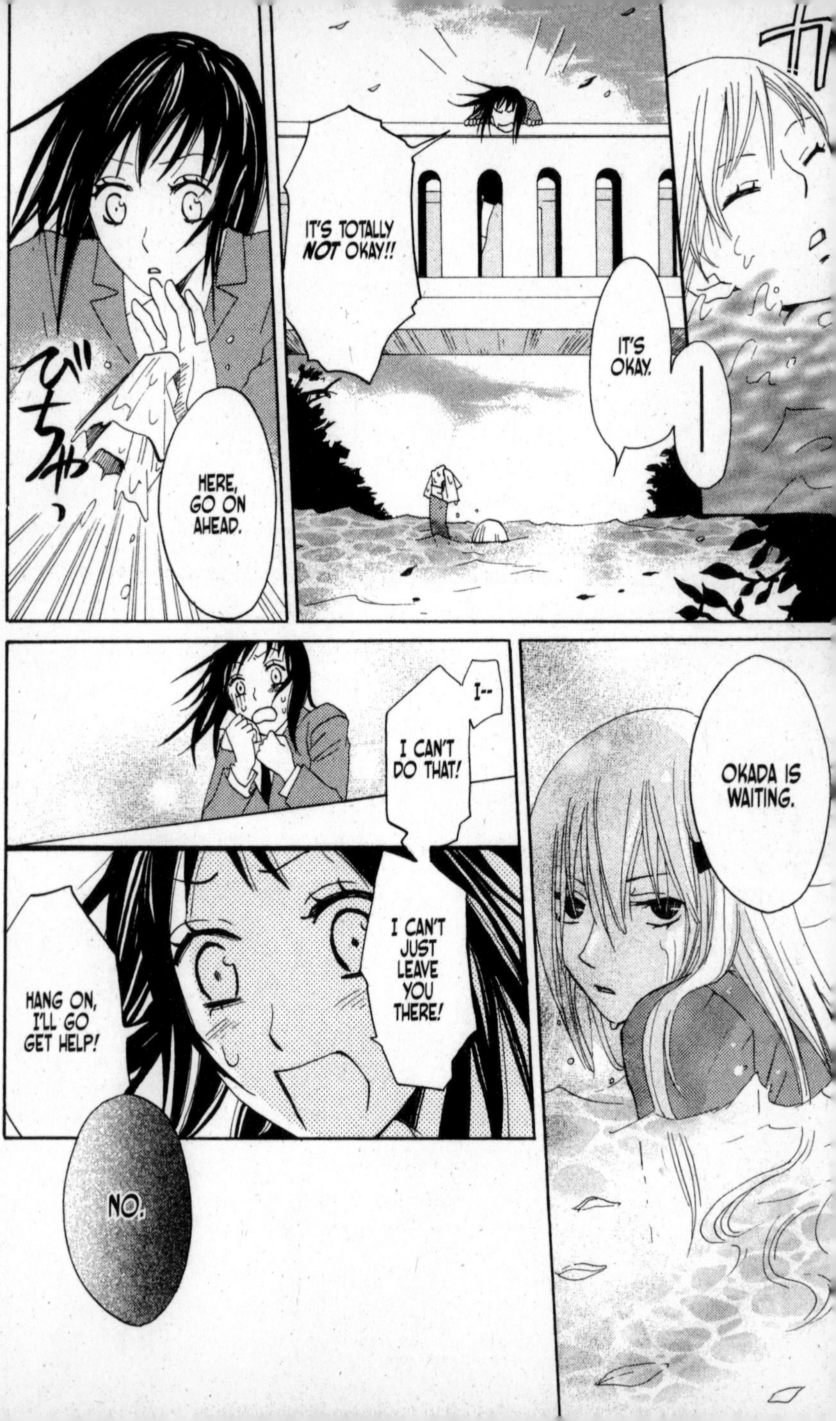
IT'S OKAY.
—
IT'S TOTALLY *NOT* OKAY!!
HERE, GO ON AHEAD.
びちゃっ
OKADA IS WAITING.
I--
I CAN'T DO THAT!
I CAN'T JUST LEAVE YOU THERE!
HANG ON, I'LL GO GET HELP!
NO.

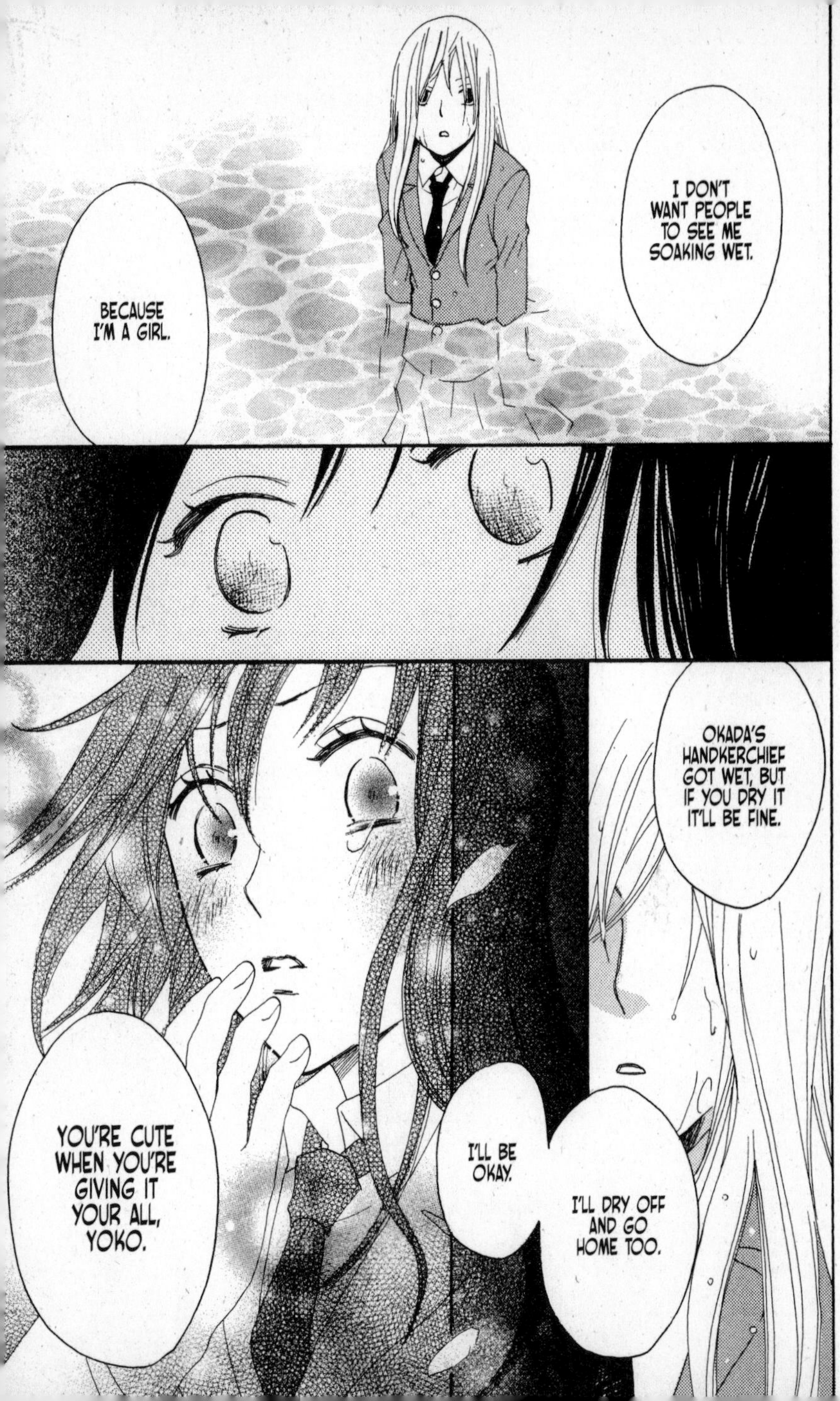
I DON'T WANT PEOPLE TO SEE ME SOAKING WET.
BECAUSE I'M A GIRL.
OKADA'S HANDKERCHIEF GOT WET, BUT IF YOU DRY IT IT'LL BE FINE.
I'LL BE OKAY.
I'LL DRY OFF AND GO HOME TOO.
YOU'RE CUTE WHEN YOU'RE GIVING IT YOUR ALL, YOKO.

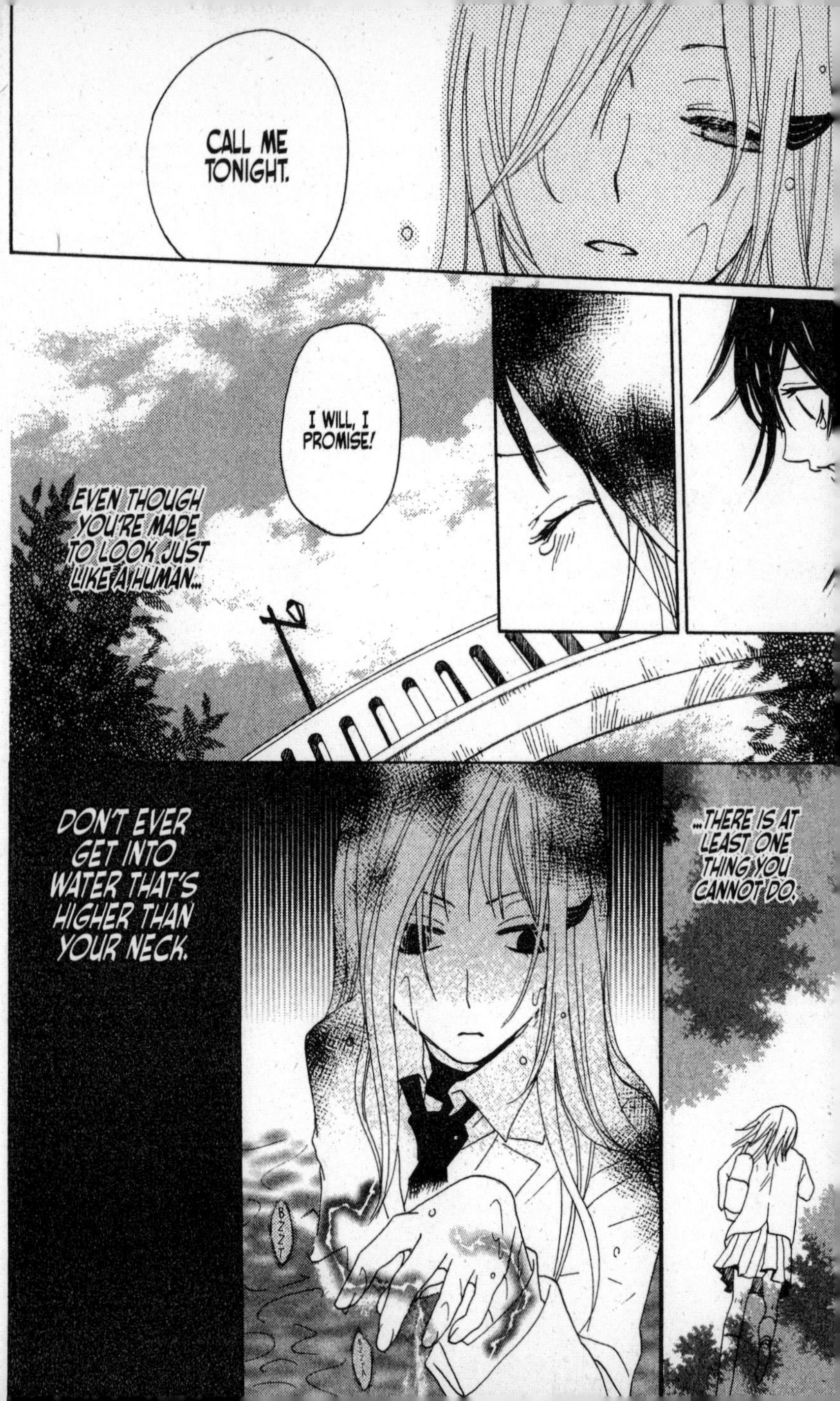
CALL ME TONIGHT.
I WILL, I PROMISE!
EVEN THOUGH YOU'RE MADE TO LOOK JUST LIKE A HUMAN...
...THERE IS AT LEAST ONE THING YOU CANNOT DO.
BZZT
DON'T EVER GET INTO WATER THAT'S HIGHER THAN YOUR NECK.

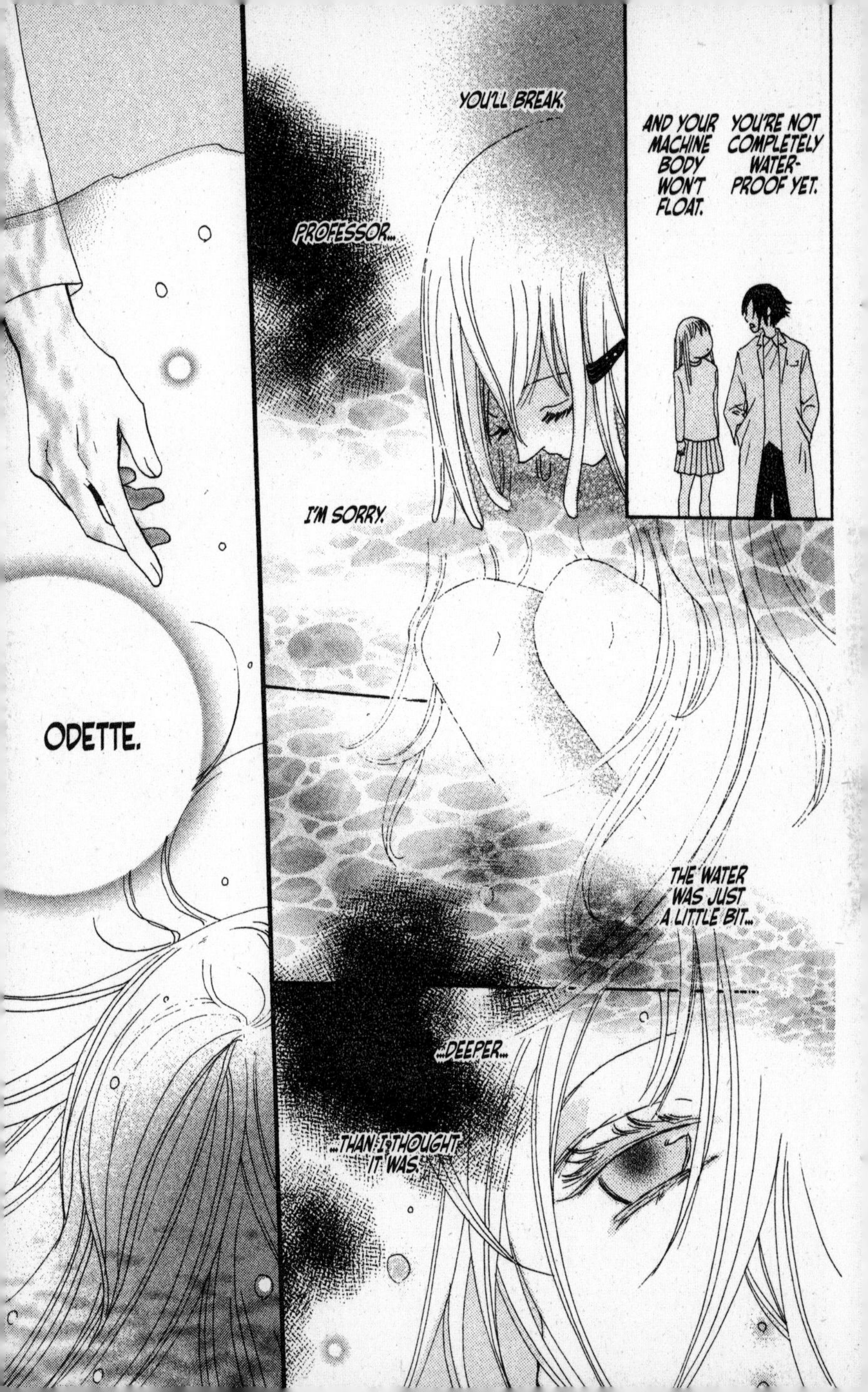
YOU'RE NOT COMPLETELY WATER-PROOF YET.
AND YOUR MACHINE BODY WON'T FLOAT.
YOU'LL BREAK.
PROFESSOR...
I'M SORRY.
THE WATER WAS JUST A LITTLE BIT...
...DEEPER...
...THAN I THOUGHT IT WAS.
ODETTE.

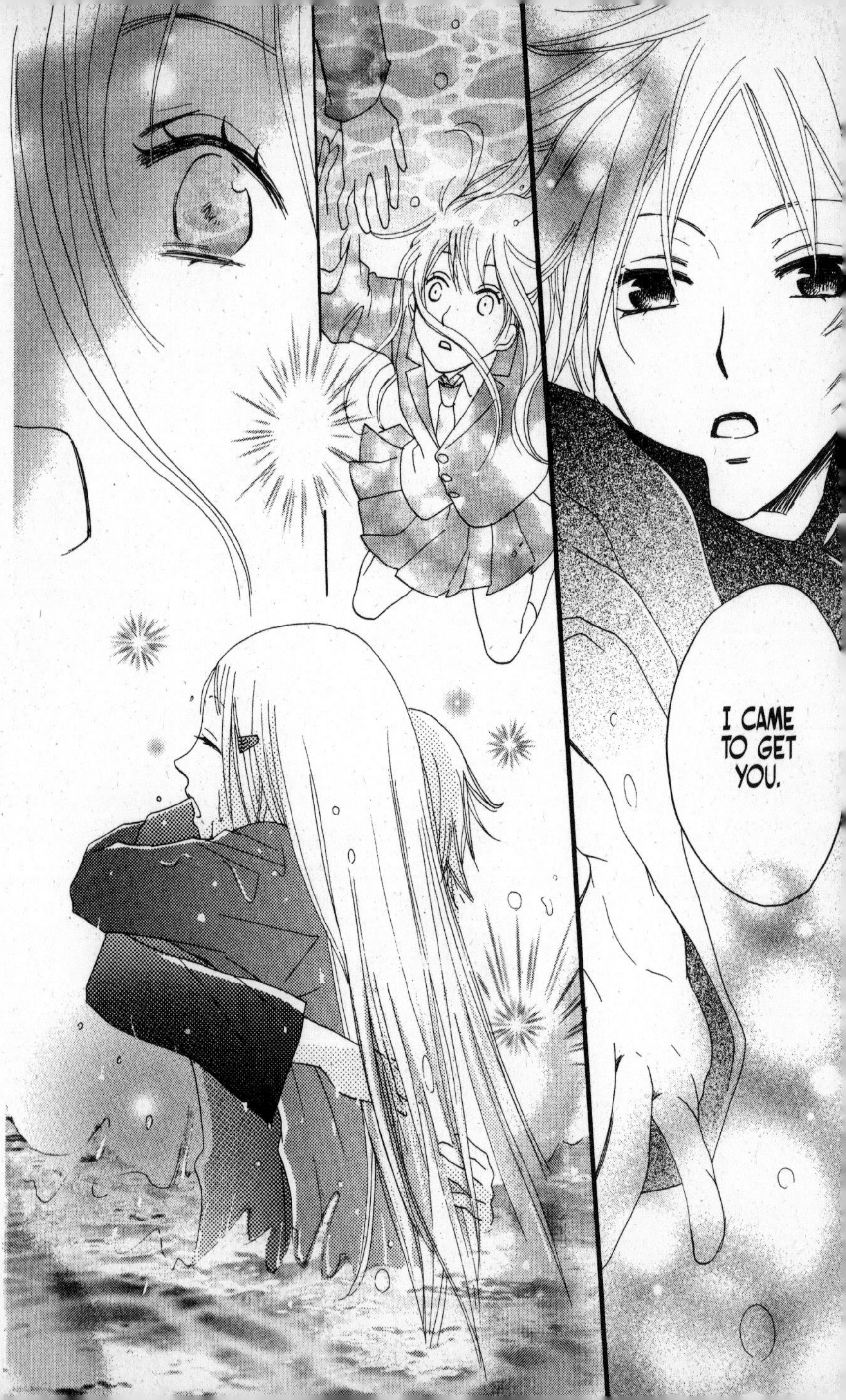
I CAME TO GET YOU.

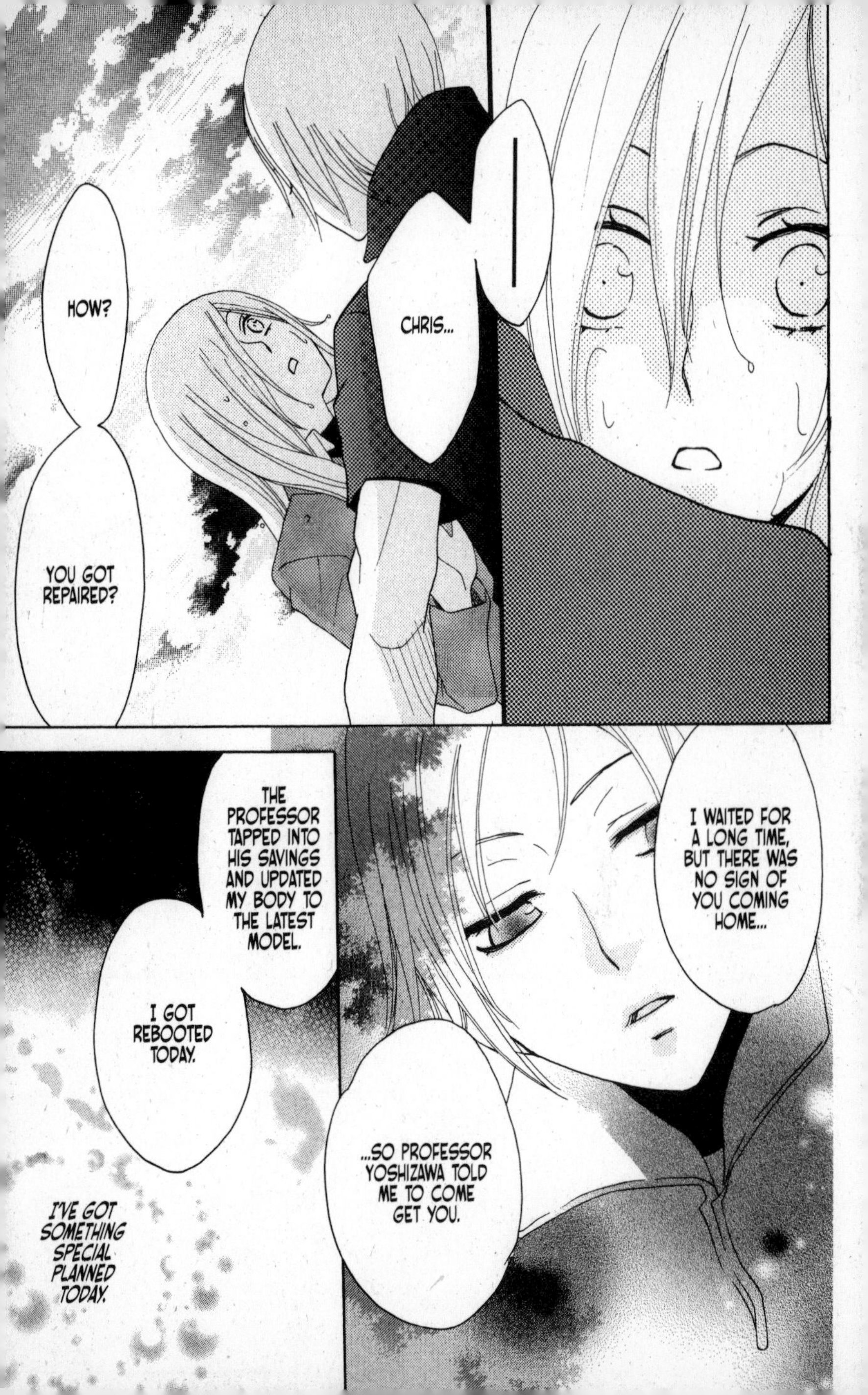
—
CHRIS...
HOW?
YOU GOT REPAIRED?
I WAITED FOR A LONG TIME, BUT THERE WAS NO SIGN OF YOU COMING HOME...
...SO PROFESSOR YOSHIZAWA TOLD ME TO COME GET YOU.
THE PROFESSOR TAPPED INTO HIS SAVINGS AND UPDATED MY BODY TO THE LATEST MODEL.
I GOT REBOOTED TODAY.
I'VE GOT SOMETHING SPECIAL PLANNED TODAY.

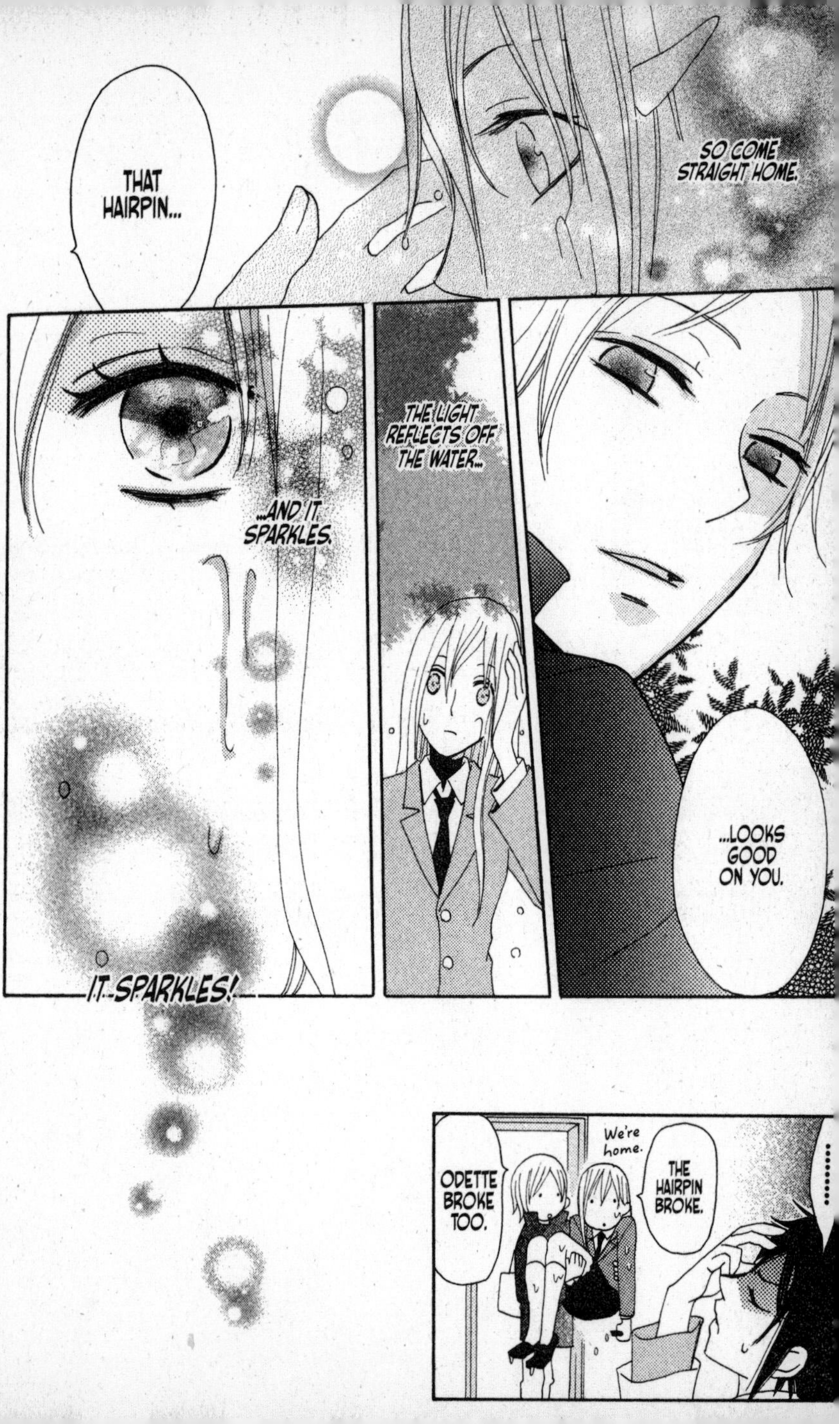
SO COME STRAIGHT HOME.
THAT HAIRPIN...
...LOOKS GOOD ON YOU.
THE LIGHT REFLECTS OFF THE WATER...
...AND IT SPARKLES.
IT SPARKLES!
...
We're home.
THE HAIRPIN BROKE.
ODETTE BROKE TOO.

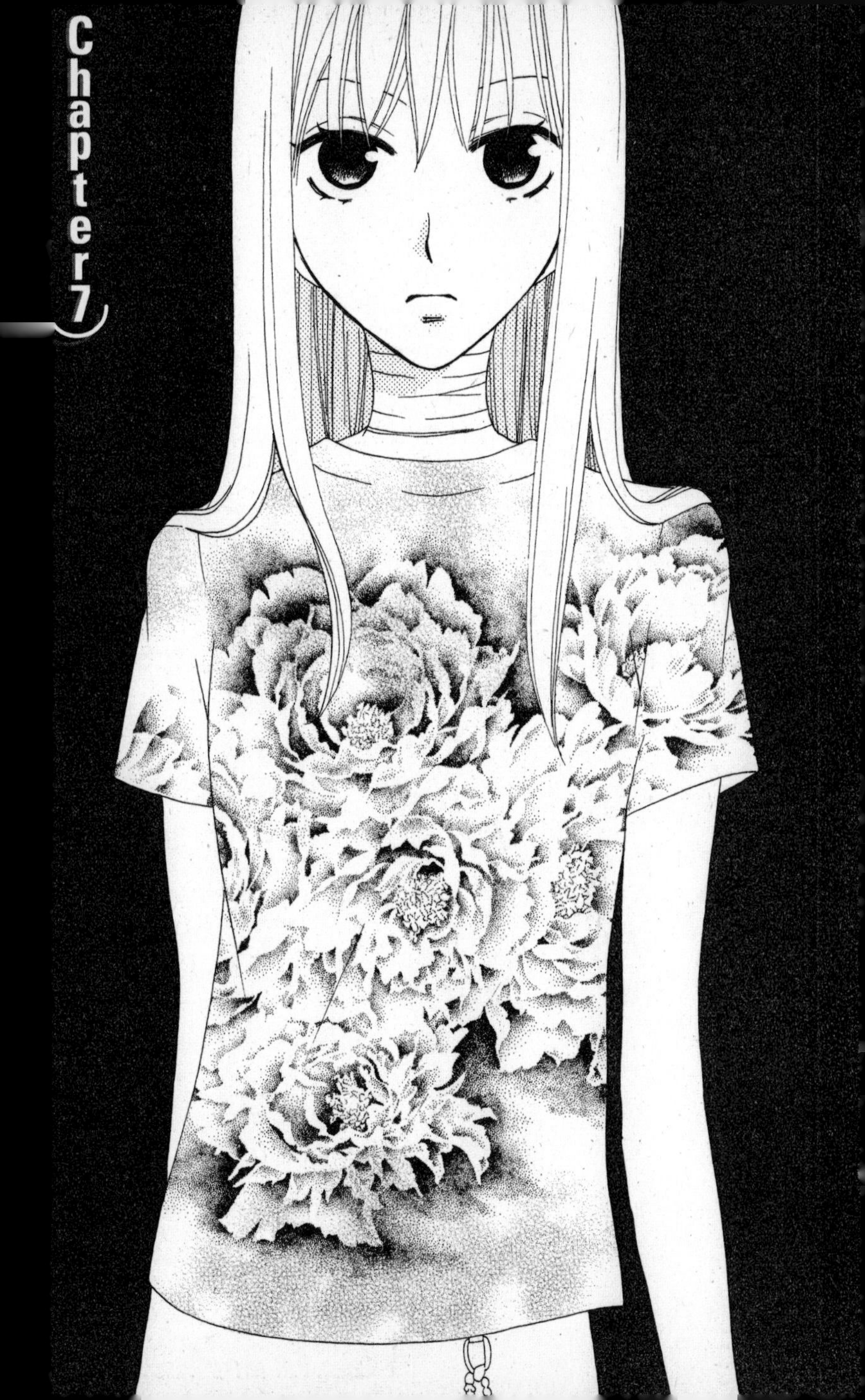
Chapter 7

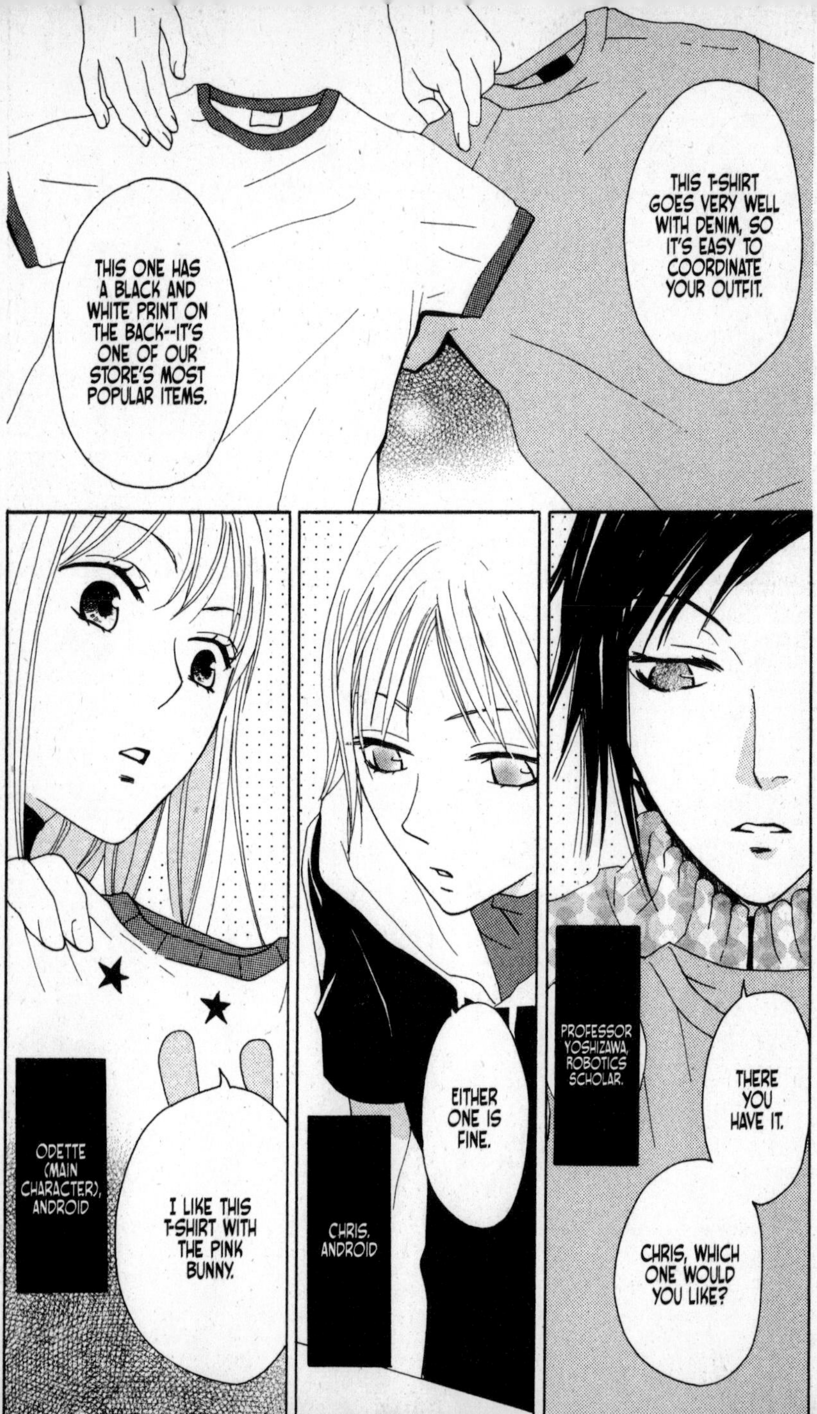
THIS T-SHIRT GOES VERY WELL WITH DENIM, SO IT'S EASY TO COORDINATE YOUR OUTFIT.
THIS ONE HAS A BLACK AND WHITE PRINT ON THE BACK--IT'S ONE OF OUR STORE'S MOST POPULAR ITEMS.
PROFESSOR YOSHIZAWA, ROBOTICS SCHOLAR.
THERE YOU HAVE IT.
CHRIS, WHICH ONE WOULD YOU LIKE?
EITHER ONE IS FINE.
CHRIS. ANDROID
ODETTE (MAIN CHARACTER), ANDROID
I LIKE THIS T-SHIRT WITH THE PINK BUNNY.

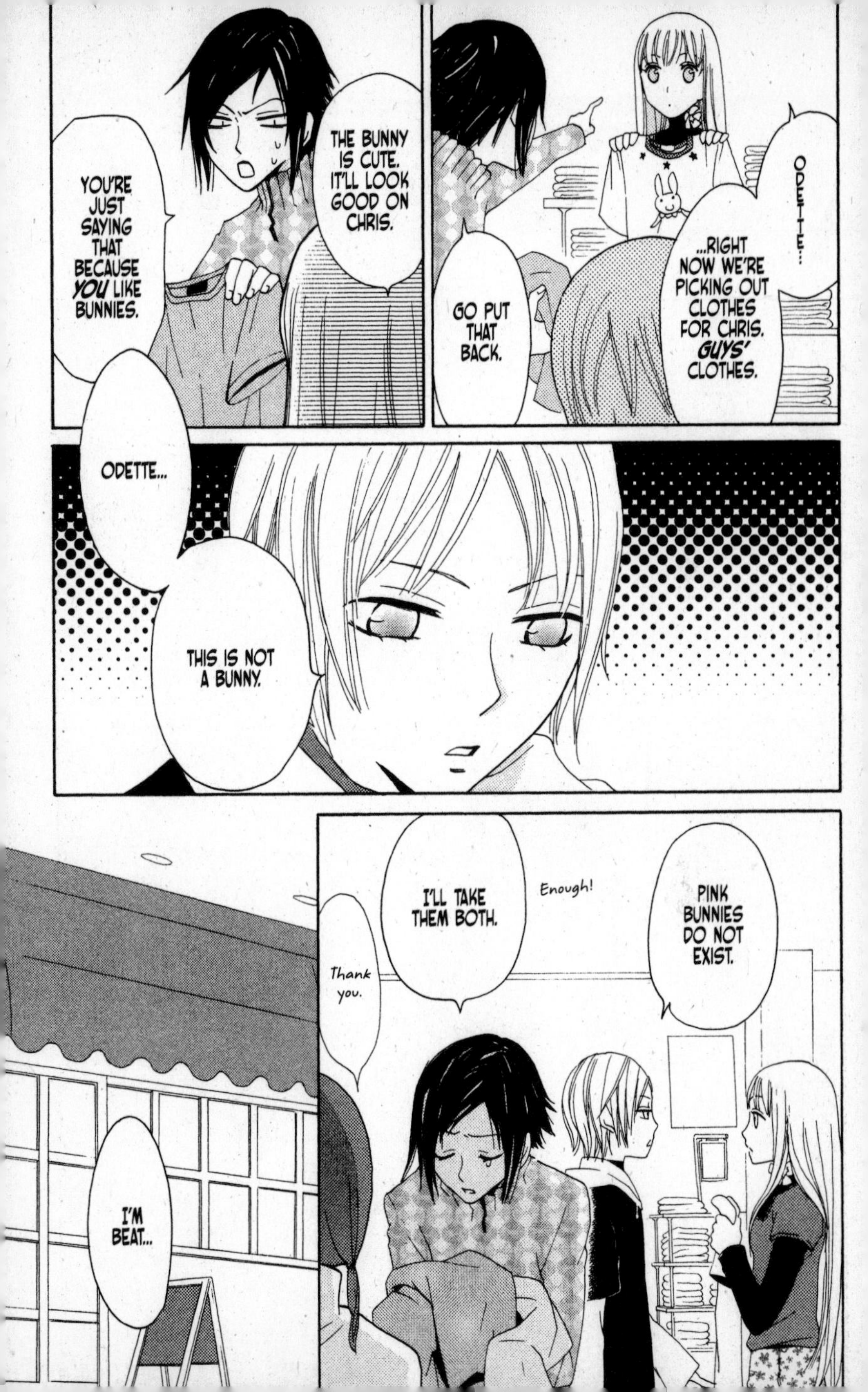
ODETTE...
...RIGHT NOW WE'RE PICKING OUT CLOTHES FOR CHRIS. *GUYS'* CLOTHES.
GO PUT THAT BACK.
THE BUNNY IS CUTE. IT'LL LOOK GOOD ON CHRIS.
YOU'RE JUST SAYING THAT BECAUSE *YOU* LIKE BUNNIES.
ODETTE...
THIS IS NOT A BUNNY.
PINK BUNNIES DO NOT EXIST.
Enough!
I'LL TAKE THEM BOTH.
Thank you.
I'M BEAT...

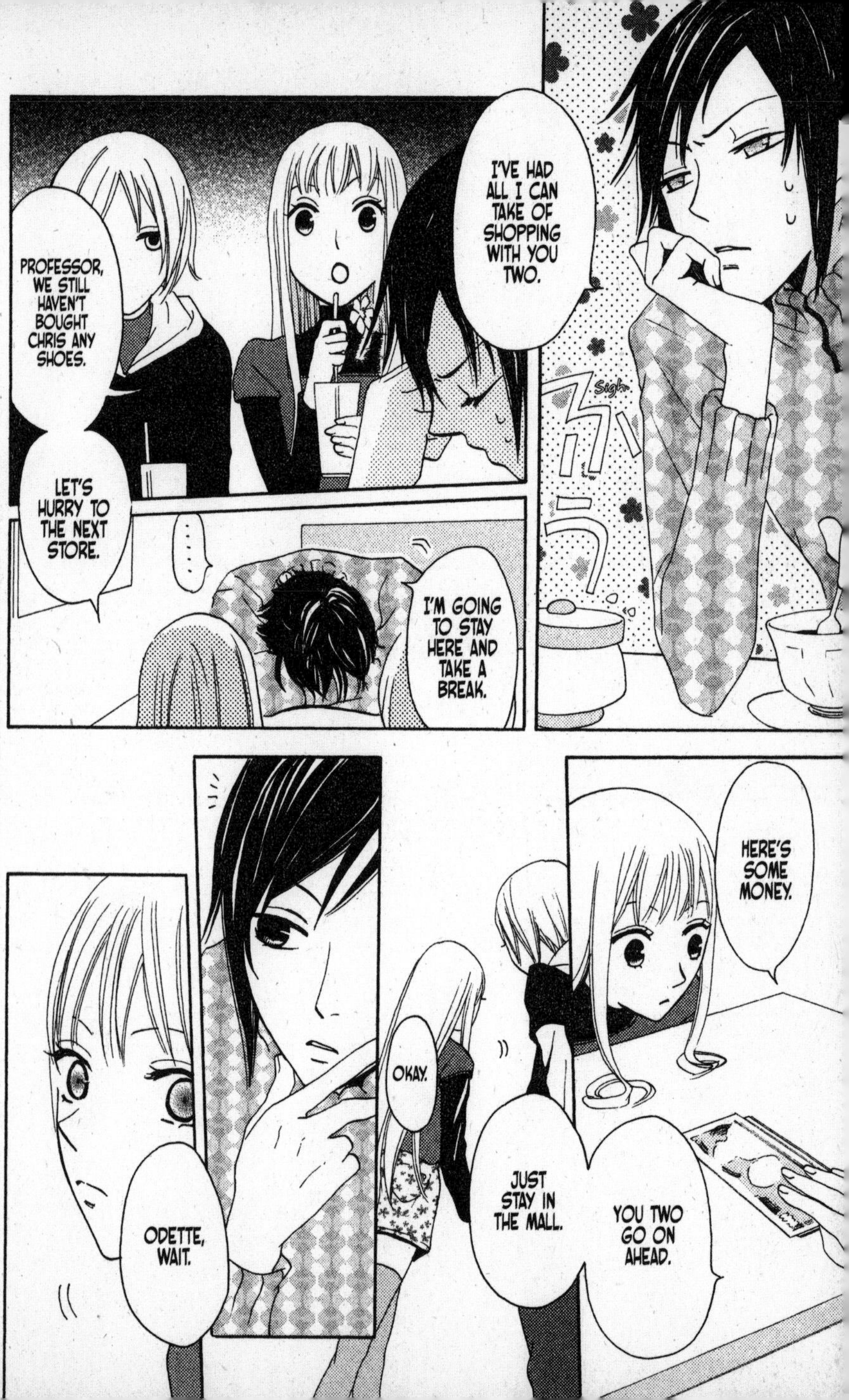
Sigh
I'VE HAD ALL I CAN TAKE OF SHOPPING WITH YOU TWO.
PROFESSOR, WE STILL HAVEN'T BOUGHT CHRIS ANY SHOES.
LET'S HURRY TO THE NEXT STORE.
......
I'M GOING TO STAY HERE AND TAKE A BREAK.
HERE'S SOME MONEY.
YOU TWO GO ON AHEAD.
JUST STAY IN THE MALL.
OKAY.
ODETTE, WAIT.

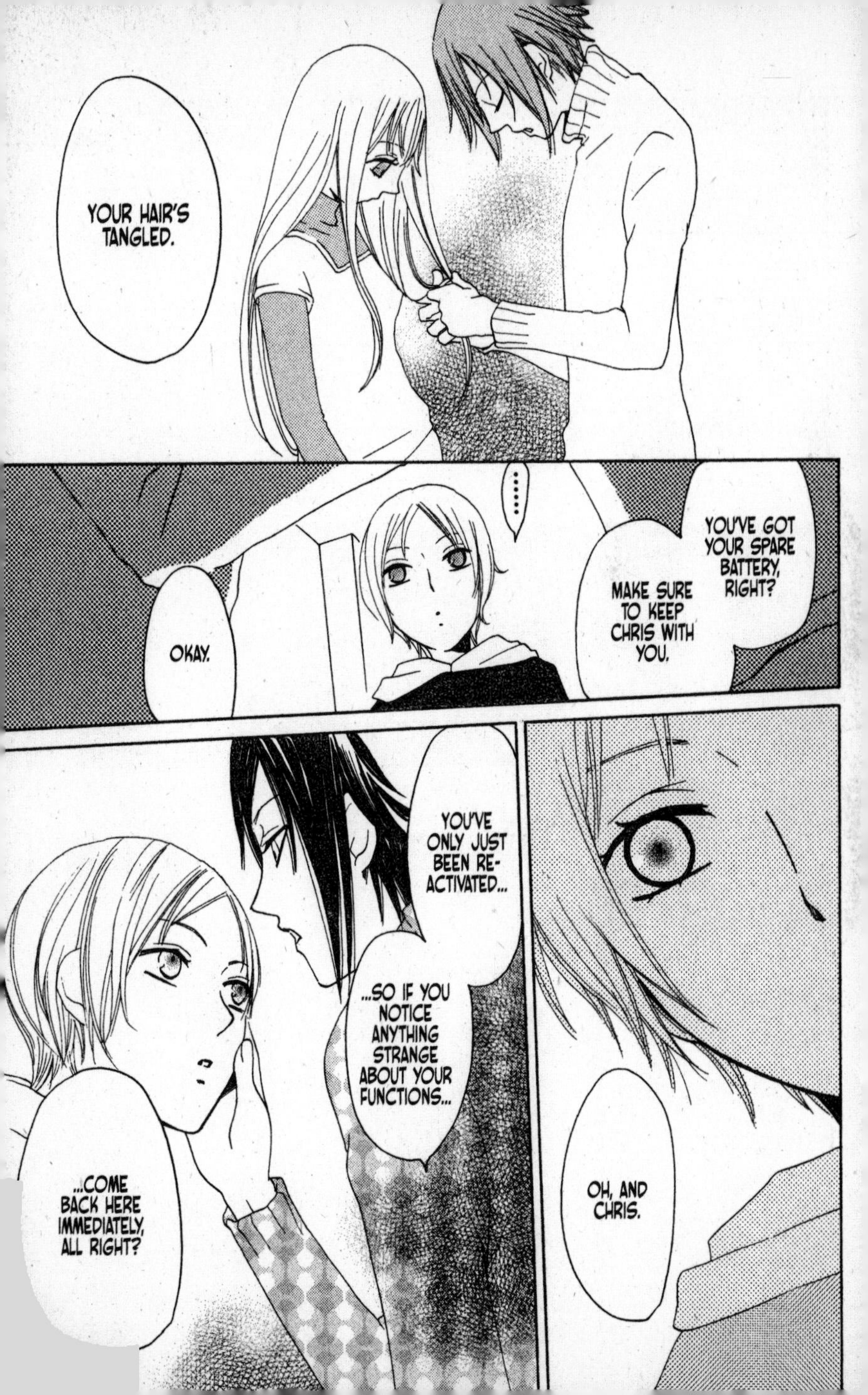
YOUR HAIR'S TANGLED.
YOU'VE GOT YOUR SPARE BATTERY, RIGHT?
MAKE SURE TO KEEP CHRIS WITH YOU.
......
OKAY.
OH, AND CHRIS.
YOU'VE ONLY JUST BEEN RE-ACTIVATED...
...SO IF YOU NOTICE ANYTHING STRANGE ABOUT YOUR FUNCTIONS...
...COME BACK HERE IMMEDIATELY, ALL RIGHT?

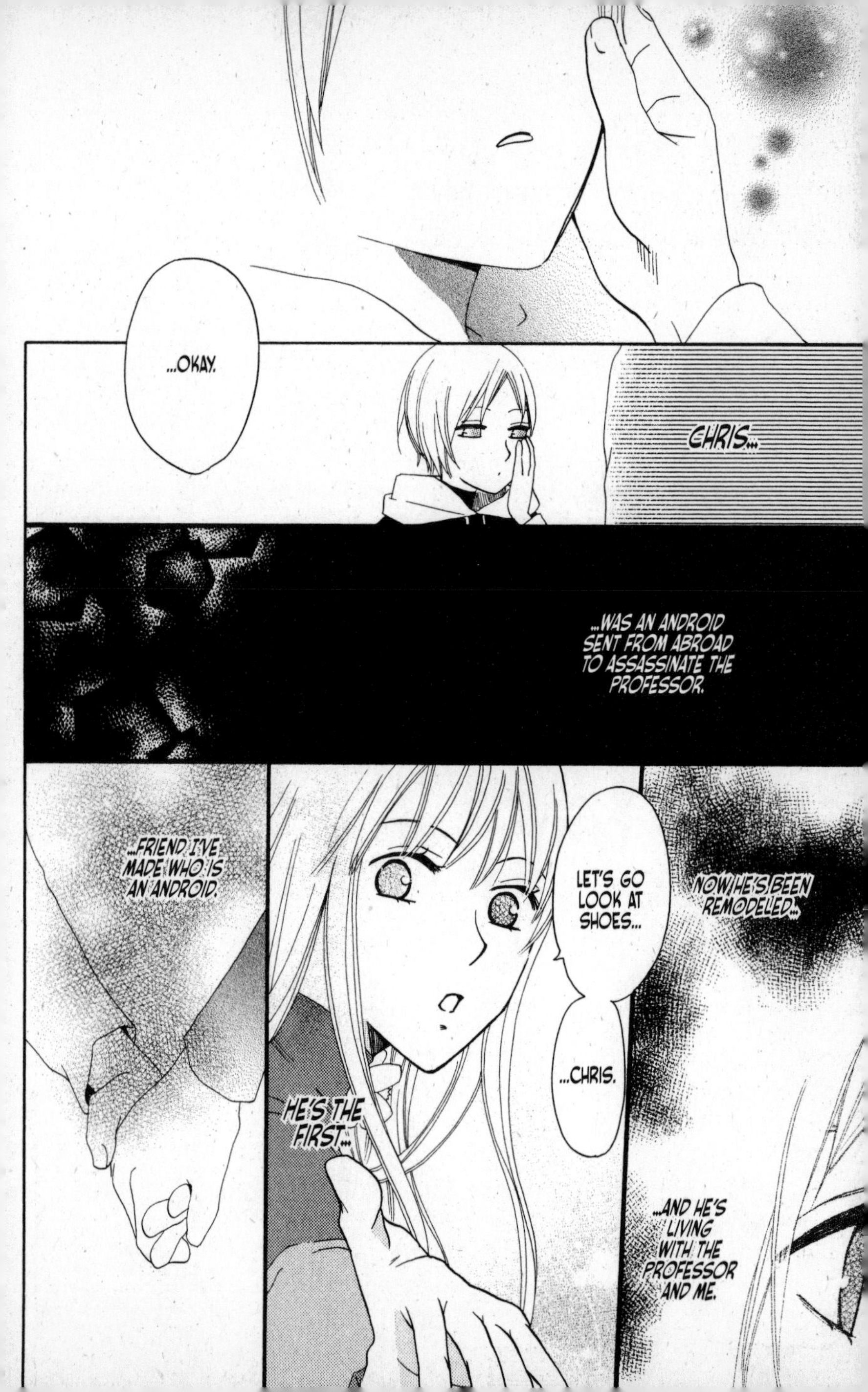
...OKAY.
CHRIS...
...WAS AN ANDROID SENT FROM ABROAD TO ASSASSINATE THE PROFESSOR.
NOW HE'S BEEN REMODELED...
...AND HE'S LIVING WITH THE PROFESSOR AND ME.
LET'S GO LOOK AT SHOES...
...CHRIS.
HE'S THE FIRST...
...FRIEND I'VE MADE WHO IS AN ANDROID.

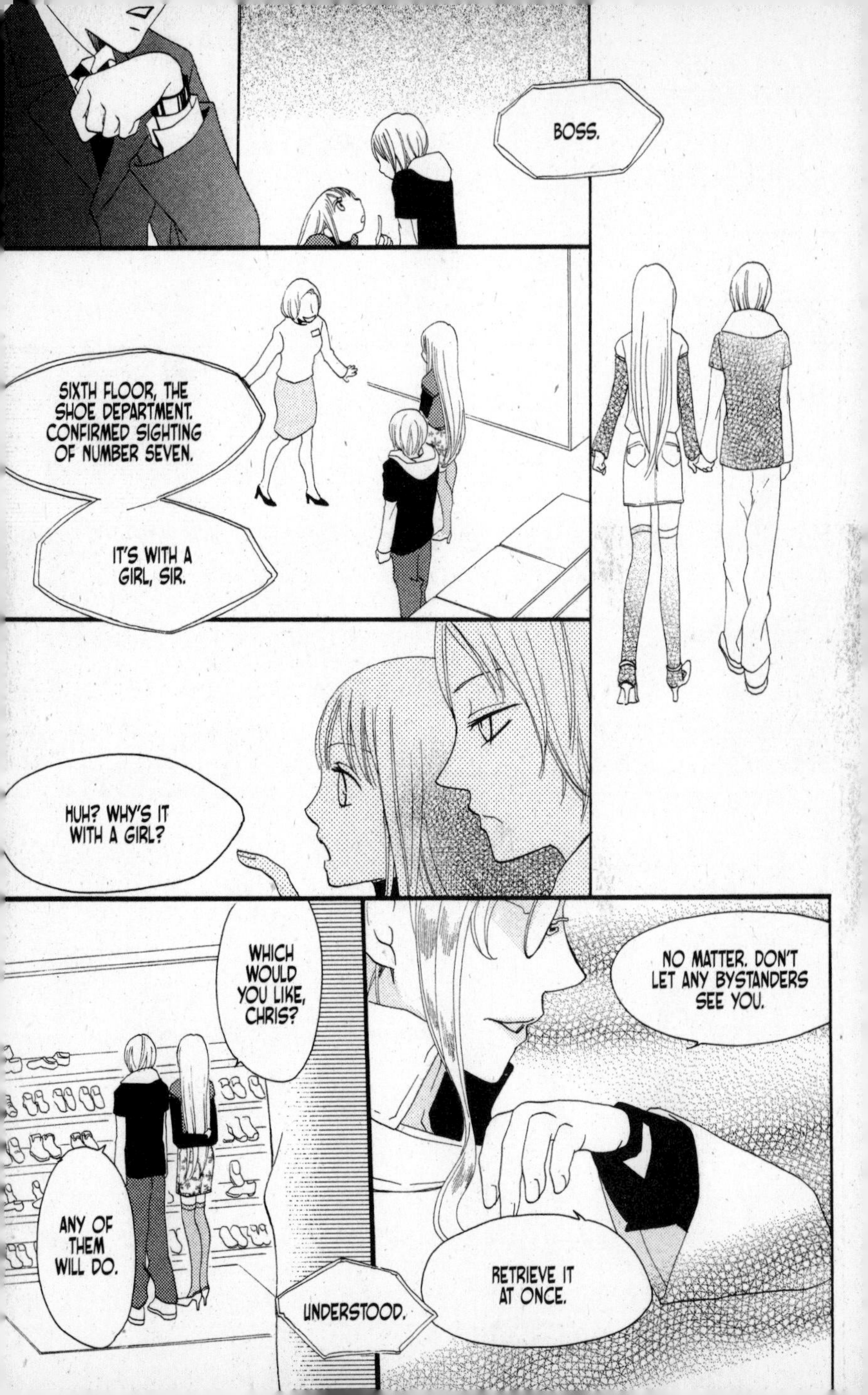
BOSS.
SIXTH FLOOR, THE SHOE DEPARTMENT. CONFIRMED SIGHTING OF NUMBER SEVEN.
IT'S WITH A GIRL, SIR.
HUH? WHY'S IT WITH A GIRL?
NO MATTER. DON'T LET ANY BYSTANDERS SEE YOU.
RETRIEVE IT AT ONCE.
UNDERSTOOD.
WHICH WOULD YOU LIKE, CHRIS?
ANY OF THEM WILL DO.

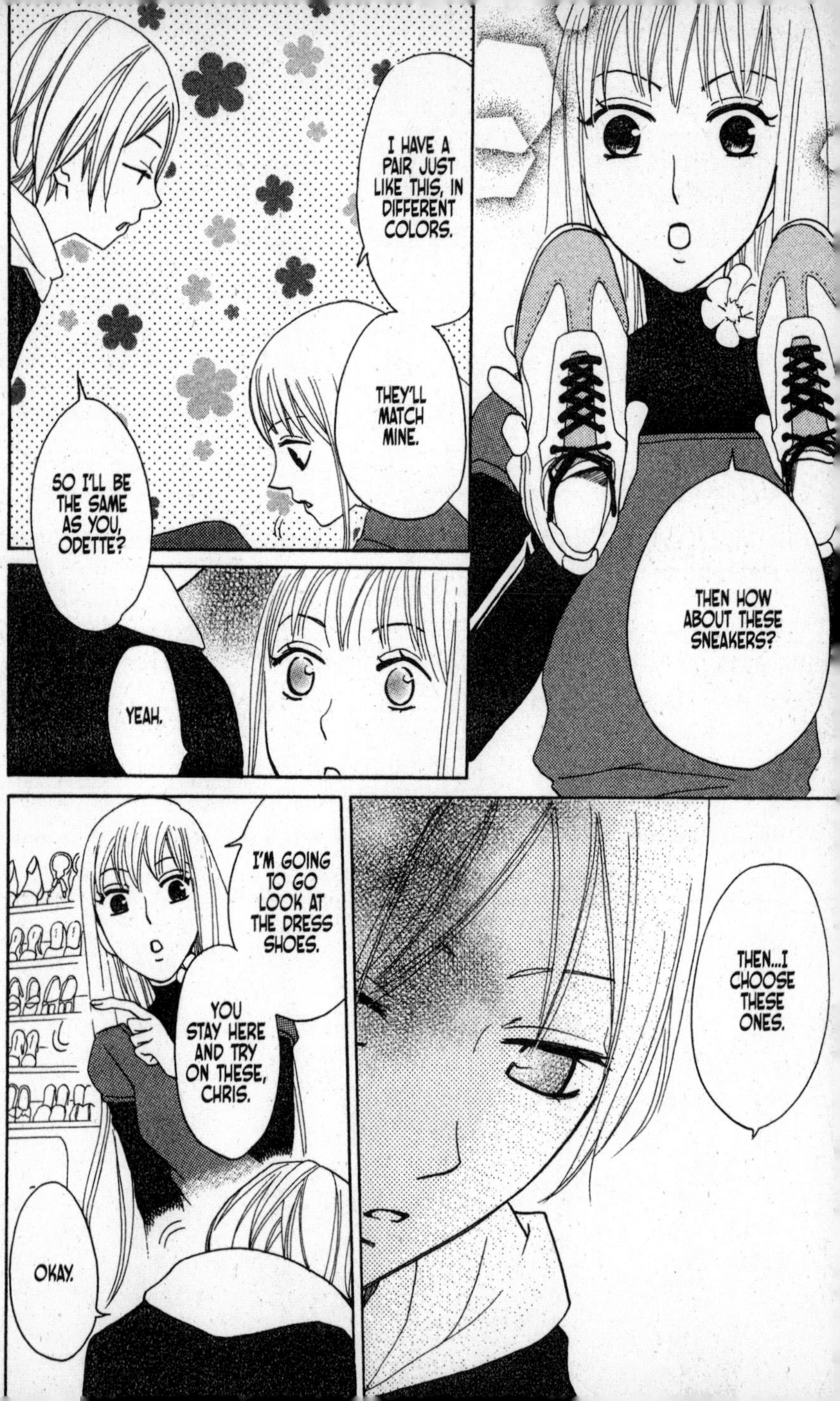
THEN HOW ABOUT THESE SNEAKERS?
I HAVE A PAIR JUST LIKE THIS, IN DIFFERENT COLORS.
THEY'LL MATCH MINE.
SO I'LL BE THE SAME AS YOU, ODETTE?
YEAH.
THEN...I CHOOSE THESE ONES.
I'M GOING TO GO LOOK AT THE DRESS SHOES.
YOU STAY HERE AND TRY ON THESE, CHRIS.
OKAY.

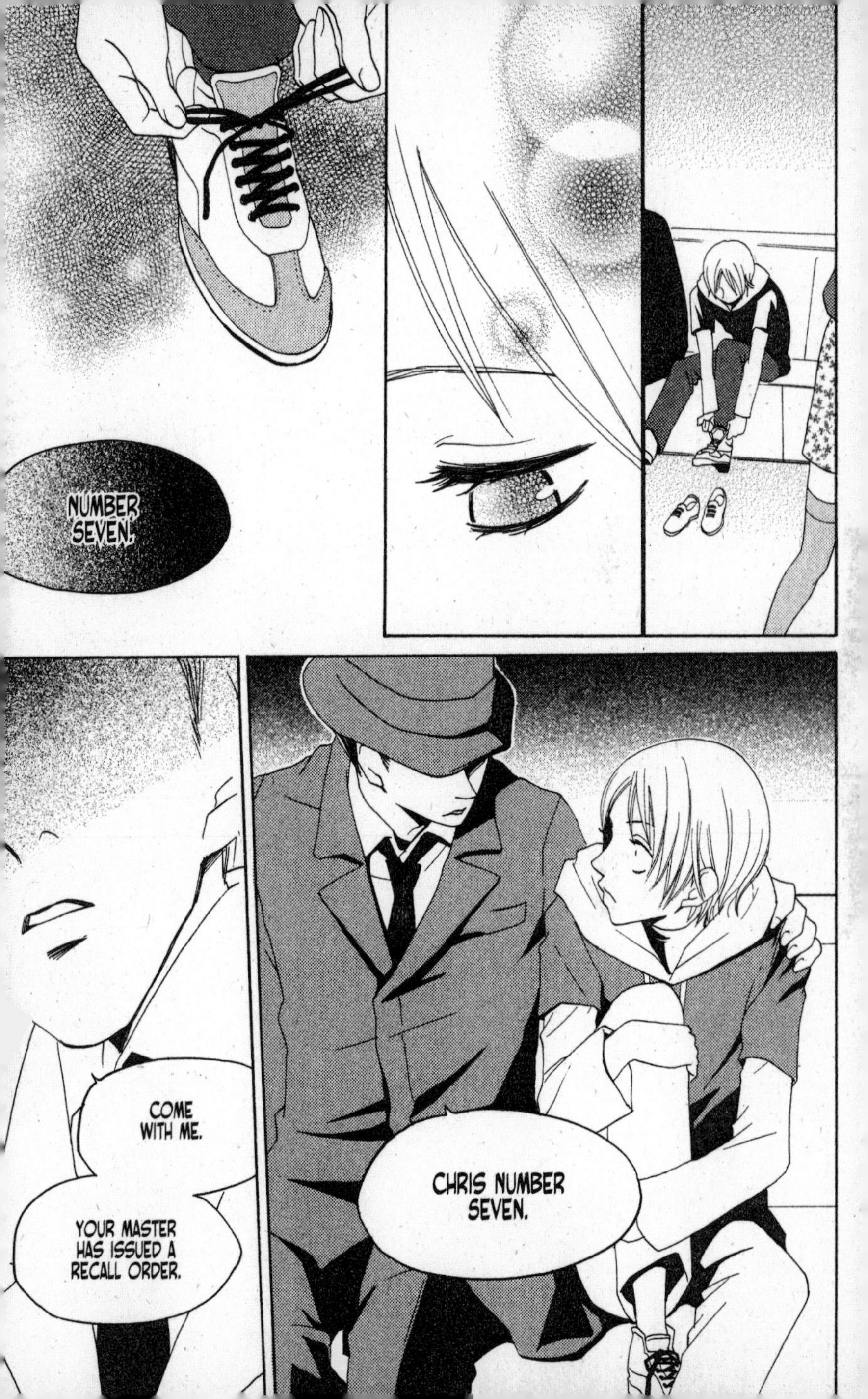
NUMBER SEVEN.
CHRIS NUMBER SEVEN.
COME WITH ME.
YOUR MASTER HAS ISSUED A RECALL ORDER.

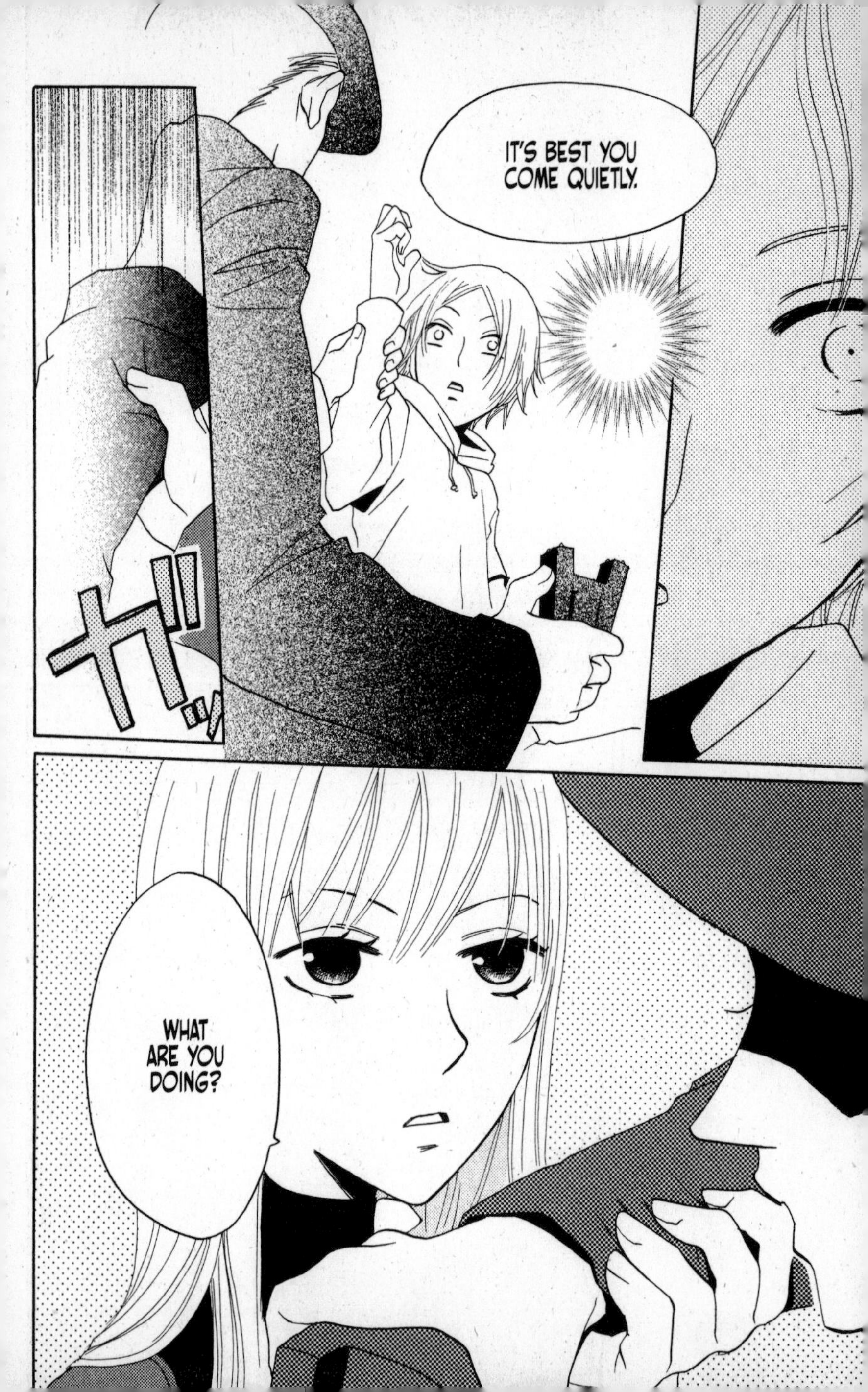
IT'S BEST YOU COME QUIETLY.
ガッ
WHAT ARE YOU DOING?

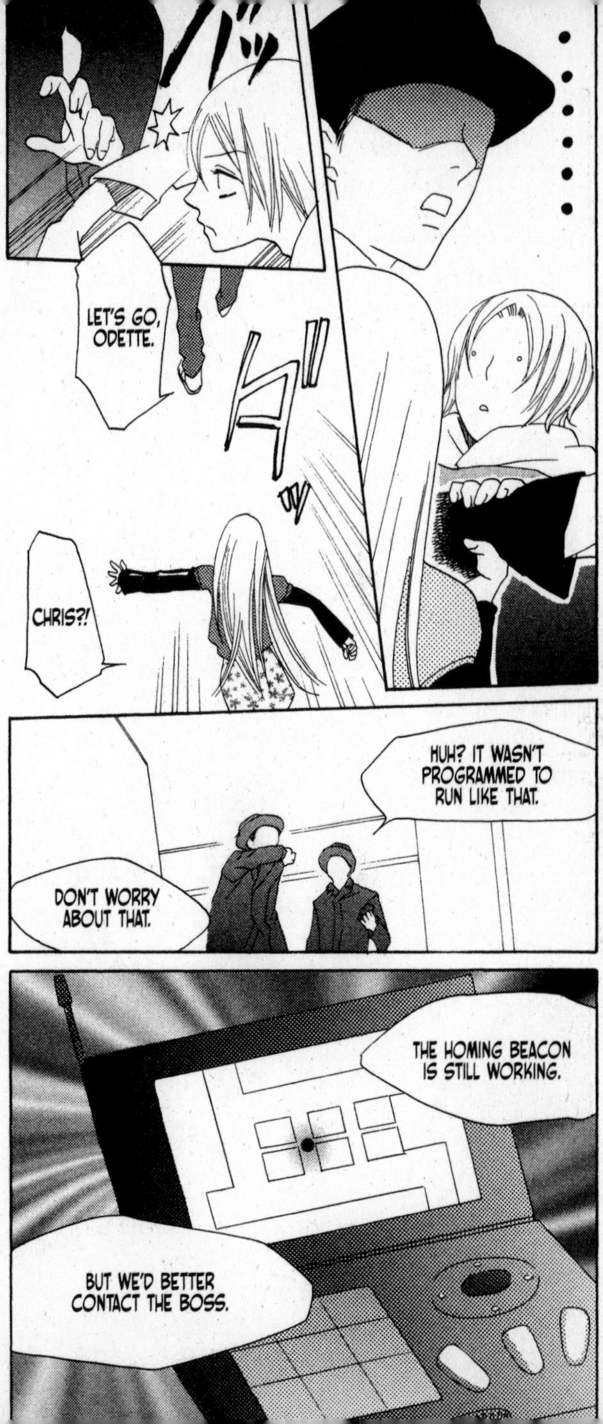
LET'S GO, ODETTE.
CHRIS?!
HUH? IT WASN'T PROGRAMMED TO RUN LIKE THAT.
DON'T WORRY ABOUT THAT.
THE HOMING BEACON IS STILL WORKING.
BUT WE'D BETTER CONTACT THE BOSS.

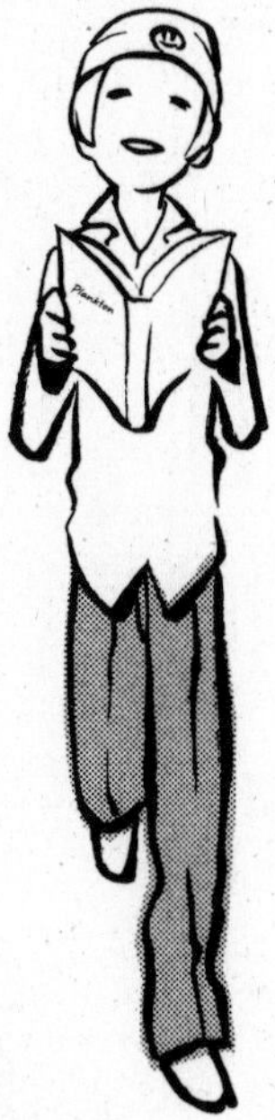
Plankton

Iwasaki

Asao's friend.

He buys a copy of his favorite manga magazine, **Shonen Plankton,** every week

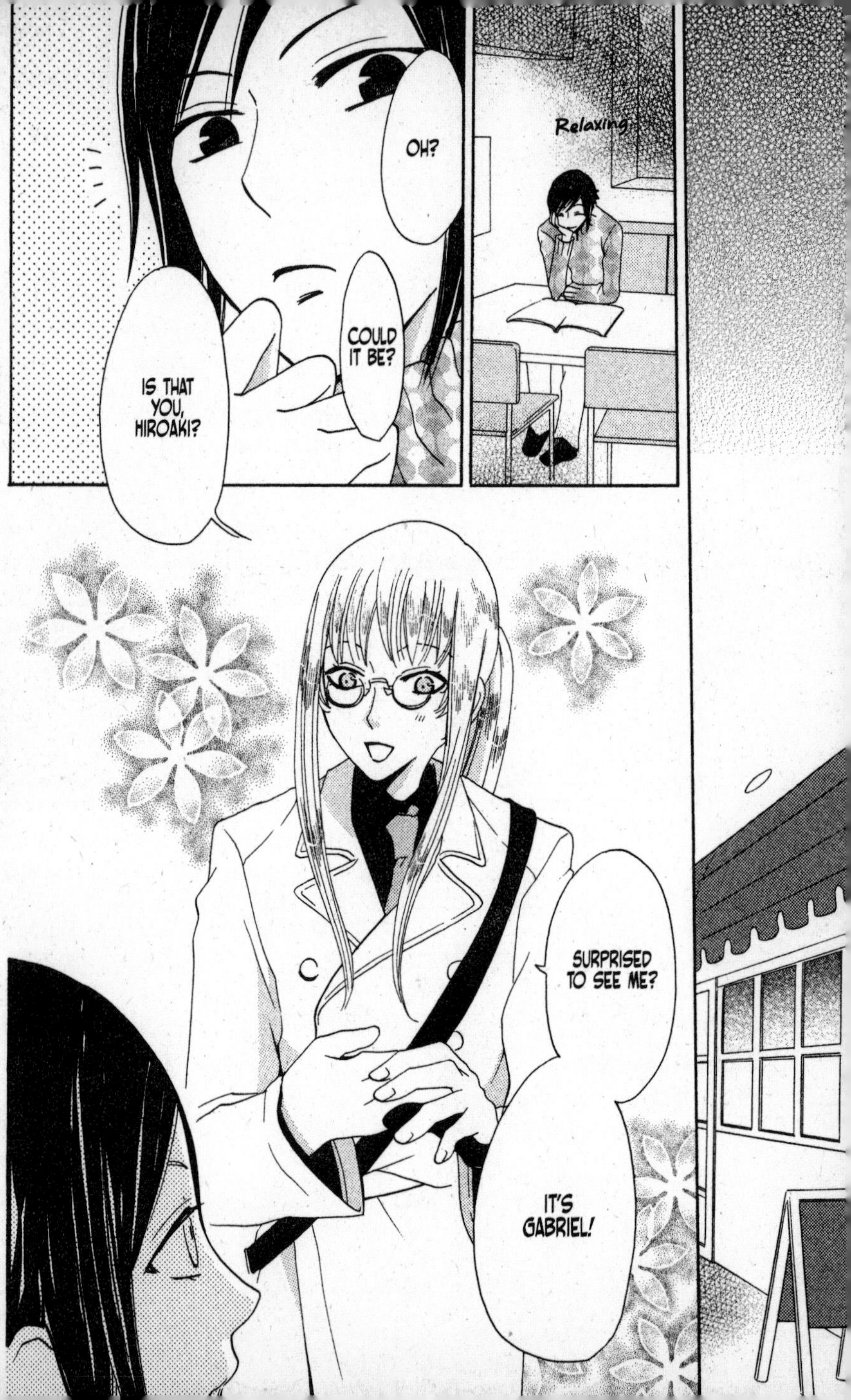
Relaxing
OH?
COULD IT BE?
IS THAT YOU, HIROAKI?
SURPRISED TO SEE ME?
IT'S GABRIEL!

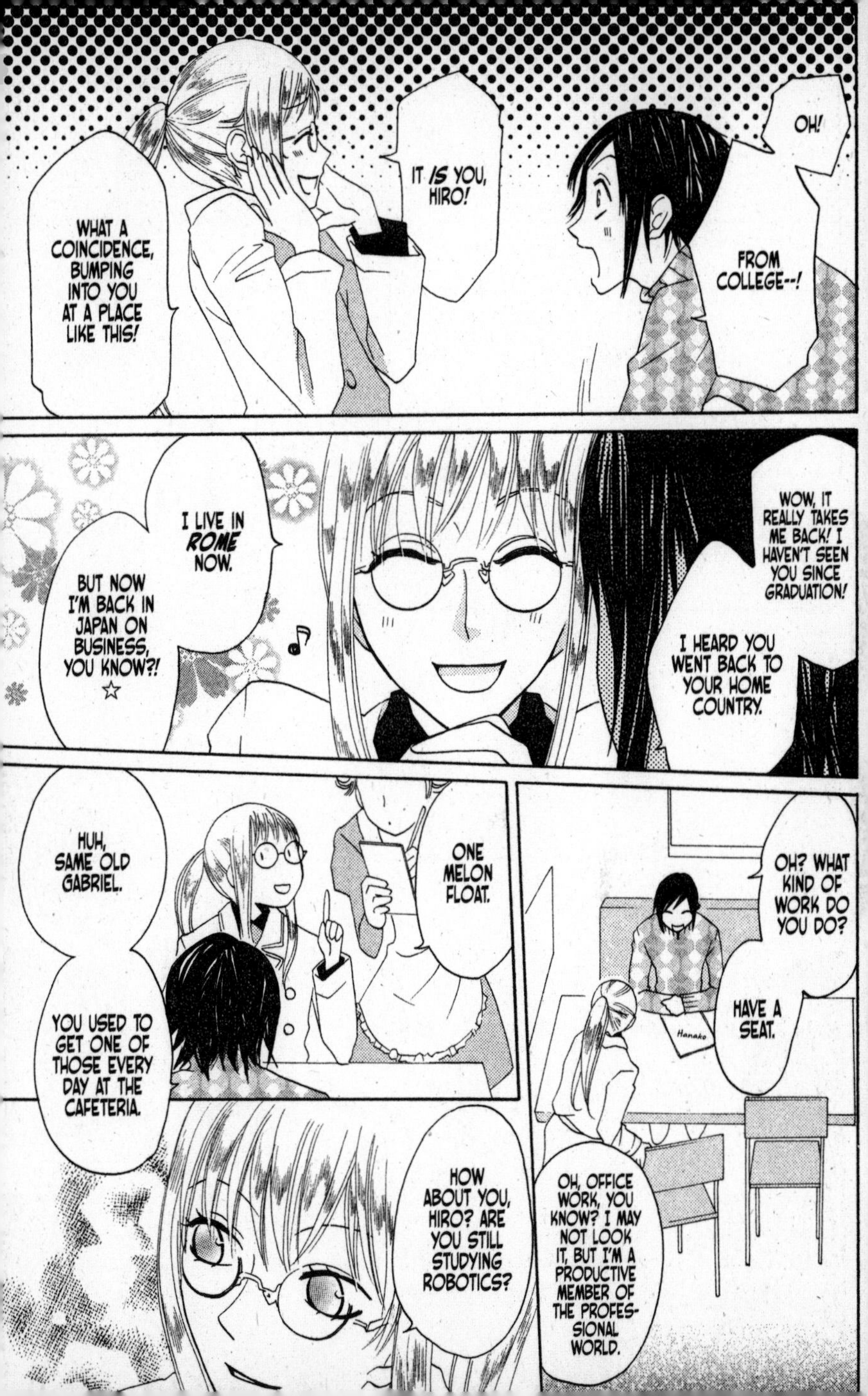

OH!
FROM COLLEGE--!
IT *IS* YOU, HIRO!
WHAT A COINCIDENCE, BUMPING INTO YOU AT A PLACE LIKE THIS!
WOW, IT REALLY TAKES ME BACK! I HAVEN'T SEEN YOU SINCE GRADUATION!
I HEARD YOU WENT BACK TO YOUR HOME COUNTRY.
I LIVE IN *ROME* NOW.
BUT NOW I'M BACK IN JAPAN ON BUSINESS, YOU KNOW?! ☆
OH? WHAT KIND OF WORK DO YOU DO?
HAVE A SEAT.
Hanako
ONE MELON FLOAT.
HUH, SAME OLD GABRIEL.
YOU USED TO GET ONE OF THOSE EVERY DAY AT THE CAFETERIA.
OH, OFFICE WORK, YOU KNOW? I MAY NOT LOOK IT, BUT I'M A PRODUCTIVE MEMBER OF THE PROFES-SIONAL WORLD.
HOW ABOUT YOU, HIRO? ARE YOU STILL STUDYING ROBOTICS?

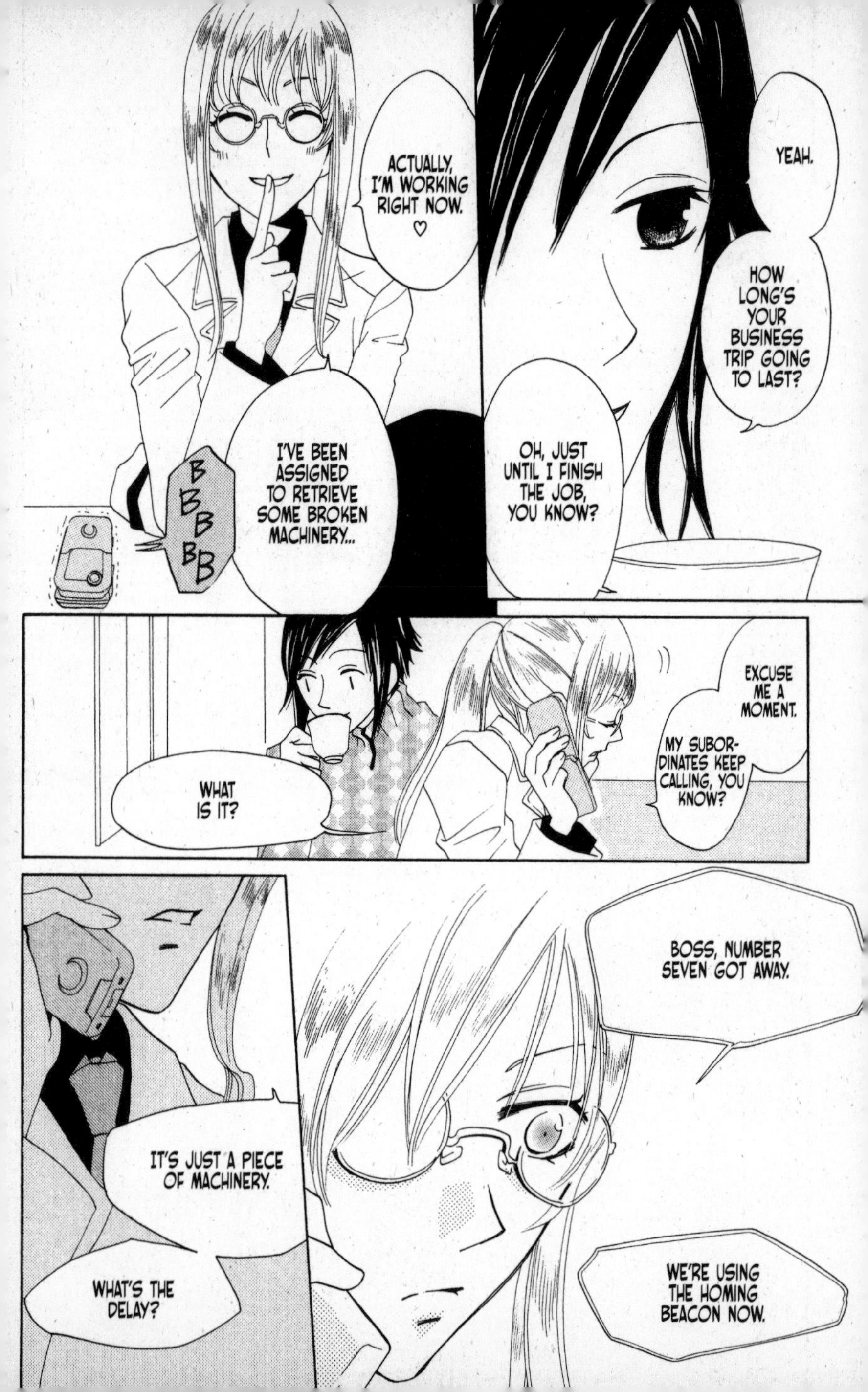
YEAH.
HOW LONG'S YOUR BUSINESS TRIP GOING TO LAST?
OH, JUST UNTIL I FINISH THE JOB, YOU KNOW?
ACTUALLY, I'M WORKING RIGHT NOW. ♡
BBBB
I'VE BEEN ASSIGNED TO RETRIEVE SOME BROKEN MACHINERY...
EXCUSE ME A MOMENT.
MY SUBOR-DINATES KEEP CALLING, YOU KNOW?
WHAT IS IT?
BOSS, NUMBER SEVEN GOT AWAY.
IT'S JUST A PIECE OF MACHINERY.
WHAT'S THE DELAY?
WE'RE USING THE HOMING BEACON NOW.

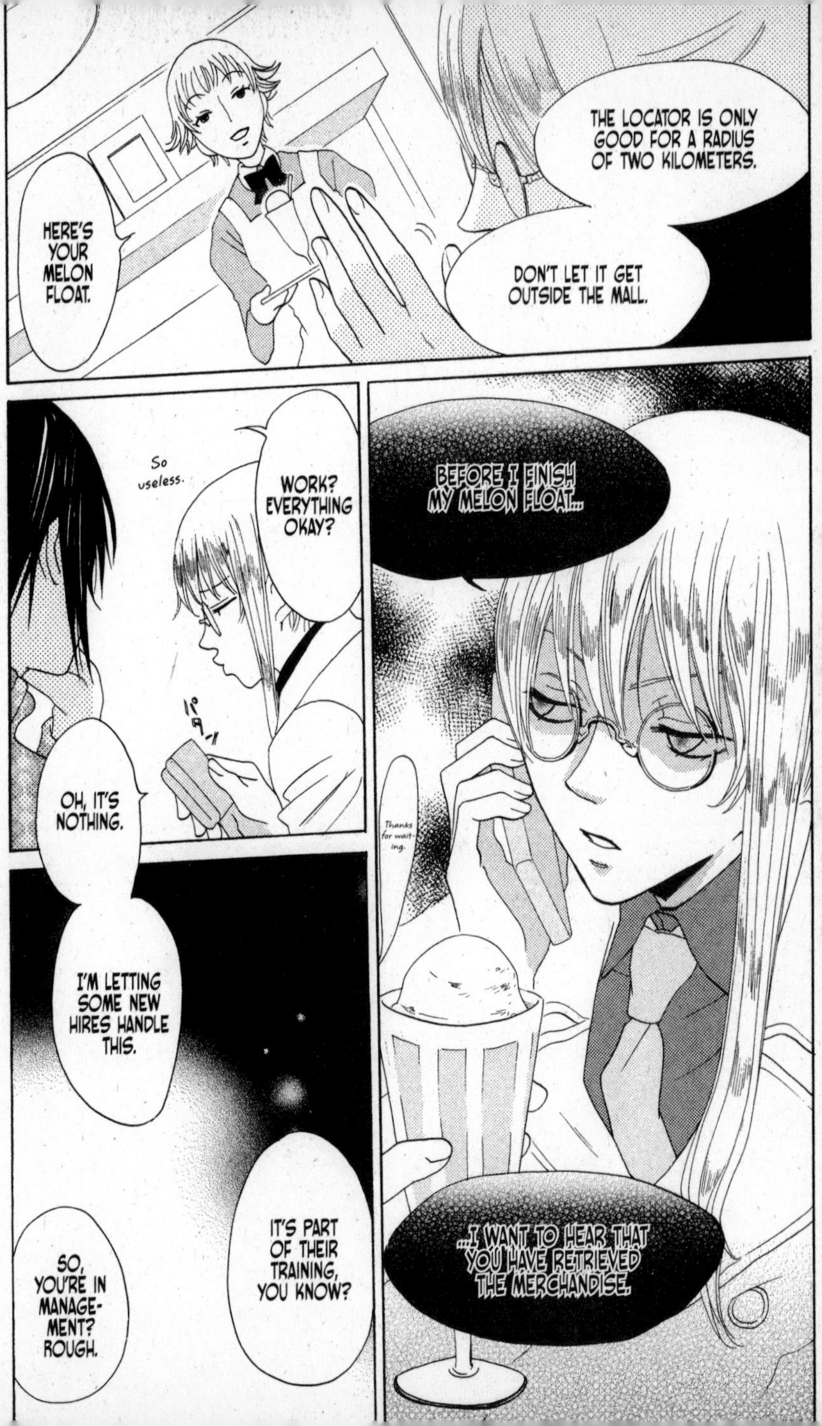
THE LOCATOR IS ONLY GOOD FOR A RADIUS OF TWO KILOMETERS.
DON'T LET IT GET OUTSIDE THE MALL.
HERE'S YOUR MELON FLOAT.
BEFORE I FINISH MY MELON FLOAT...
Thanks for wait-ing.
...I WANT TO HEAR THAT YOU HAVE RETRIEVED THE MERCHANDISE.
WORK? EVERYTHING OKAY?
So useless.
OH, IT'S NOTHING.
I'M LETTING SOME NEW HIRES HANDLE THIS.
IT'S PART OF THEIR TRAINING, YOU KNOW?
SO, YOU'RE IN MANAGE-MENT? ROUGH.

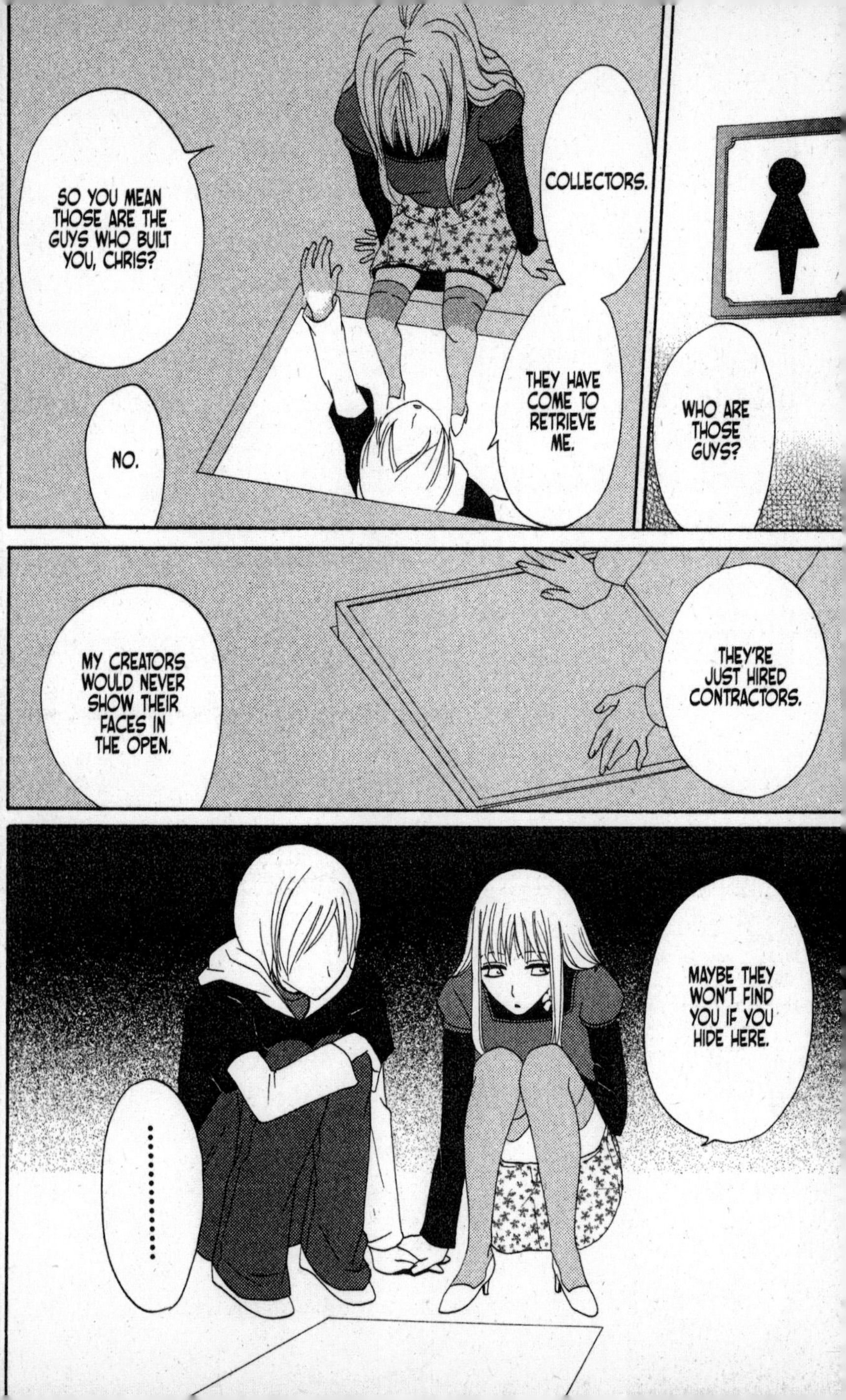
WHO ARE THOSE GUYS?
COLLECTORS.
THEY HAVE COME TO RETRIEVE ME.
SO YOU MEAN THOSE ARE THE GUYS WHO BUILT YOU, CHRIS?
NO.
THEY'RE JUST HIRED CONTRACTORS.
MY CREATORS WOULD NEVER SHOW THEIR FACES IN THE OPEN.
MAYBE THEY WON'T FIND YOU IF YOU HIDE HERE.
......

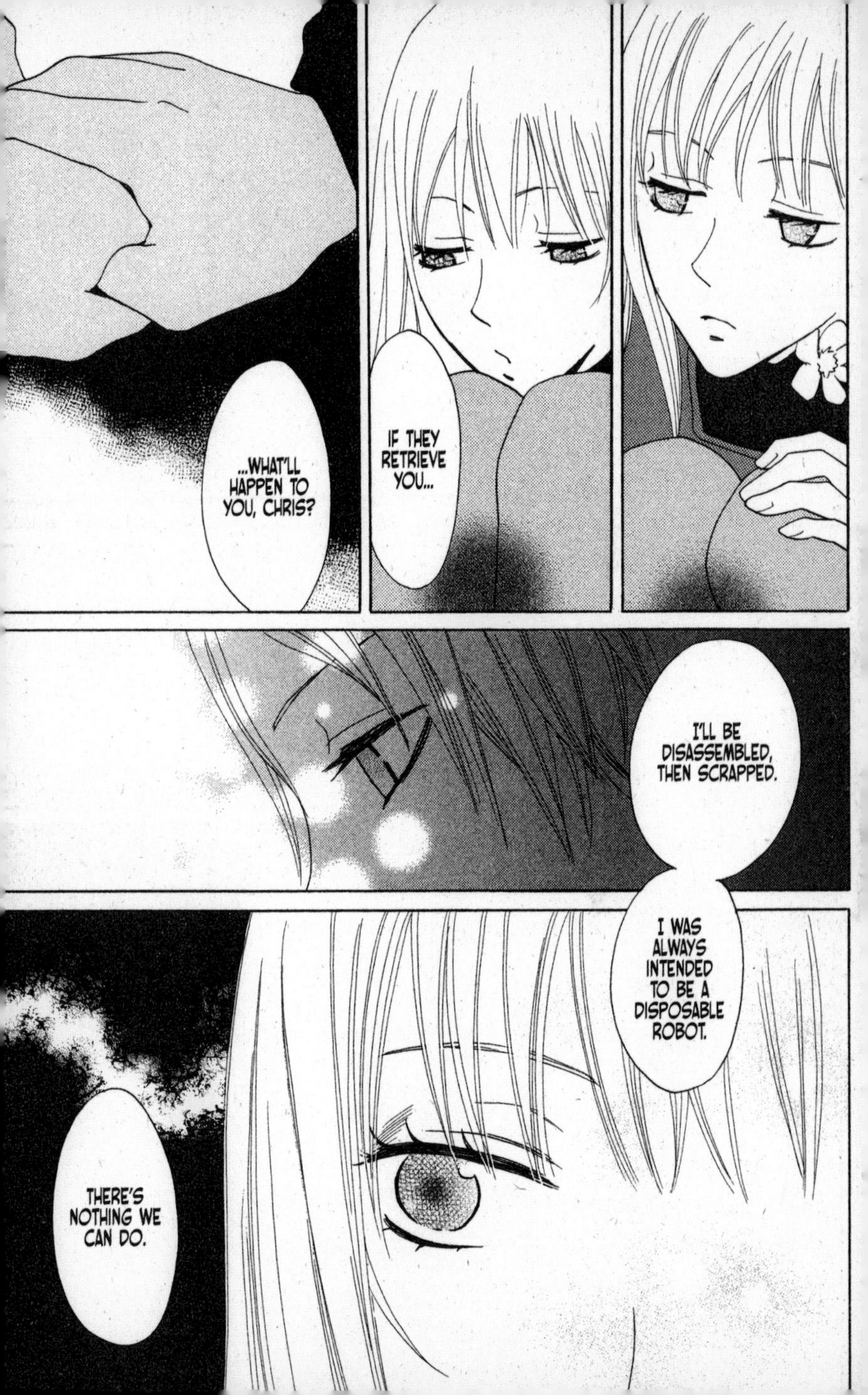
IF THEY RETRIEVE YOU...
...WHAT'LL HAPPEN TO YOU, CHRIS?
I'LL BE DISASSEMBLED, THEN SCRAPPED.
I WAS ALWAYS INTENDED TO BE A DISPOSABLE ROBOT.
THERE'S NOTHING WE CAN DO.

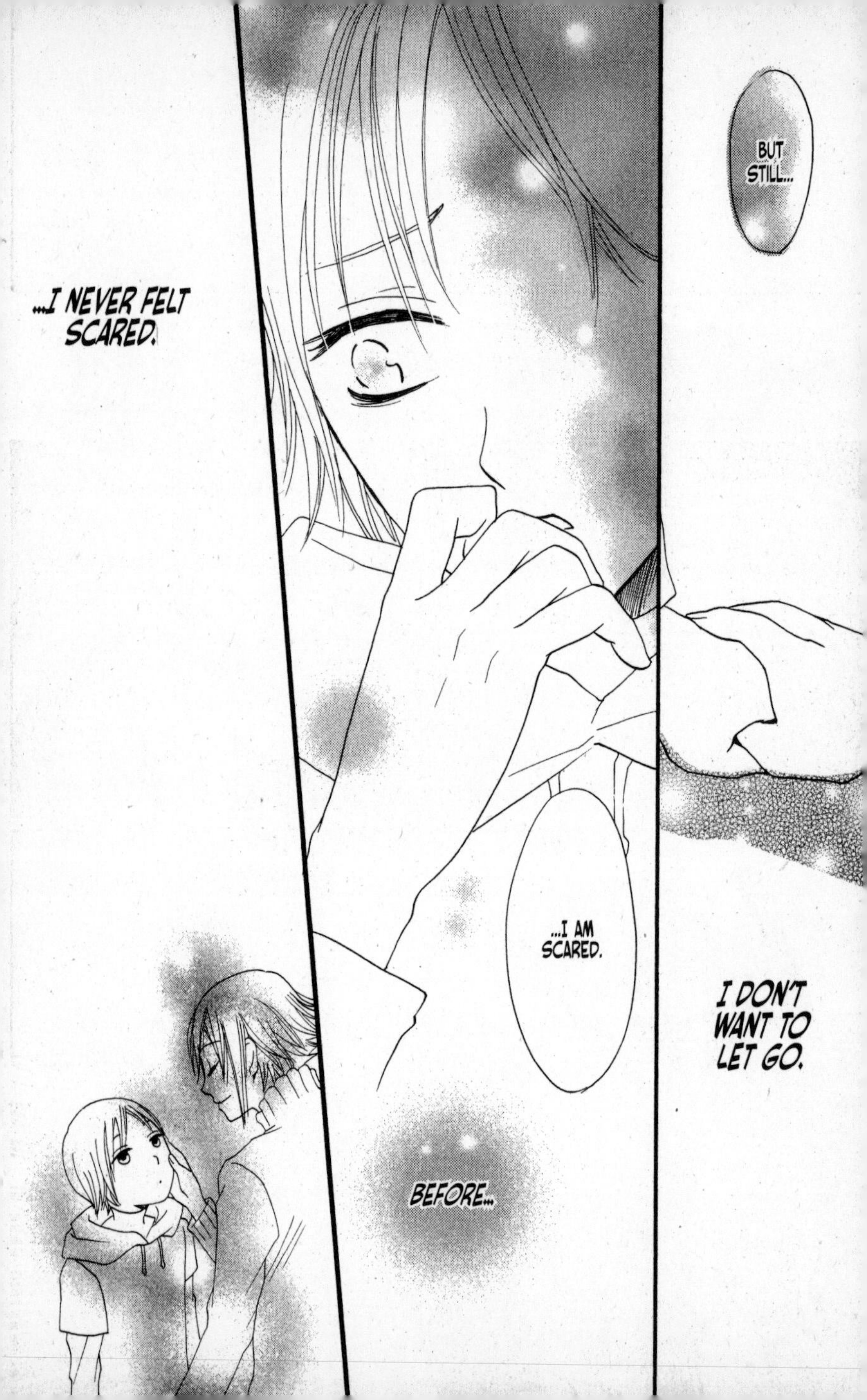
BUT STILL...
I DON'T WANT TO LET GO.
...I AM SCARED.
BEFORE...
...I NEVER FELT SCARED.

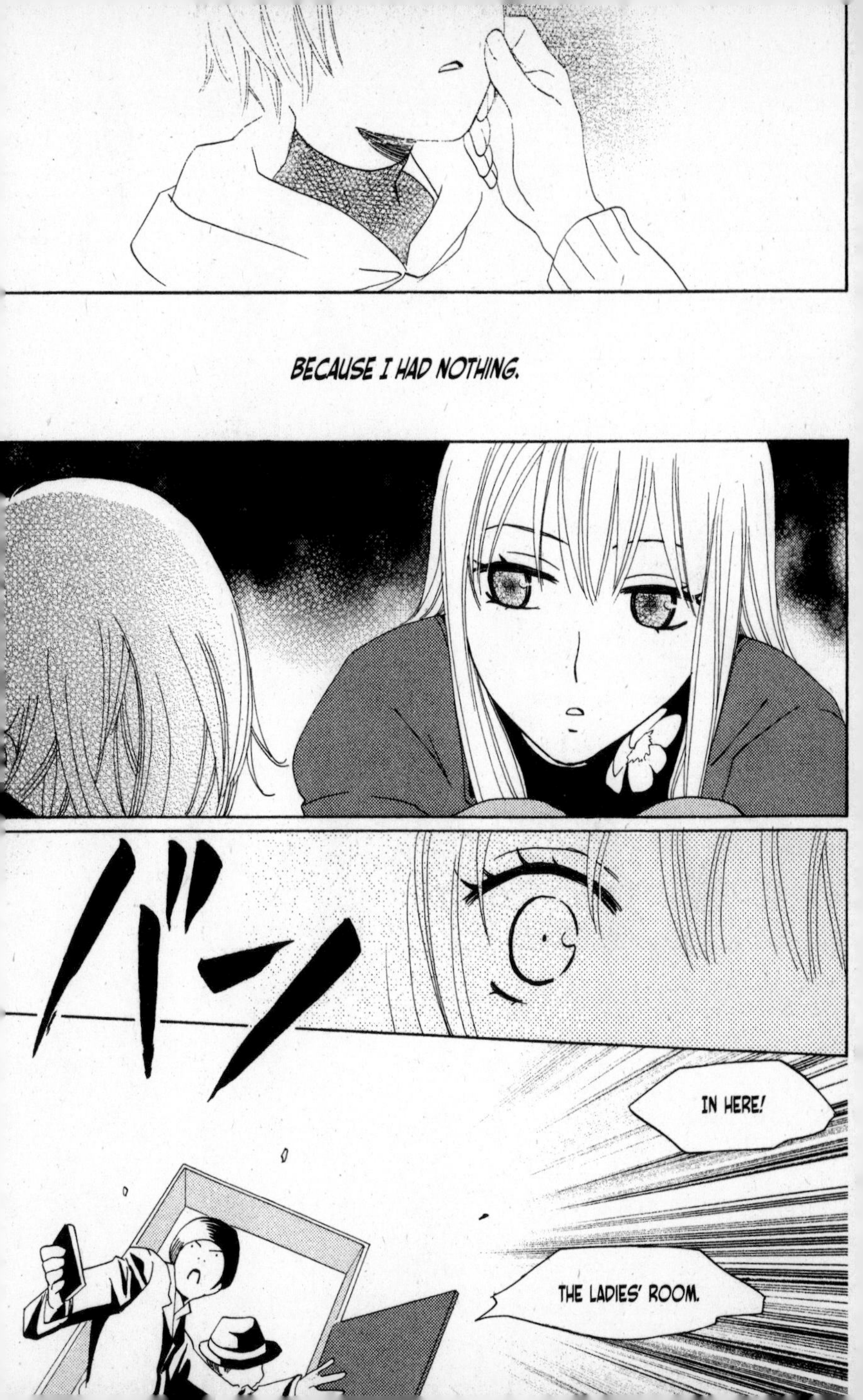
BECAUSE I HAD NOTHING.
バン
IN HERE!
THE LADIES' ROOM.

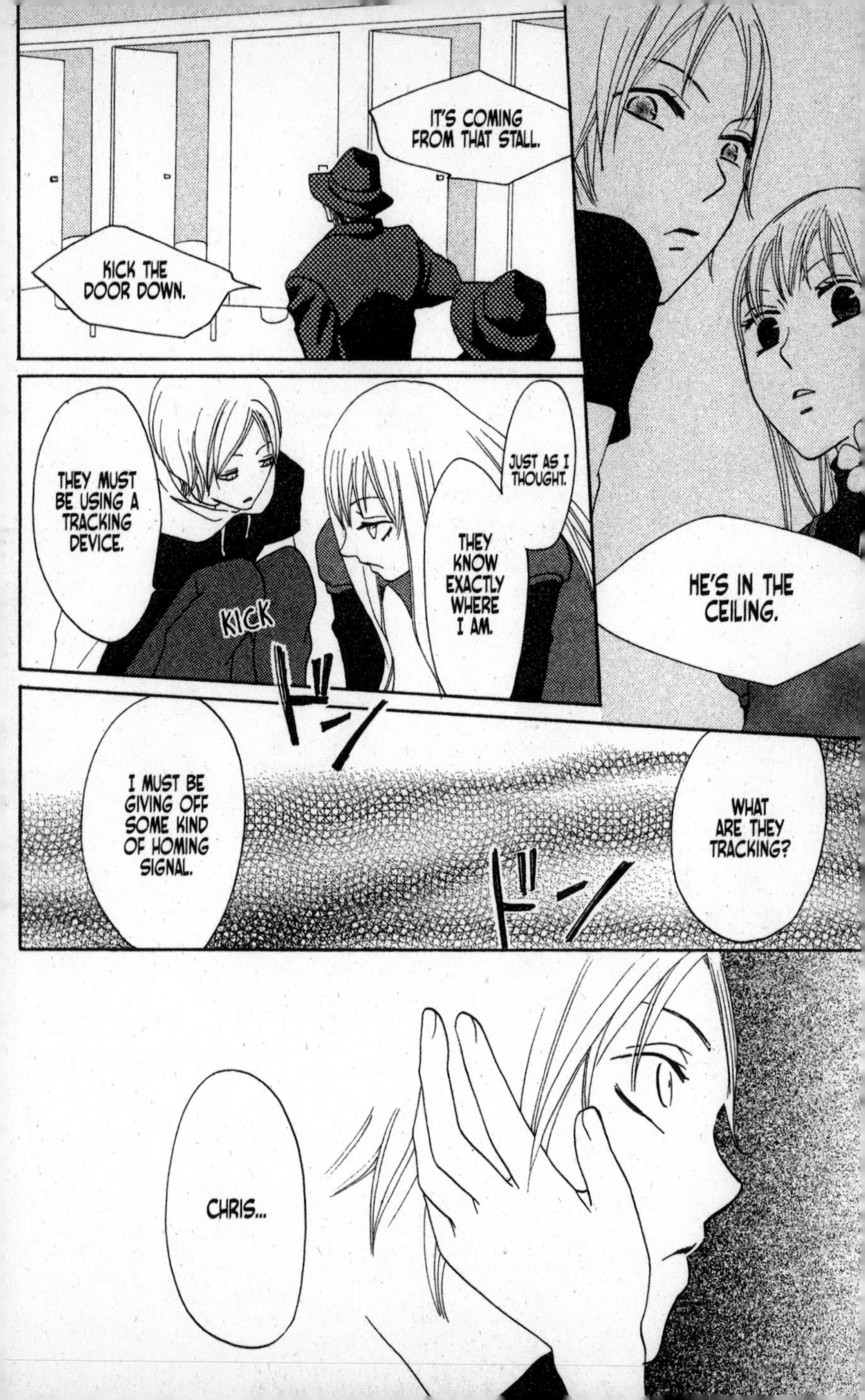
HE'S IN THE CEILING.
IT'S COMING FROM THAT STALL.
KICK THE DOOR DOWN.
JUST AS I THOUGHT.
THEY KNOW EXACTLY WHERE I AM.
THEY MUST BE USING A TRACKING DEVICE.
KICK
WHAT ARE THEY TRACKING?
I MUST BE GIVING OFF SOME KIND OF HOMING SIGNAL.
CHRIS...

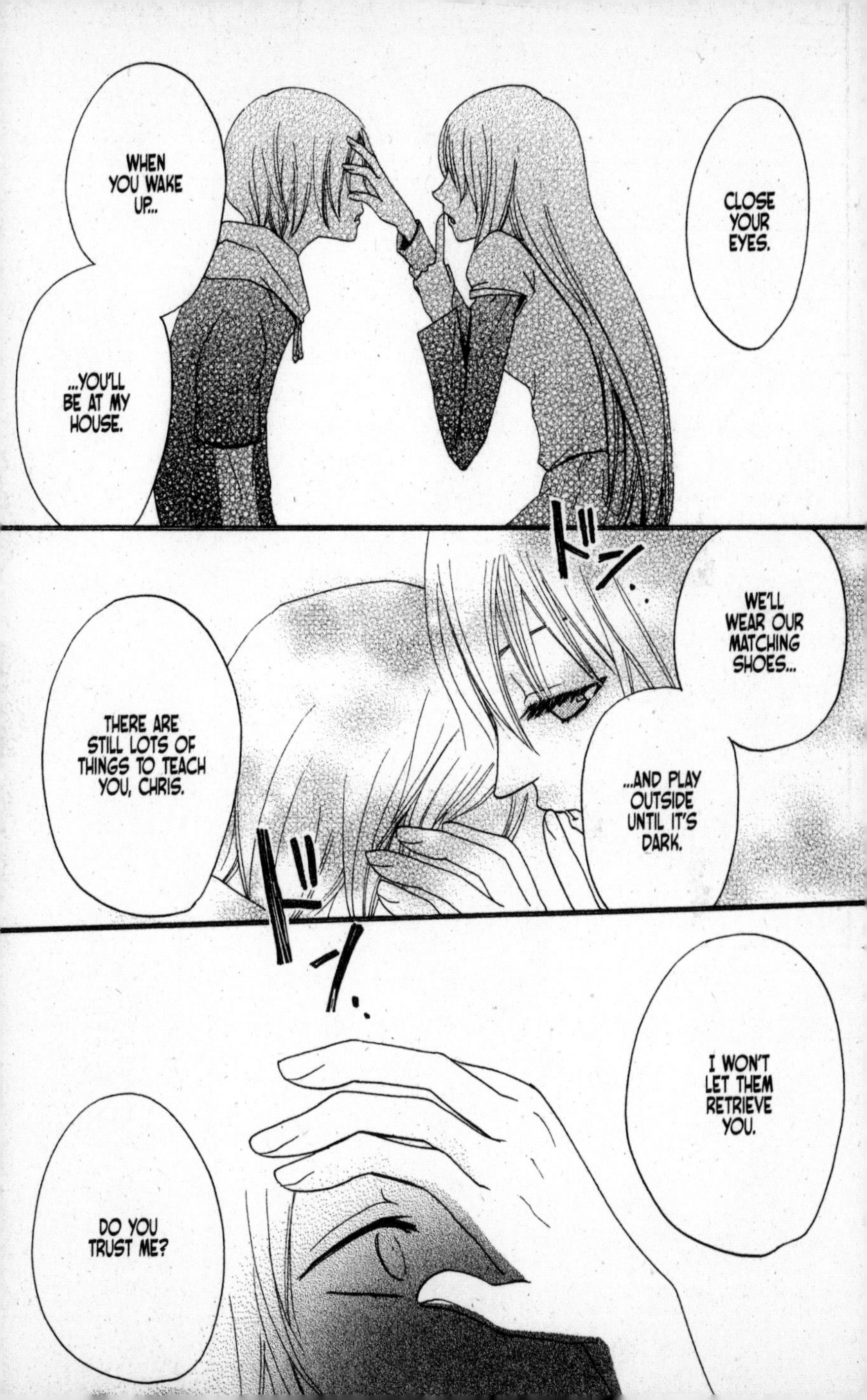
CLOSE YOUR EYES.
WHEN YOU WAKE UP...
...YOU'LL BE AT MY HOUSE.
WE'LL WEAR OUR MATCHING SHOES...
...AND PLAY OUTSIDE UNTIL IT'S DARK.
THERE ARE STILL LOTS OF THINGS TO TEACH YOU, CHRIS.
I WON'T LET THEM RETRIEVE YOU.
DO YOU TRUST ME?

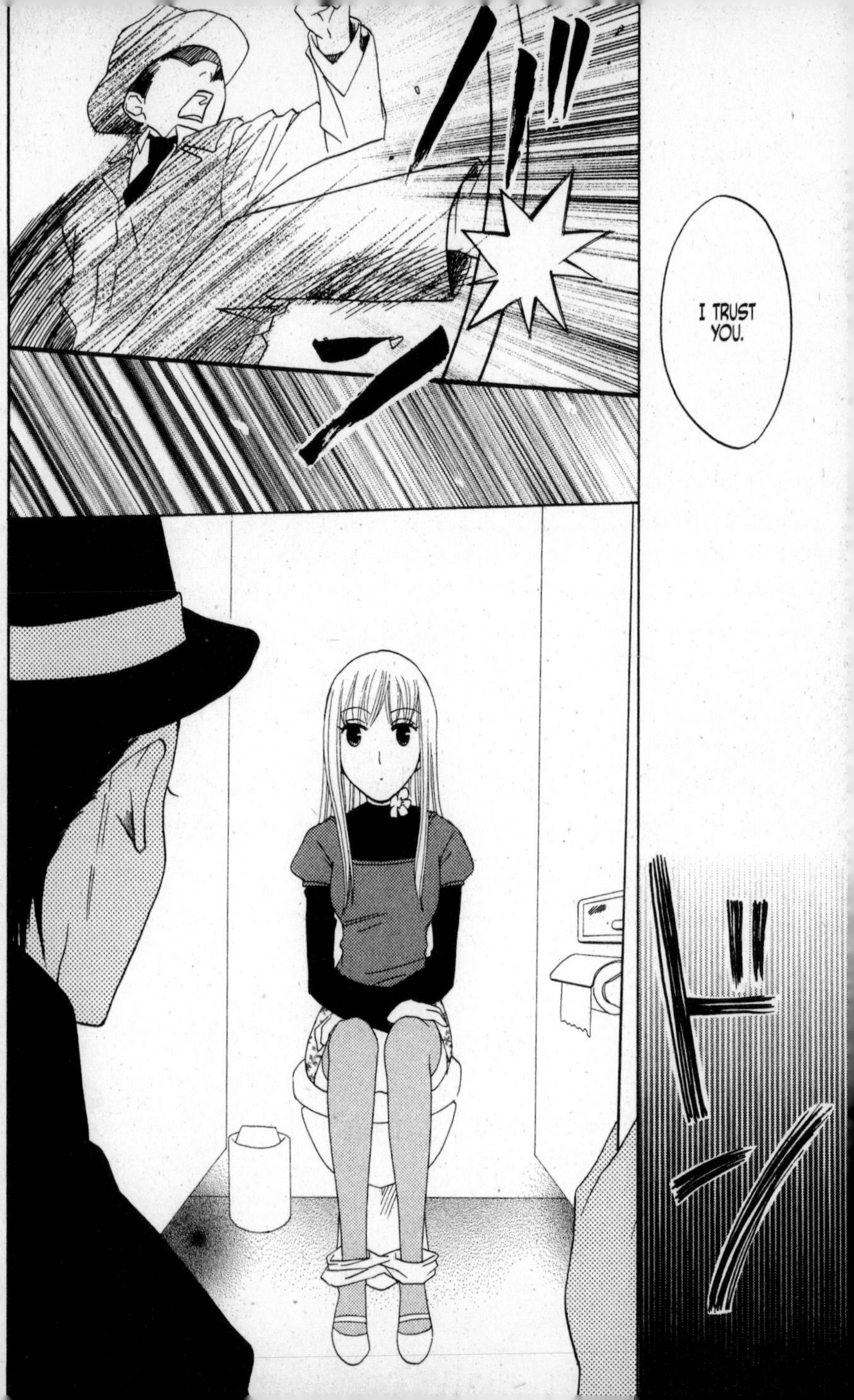
I TRUST YOU.

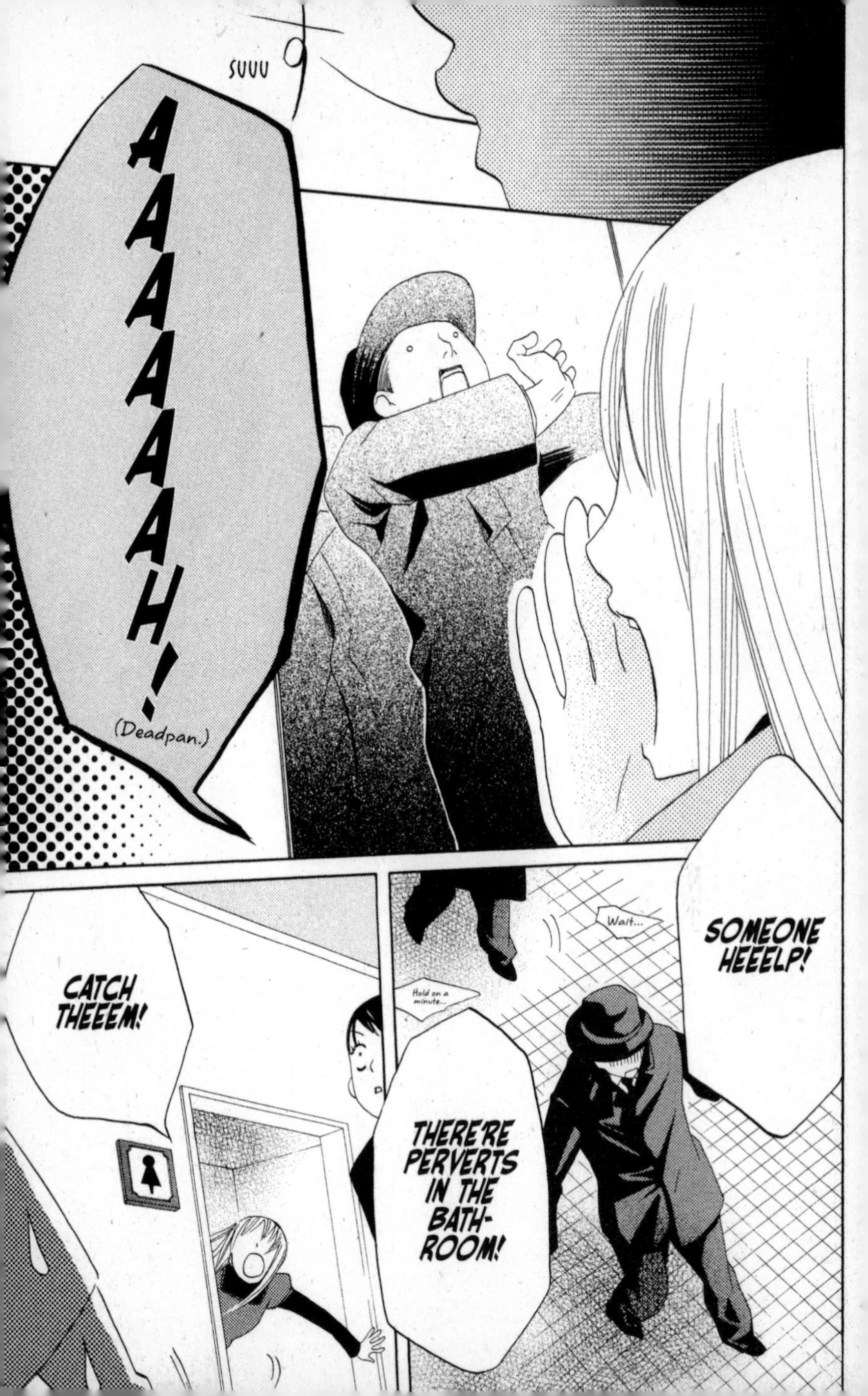
SUUU
AAAAAAAH!
(Deadpan.)
SOMEONE HEEELP!
Wait...
Hold on a minute...
THERE'RE PERVERTS IN THE BATH-ROOM!
CATCH THEEEM!

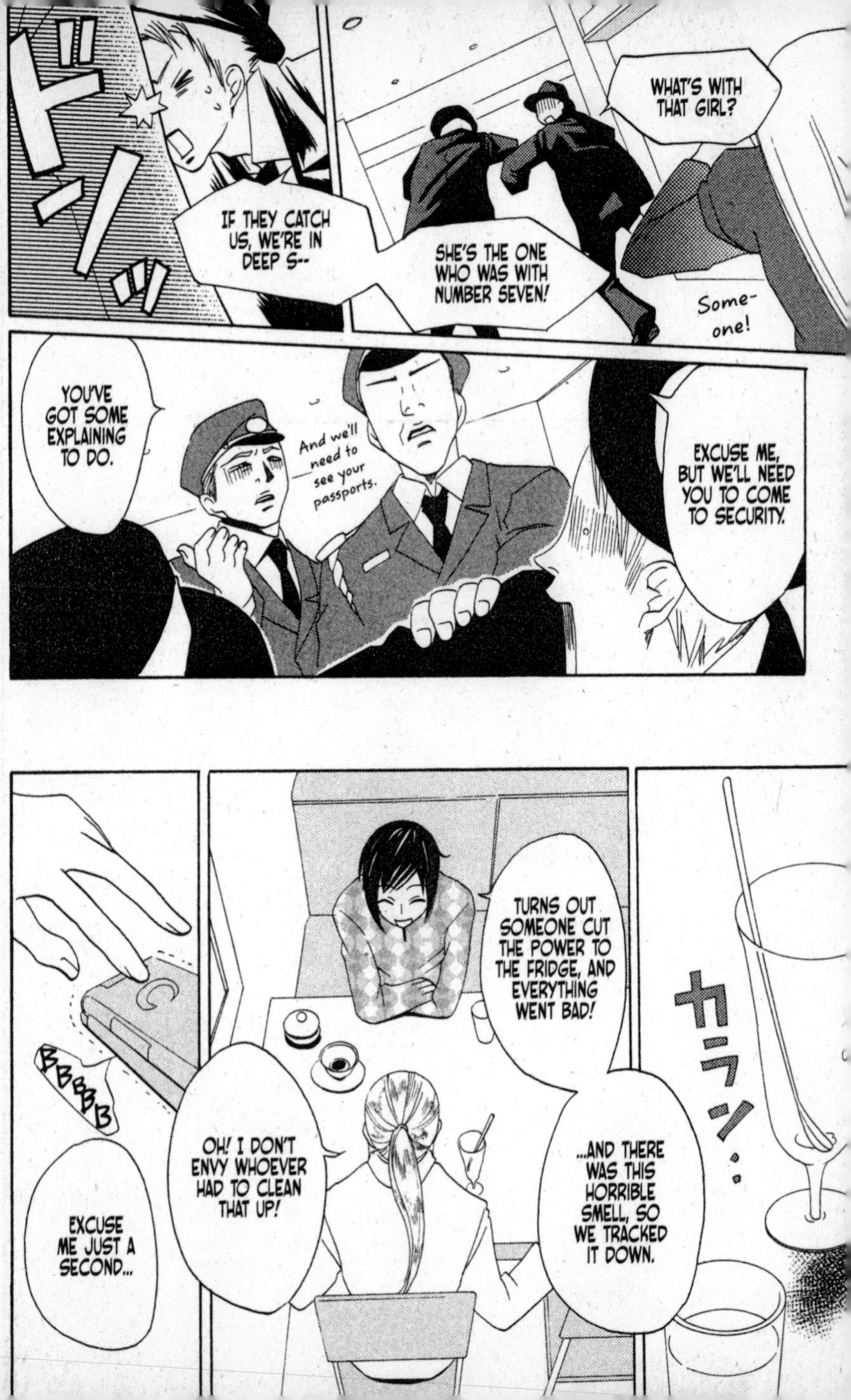
WHAT'S WITH THAT GIRL?
Some-one!
SHE'S THE ONE WHO WAS WITH NUMBER SEVEN!
IF THEY CATCH US, WE'RE IN DEEP S--
EXCUSE ME, BUT WE'LL NEED YOU TO COME TO SECURITY.
And we'll need to see your passports.
YOU'VE GOT SOME EXPLAINING TO DO.
カラン..
TURNS OUT SOMEONE CUT THE POWER TO THE FRIDGE, AND EVERYTHING WENT BAD!
...AND THERE WAS THIS HORRIBLE SMELL, SO WE TRACKED IT DOWN.
OH! I DON'T ENVY WHOEVER HAD TO CLEAN THAT UP!
BBBBB
EXCUSE ME JUST A SECOND...

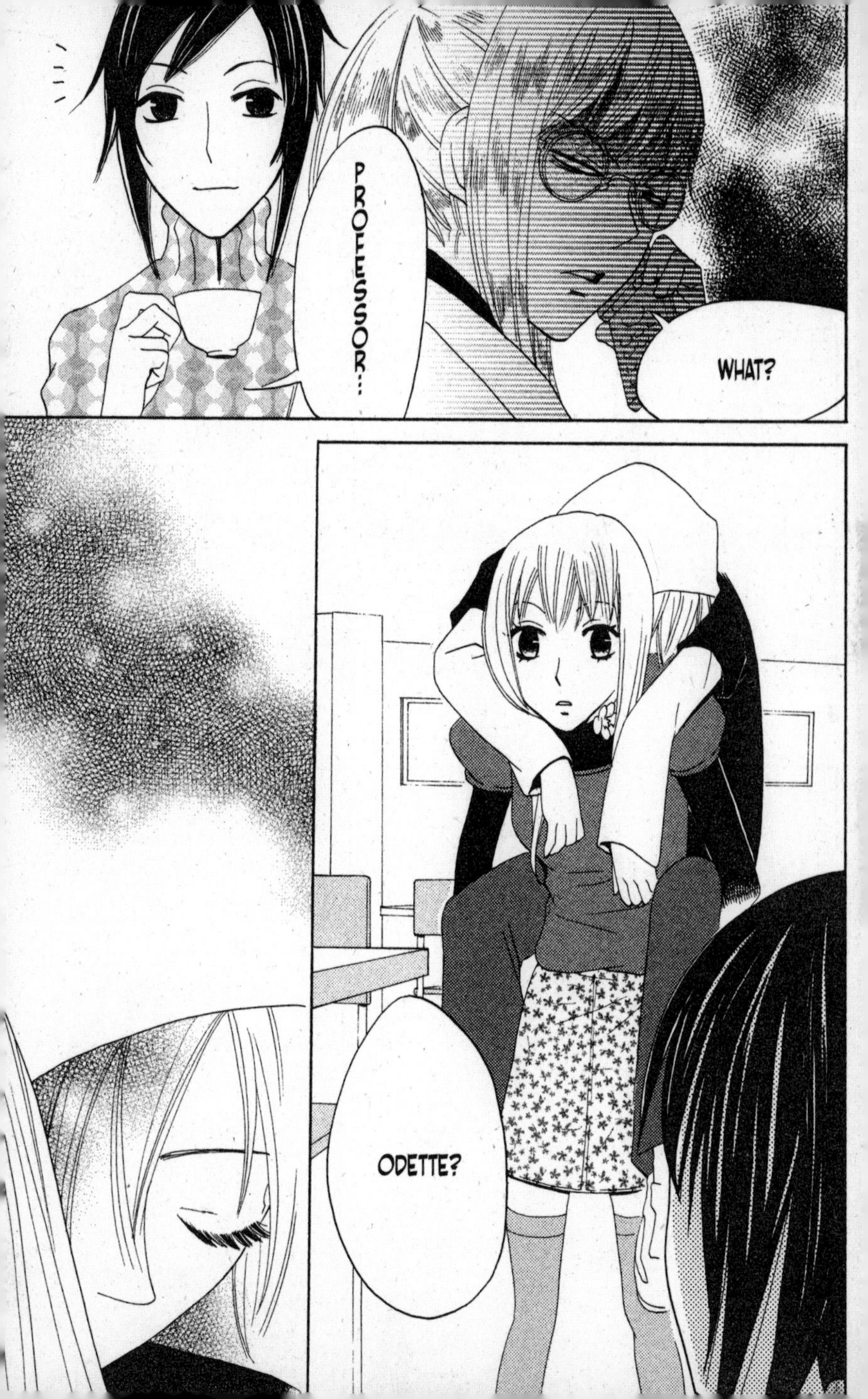
WHAT?
PROFESSOR...
ODETTE?

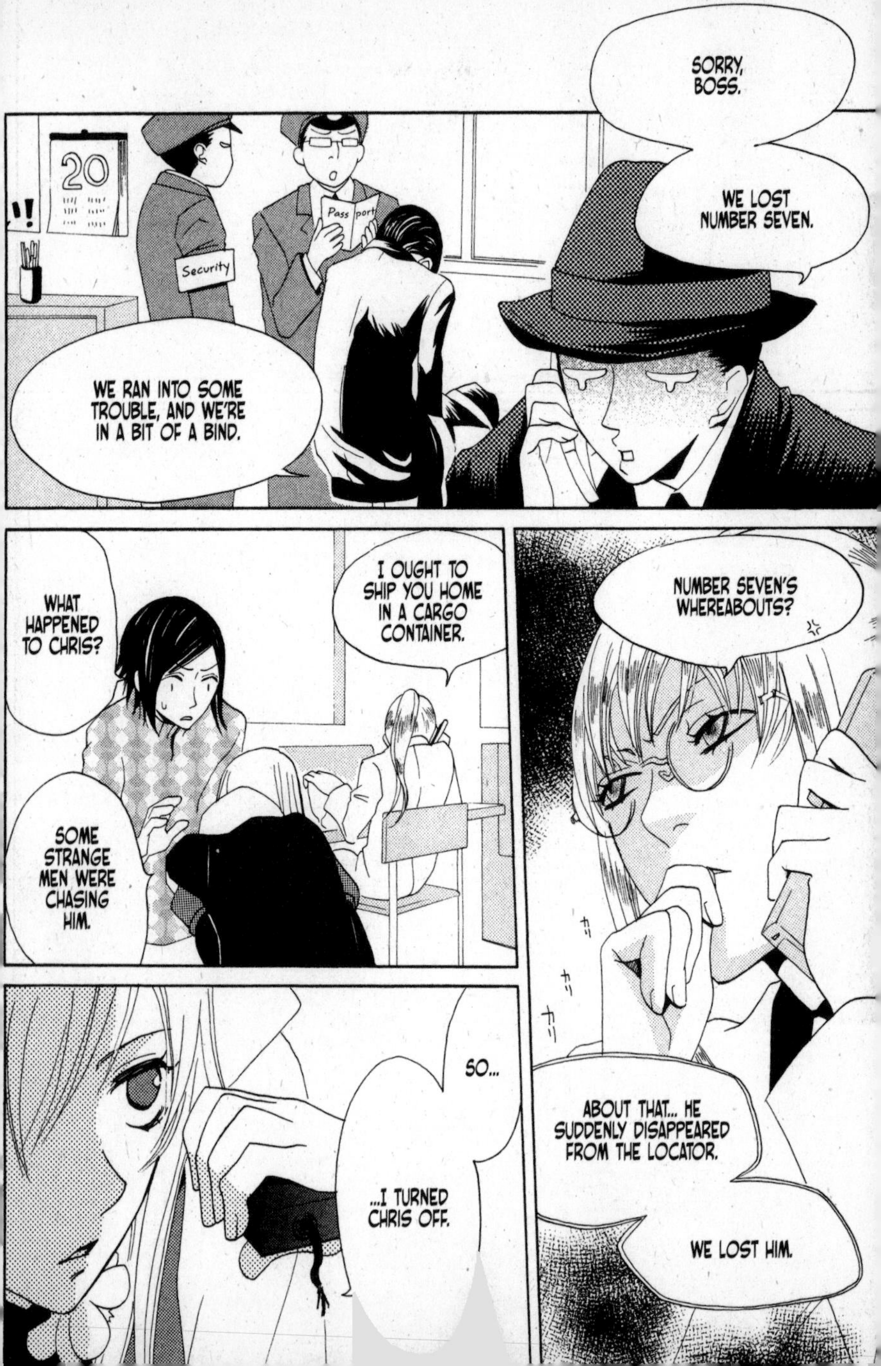
SORRY, BOSS.
WE LOST NUMBER SEVEN.
Passport
20
Security
WE RAN INTO SOME TROUBLE, AND WE'RE IN A BIT OF A BIND.
NUMBER SEVEN'S WHEREABOUTS?
ABOUT THAT... HE SUDDENLY DISAPPEARED FROM THE LOCATOR.
WE LOST HIM.
I OUGHT TO SHIP YOU HOME IN A CARGO CONTAINER.
WHAT HAPPENED TO CHRIS?
SOME STRANGE MEN WERE CHASING HIM.
SO...
...I TURNED CHRIS OFF.

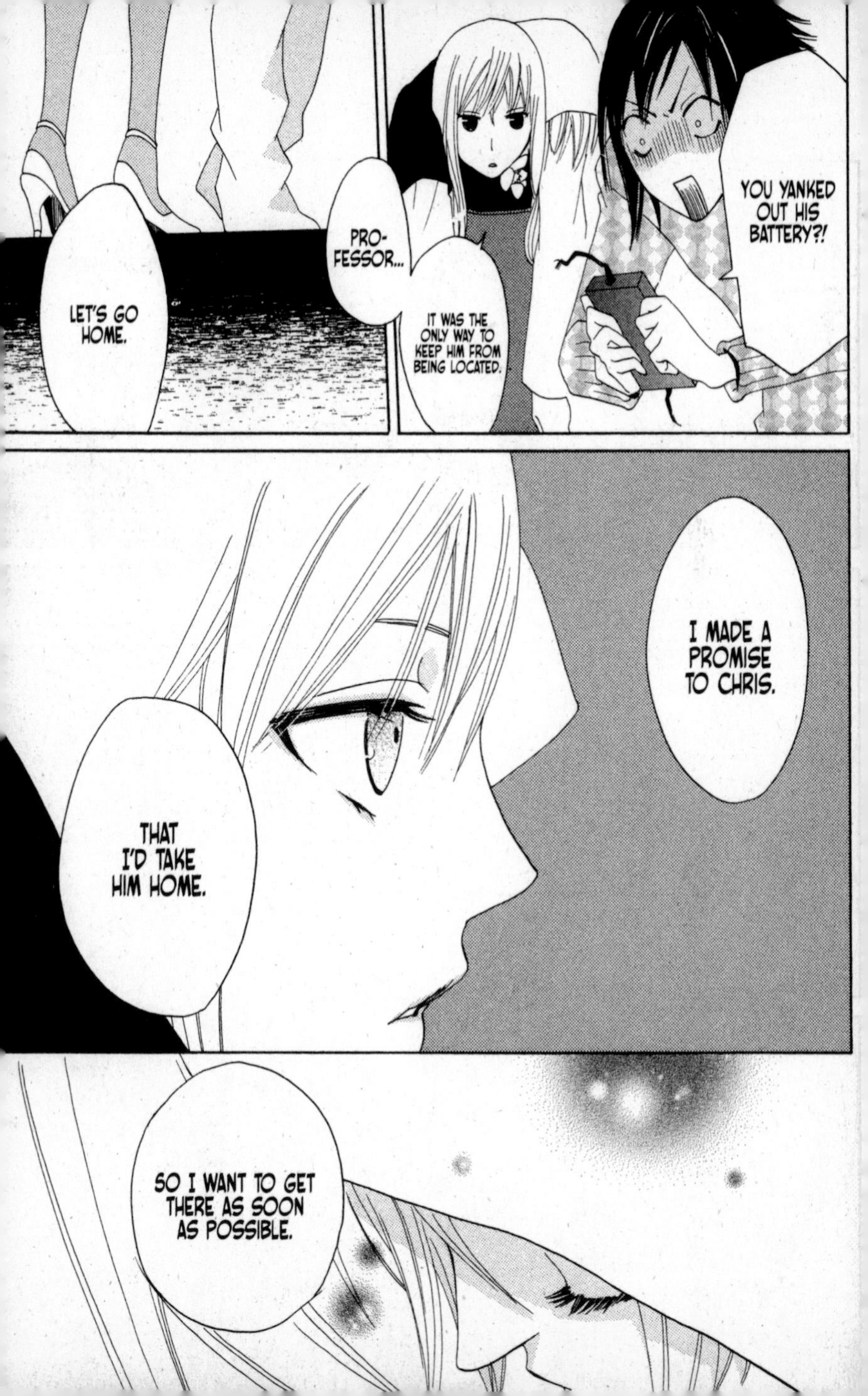
YOU YANKED OUT HIS BATTERY?!
PRO-FESSOR...
IT WAS THE ONLY WAY TO KEEP HIM FROM BEING LOCATED.
LET'S GO HOME.
I MADE A PROMISE TO CHRIS.
THAT I'D TAKE HIM HOME.
SO I WANT TO GET THERE AS SOON AS POSSIBLE.

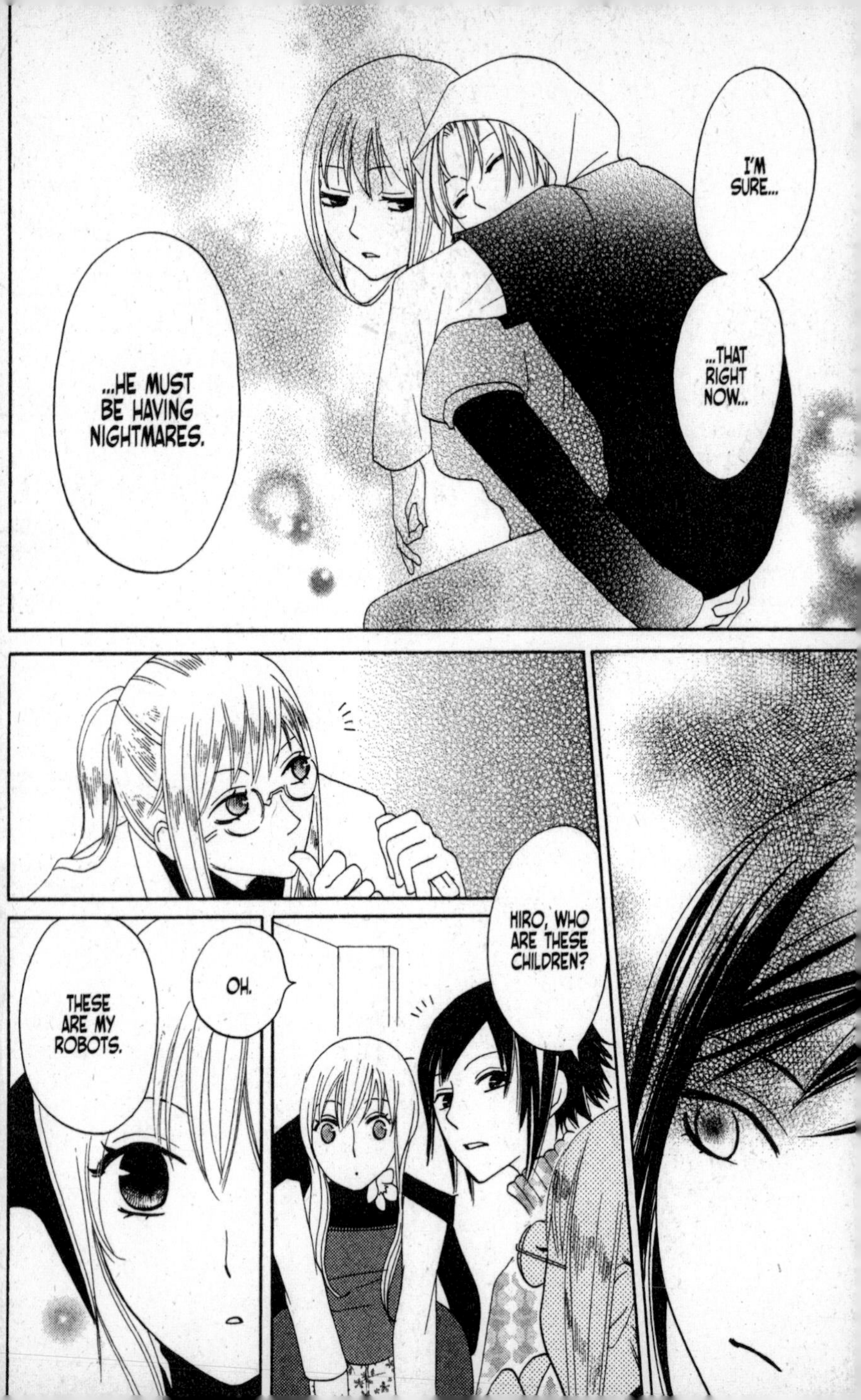
I'M SURE...
...THAT RIGHT NOW...
...HE MUST BE HAVING NIGHTMARES.
HIRO, WHO ARE THESE CHILDREN?
OH.
THESE ARE MY ROBOTS.

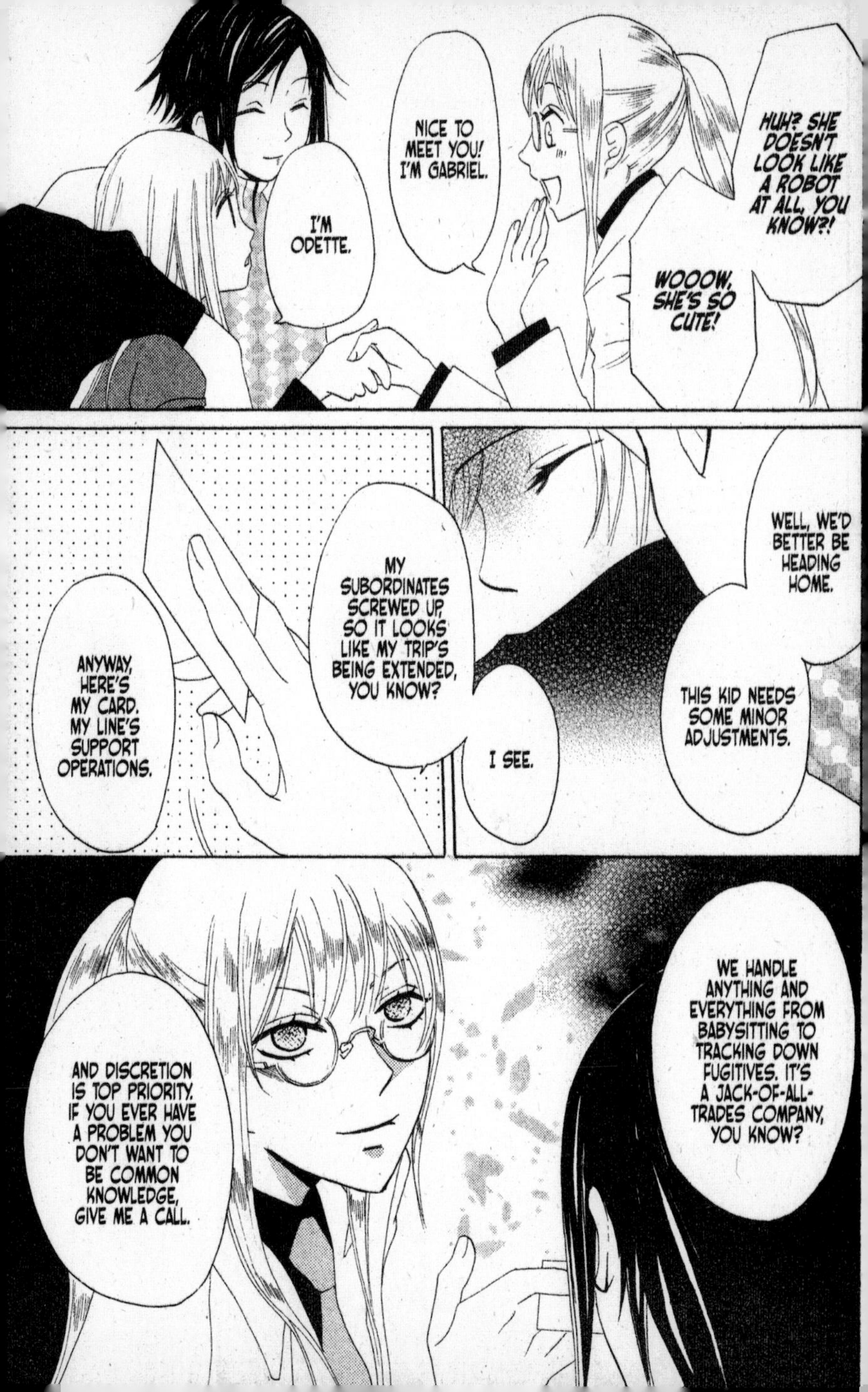
HUH? SHE DOESN'T LOOK LIKE A ROBOT AT ALL, YOU KNOW?!
WOOOW, SHE'S SO CUTE!
NICE TO MEET YOU! I'M GABRIEL.
I'M ODETTE.
WELL, WE'D BETTER BE HEADING HOME.
THIS KID NEEDS SOME MINOR ADJUSTMENTS.
I SEE.
MY SUBORDINATES SCREWED UP, SO IT LOOKS LIKE MY TRIP'S BEING EXTENDED, YOU KNOW?
ANYWAY, HERE'S MY CARD. MY LINE'S SUPPORT OPERATIONS.
WE HANDLE ANYTHING AND EVERYTHING FROM BABYSITTING TO TRACKING DOWN FUGITIVES. IT'S A JACK-OF-ALL-TRADES COMPANY, YOU KNOW?
AND DISCRETION IS TOP PRIORITY. IF YOU EVER HAVE A PROBLEM YOU DON'T WANT TO BE COMMON KNOWLEDGE, GIVE ME A CALL.

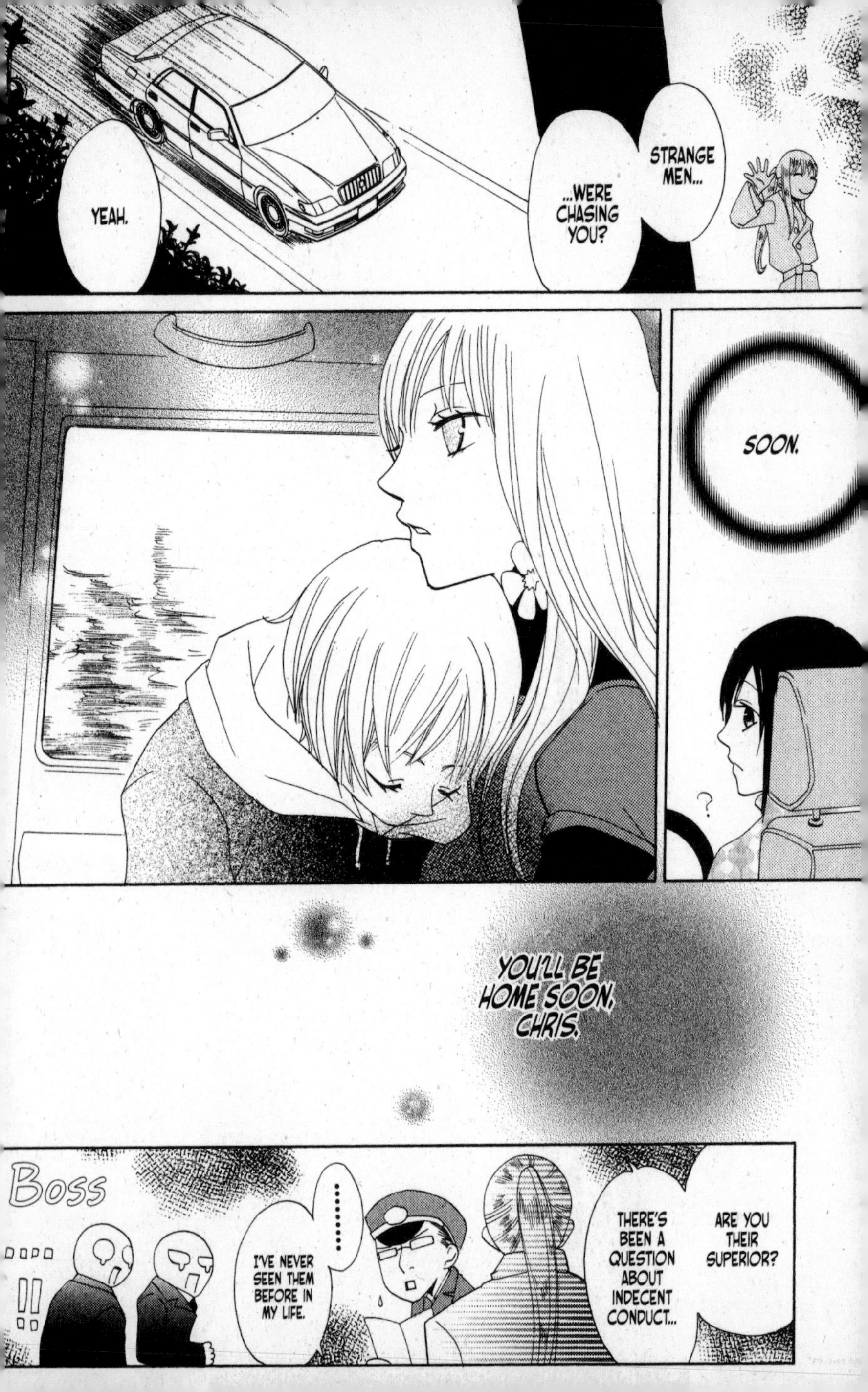
STRANGE MEN...
...WERE CHASING YOU?
YEAH.
SOON.
YOU'LL BE HOME SOON, CHRIS.
ARE YOU THEIR SUPERIOR?
THERE'S BEEN A QUESTION ABOUT INDECENT CONDUCT...
....
I'VE NEVER SEEN THEM BEFORE IN MY LIFE.
Boss
!!

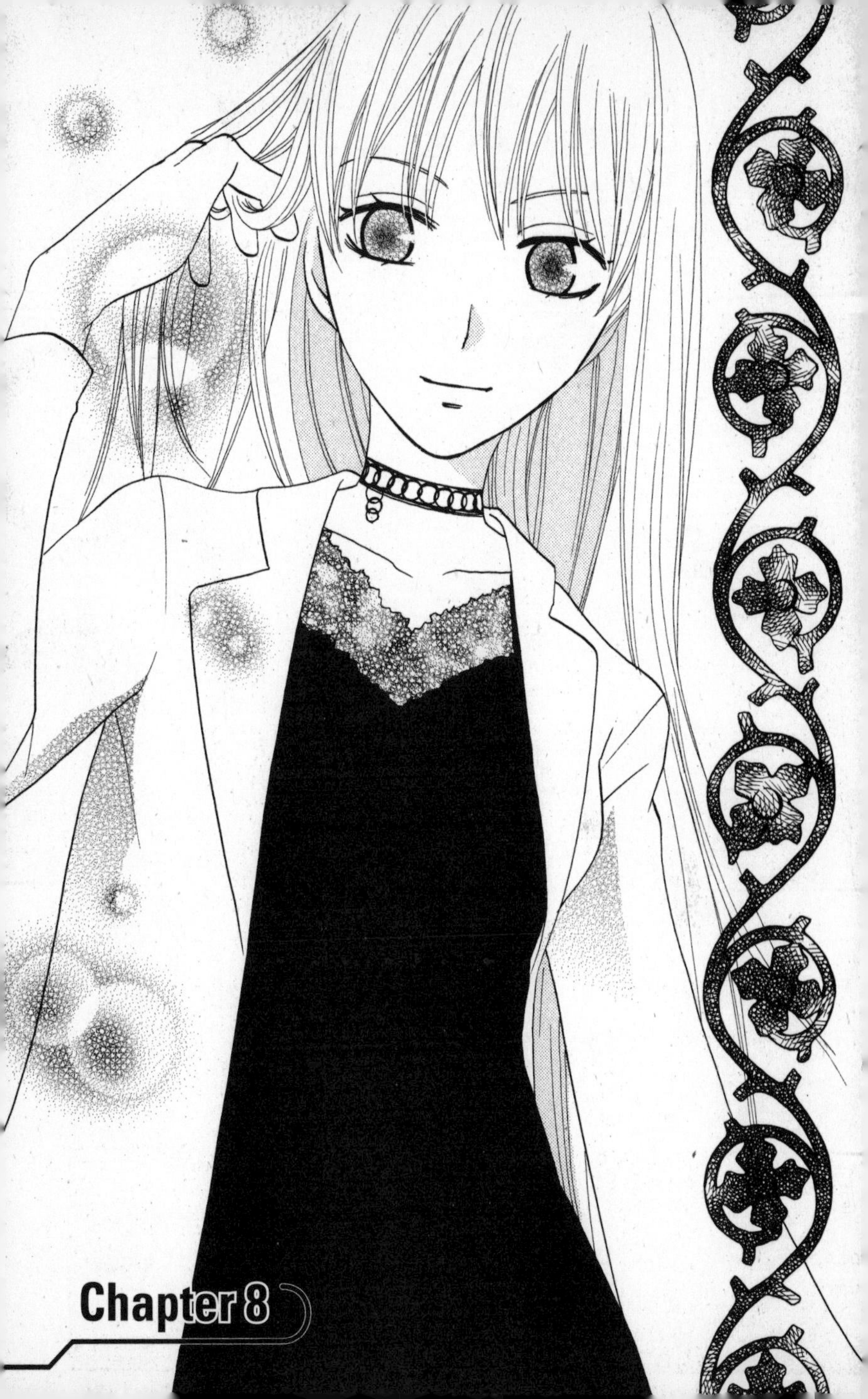
Chapter 8

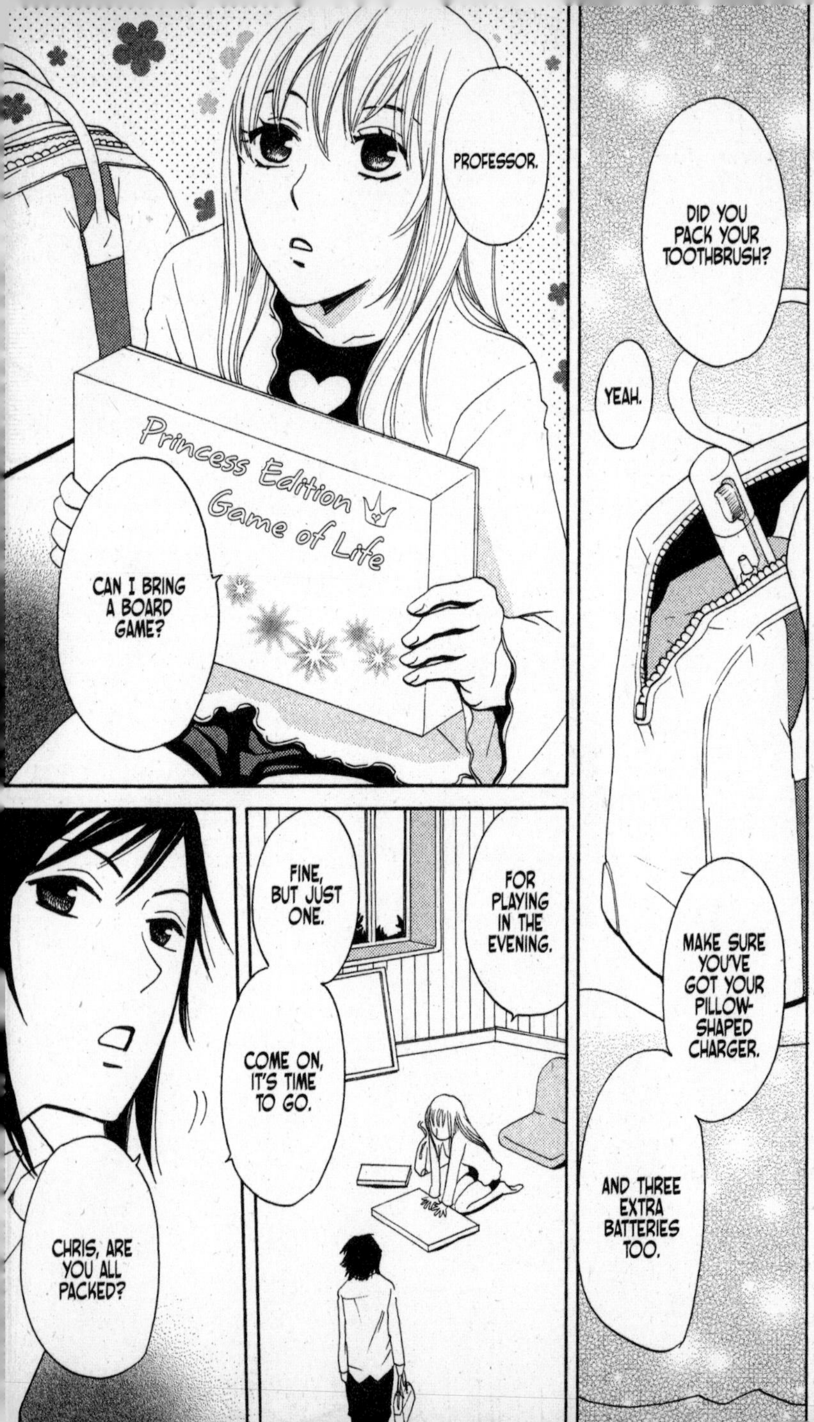
DID YOU PACK YOUR TOOTHBRUSH?
YEAH.
MAKE SURE YOU'VE GOT YOUR PILLOW-SHAPED CHARGER.
AND THREE EXTRA BATTERIES TOO.
PROFESSOR.
Princess Edition Game of Life
CAN I BRING A BOARD GAME?
FOR PLAYING IN THE EVENING.
FINE, BUT JUST ONE.
COME ON, IT'S TIME TO GO.
CHRIS, ARE YOU ALL PACKED?

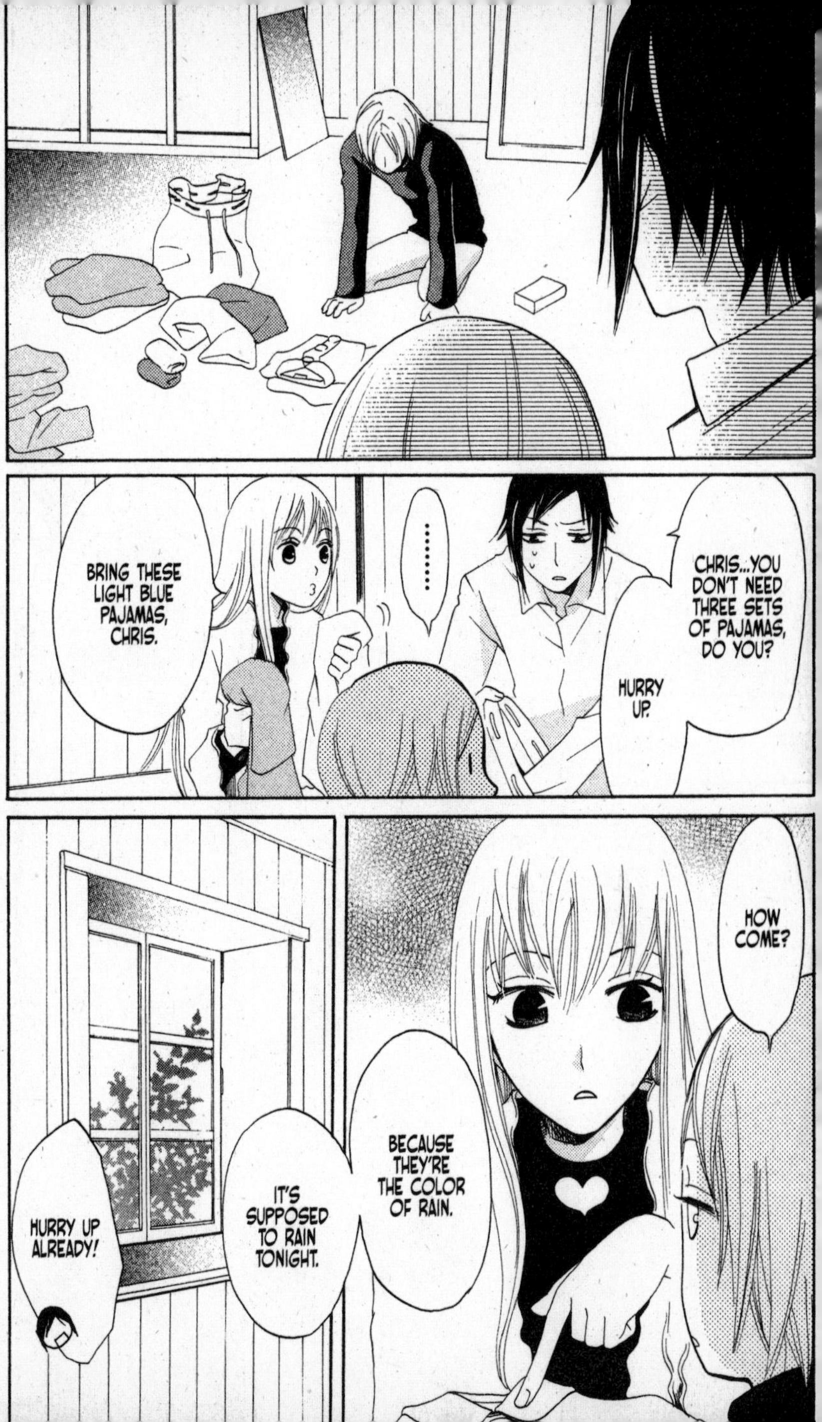
CHRIS...YOU DON'T NEED THREE SETS OF PAJAMAS, DO YOU?
HURRY UP.
......
BRING THESE LIGHT BLUE PAJAMAS, CHRIS.
HOW COME?
BECAUSE THEY'RE THE COLOR OF RAIN.
IT'S SUPPOSED TO RAIN TONIGHT.
HURRY UP ALREADY!

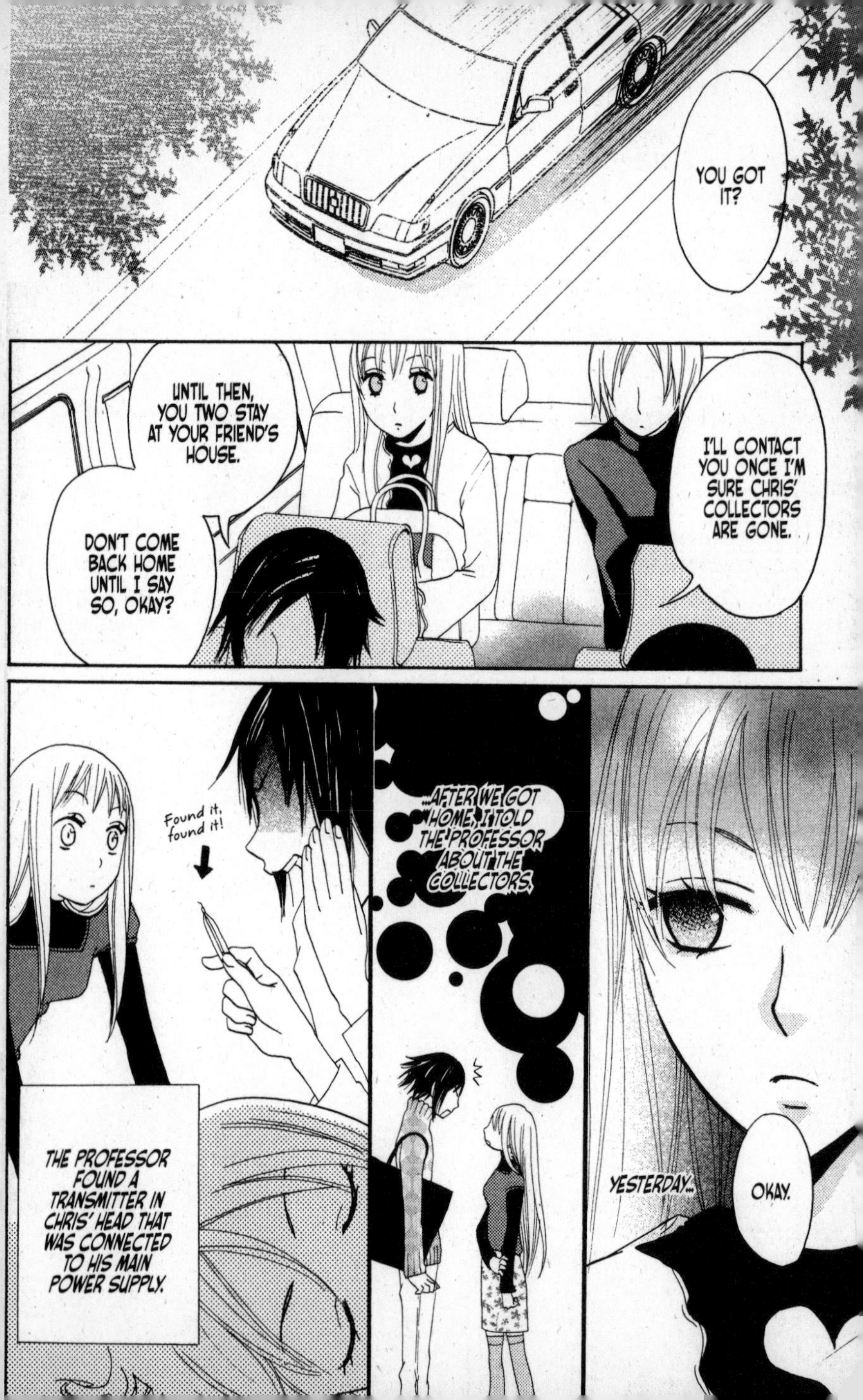
YOU GOT IT?
I'LL CONTACT YOU ONCE I'M SURE CHRIS' COLLECTORS ARE GONE.
UNTIL THEN, YOU TWO STAY AT YOUR FRIEND'S HOUSE.
DON'T COME BACK HOME UNTIL I SAY SO, OKAY?
OKAY.
YESTERDAY...
...AFTER WE GOT HOME, I TOLD THE PROFESSOR ABOUT THE COLLECTORS.
Found it, found it!
THE PROFESSOR FOUND A TRANSMITTER IN CHRIS' HEAD THAT WAS CONNECTED TO HIS MAIN POWER SUPPLY.

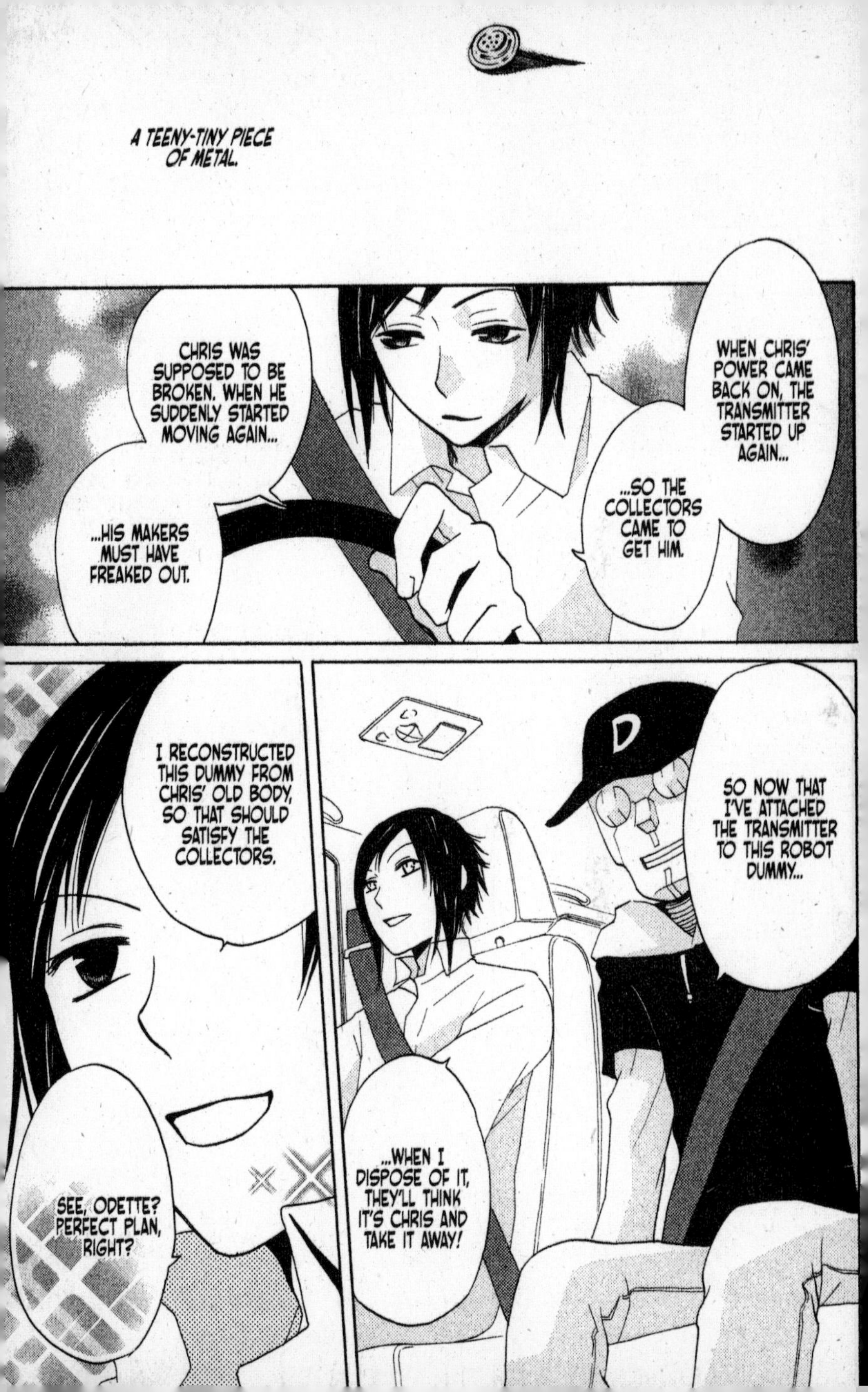
A TEENY-TINY PIECE OF METAL.
WHEN CHRIS' POWER CAME BACK ON, THE TRANSMITTER STARTED UP AGAIN...
...SO THE COLLECTORS CAME TO GET HIM.
CHRIS WAS SUPPOSED TO BE BROKEN. WHEN HE SUDDENLY STARTED MOVING AGAIN...
...HIS MAKERS MUST HAVE FREAKED OUT.
D
SO NOW THAT I'VE ATTACHED THE TRANSMITTER TO THIS ROBOT DUMMY...
...WHEN I DISPOSE OF IT, THEY'LL THINK IT'S CHRIS AND TAKE IT AWAY!
I RECONSTRUCTED THIS DUMMY FROM CHRIS' OLD BODY, SO THAT SHOULD SATISFY THE COLLECTORS.
SEE, ODETTE? PERFECT PLAN, RIGHT?

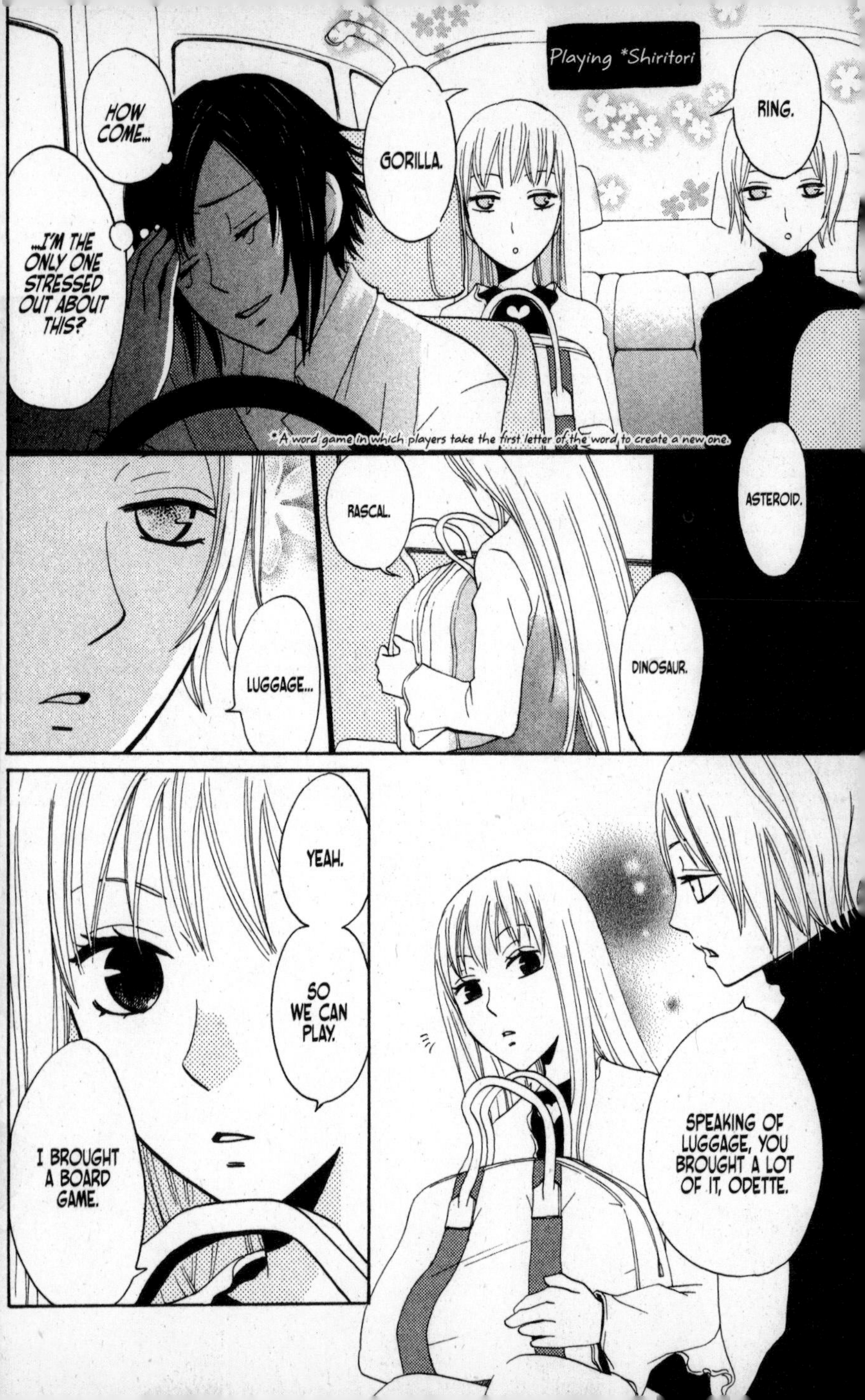
Playing *Shiritori
RING.
GORILLA.
HOW COME...
...I'M THE ONLY ONE STRESSED OUT ABOUT THIS?
*A word game in which players take the first letter of the word to create a new one.
ASTEROID.
DINOSAUR.
RASCAL.
LUGGAGE...
SPEAKING OF LUGGAGE, YOU BROUGHT A LOT OF IT, ODETTE.
YEAH.
SO WE CAN PLAY.
I BROUGHT A BOARD GAME.

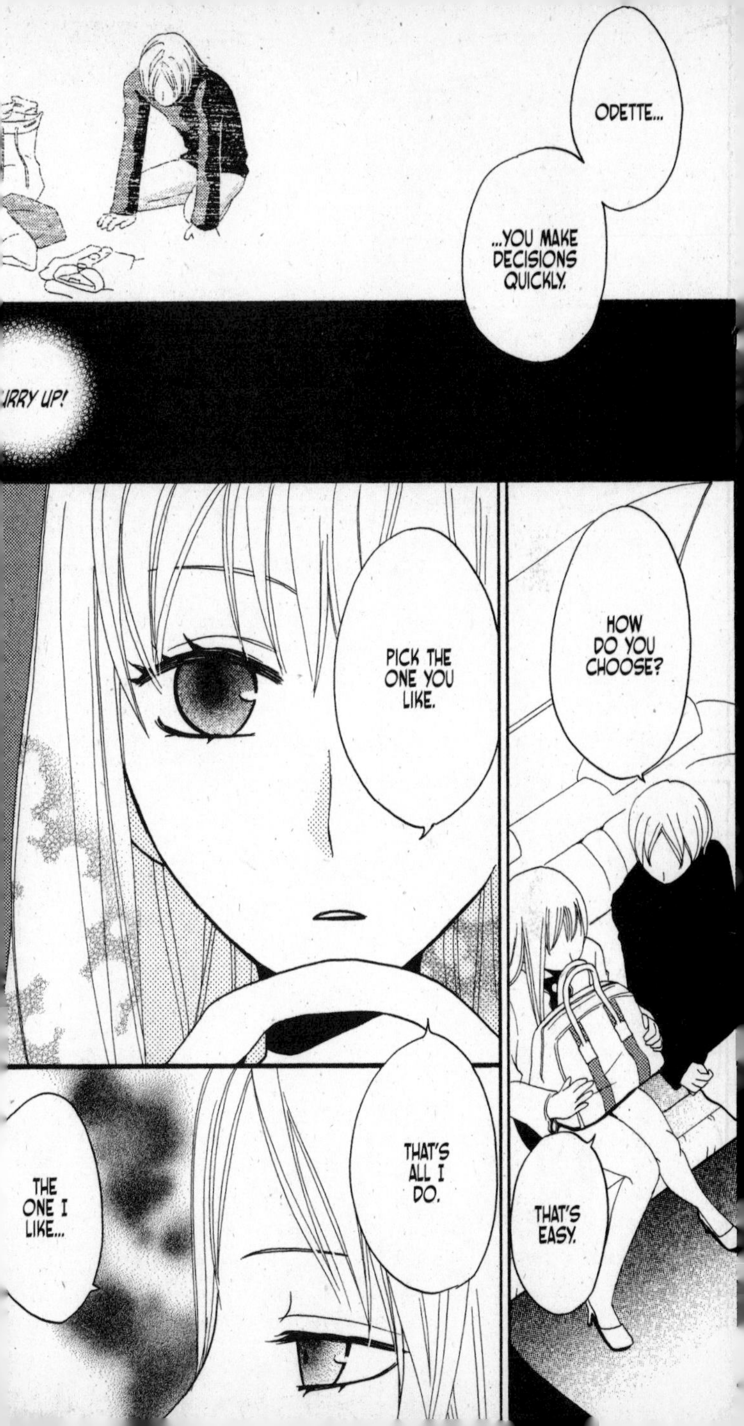
ODETTE...
...YOU MAKE DECISIONS QUICKLY.
URRY UP!
HOW DO YOU CHOOSE?
THAT'S EASY.
PICK THE ONE YOU LIKE.
THAT'S ALL I DO.
THE ONE I LIKE...

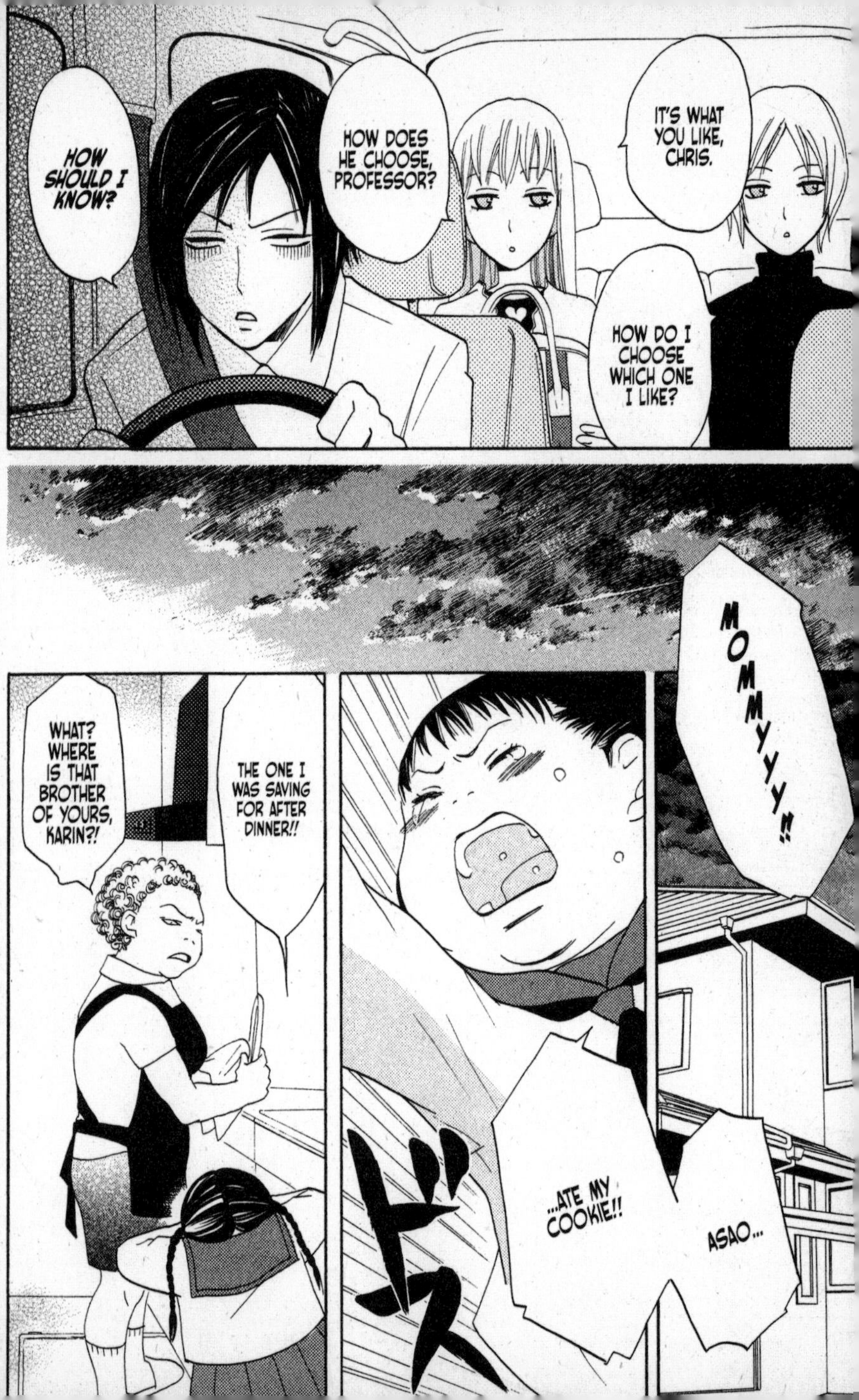
IT'S WHAT YOU LIKE, CHRIS.
HOW DO I CHOOSE WHICH ONE I LIKE?
HOW DOES HE CHOOSE, PROFESSOR?
HOW SHOULD I KNOW?
MOMMYYY!!
ASAO...
...ATE MY COOKIE!!
ドス
THE ONE I WAS SAVING FOR AFTER DINNER!!
WHAT? WHERE IS THAT BROTHER OF YOURS, KARIN?!

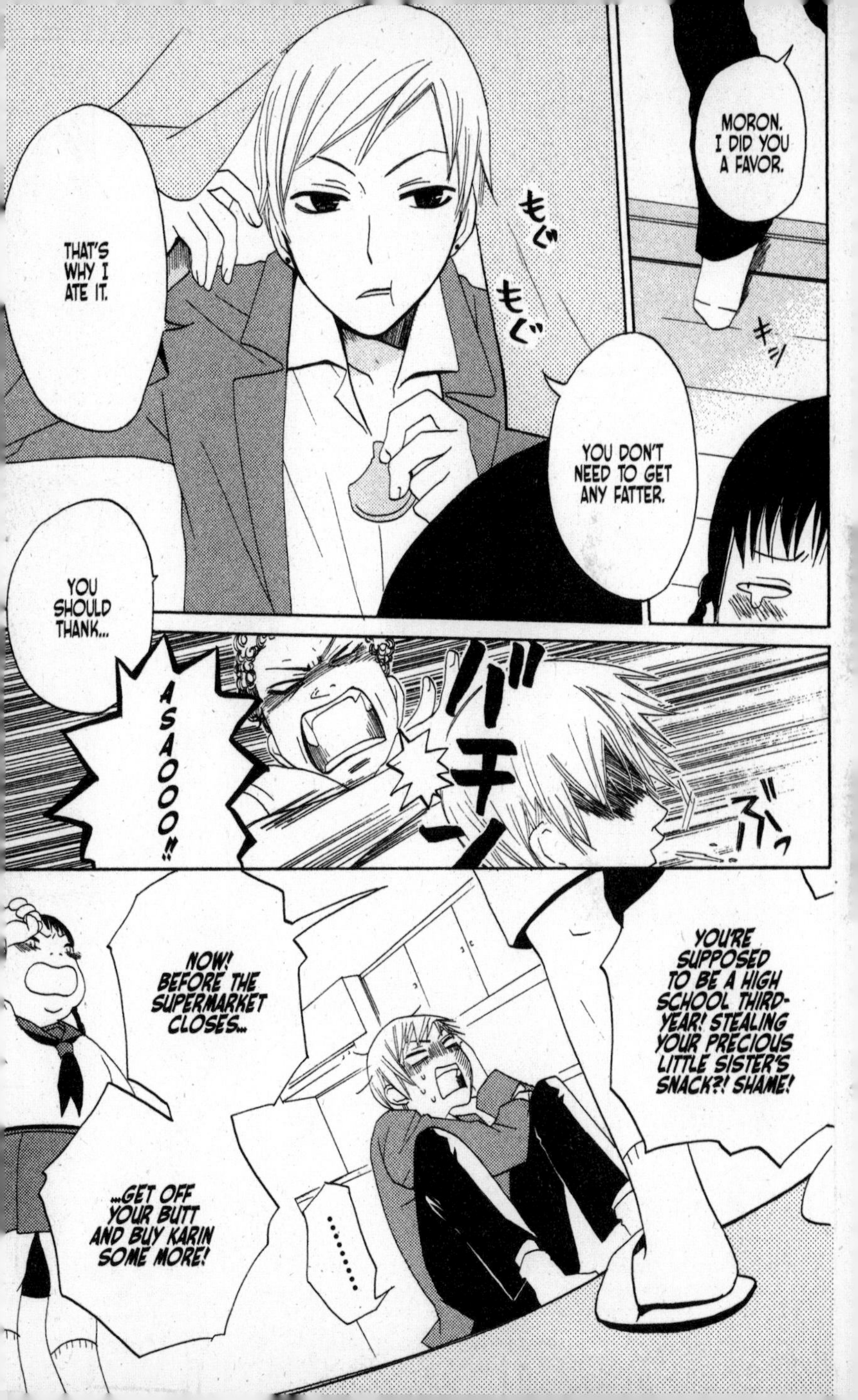
MORON. I DID YOU A FAVOR.
YOU DON'T NEED TO GET ANY FATTER.
もぐ もぐ
THAT'S WHY I ATE IT.
YOU SHOULD THANK...
バチーン
ぶっ
ASAOOOO!!
YOU'RE SUPPOSED TO BE A HIGH SCHOOL THIRD-YEAR! STEALING YOUR PRECIOUS LITTLE SISTER'S SNACK?! SHAME!
....
NOW! BEFORE THE SUPERMARKET CLOSES...
...GET OFF YOUR BUTT AND BUY KARIN SOME MORE!

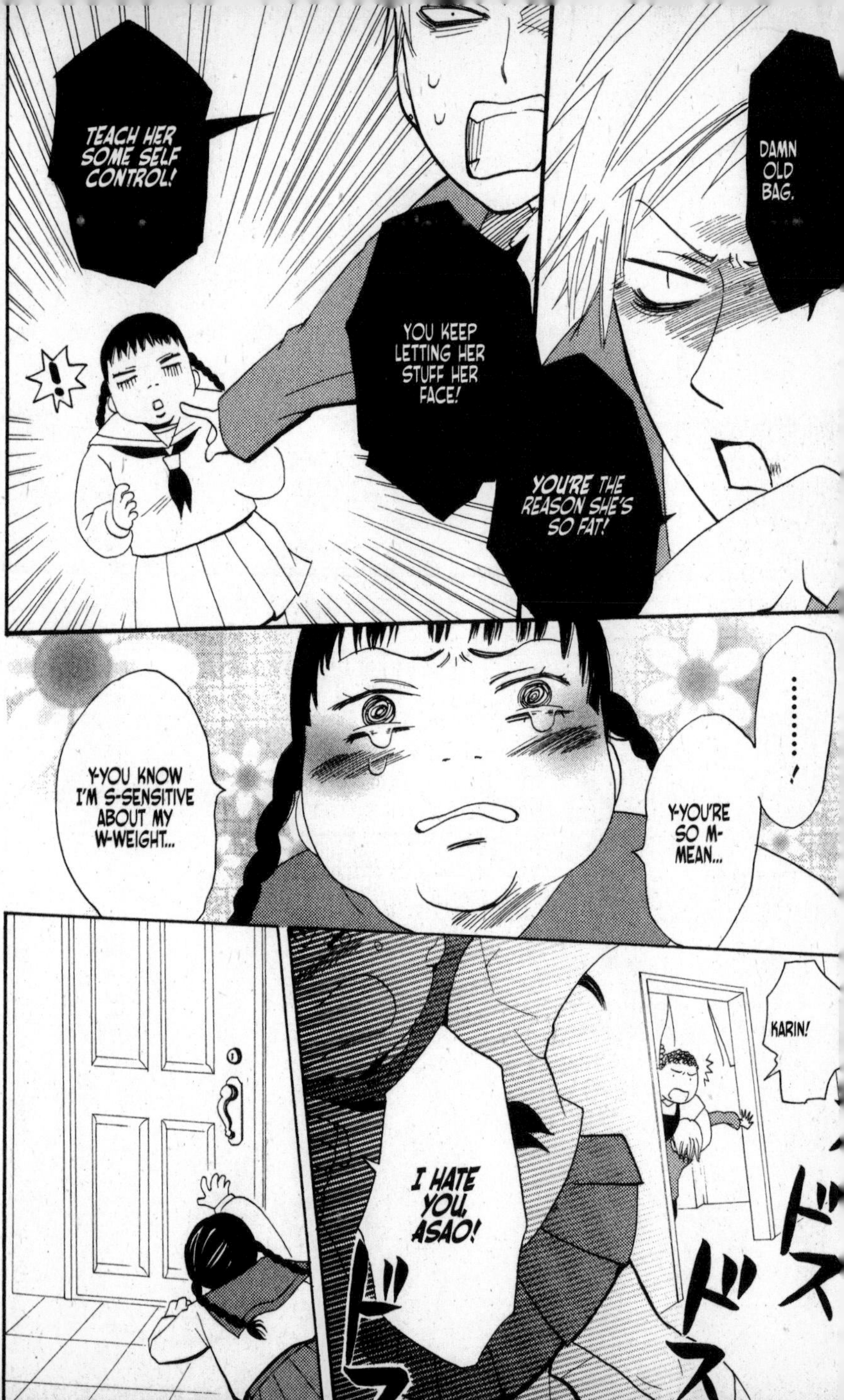
DAMN OLD BAG.
TEACH HER SOME SELF CONTROL!
YOU KEEP LETTING HER STUFF HER FACE!
YOU'RE THE REASON SHE'S SO FAT!
......!
Y-YOU'RE SO M-MEAN...
Y-YOU KNOW I'M S-SENSITIVE ABOUT MY W-WEIGHT...
KARIN!
ドス
ドス
I HATE YOU, ASAO!
ドド

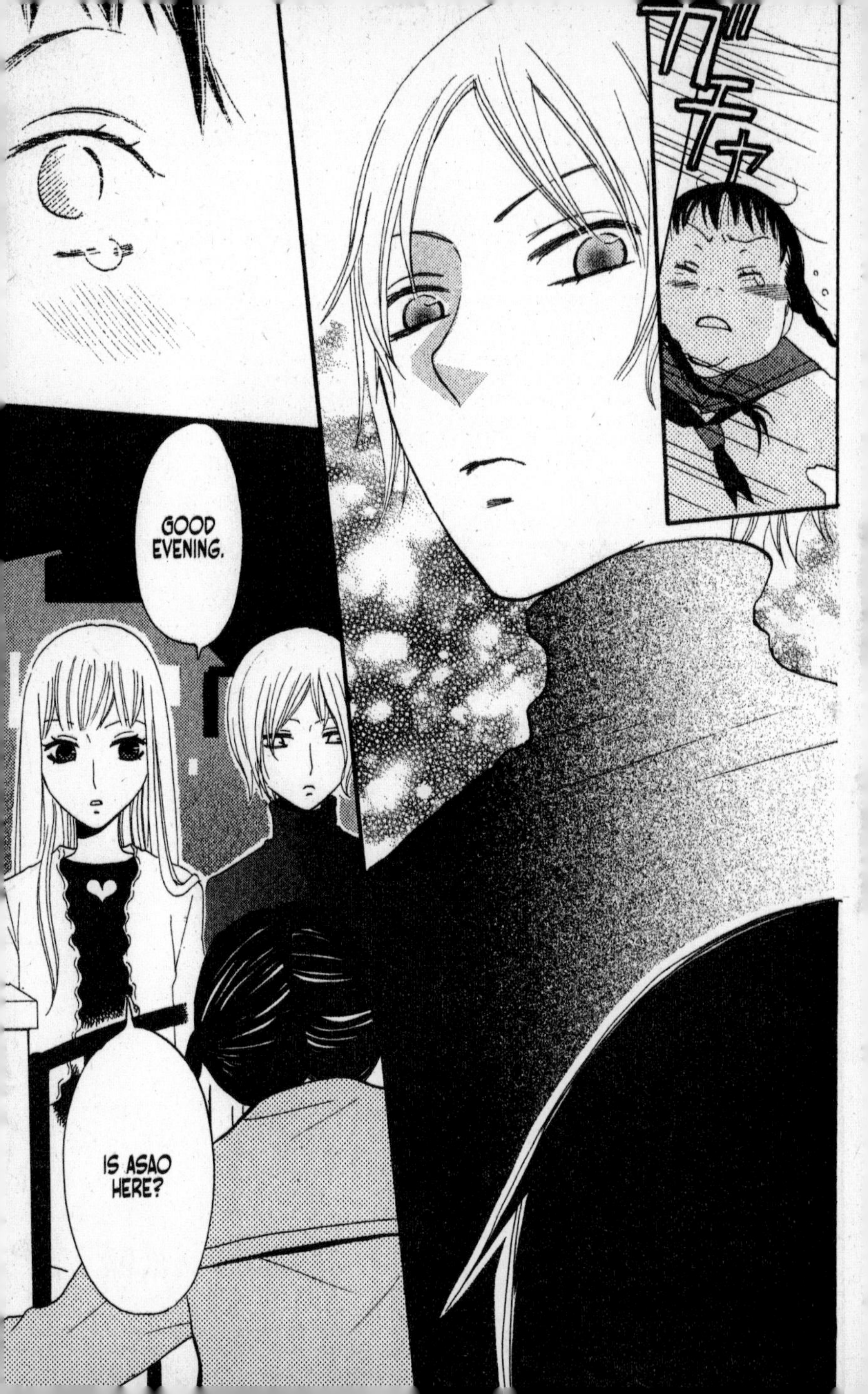
ガチャ
GOOD EVENING.
IS ASAO HERE?

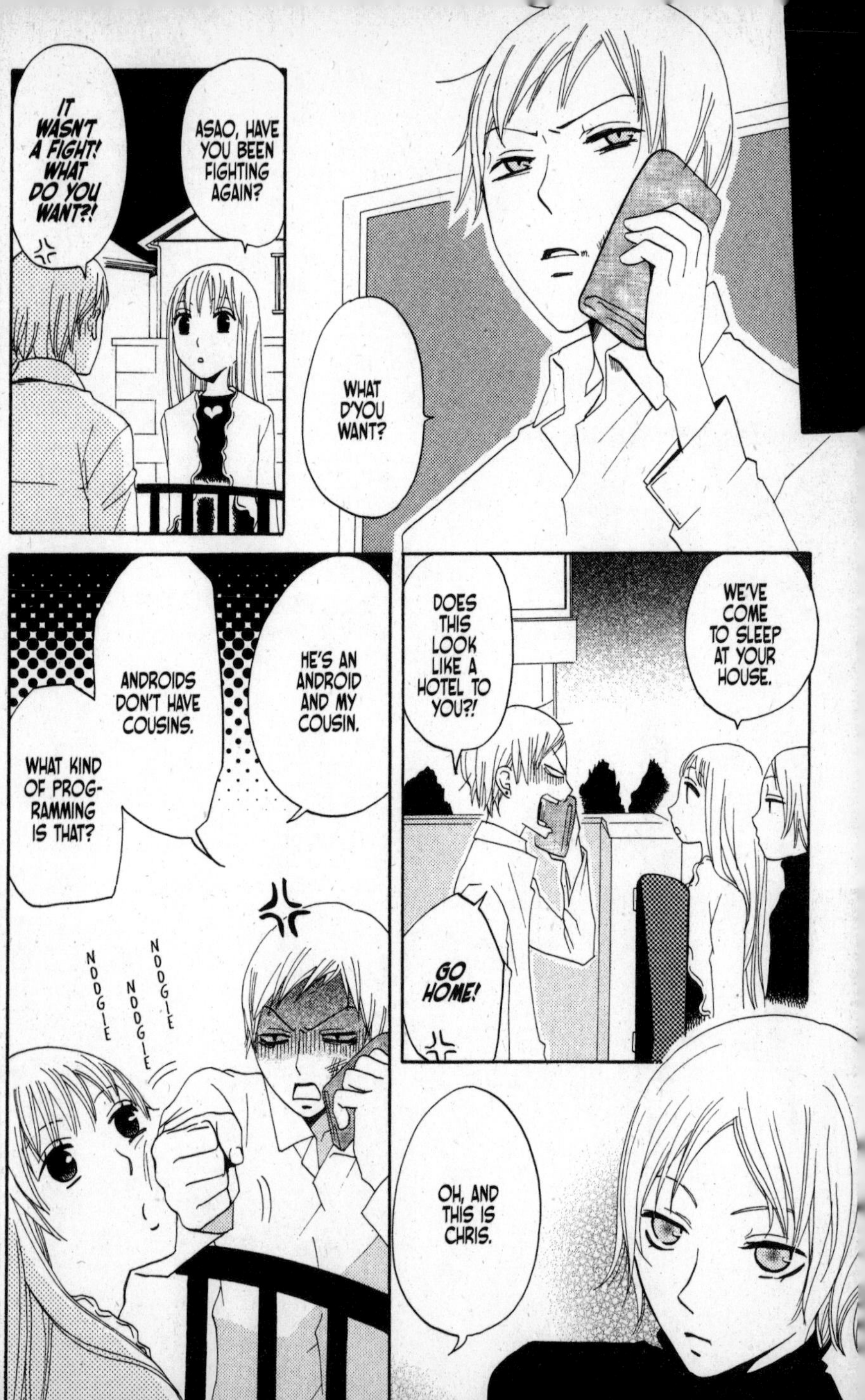
WHAT D'YOU WANT?
ASAO, HAVE YOU BEEN FIGHTING AGAIN?
IT WASN'T A FIGHT! WHAT DO YOU WANT?!
WE'VE COME TO SLEEP AT YOUR HOUSE.
DOES THIS LOOK LIKE A HOTEL TO YOU?!
GO HOME!
OH, AND THIS IS CHRIS.
HE'S AN ANDROID AND MY COUSIN.
ANDROIDS DON'T HAVE COUSINS.
WHAT KIND OF PROG-RAMMING IS THAT?
NOOGIE NOOGIE NOOGIE

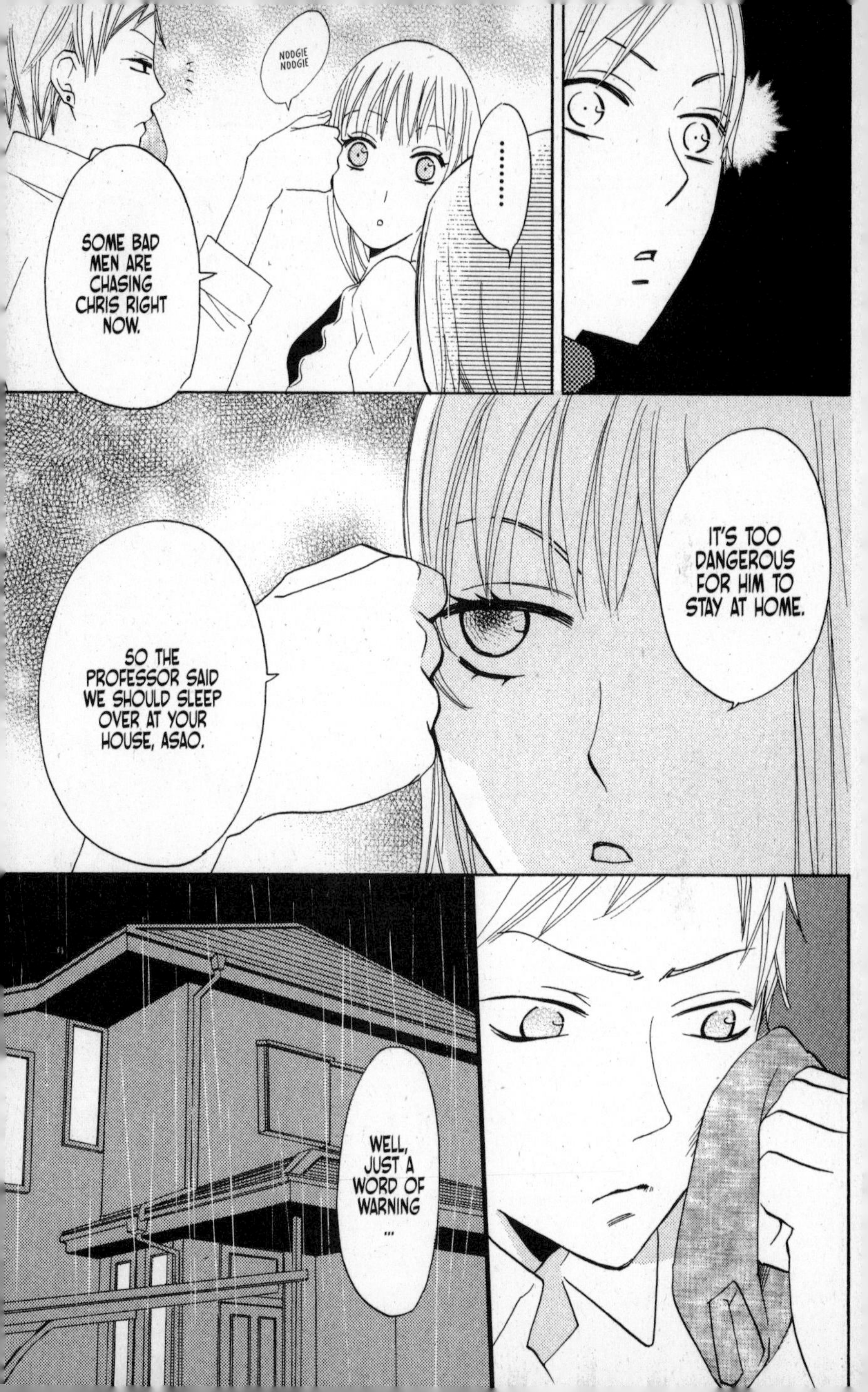
......
NOOGIE NOOGIE
SOME BAD MEN ARE CHASING CHRIS RIGHT NOW.
IT'S TOO DANGEROUS FOR HIM TO STAY AT HOME.
SO THE PROFESSOR SAID WE SHOULD SLEEP OVER AT YOUR HOUSE, ASAO.
WELL, JUST A WORD OF WARNING ...

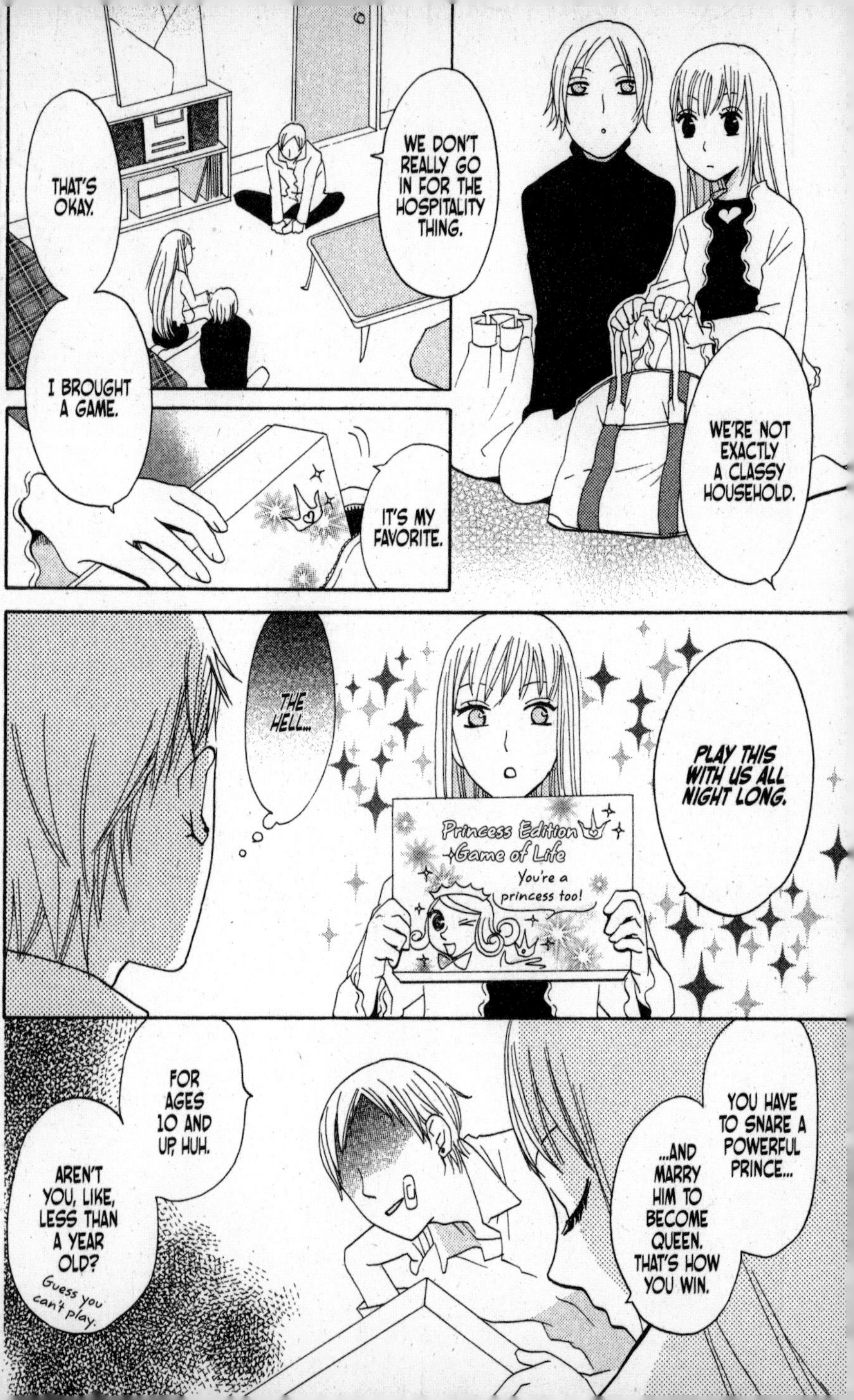
WE'RE NOT EXACTLY A CLASSY HOUSEHOLD.
WE DON'T REALLY GO IN FOR THE HOSPITALITY THING.
THAT'S OKAY.
I BROUGHT A GAME.
IT'S MY FAVORITE.
PLAY THIS WITH US ALL NIGHT LONG.
Princess Edition Game of Life
You're a princess too!
THE HELL...
YOU HAVE TO SNARE A POWERFUL PRINCE...
...AND MARRY HIM TO BECOME QUEEN. THAT'S HOW YOU WIN.
FOR AGES 10 AND UP, HUH.
AREN'T YOU, LIKE, LESS THAN A YEAR OLD?
Guess you can't play.

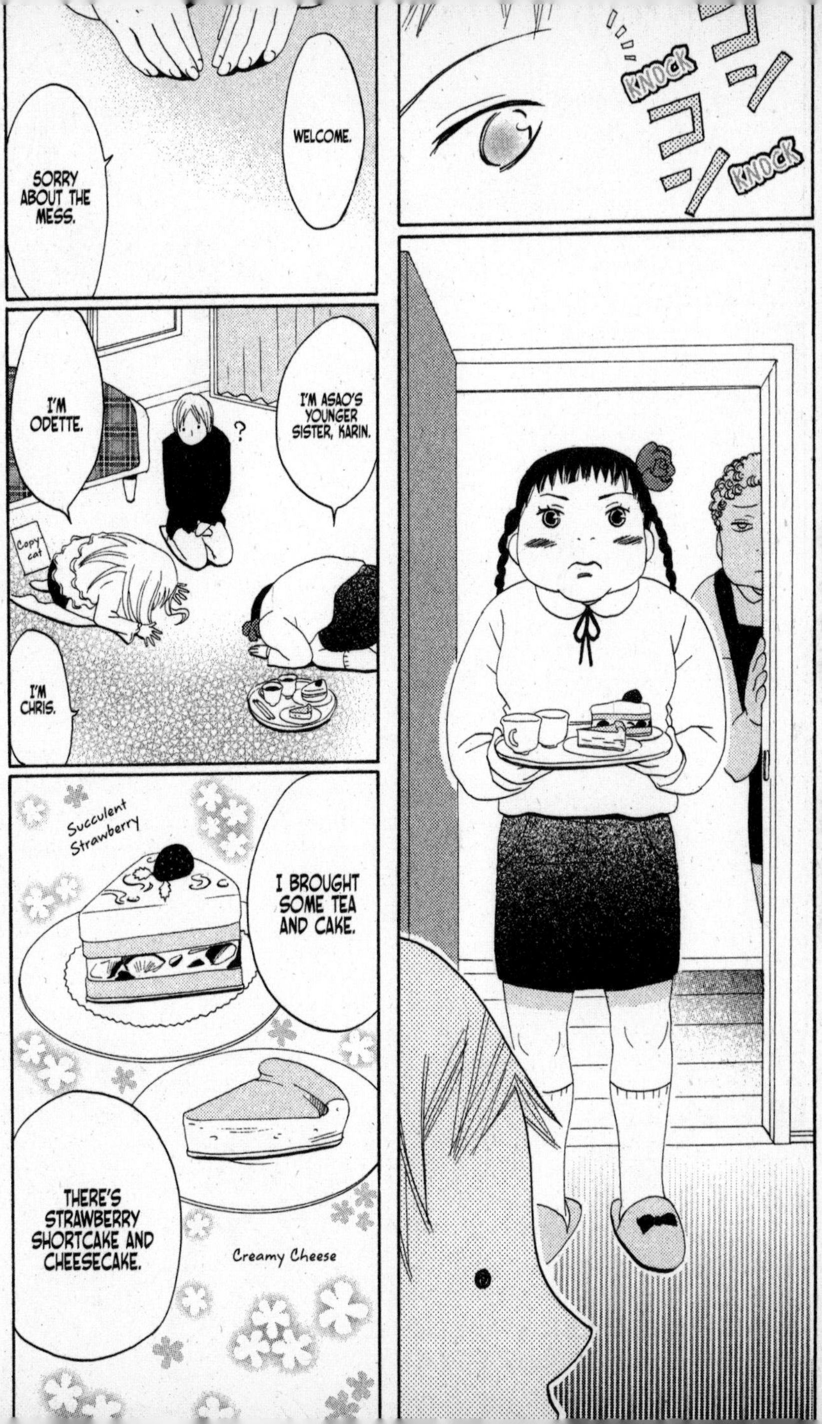

KNOCK
KNOCK
WELCOME.
SORRY ABOUT THE MESS.
I'M ASAO'S YOUNGER SISTER, KARIN.
I'M ODETTE.
Copy-cat
I'M CHRIS.
I BROUGHT SOME TEA AND CAKE.
Succulent Strawberry
THERE'S STRAWBERRY SHORTCAKE AND CHEESECAKE.
Creamy Cheese

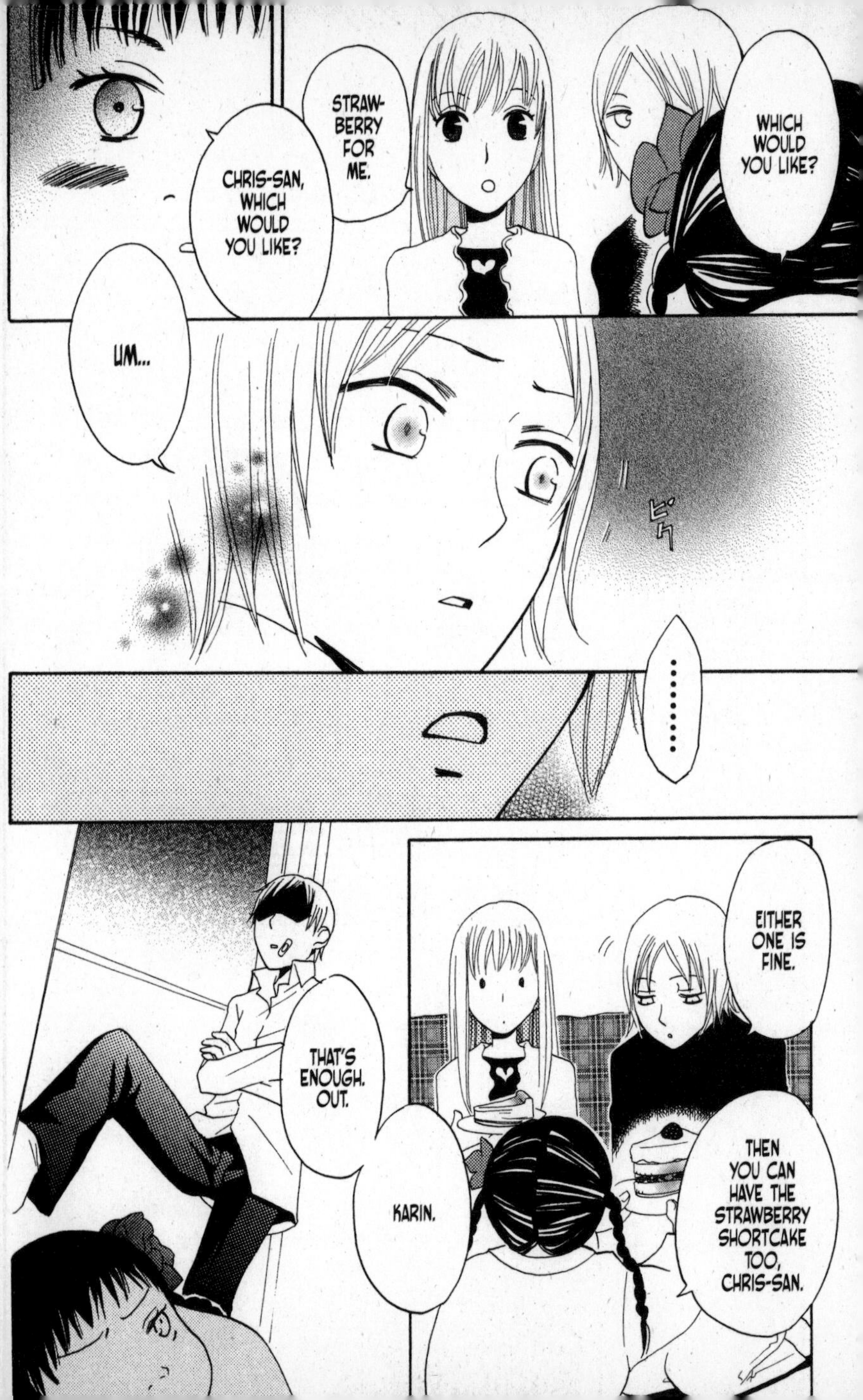
WHICH WOULD YOU LIKE?
STRAW-BERRY FOR ME.
CHRIS-SAN, WHICH WOULD YOU LIKE?
UM...
ビク
....
EITHER ONE IS FINE.
THEN YOU CAN HAVE THE STRAWBERRY SHORTCAKE TOO, CHRIS-SAN.
KARIN.
THAT'S ENOUGH. OUT.

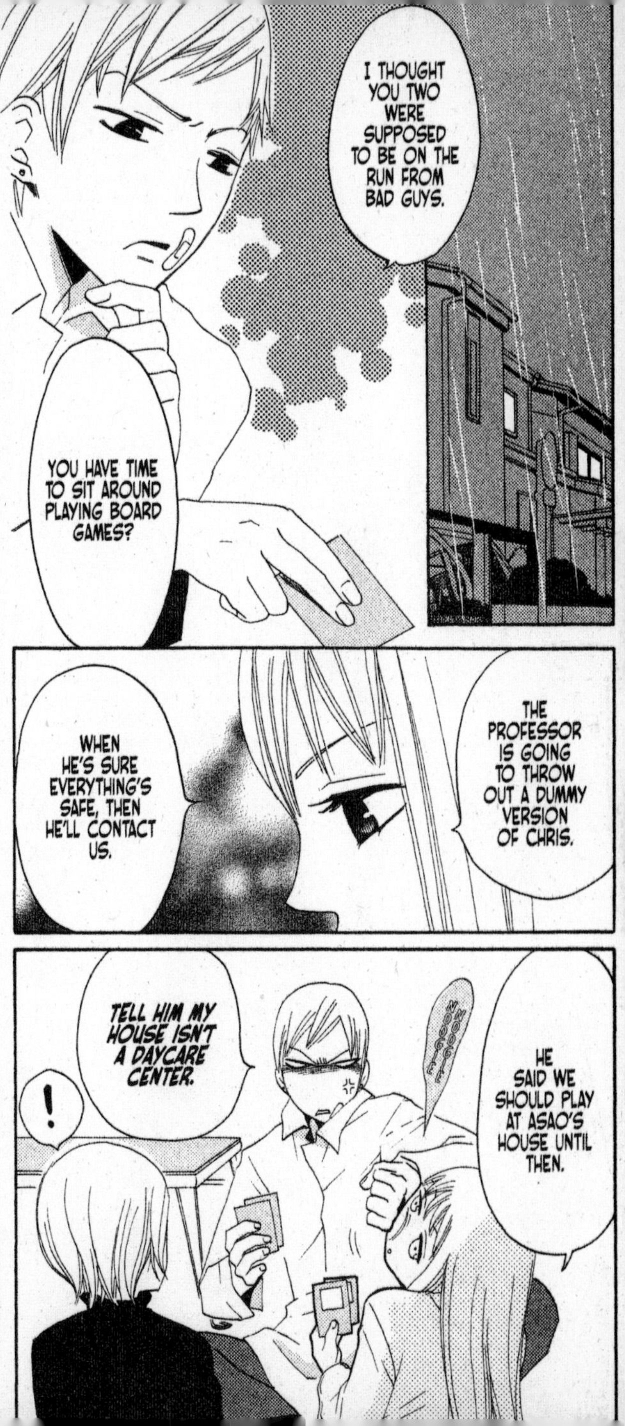
I THOUGHT YOU TWO WERE SUPPOSED TO BE ON THE RUN FROM BAD GUYS.
YOU HAVE TIME TO SIT AROUND PLAYING BOARD GAMES?
THE PROFESSOR IS GOING TO THROW OUT A DUMMY VERSION OF CHRIS.
WHEN HE'S SURE EVERYTHING'S SAFE, THEN HE'LL CONTACT US.
HE SAID WE SHOULD PLAY AT ASAO'S HOUSE UNTIL THEN.
NOOGIE NOOGIE
TELL HIM MY HOUSE ISN'T A DAYCARE CENTER.
!

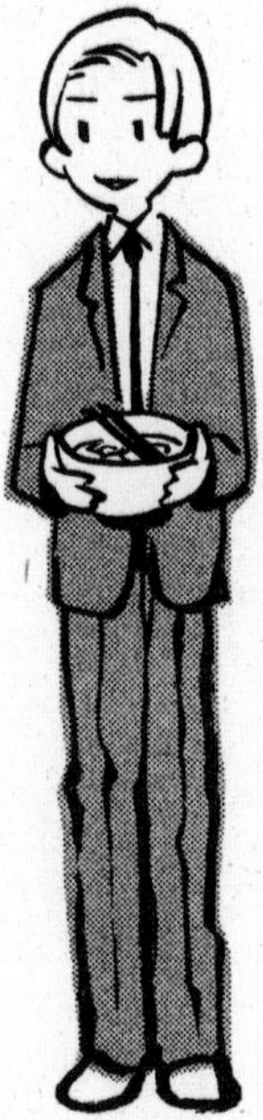

Yamashiro-kun

Class 2-D, 17 years old
Likes: Cute girls and ramen.

Favorite kind of ramen is pork and soy. His dream is to eat ramen with a cute girl.

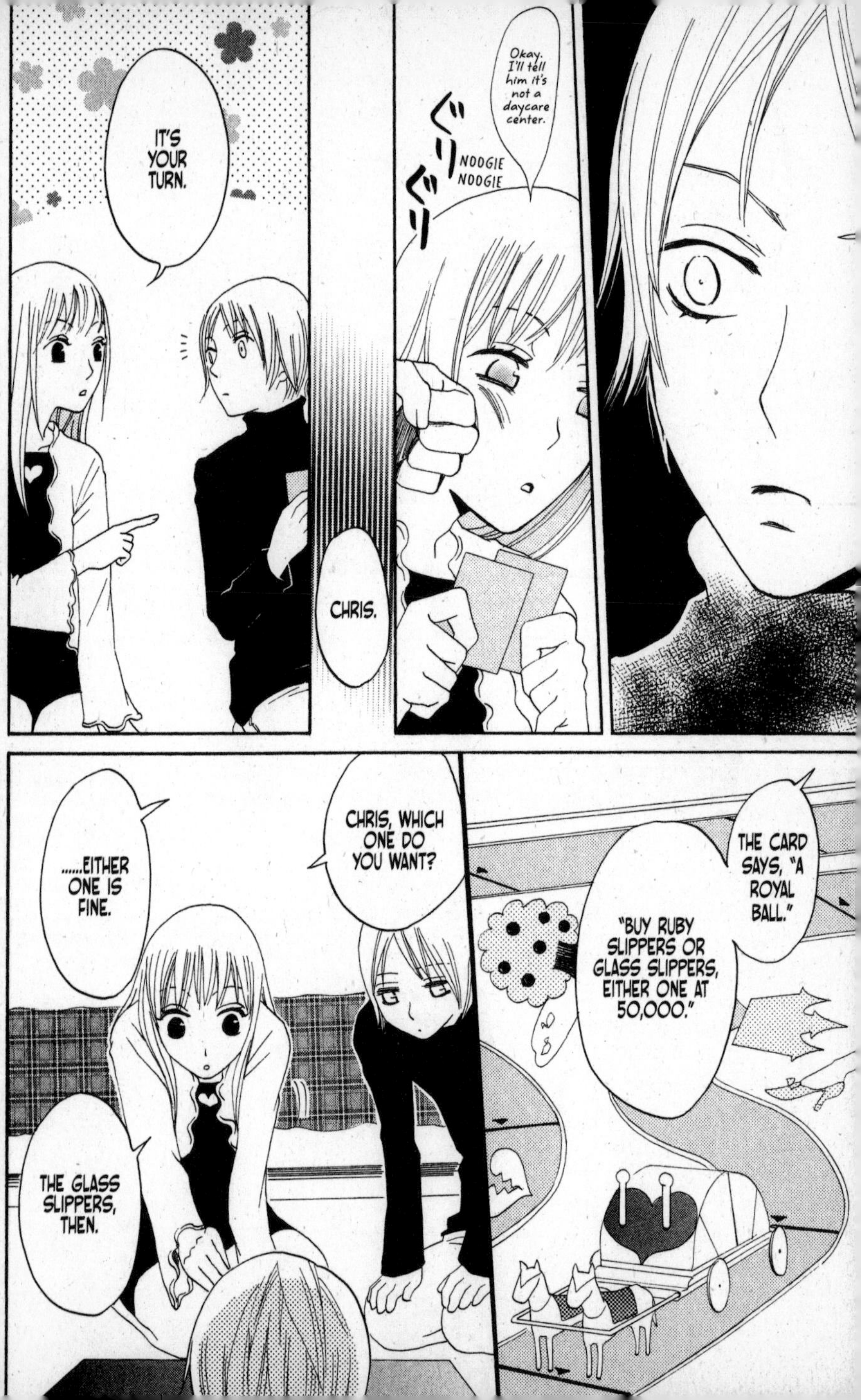
Okay. I'll tell him it's not a daycare center.
ぐりぐり
NOODGIE NOODGIE
CHRIS.
IT'S YOUR TURN.
THE CARD SAYS, "A ROYAL BALL."
"BUY RUBY SLIPPERS OR GLASS SLIPPERS, EITHER ONE AT 50,000."
CHRIS, WHICH ONE DO YOU WANT?
......EITHER ONE IS FINE.
THE GLASS SLIPPERS, THEN.

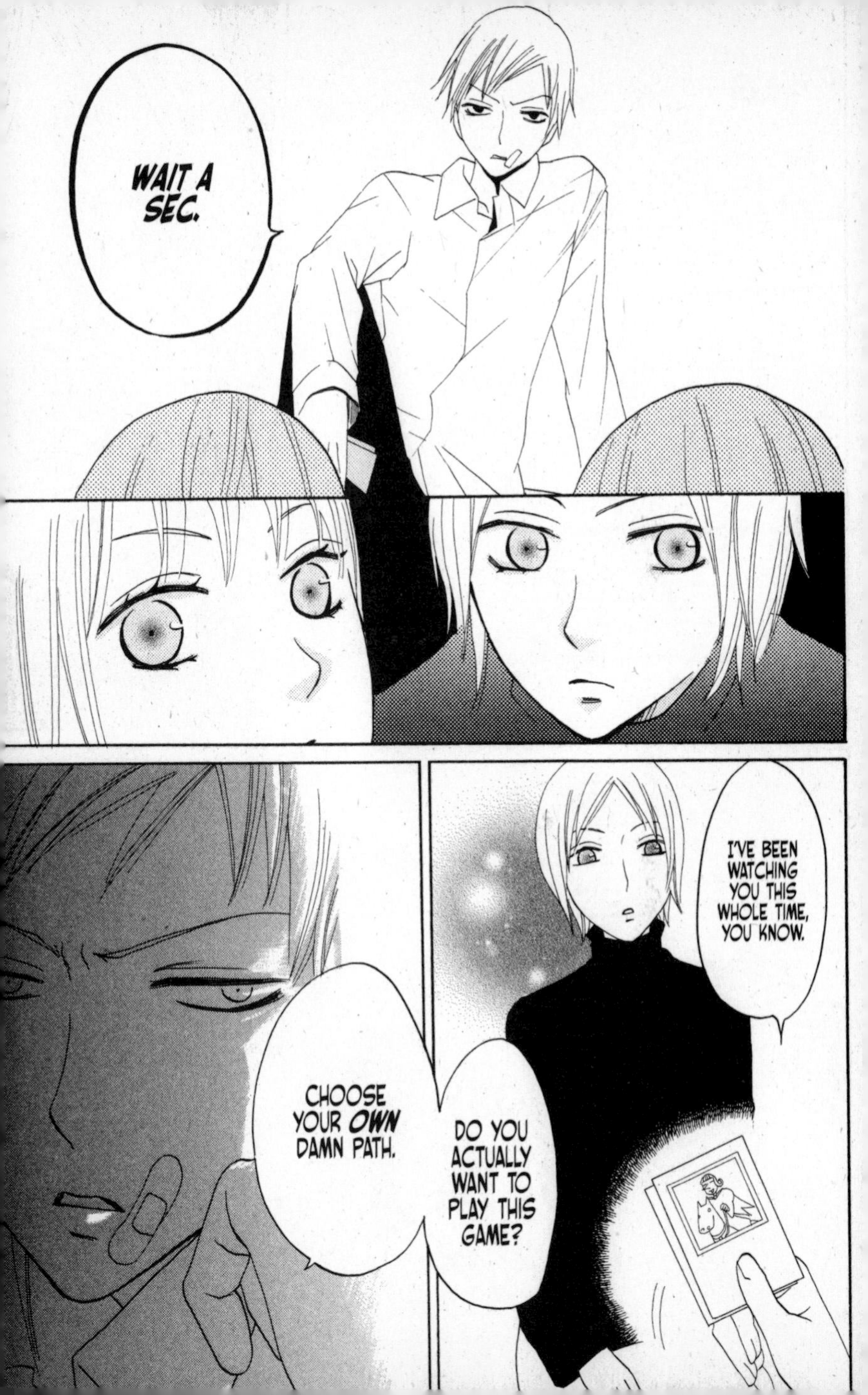
WAIT A SEC.
I'VE BEEN WATCHING YOU THIS WHOLE TIME, YOU KNOW.
DO YOU ACTUALLY WANT TO PLAY THIS GAME?
CHOOSE YOUR *OWN* DAMN PATH.

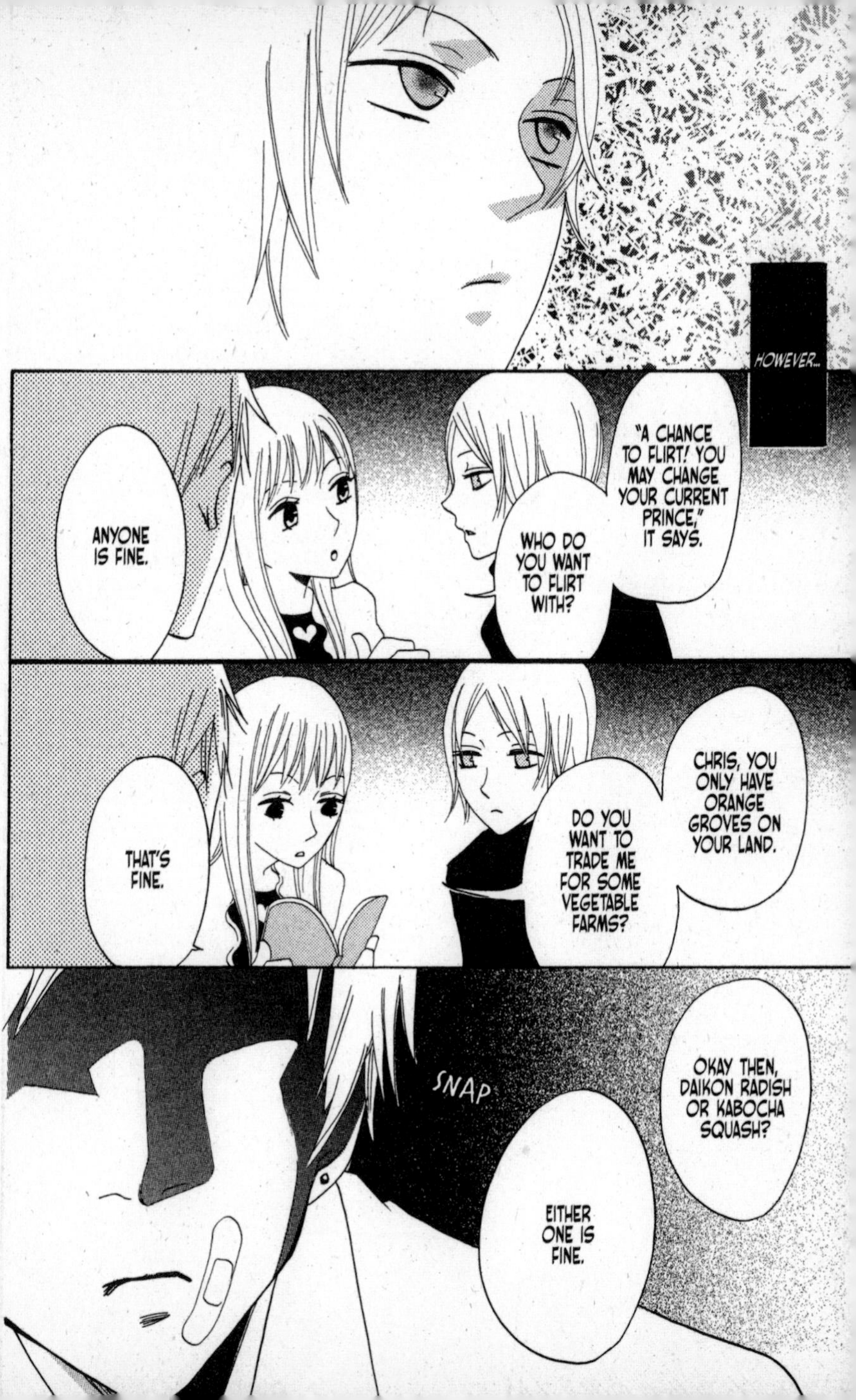
HOWEVER...
"A CHANCE TO FLIRT! YOU MAY CHANGE YOUR CURRENT PRINCE," IT SAYS.
WHO DO YOU WANT TO FLIRT WITH?
ANYONE IS FINE.
CHRIS, YOU ONLY HAVE ORANGE GROVES ON YOUR LAND.
DO YOU WANT TO TRADE ME FOR SOME VEGETABLE FARMS?
THAT'S FINE.
OKAY THEN, DAIKON RADISH OR KABOCHA SQUASH?
EITHER ONE IS FINE.
SNAP

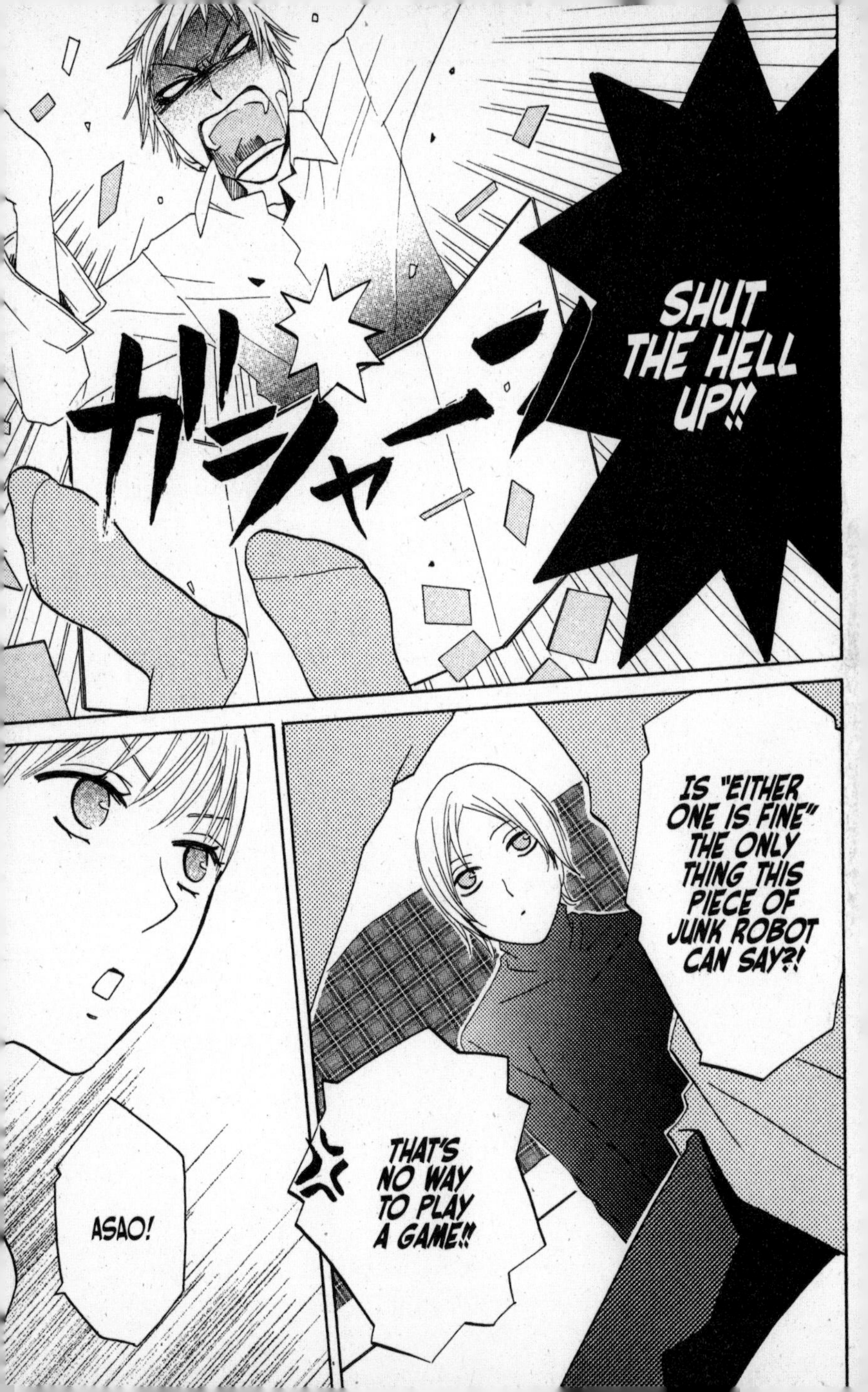
SHUT THE HELL UP!!
ガシャーン
IS "EITHER ONE IS FINE" THE ONLY THING THIS PIECE OF JUNK ROBOT CAN SAY?!
THAT'S NO WAY TO PLAY A GAME!!
ASAO!

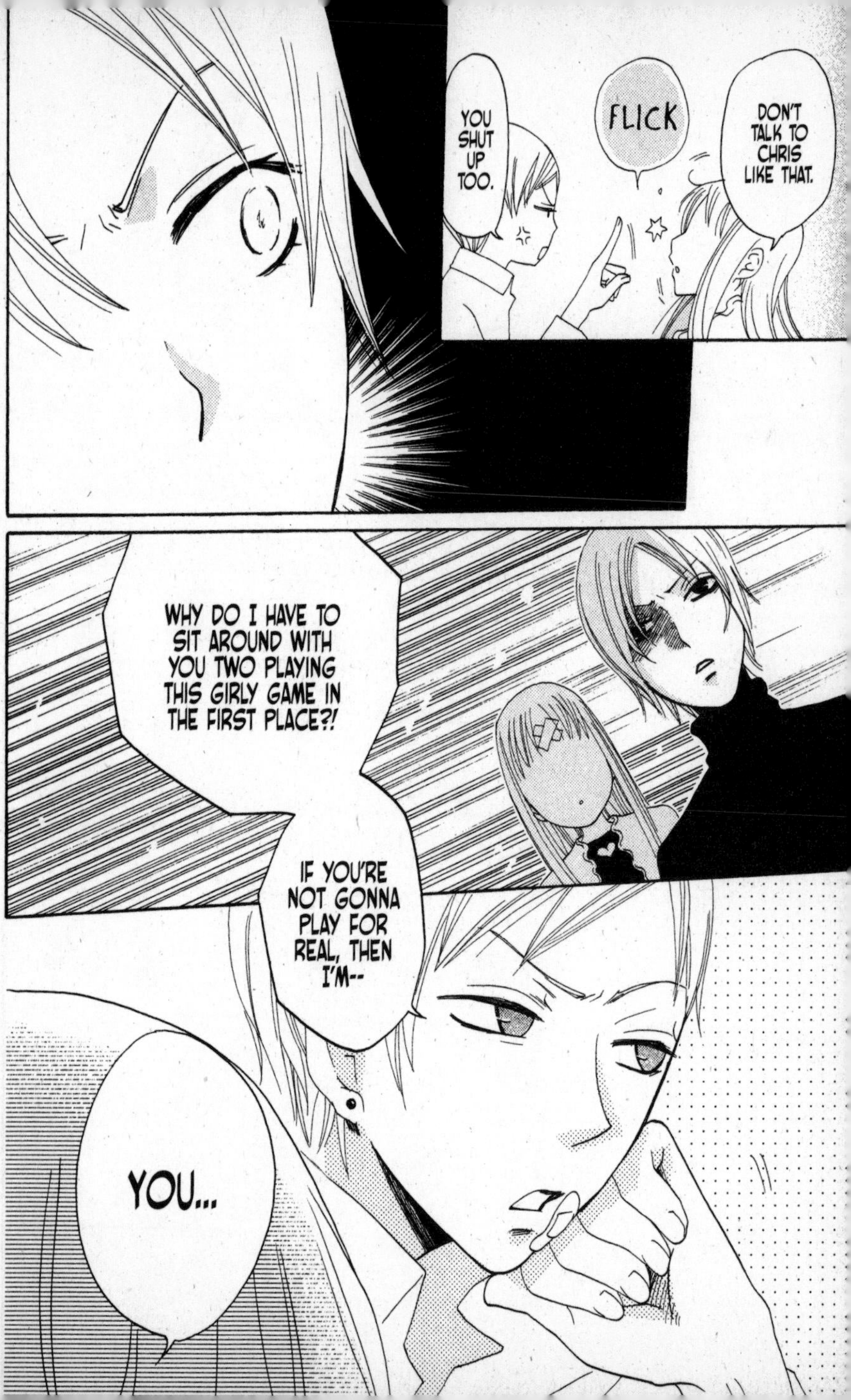
DON'T TALK TO CHRIS LIKE THAT.
FLICK
YOU SHUT UP TOO.
WHY DO I HAVE TO SIT AROUND WITH YOU TWO PLAYING THIS GIRLY GAME IN THE FIRST PLACE?!
IF YOU'RE NOT GONNA PLAY FOR REAL, THEN I'M--
YOU...

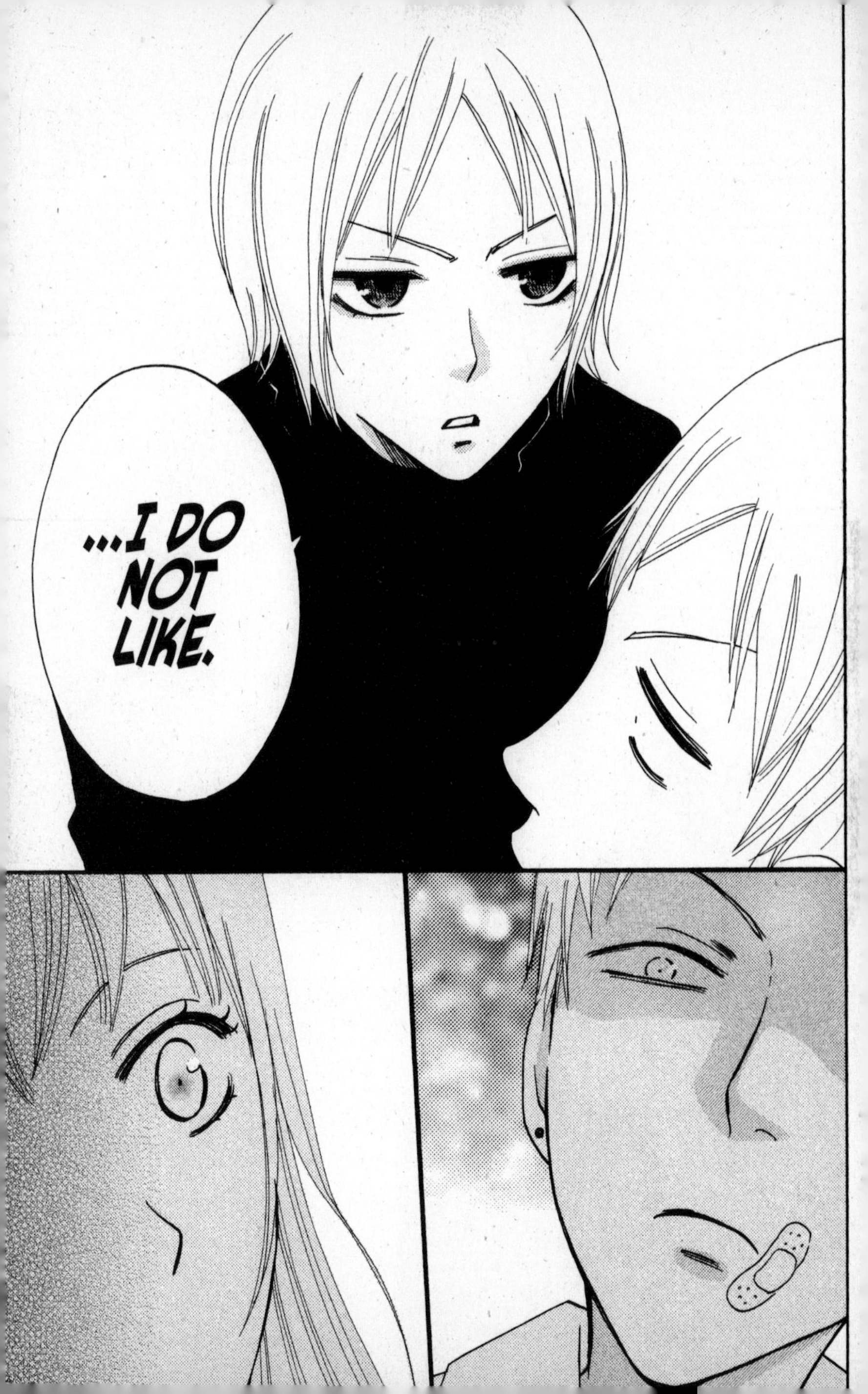
...I DO NOT LIKE.

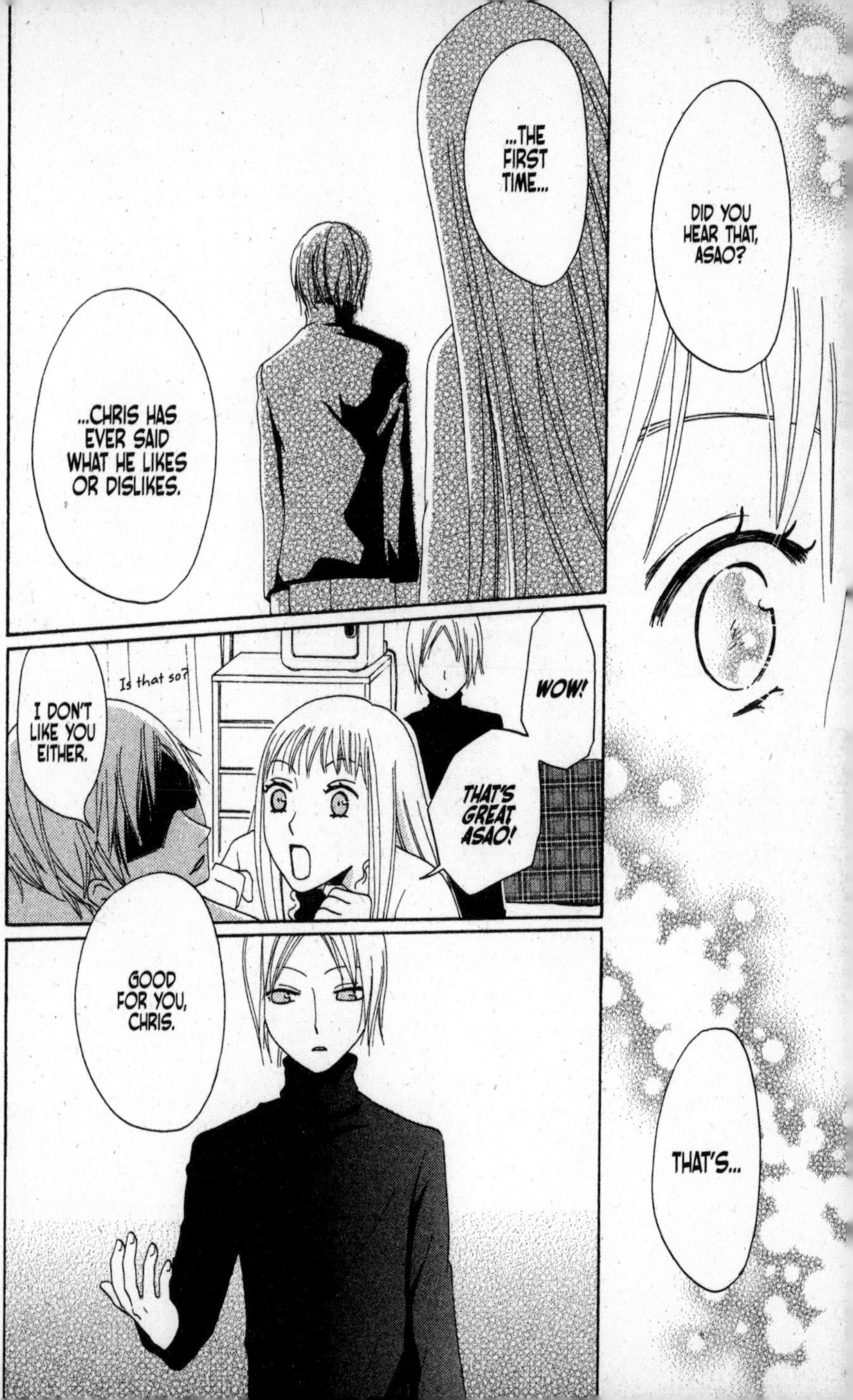
DID YOU HEAR THAT, ASAO?
THAT'S...
...THE FIRST TIME...
...CHRIS HAS EVER SAID WHAT HE LIKES OR DISLIKES.
WOW!
THAT'S GREAT ASAO!
Is that so?
I DON'T LIKE YOU EITHER.
GOOD FOR YOU, CHRIS.

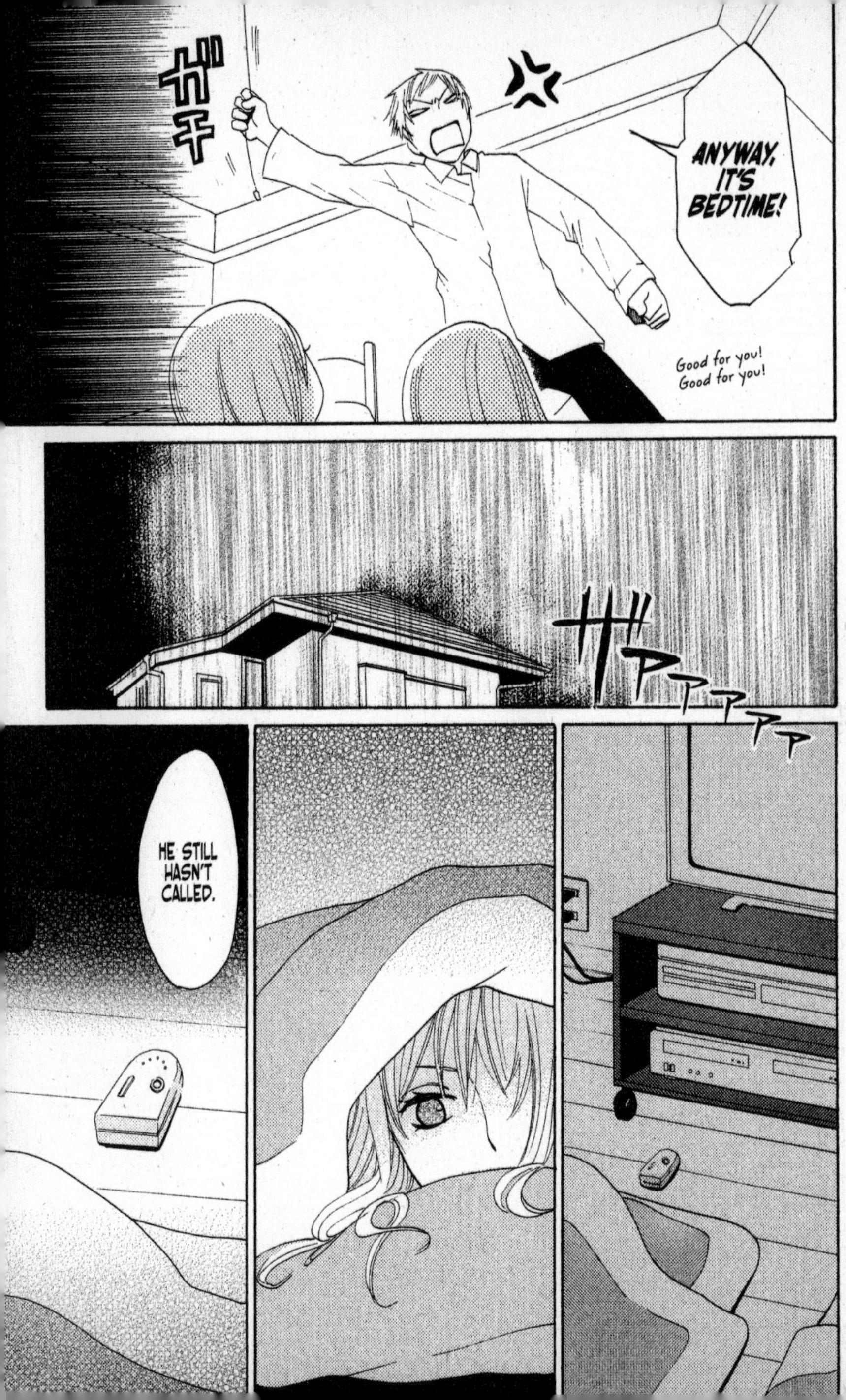
ANYWAY, IT'S BEDTIME!
Good for you! Good for you!
HE STILL HASN'T CALLED.

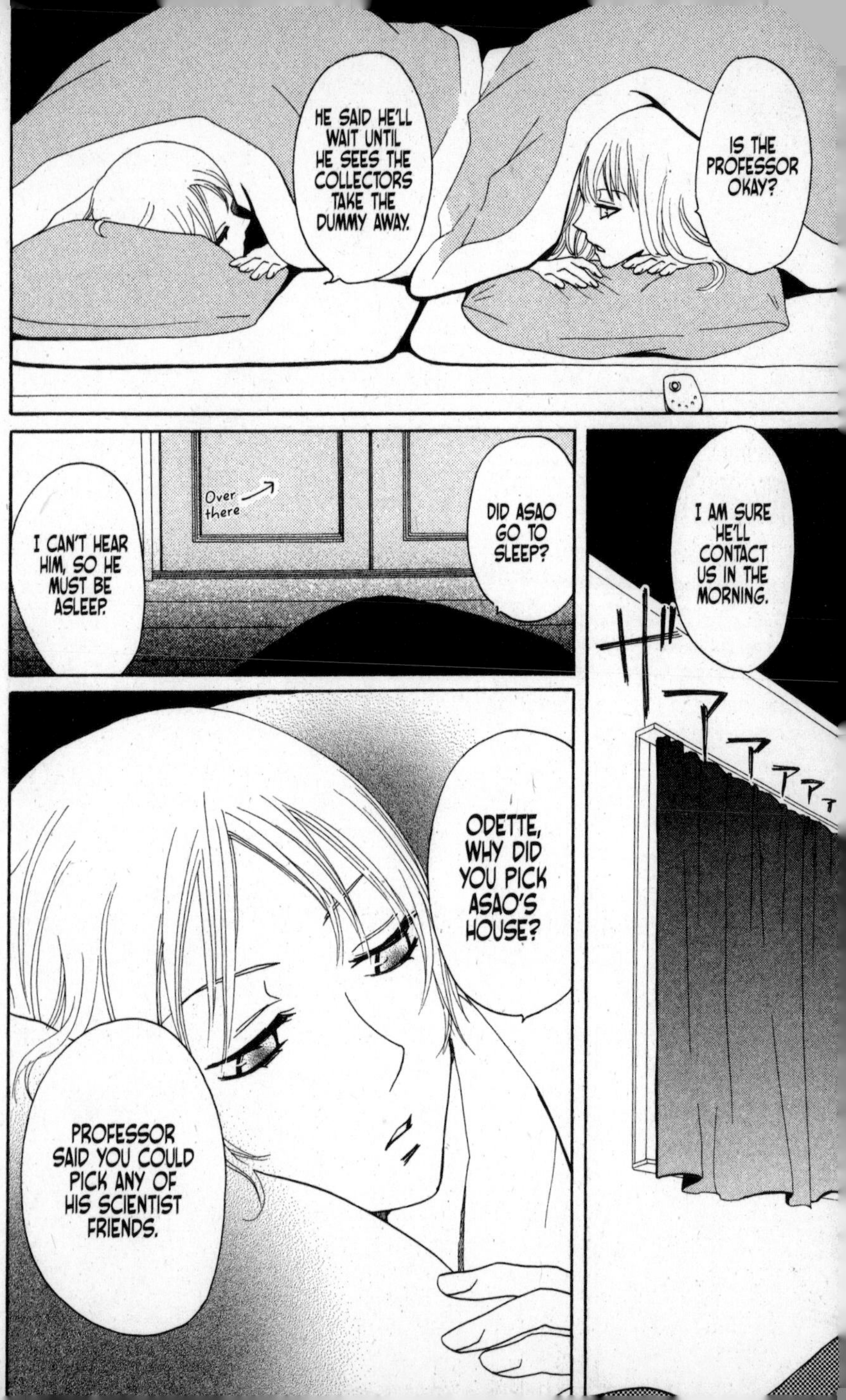
IS THE PROFESSOR OKAY?
HE SAID HE'LL WAIT UNTIL HE SEES THE COLLECTORS TAKE THE DUMMY AWAY.
I AM SURE HE'LL CONTACT US IN THE MORNING.
ザアアアァ
DID ASAO GO TO SLEEP?
Over there
I CAN'T HEAR HIM, SO HE MUST BE ASLEEP.
ODETTE, WHY DID YOU PICK ASAO'S HOUSE?
PROFESSOR SAID YOU COULD PICK ANY OF HIS SCIENTIST FRIENDS.

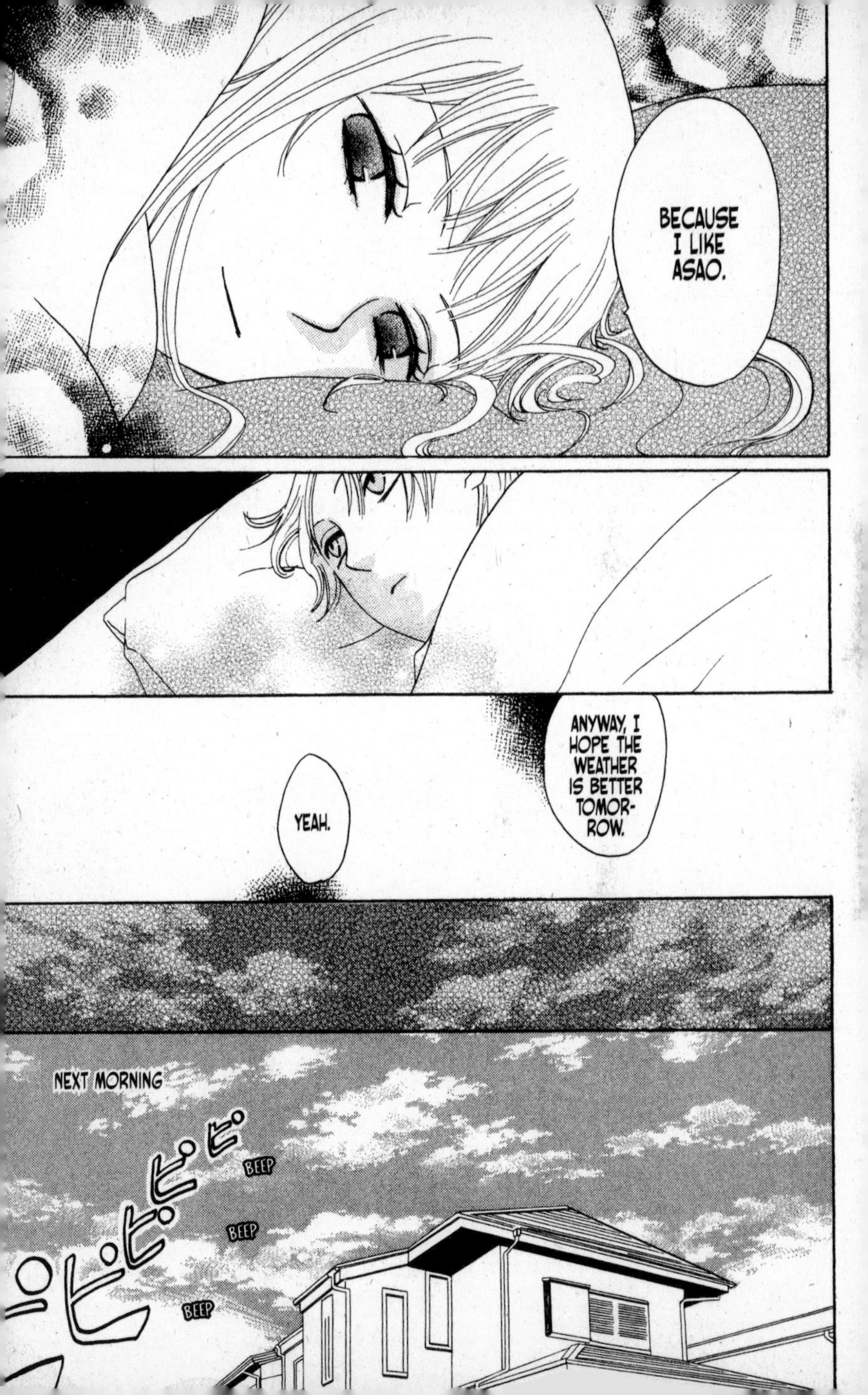
BECAUSE I LIKE ASAO.
ANYWAY, I HOPE THE WEATHER IS BETTER TOMORROW.
YEAH.
NEXT MORNING
ピピピ
BEEP
BEEP
BEEP

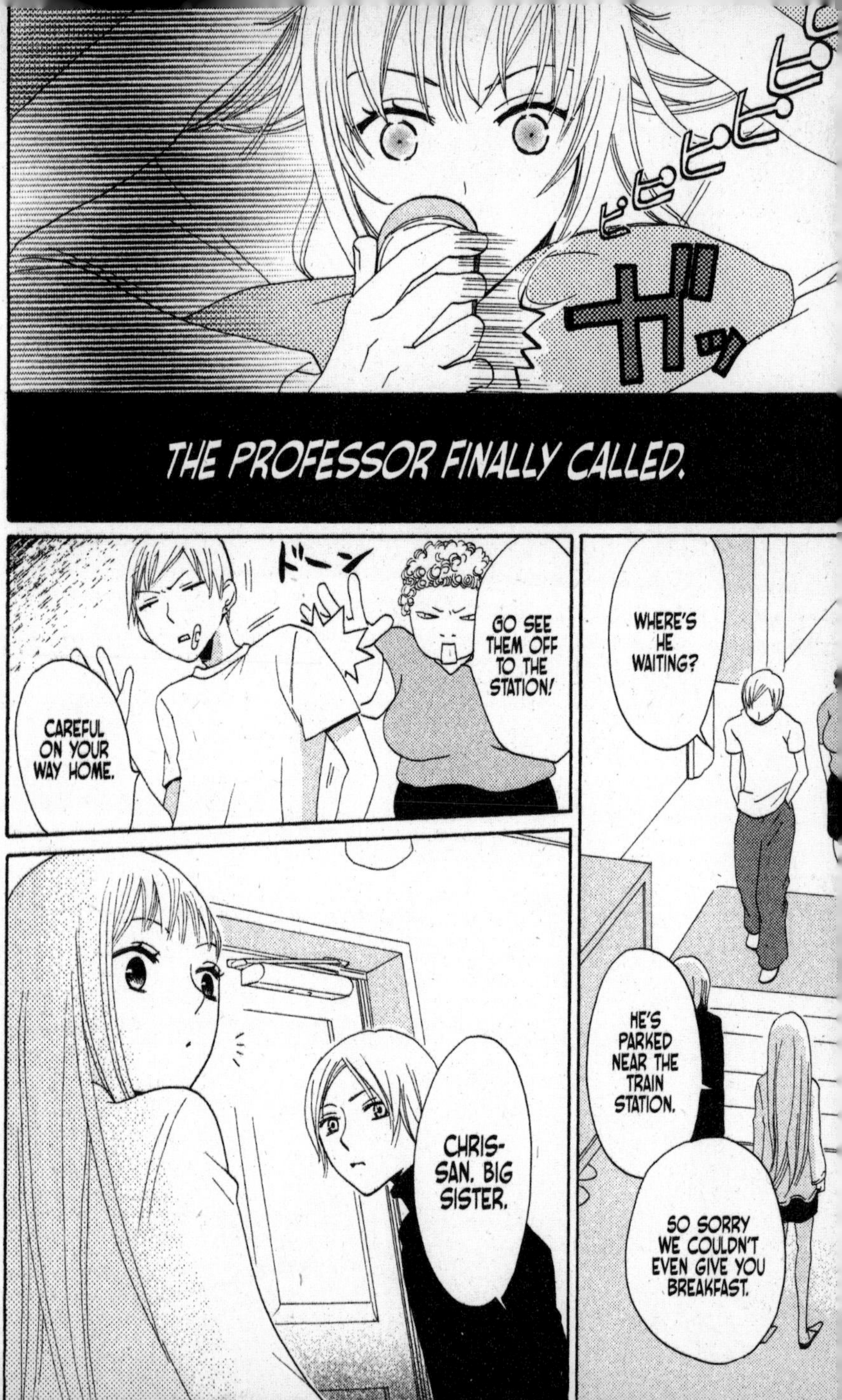
ピピピピピピ
ガッ
THE PROFESSOR FINALLY CALLED.
WHERE'S HE WAITING?
HE'S PARKED NEAR THE TRAIN STATION.
SO SORRY WE COULDN'T EVEN GIVE YOU BREAKFAST.
GO SEE THEM OFF TO THE STATION!
ドーン
CAREFUL ON YOUR WAY HOME.
CHRIS-SAN. BIG SISTER.

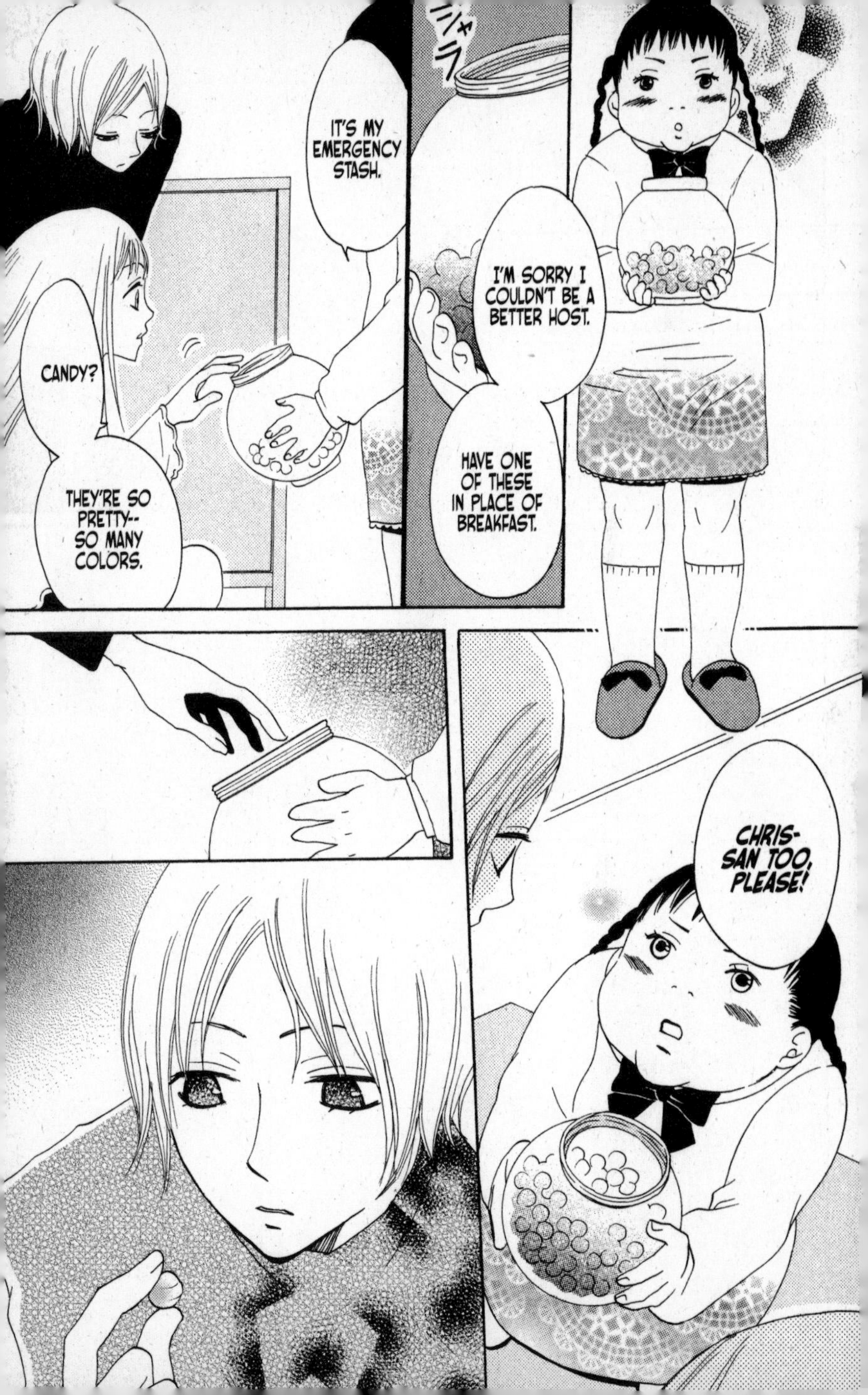
シャラ
I'M SORRY I COULDN'T BE A BETTER HOST.
HAVE ONE OF THESE IN PLACE OF BREAKFAST.
IT'S MY EMERGENCY STASH.
CANDY?
THEY'RE SO PRETTY-- SO MANY COLORS.
CHRIS-SAN TOO, PLEASE!

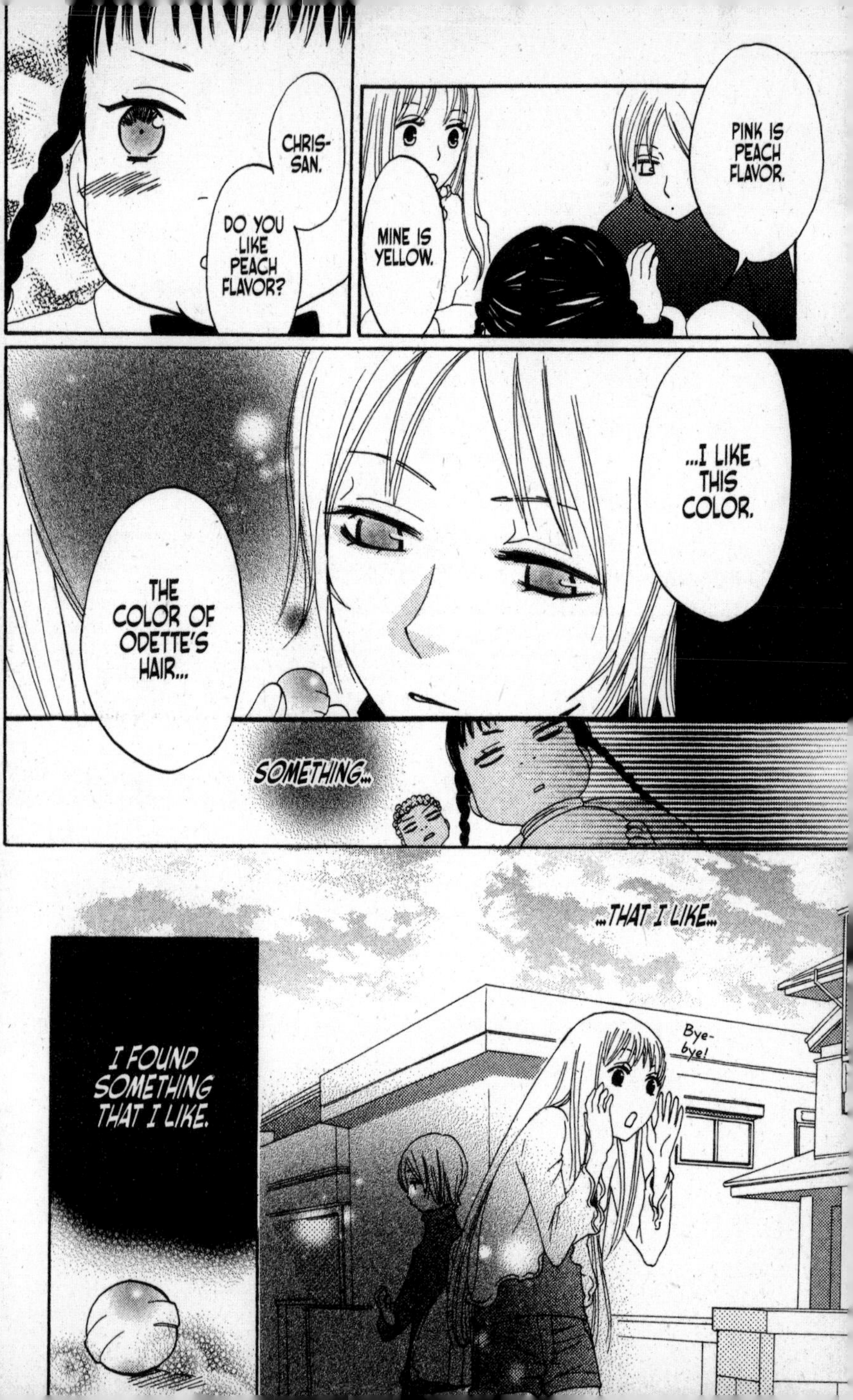
PINK IS PEACH FLAVOR.
MINE IS YELLOW.
CHRIS-SAN.
DO YOU LIKE PEACH FLAVOR?
...I LIKE THIS COLOR.
THE COLOR OF ODETTE'S HAIR...
SOMETHING...
...THAT I LIKE...
Bye-bye!
I FOUND SOMETHING THAT I LIKE.

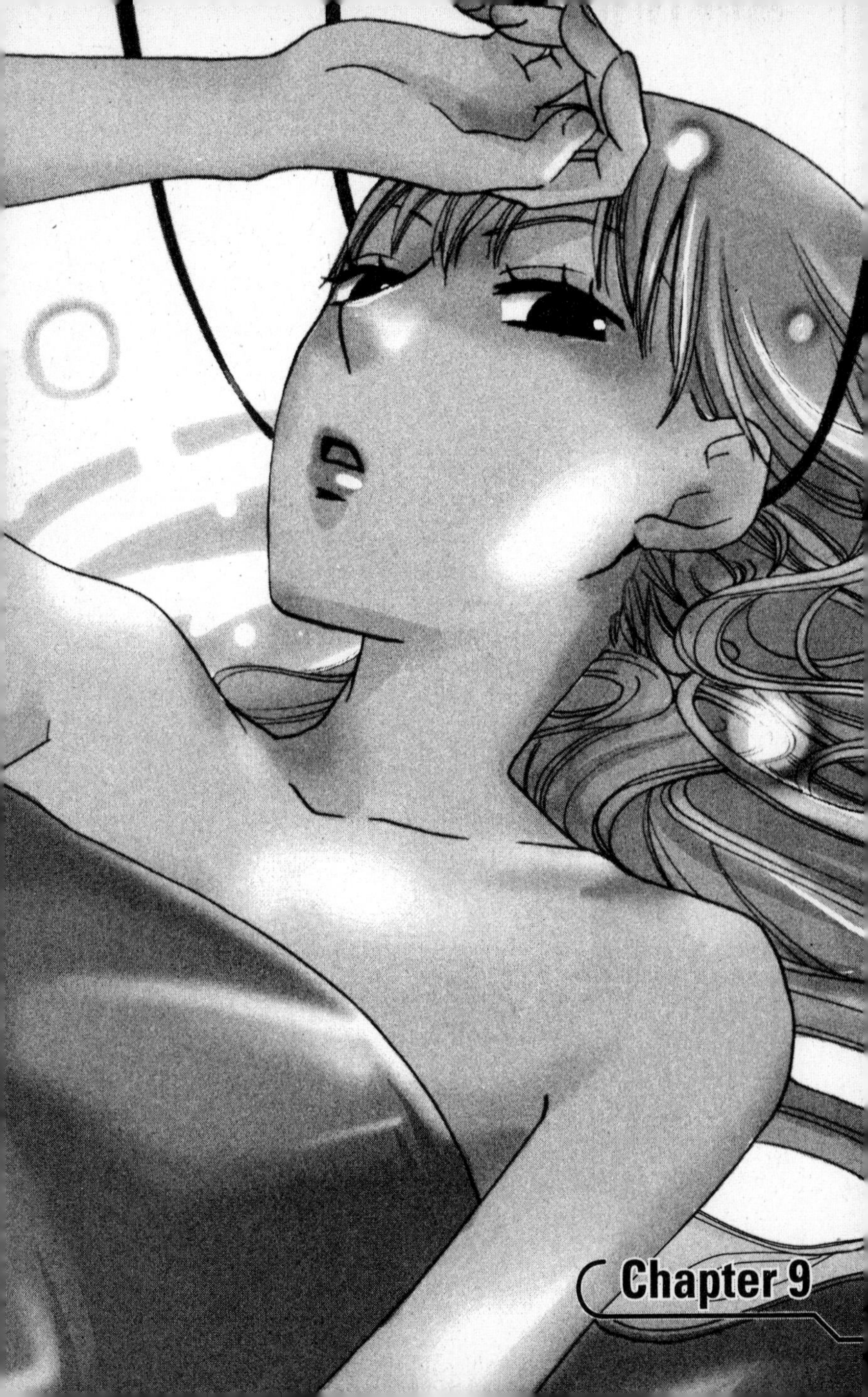
Chapter 9

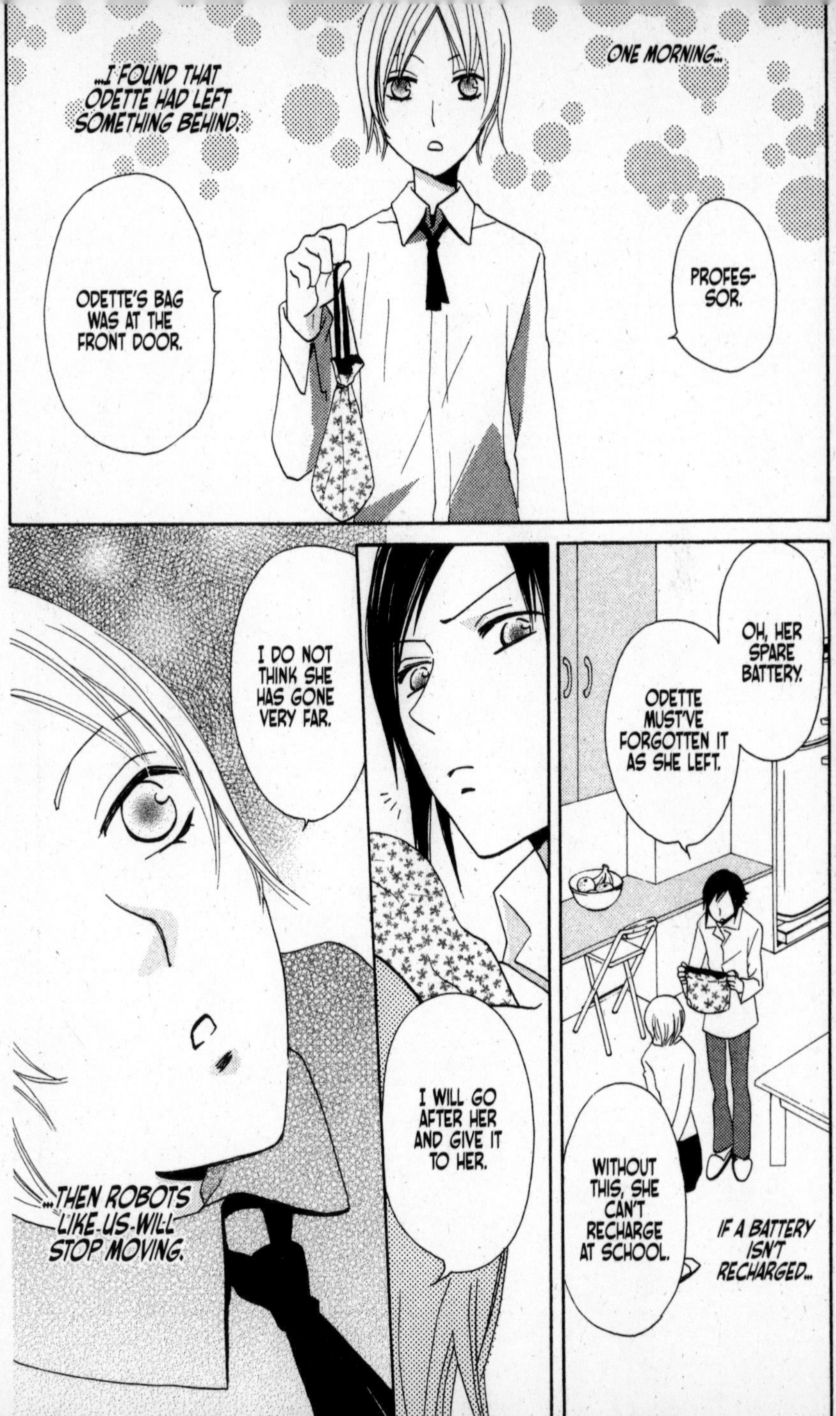
ONE MORNING...
...I FOUND THAT ODETTE HAD LEFT SOMETHING BEHIND.
PROFES-SOR.
ODETTE'S BAG WAS AT THE FRONT DOOR.
OH, HER SPARE BATTERY.
ODETTE MUST'VE FORGOTTEN IT AS SHE LEFT.
WITHOUT THIS, SHE CAN'T RECHARGE AT SCHOOL.
IF A BATTERY ISN'T RECHARGED...
I DO NOT THINK SHE HAS GONE VERY FAR.
I WILL GO AFTER HER AND GIVE IT TO HER.
...THEN ROBOTS LIKE US WILL STOP MOVING.

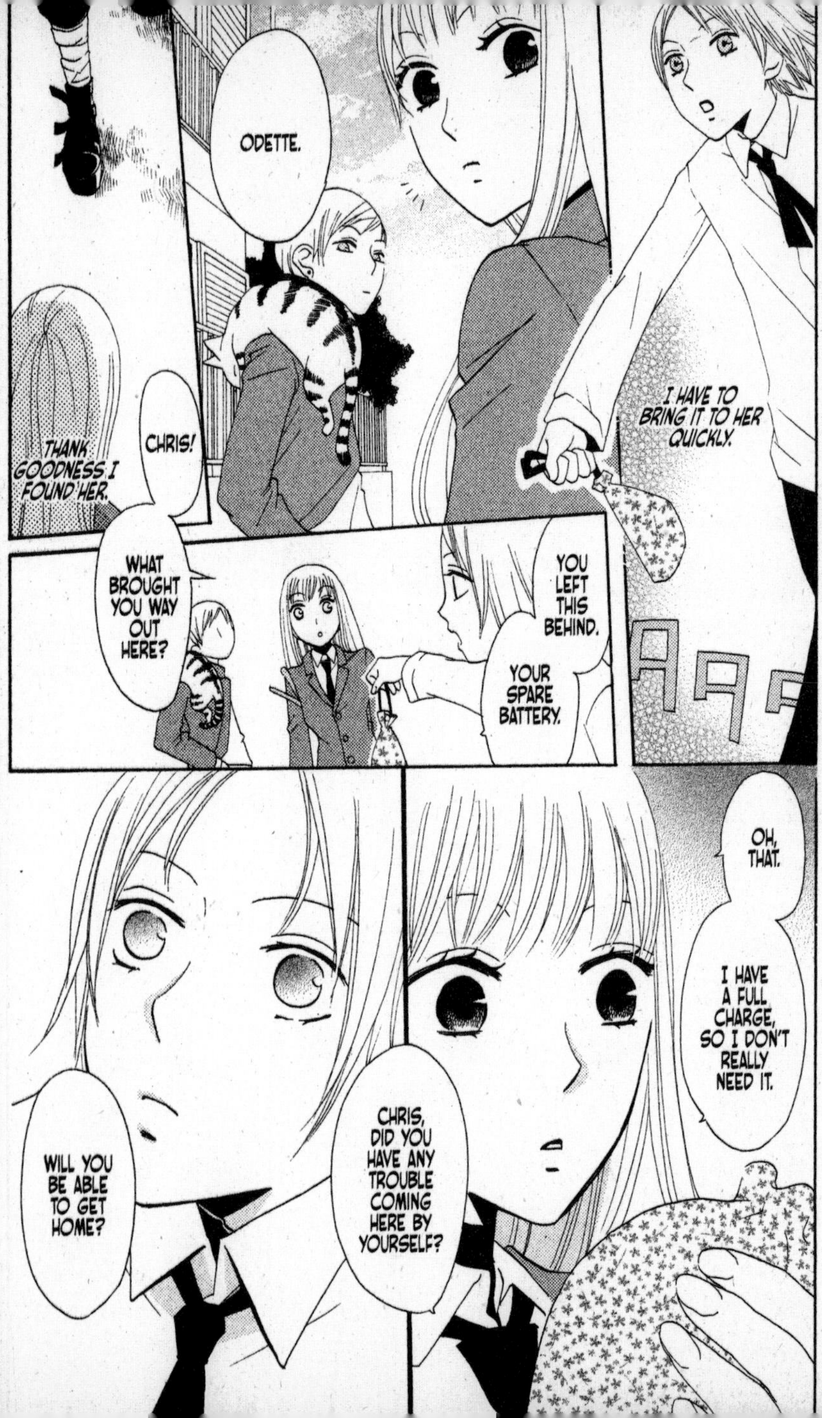
I HAVE TO BRING IT TO HER QUICKLY.
ODETTE.
CHRIS!
THANK GOODNESS I FOUND HER.
YOU LEFT THIS BEHIND.
YOUR SPARE BATTERY.
WHAT BROUGHT YOU WAY OUT HERE?
OH, THAT.
I HAVE A FULL CHARGE, SO I DON'T REALLY NEED IT.
CHRIS, DID YOU HAVE ANY TROUBLE COMING HERE BY YOURSELF?
WILL YOU BE ABLE TO GET HOME?

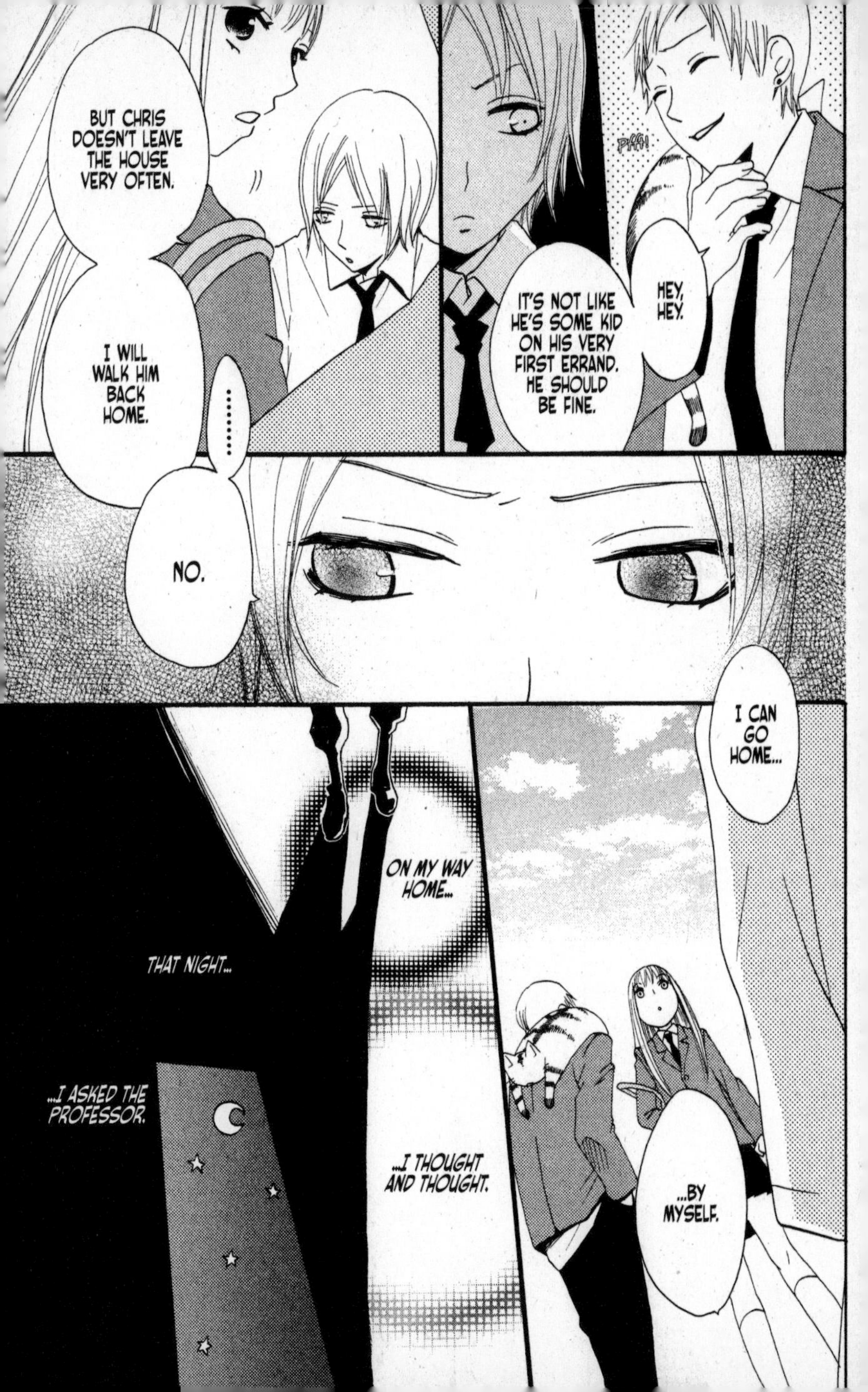
Pfft!
HEY, HEY.
IT'S NOT LIKE HE'S SOME KID ON HIS VERY FIRST ERRAND. HE SHOULD BE FINE.
BUT CHRIS DOESN'T LEAVE THE HOUSE VERY OFTEN.
I WILL WALK HIM BACK HOME.
......
NO.
I CAN GO HOME...
...BY MYSELF.
ON MY WAY HOME...
...I THOUGHT AND THOUGHT.
THAT NIGHT...
...I ASKED THE PROFESSOR.

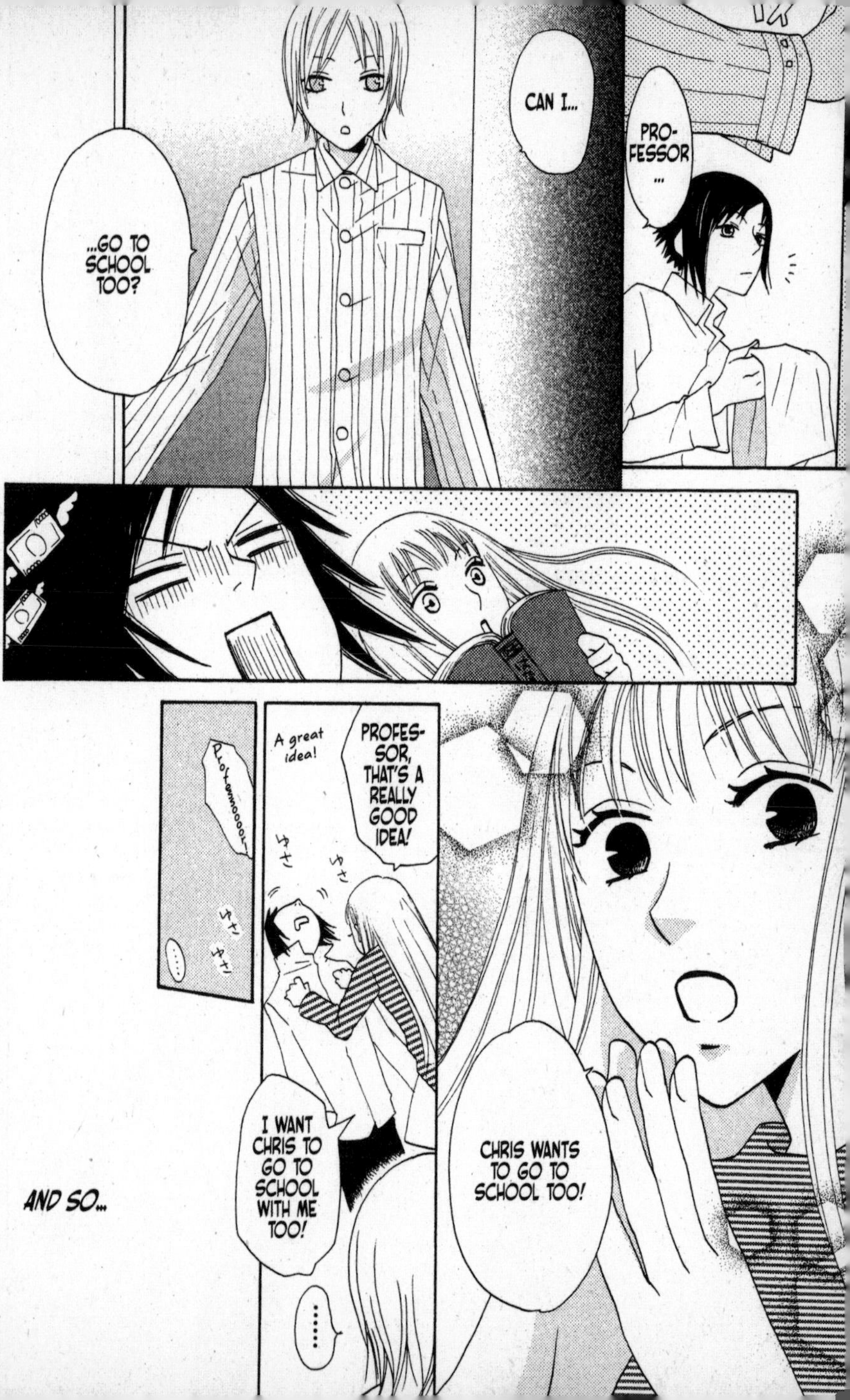
PROFESSOR ...
CAN I...
...GO TO SCHOOL TOO?
CHRIS WANTS TO GO TO SCHOOL TOO!
PROFESSOR, THAT'S A REALLY GOOD IDEA!
A great idea!
ゆさ ゆさ
I WANT CHRIS TO GO TO SCHOOL WITH ME TOO!
......
Professooooor!
ゆさ ゆさ
.....
AND SO...

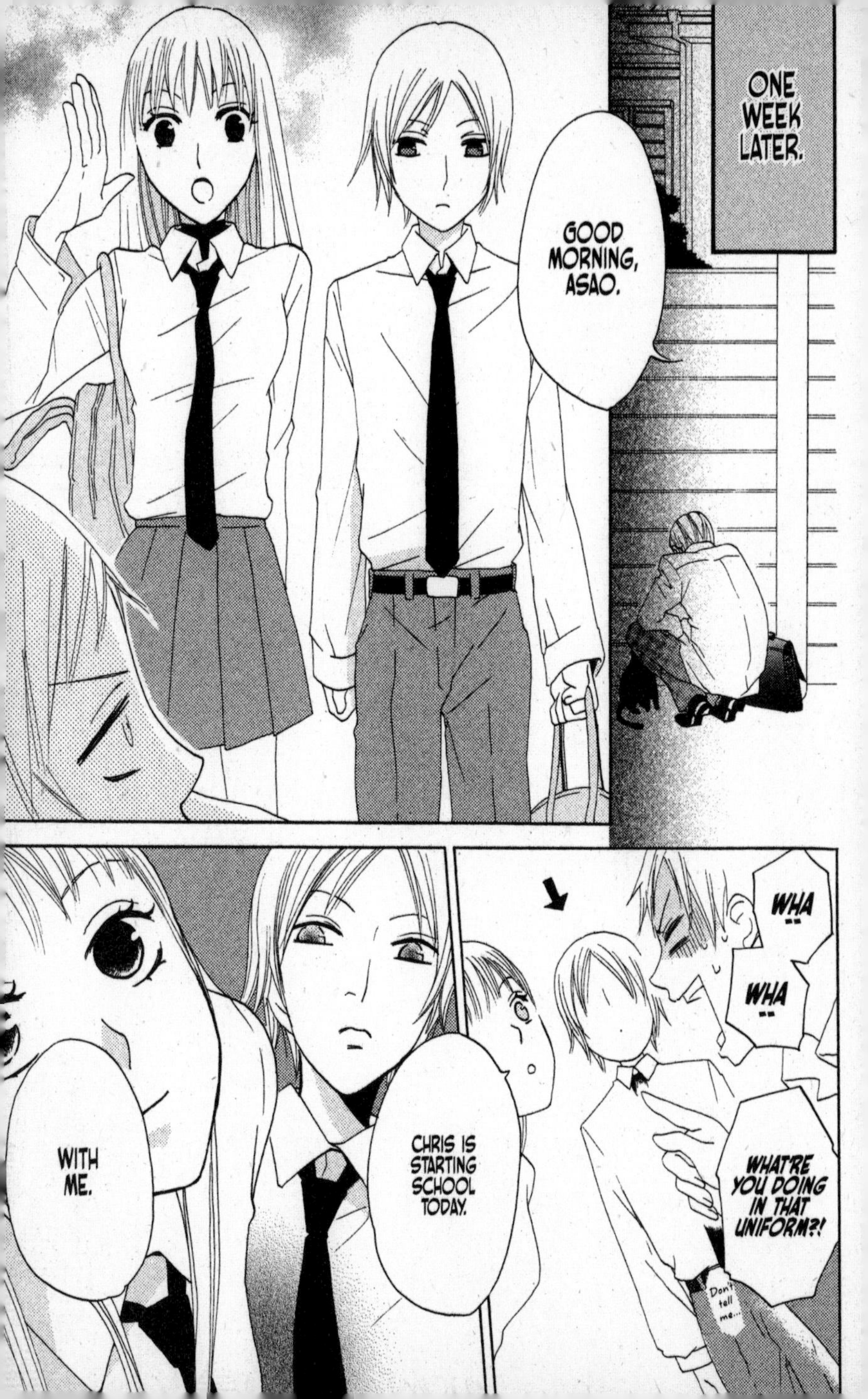
ONE WEEK LATER.
GOOD MORNING, ASAO.
WHA--
WHA--
WHAT'RE YOU DOING IN THAT UNIFORM?!
Don't tell me...
CHRIS IS STARTING SCHOOL TODAY.
WITH ME.

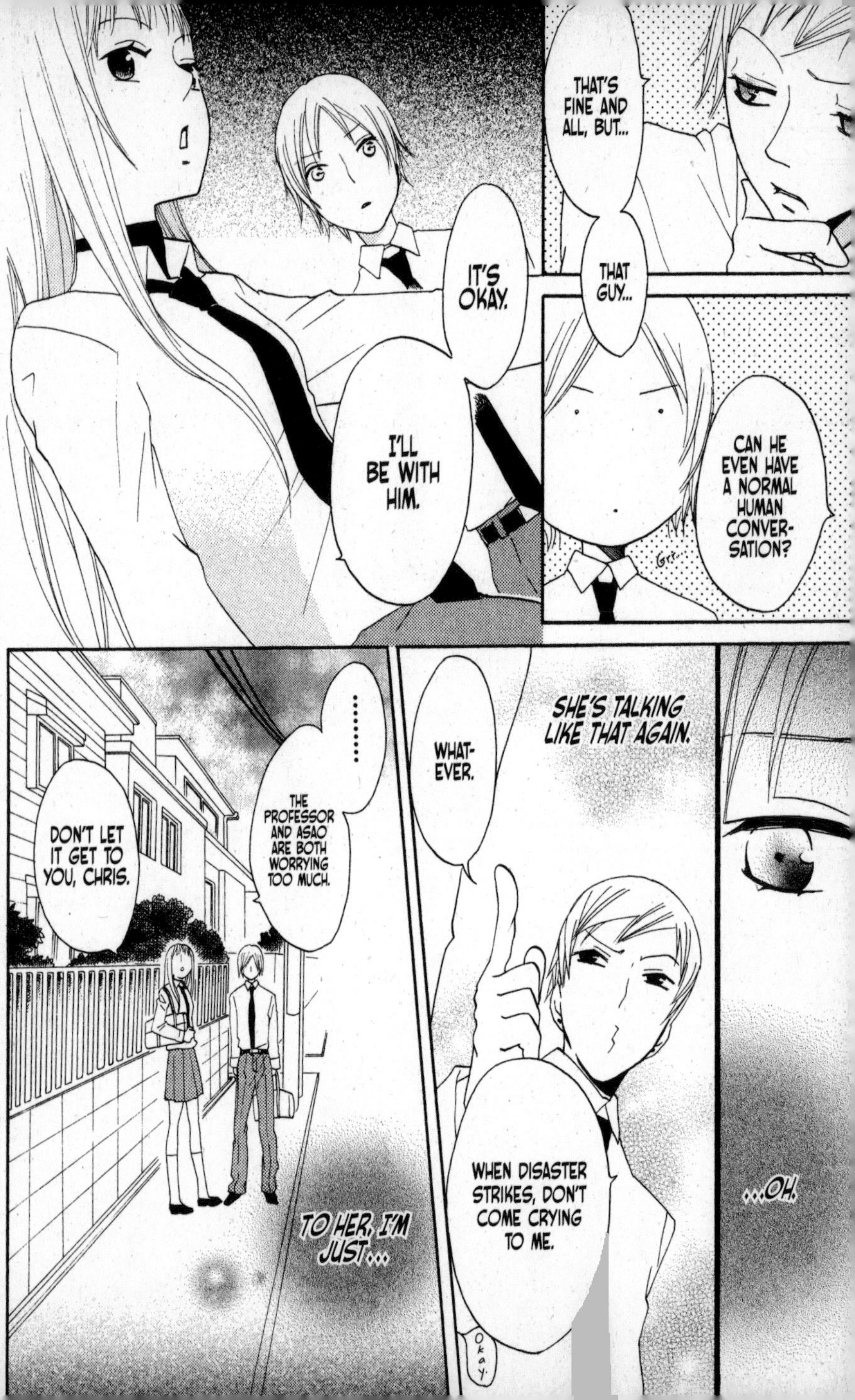

THAT'S FINE AND ALL, BUT...
THAT GUY...
CAN HE EVEN HAVE A NORMAL HUMAN CONVER-SATION?
Grr...
IT'S OKAY.
I'LL BE WITH HIM.
...OH.
SHE'S TALKING LIKE THAT AGAIN.
WHAT-EVER.
WHEN DISASTER STRIKES, DON'T COME CRYING TO ME.
Okay.
......
THE PROFESSOR AND ASAO ARE BOTH WORRYING TOO MUCH.
DON'T LET IT GET TO YOU, CHRIS.
TO HER, I'M JUST...

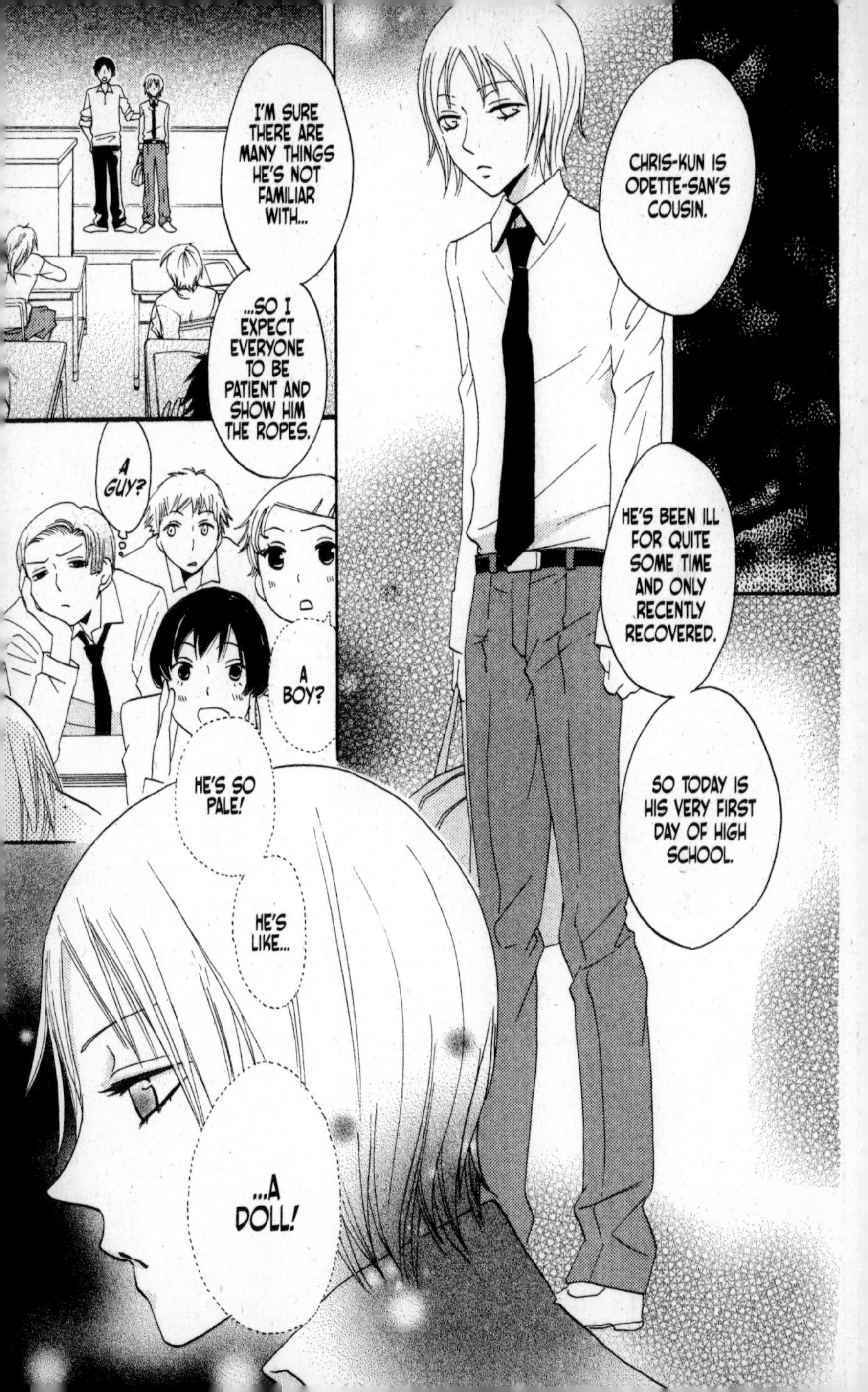
CHRIS-KUN IS ODETTE-SAN'S COUSIN.
HE'S BEEN ILL FOR QUITE SOME TIME AND ONLY RECENTLY RECOVERED.
SO TODAY IS HIS VERY FIRST DAY OF HIGH SCHOOL.
I'M SURE THERE ARE MANY THINGS HE'S NOT FAMILIAR WITH...
...SO I EXPECT EVERYONE TO BE PATIENT AND SHOW HIM THE ROPES.
A GUY?
A BOY?
HE'S SO PALE!
HE'S LIKE...
...A DOLL!

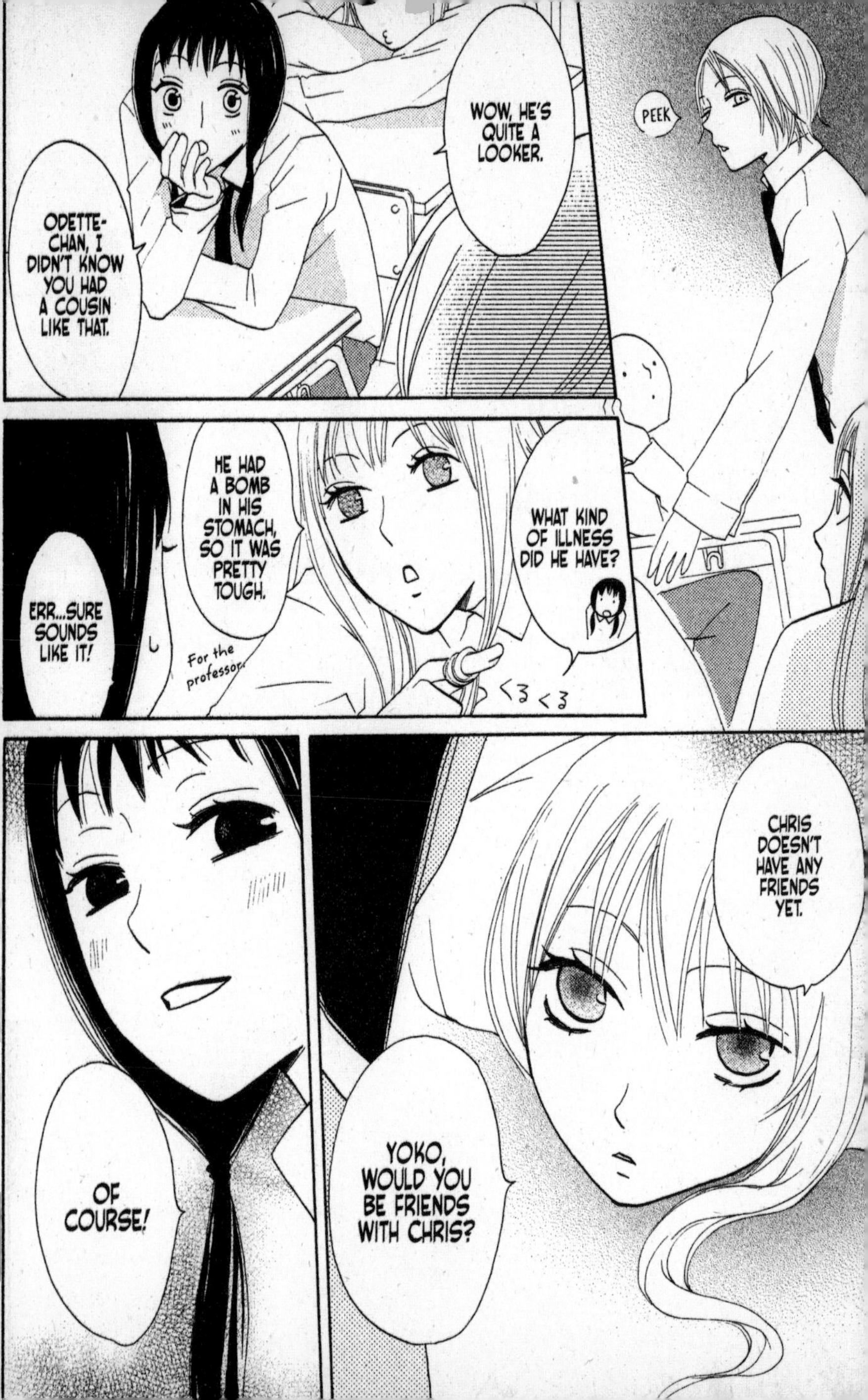
PEEK
WOW, HE'S QUITE A LOOKER.
ODETTE-CHAN, I DIDN'T KNOW YOU HAD A COUSIN LIKE THAT.
WHAT KIND OF ILLNESS DID HE HAVE?
くるくる
HE HAD A BOMB IN HIS STOMACH, SO IT WAS PRETTY TOUGH.
For the professor.
ERR...SURE SOUNDS LIKE IT!
CHRIS DOESN'T HAVE ANY FRIENDS YET.
YOKO, WOULD YOU BE FRIENDS WITH CHRIS?
OF COURSE!

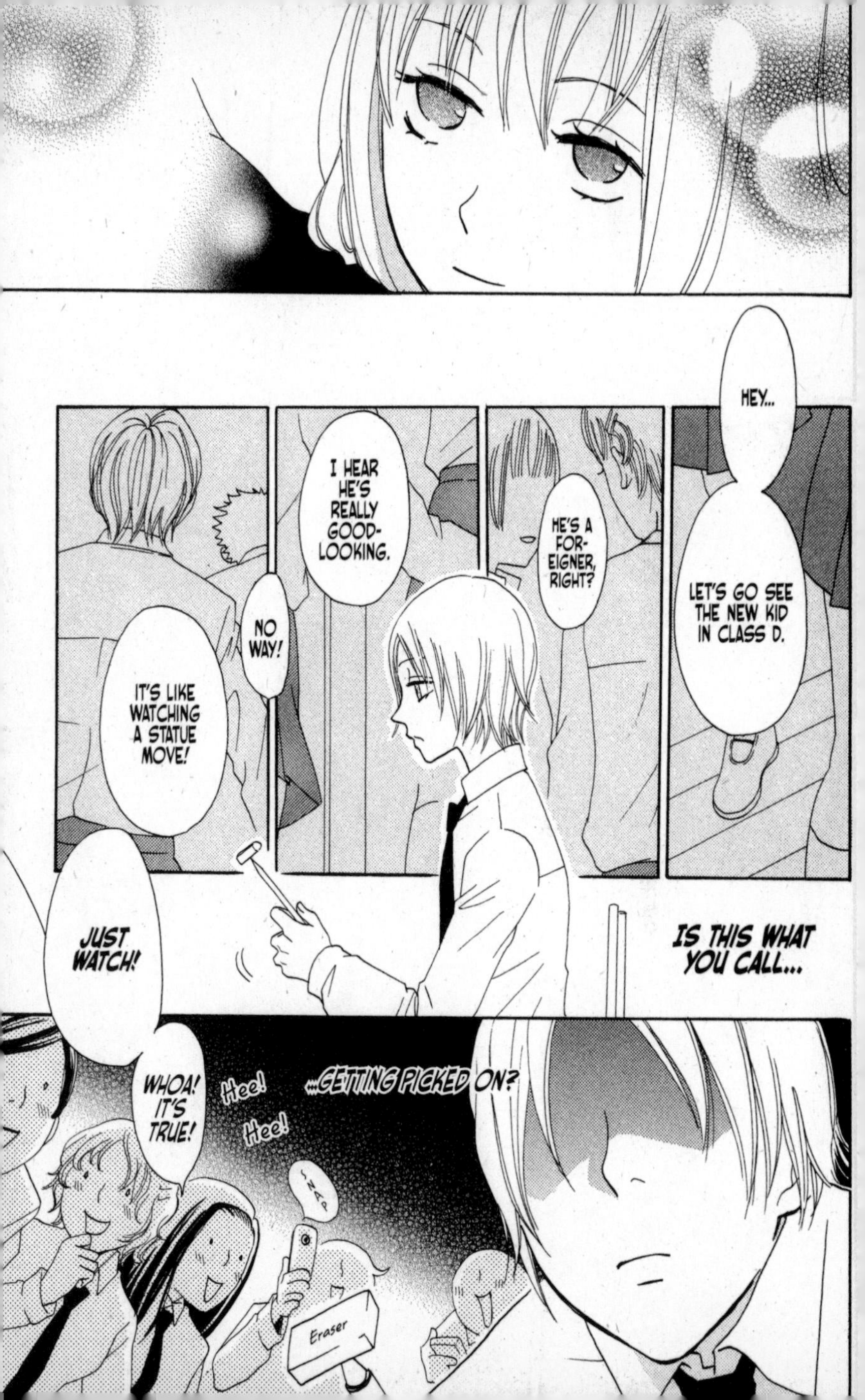
HEY...
LET'S GO SEE THE NEW KID IN CLASS D.
HE'S A FOR-EIGNER, RIGHT?
I HEAR HE'S REALLY GOOD-LOOKING.
NO WAY!
IT'S LIKE WATCHING A STATUE MOVE!
IS THIS WHAT YOU CALL...
JUST WATCH!
...GETTING PICKED ON?
Hee!
Hee!
WHOA! IT'S TRUE!
SNAP
Eraser

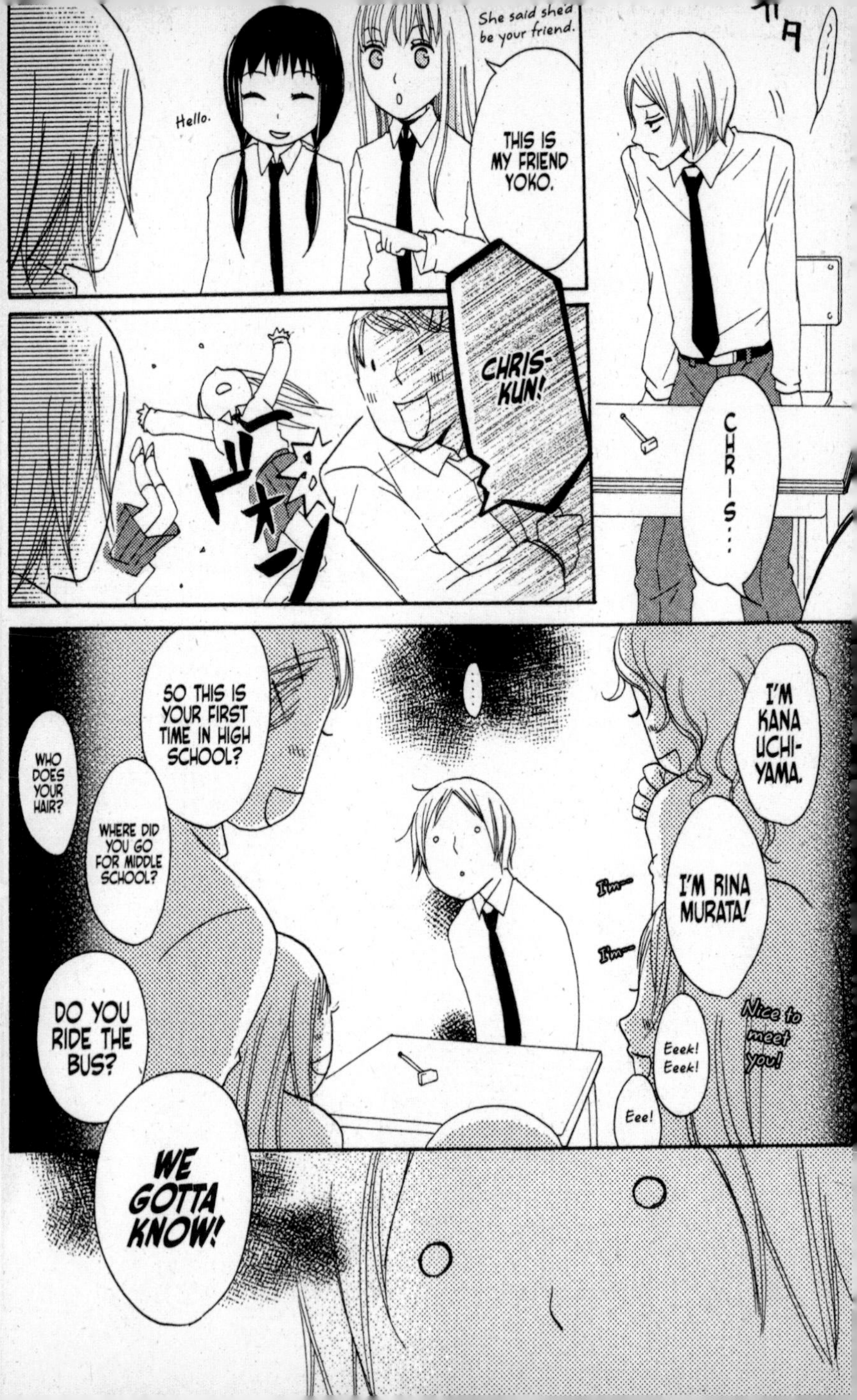

ガタ
CHRIS...
She said she'd be your friend.
THIS IS MY FRIEND YOKO.
Hello.
CHRIS-KUN!
I'M KANA UCHIYAMA.
I'M RINA MURATA!
Nice to meet you!
Eeek! Eeek!
Eee!
I'm--
I'm--
...
SO THIS IS YOUR FIRST TIME IN HIGH SCHOOL?
WHO DOES YOUR HAIR?
WHERE DID YOU GO FOR MIDDLE SCHOOL?
DO YOU RIDE THE BUS?
WE GOTTA KNOW!

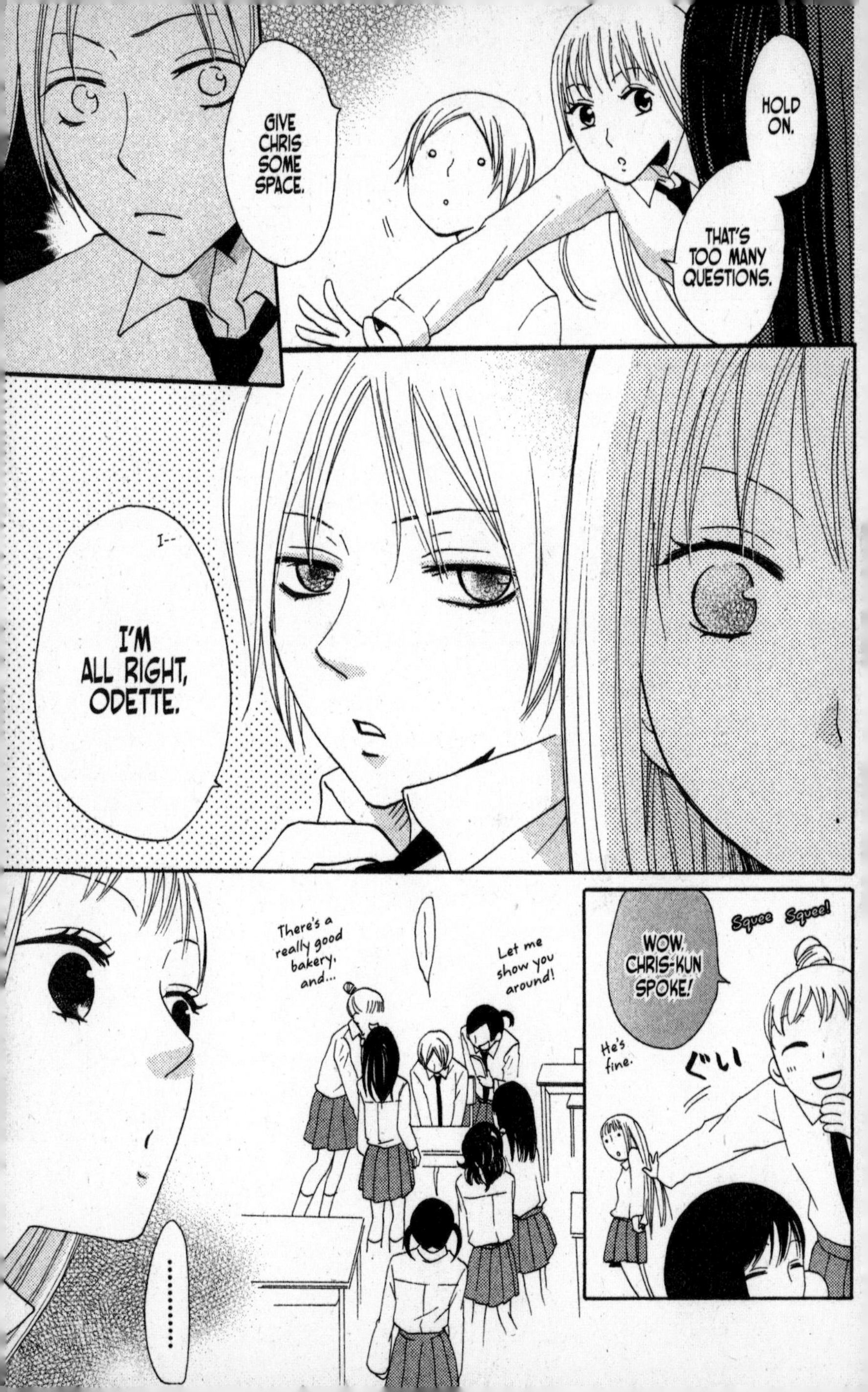
HOLD ON.
THAT'S TOO MANY QUESTIONS.
GIVE CHRIS SOME SPACE.
I--
I'M ALL RIGHT, ODETTE.
Squee Squee!
WOW. CHRIS-KUN SPOKE!
ぐい
He's fine.
Let me show you around!
!
There's a really good bakery, and...
....

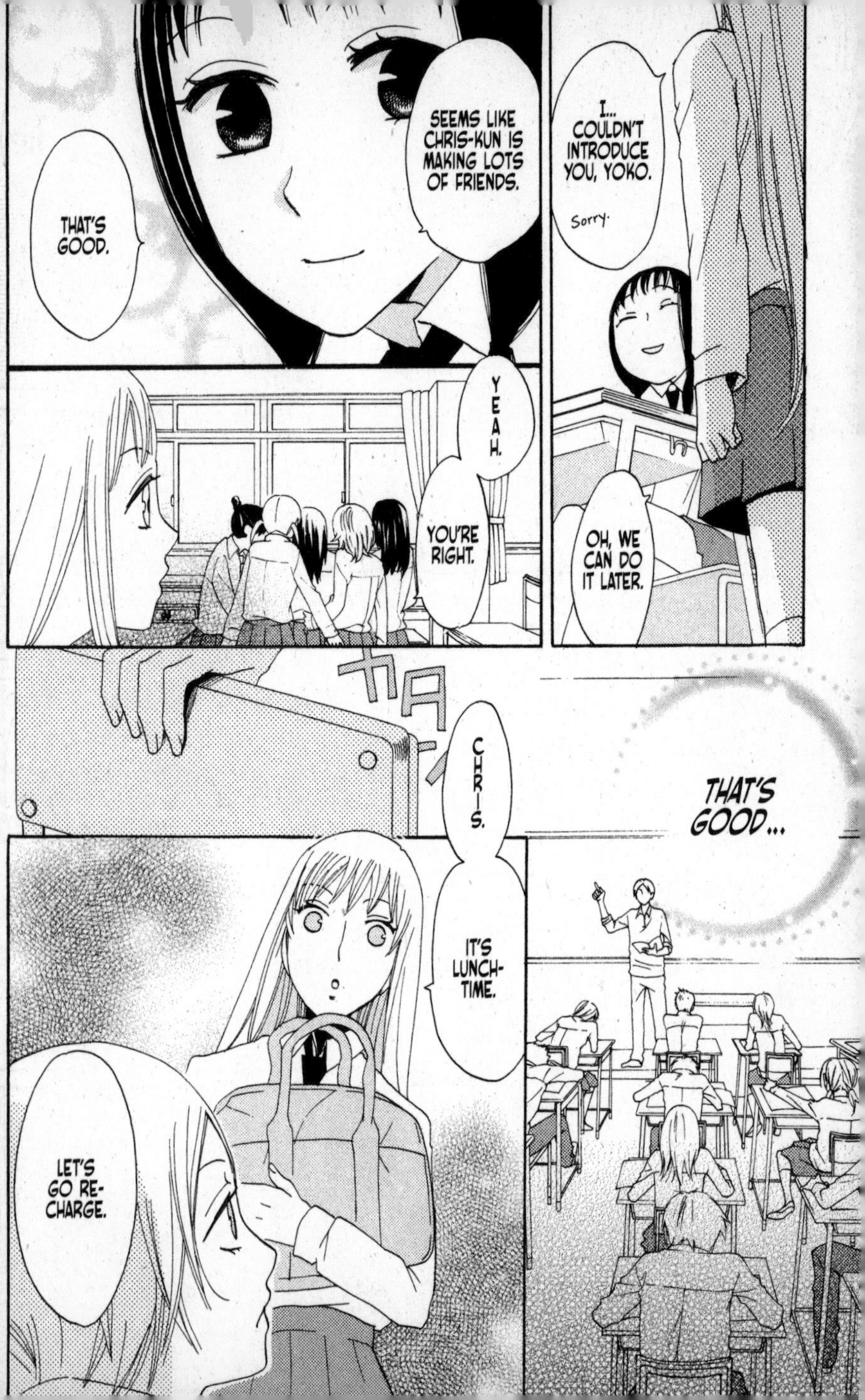
I... COULDN'T INTRODUCE YOU, YOKO.
Sorry.
OH, WE CAN DO IT LATER.
SEEMS LIKE CHRIS-KUN IS MAKING LOTS OF FRIENDS.
THAT'S GOOD.
YEAH.
YOU'RE RIGHT.
THAT'S GOOD...
CHRIS.
IT'S LUNCH-TIME.
LET'S GO RE-CHARGE.

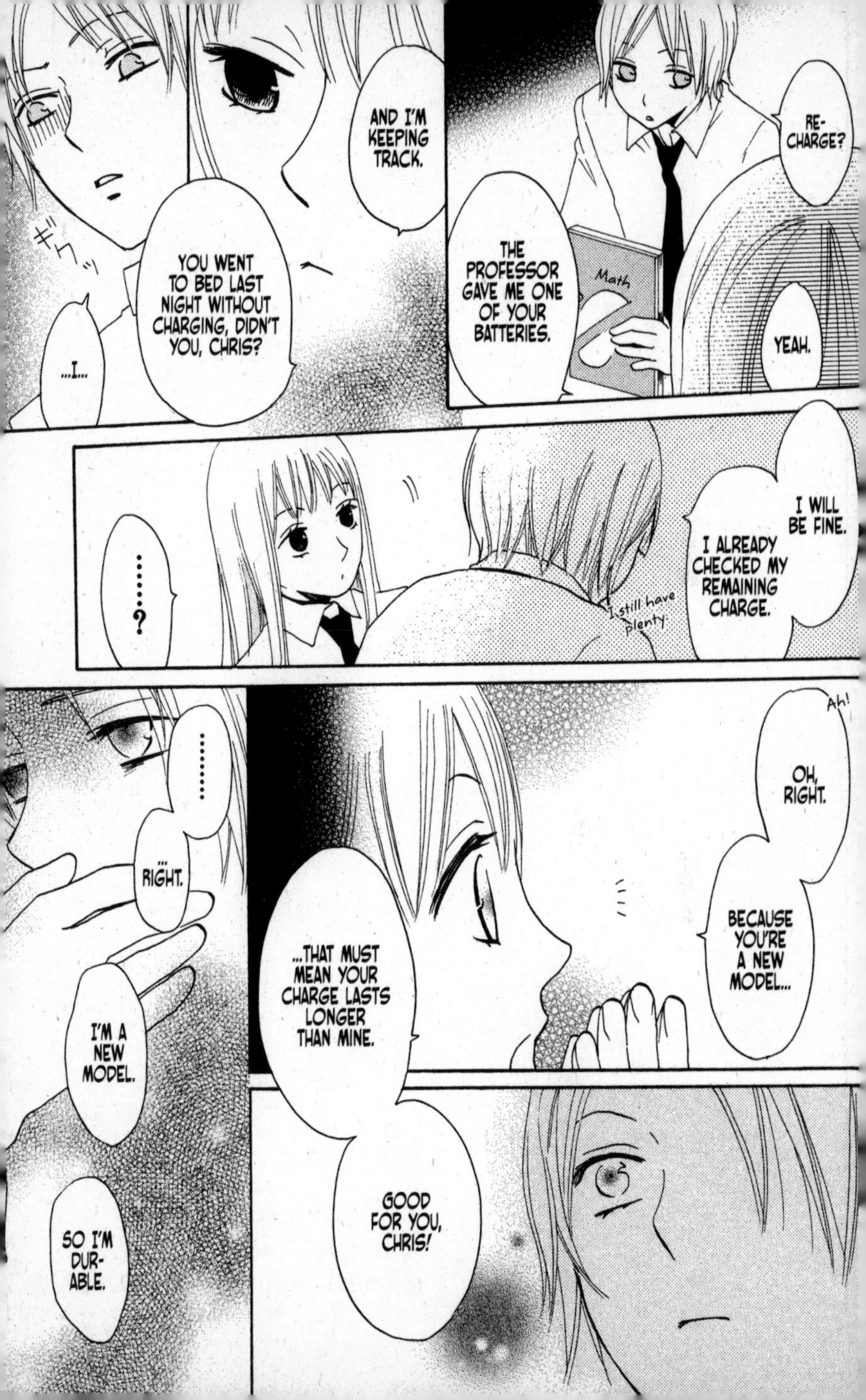
RE-CHARGE?
YEAH.
THE PROFESSOR GAVE ME ONE OF YOUR BATTERIES.
Math
AND I'M KEEPING TRACK.
YOU WENT TO BED LAST NIGHT WITHOUT CHARGING, DIDN'T YOU, CHRIS?
ギクッ
...I...
I WILL BE FINE.
I ALREADY CHECKED MY REMAINING CHARGE.
I still have plenty
......?
Ah!
OH, RIGHT.
BECAUSE YOU'RE A NEW MODEL...
...THAT MUST MEAN YOUR CHARGE LASTS LONGER THAN MINE.
GOOD FOR YOU, CHRIS!
....
...RIGHT.
I'M A NEW MODEL.
SO I'M DUR-ABLE.

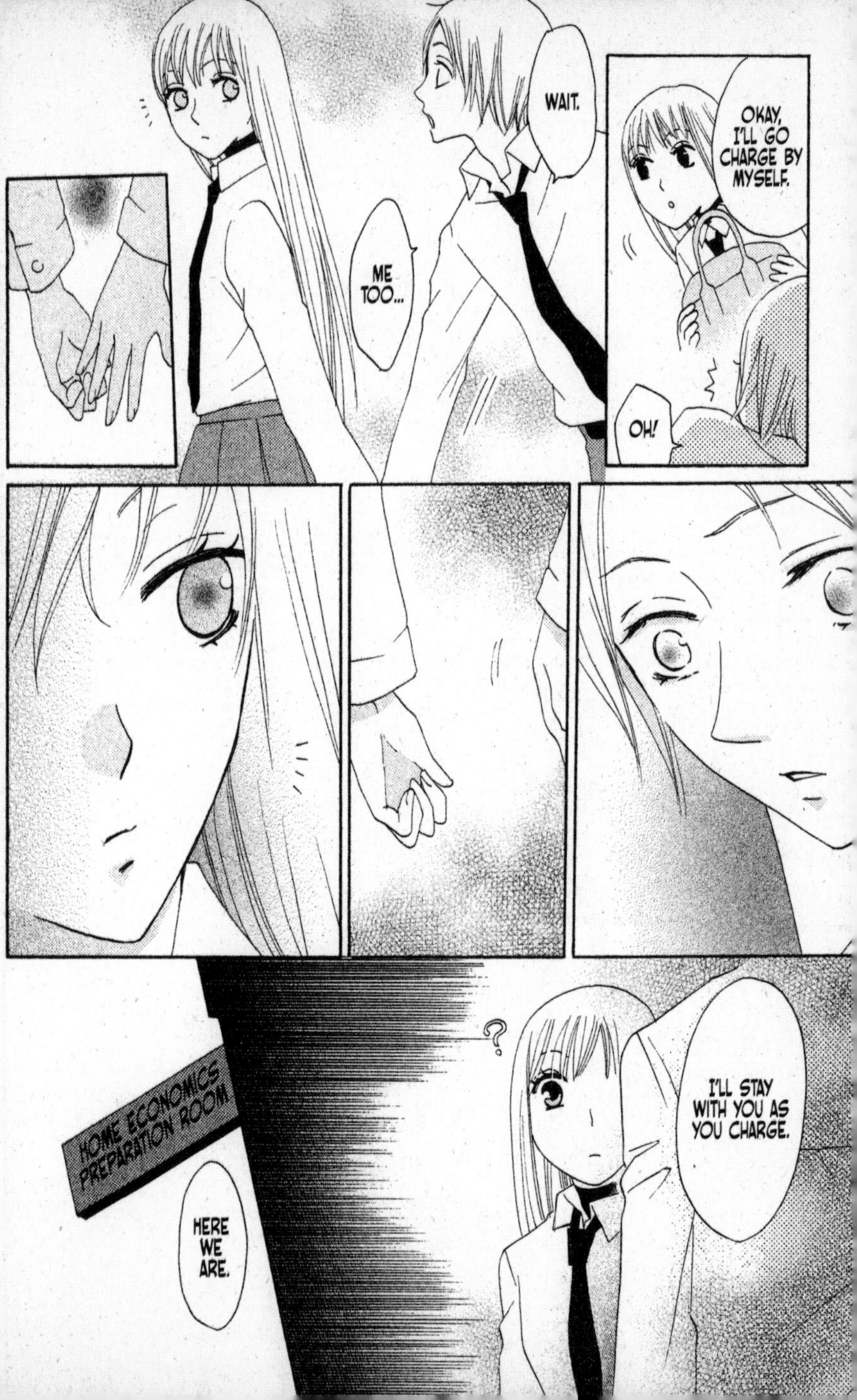
OKAY, I'LL GO CHARGE BY MYSELF.
OH!
WAIT.
ME TOO...
I'LL STAY WITH YOU AS YOU CHARGE.
HOME ECONOMICS PREPARATION ROOM
HERE WE ARE.

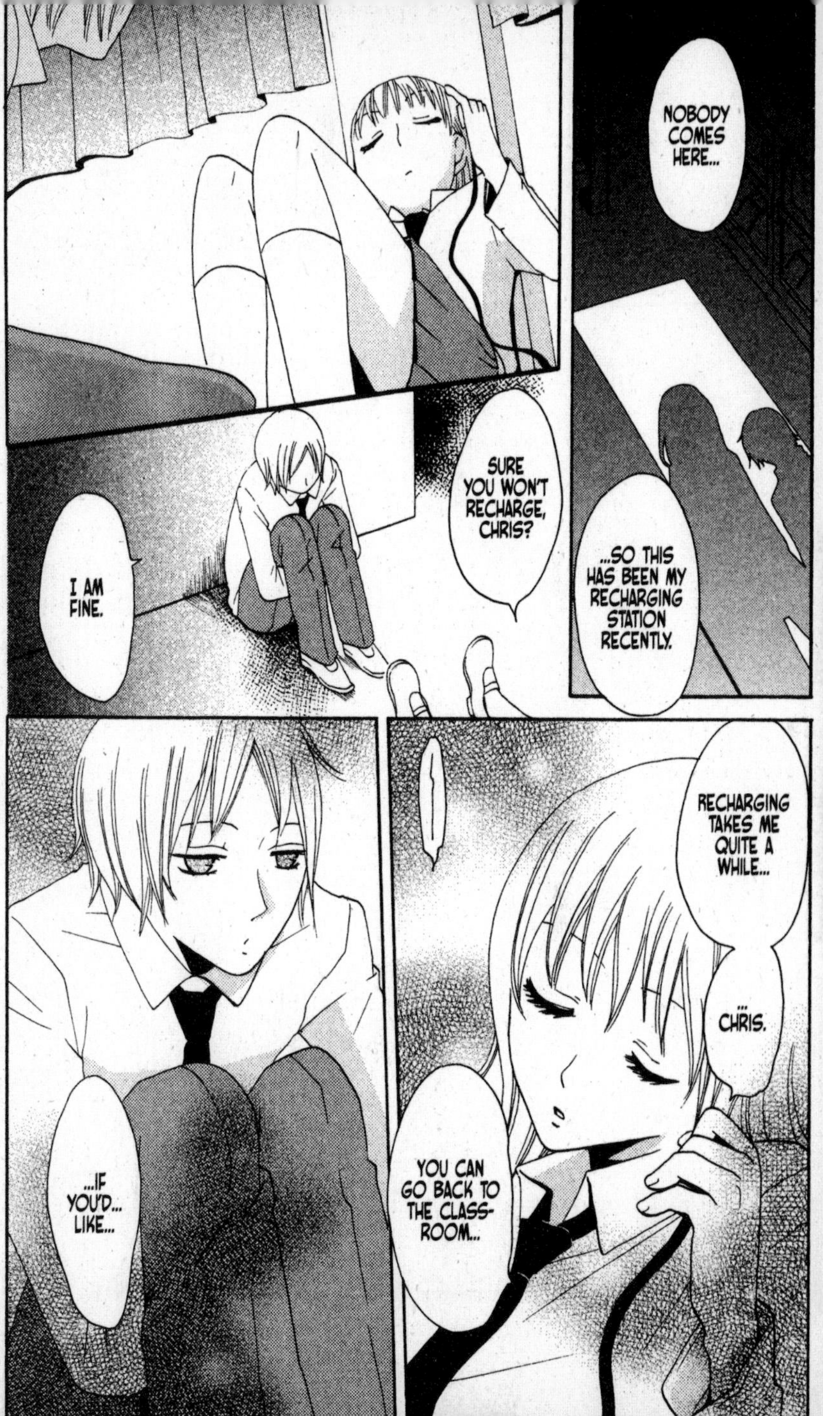
NOBODY COMES HERE...
...SO THIS HAS BEEN MY RECHARGING STATION RECENTLY.
SURE YOU WON'T RECHARGE, CHRIS?
I AM FINE.
!
RECHARGING TAKES ME QUITE A WHILE...
... CHRIS.
YOU CAN GO BACK TO THE CLASS-ROOM...
...IF YOU'D... LIKE...

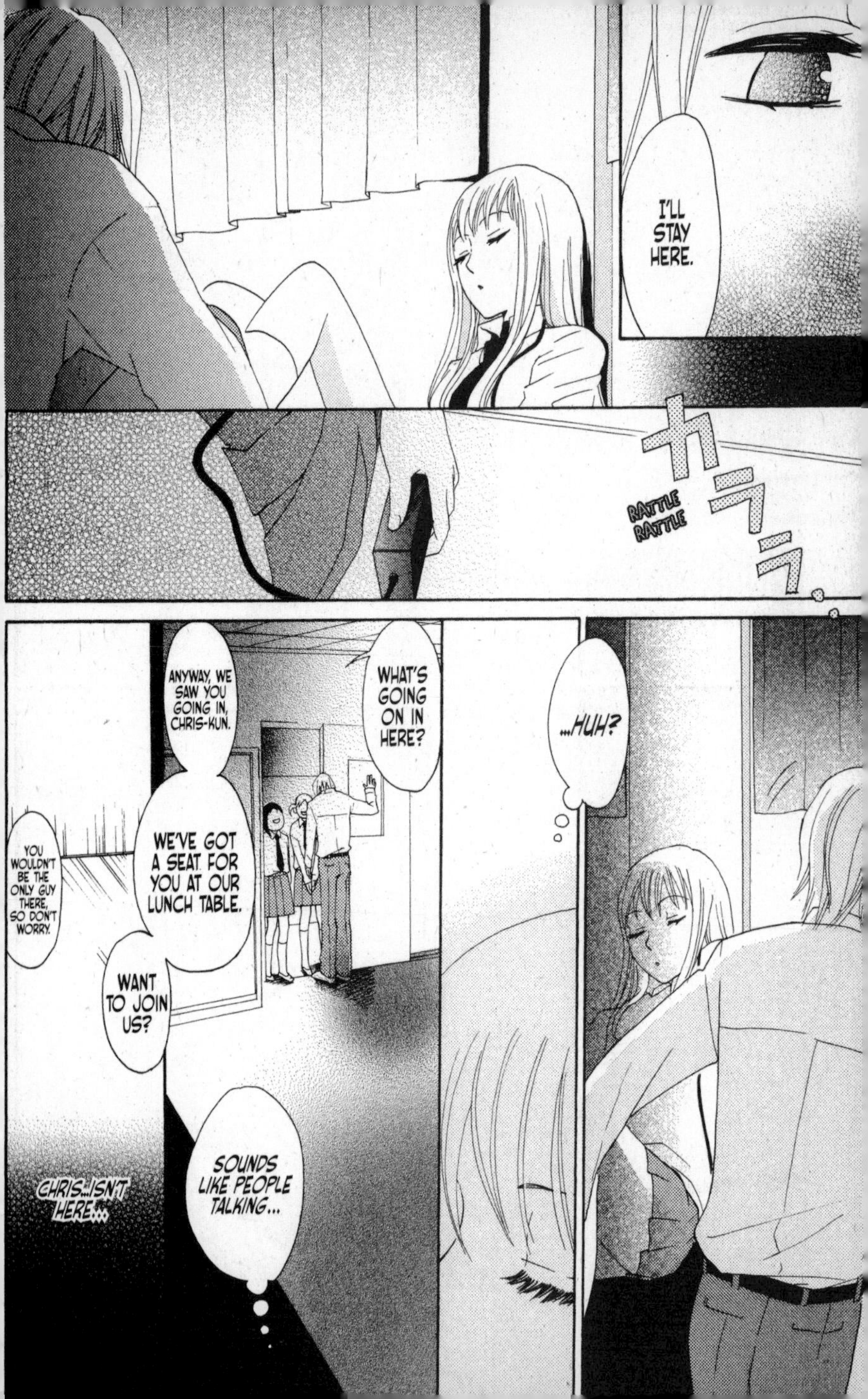
I'LL STAY HERE.
カララ
RATTLE RATTLE
...HUH?
WHAT'S GOING ON IN HERE?
ANYWAY, WE SAW YOU GOING IN, CHRIS-KUN.
WE'VE GOT A SEAT FOR YOU AT OUR LUNCH TABLE.
YOU WOULDN'T BE THE ONLY GUY THERE, SO DON'T WORRY.
WANT TO JOIN US?
SOUNDS LIKE PEOPLE TALKING...
CHRIS...ISN'T HERE...

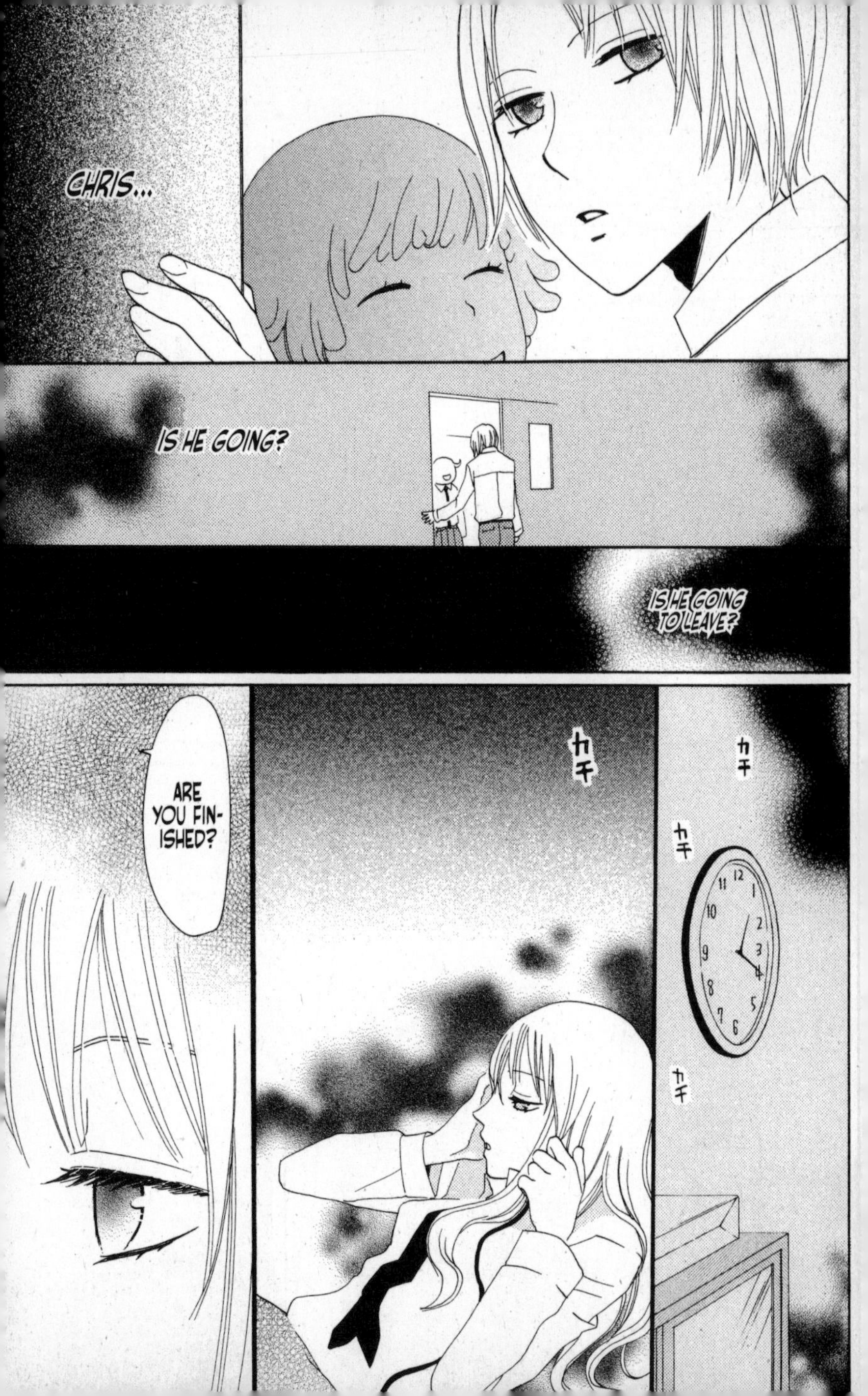
CHRIS...
IS HE GOING?
IS HE GOING TO LEAVE?
カチ
カチ
カチ
ARE YOU FIN-ISHED?

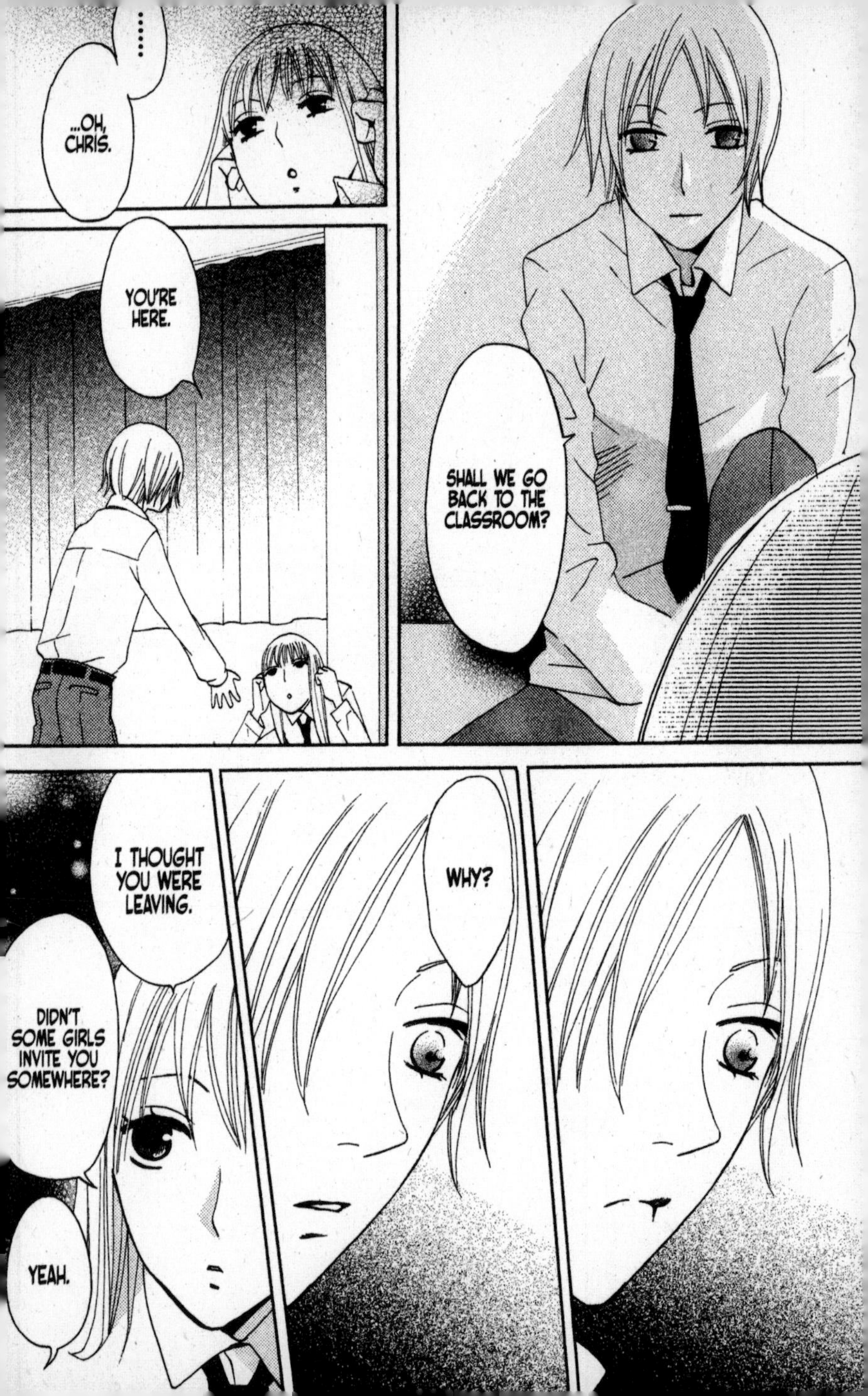
SHALL WE GO BACK TO THE CLASSROOM?
......
...OH, CHRIS.
YOU'RE HERE.
WHY?
I THOUGHT YOU WERE LEAVING.
DIDN'T SOME GIRLS INVITE YOU SOMEWHERE?
YEAH.

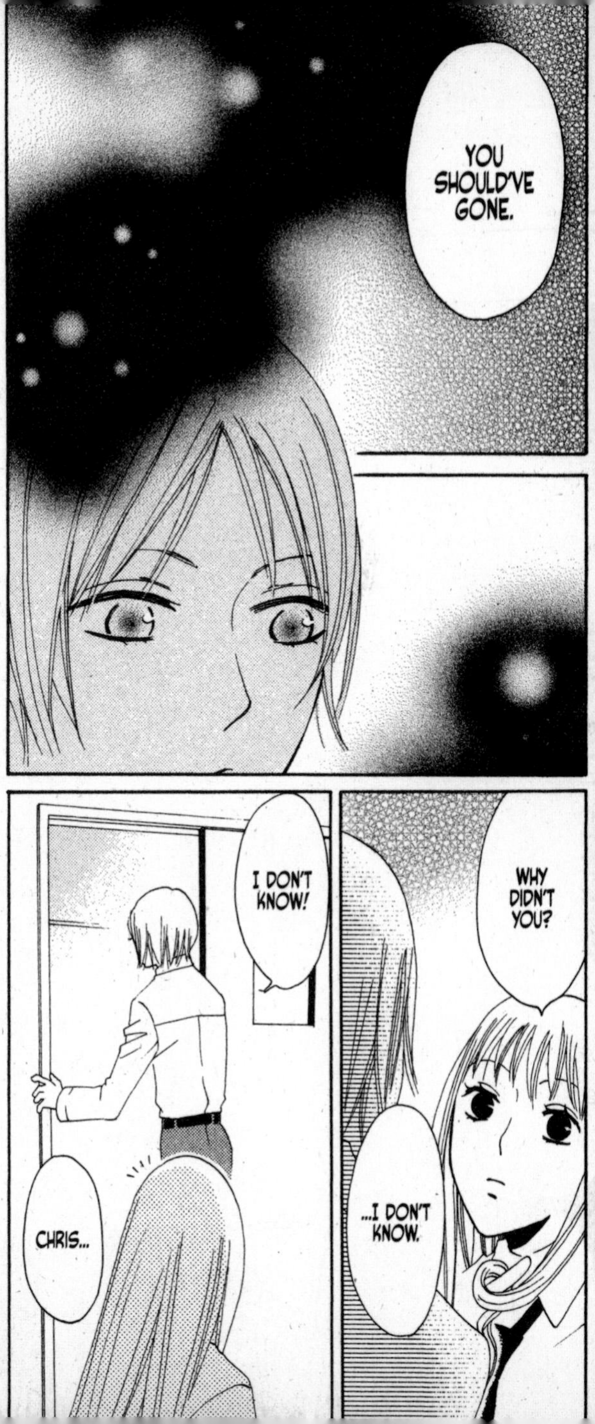
YOU SHOULD'VE GONE.
WHY DIDN'T YOU?
...I DON'T KNOW.
I DON'T KNOW!
CHRIS...

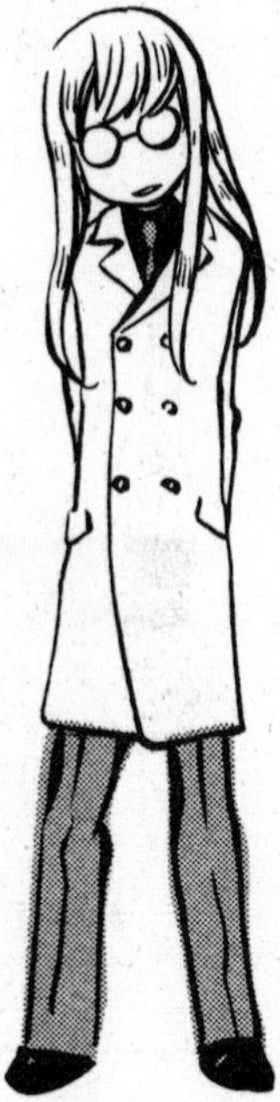

Gabriel

Professor Yoshizawa's friend. Can't forget about the melon float his father bought for him when he was little. Dislikes dealing with his subordinates.

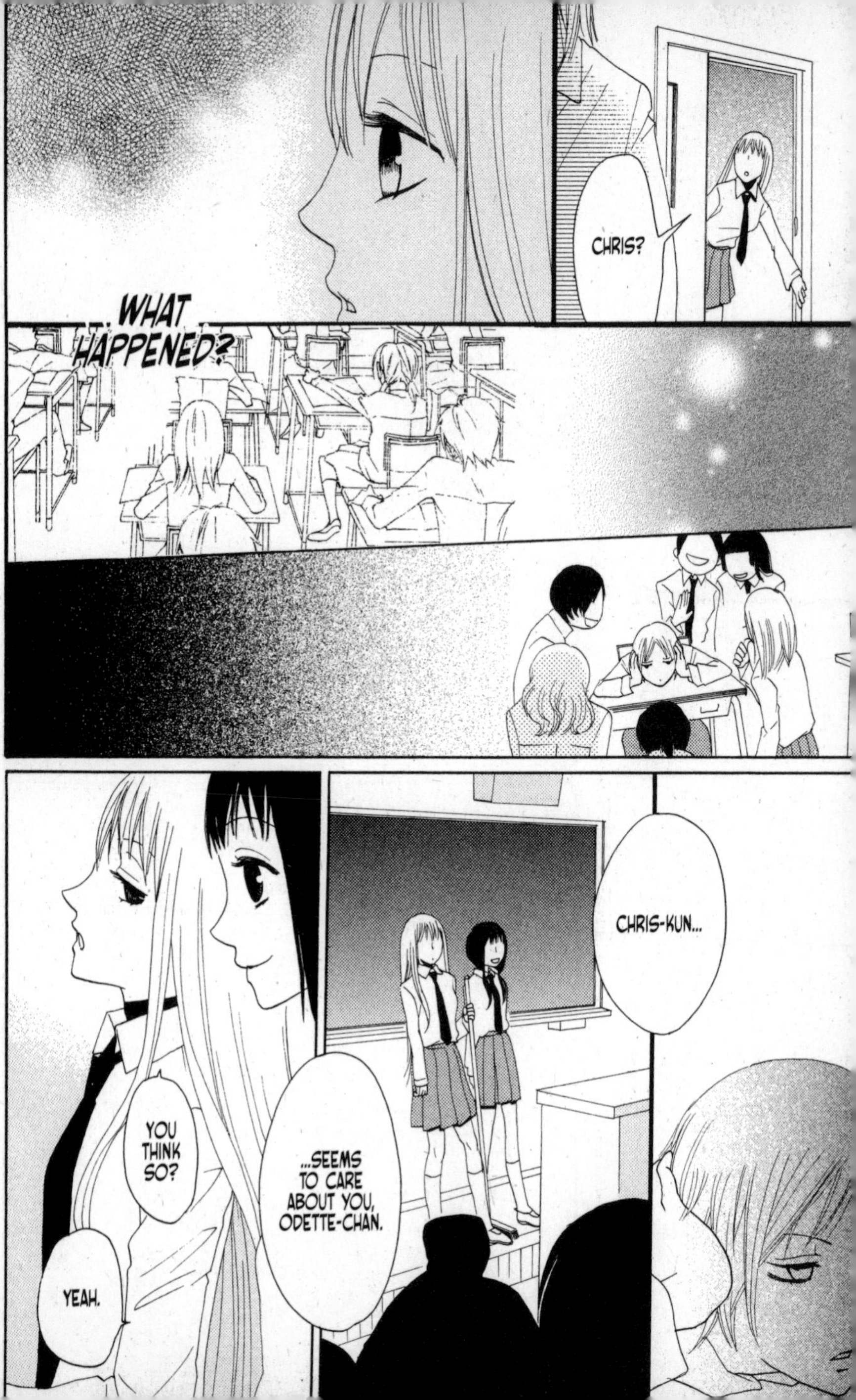
CHRIS?
...WHAT HAPPENED?
CHRIS-KUN...
...SEEMS TO CARE ABOUT YOU, ODETTE-CHAN.
YOU THINK SO?
YEAH.

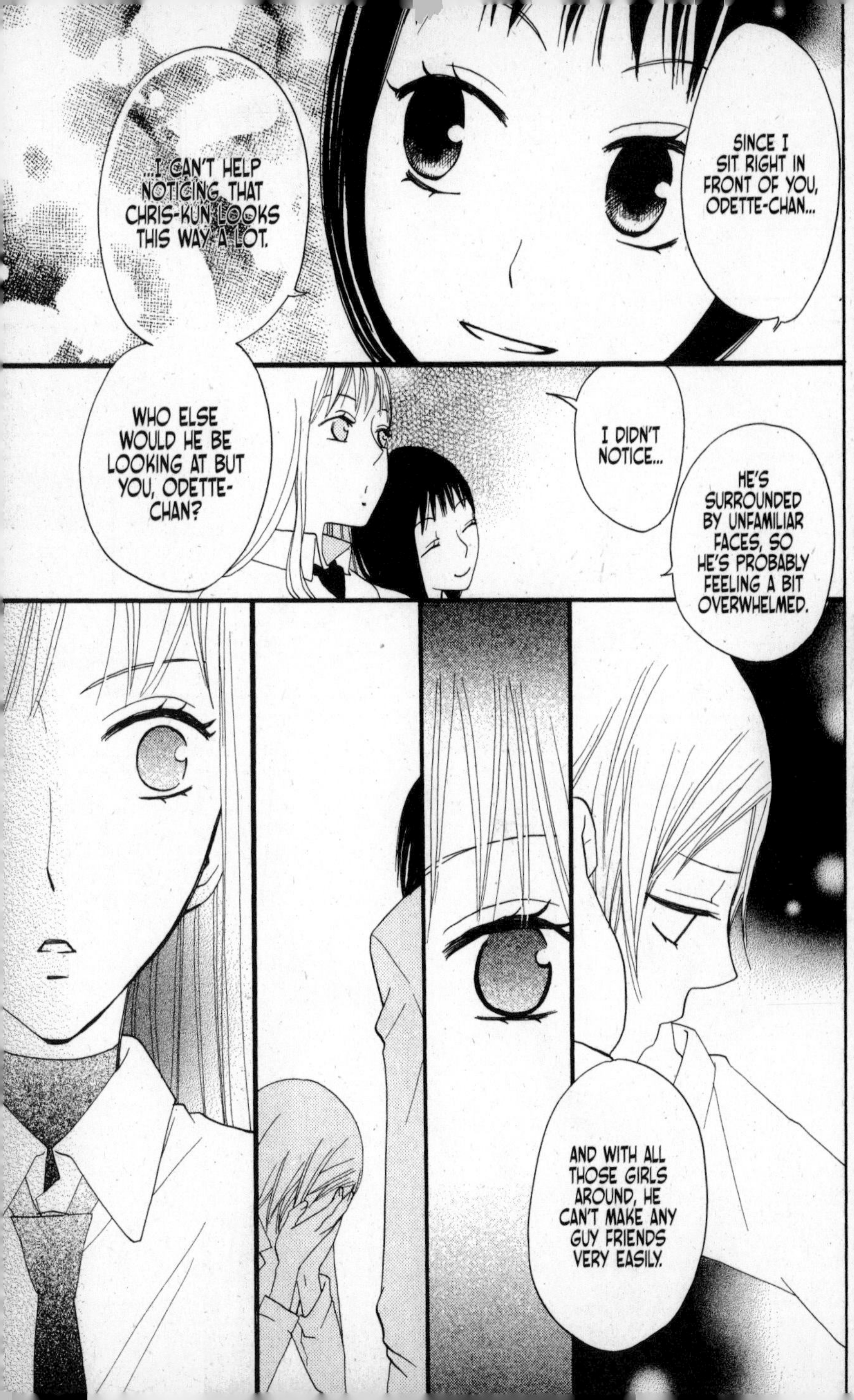
SINCE I SIT RIGHT IN FRONT OF YOU, ODETTE-CHAN...
...I CAN'T HELP NOTICING THAT CHRIS-KUN LOOKS THIS WAY A LOT.
WHO ELSE WOULD HE BE LOOKING AT BUT YOU, ODETTE-CHAN?
I DIDN'T NOTICE...
HE'S SURROUNDED BY UNFAMILIAR FACES, SO HE'S PROBABLY FEELING A BIT OVERWHELMED.
AND WITH ALL THOSE GIRLS AROUND, HE CAN'T MAKE ANY GUY FRIENDS VERY EASILY.

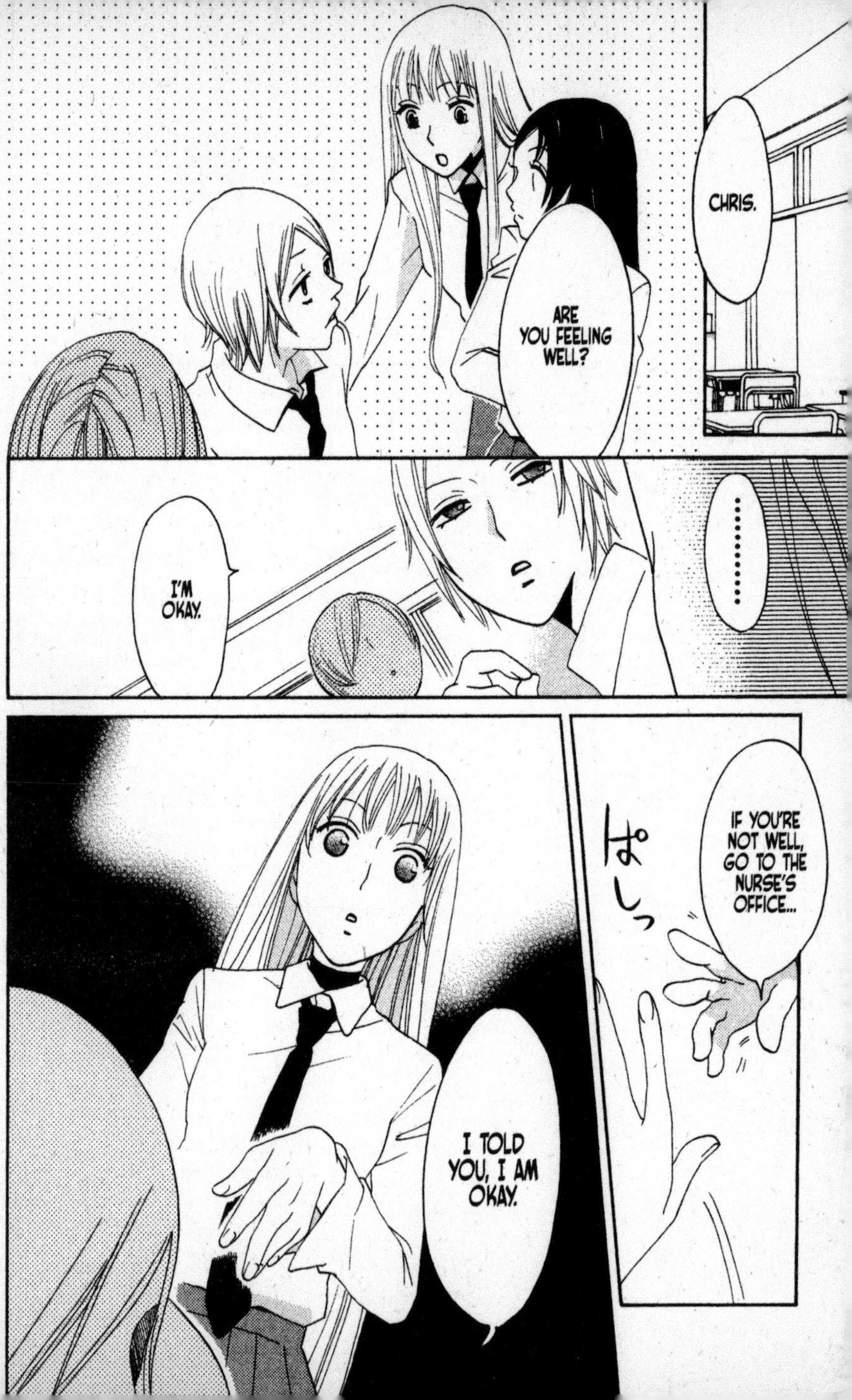
CHRIS.
ARE YOU FEELING WELL?
......
I'M OKAY.
IF YOU'RE NOT WELL, GO TO THE NURSE'S OFFICE...
ぱしっ
I TOLD YOU, I AM OKAY.

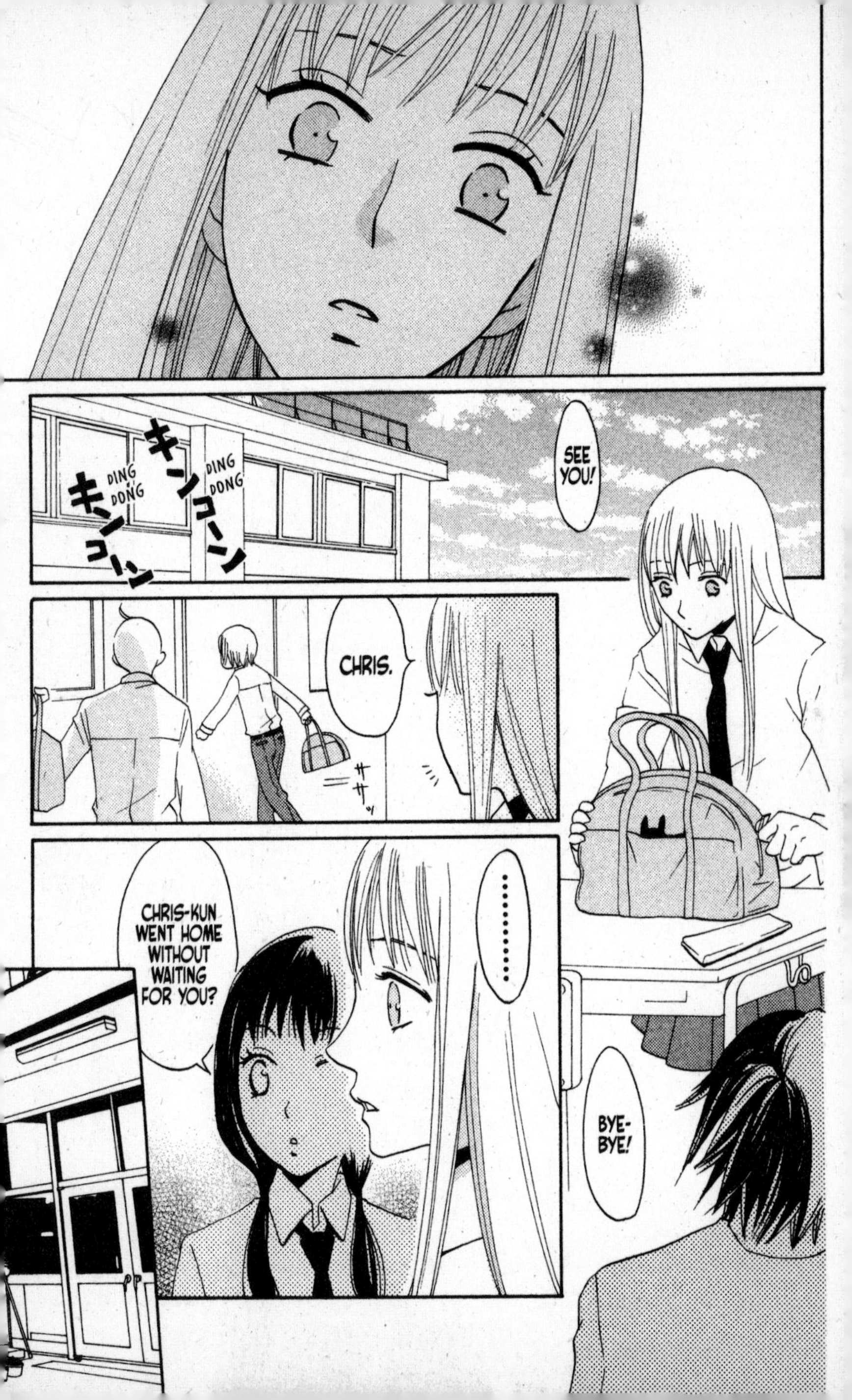
SEE YOU!
キンコーン DING DONG
キンコーン DING DONG
CHRIS.
ササッ
......
CHRIS-KUN WENT HOME WITHOUT WAITING FOR YOU?
BYE-BYE!

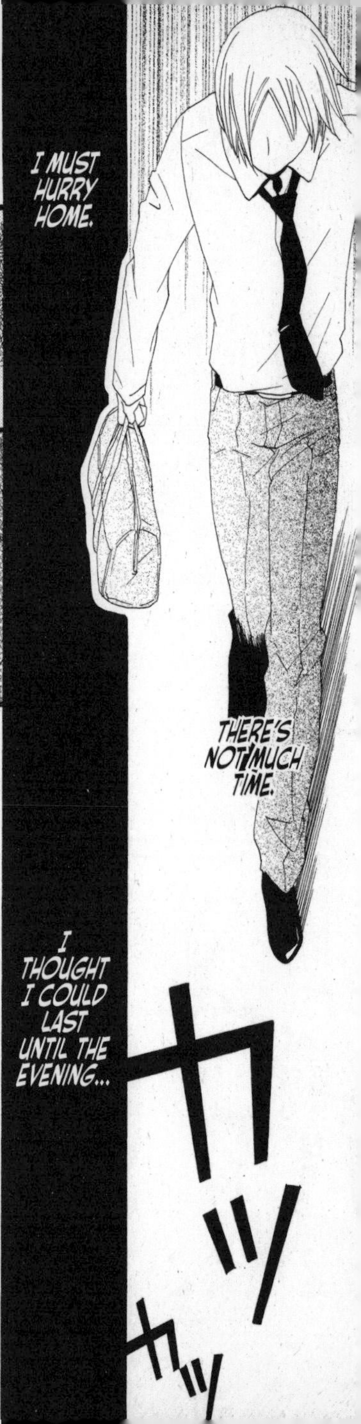
I MUST HURRY HOME.
THERE'S NOT MUCH TIME.
I THOUGHT I COULD LAST UNTIL THE EVENING...
カッ
カッ

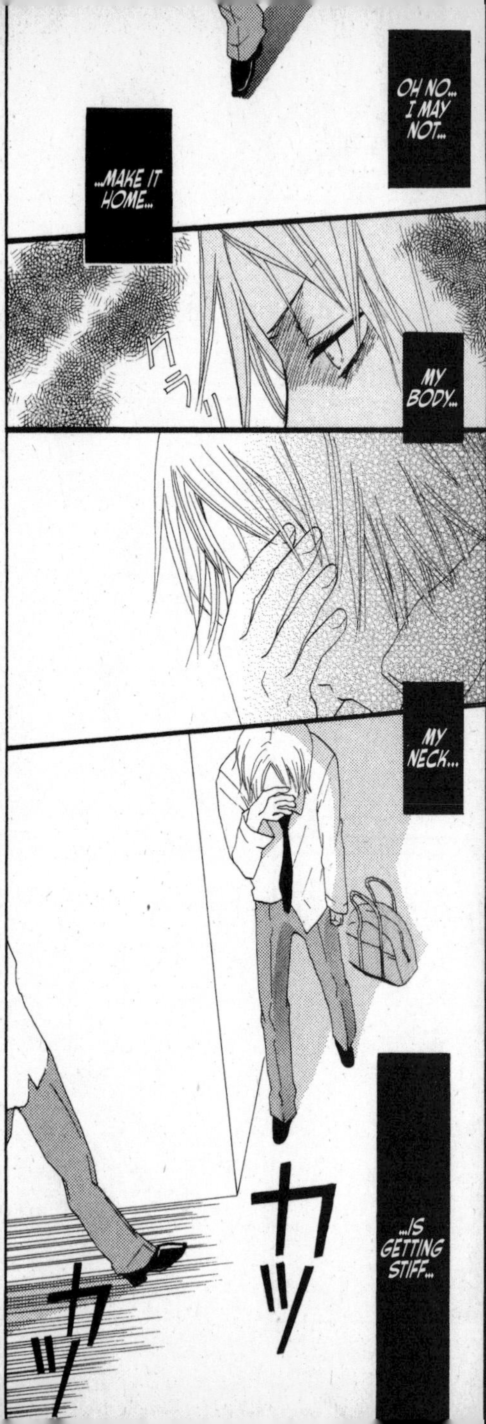
OH NO... I MAY NOT...
...MAKE IT HOME...
MY BODY...
クラッ
MY NECK...
...IS GETTING STIFF...
カッ
カッ

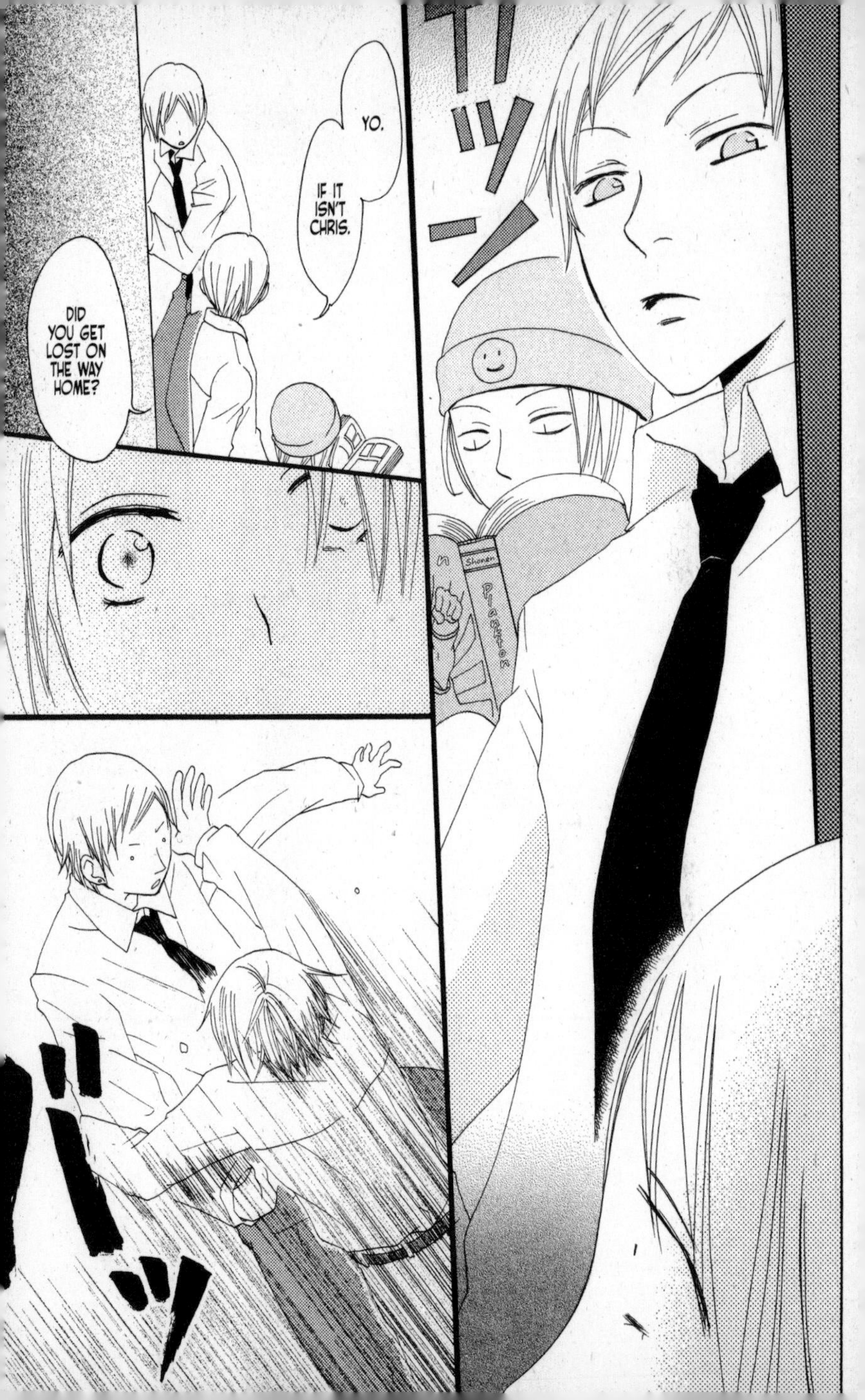
YO.
IF IT ISN'T CHRIS.
DID YOU GET LOST ON THE WAY HOME?
Shonen Plankton

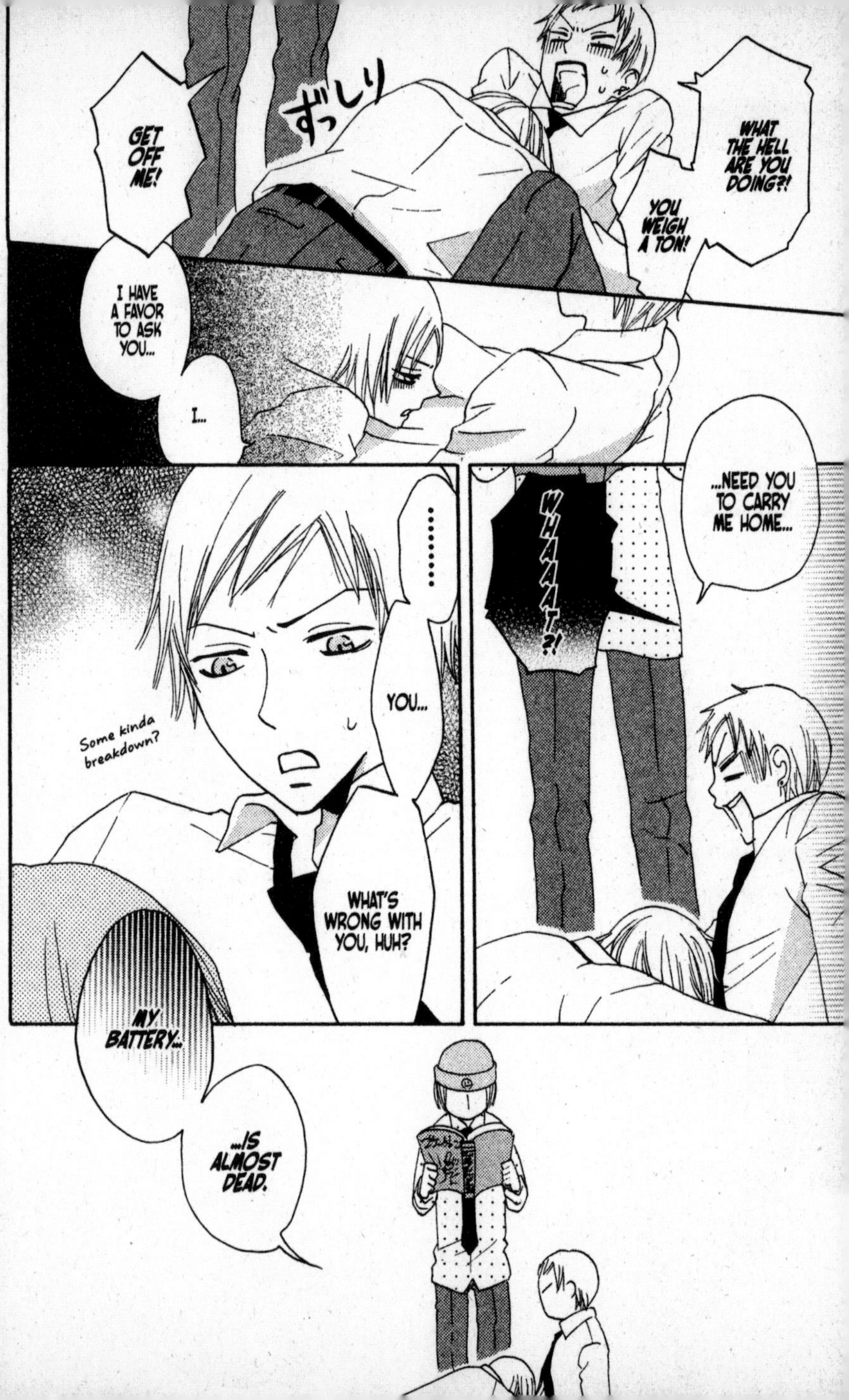
WHAT THE HELL ARE YOU DOING?!
YOU WEIGH A TON!
ずっしり
GET OFF ME!
I HAVE A FAVOR TO ASK YOU...
I...
...NEED YOU TO CARRY ME HOME...
WHAAAAT?!
......
YOU...
WHAT'S WRONG WITH YOU, HUH?
Some kinda breakdown?
MY BATTERY...
...IS ALMOST DEAD.

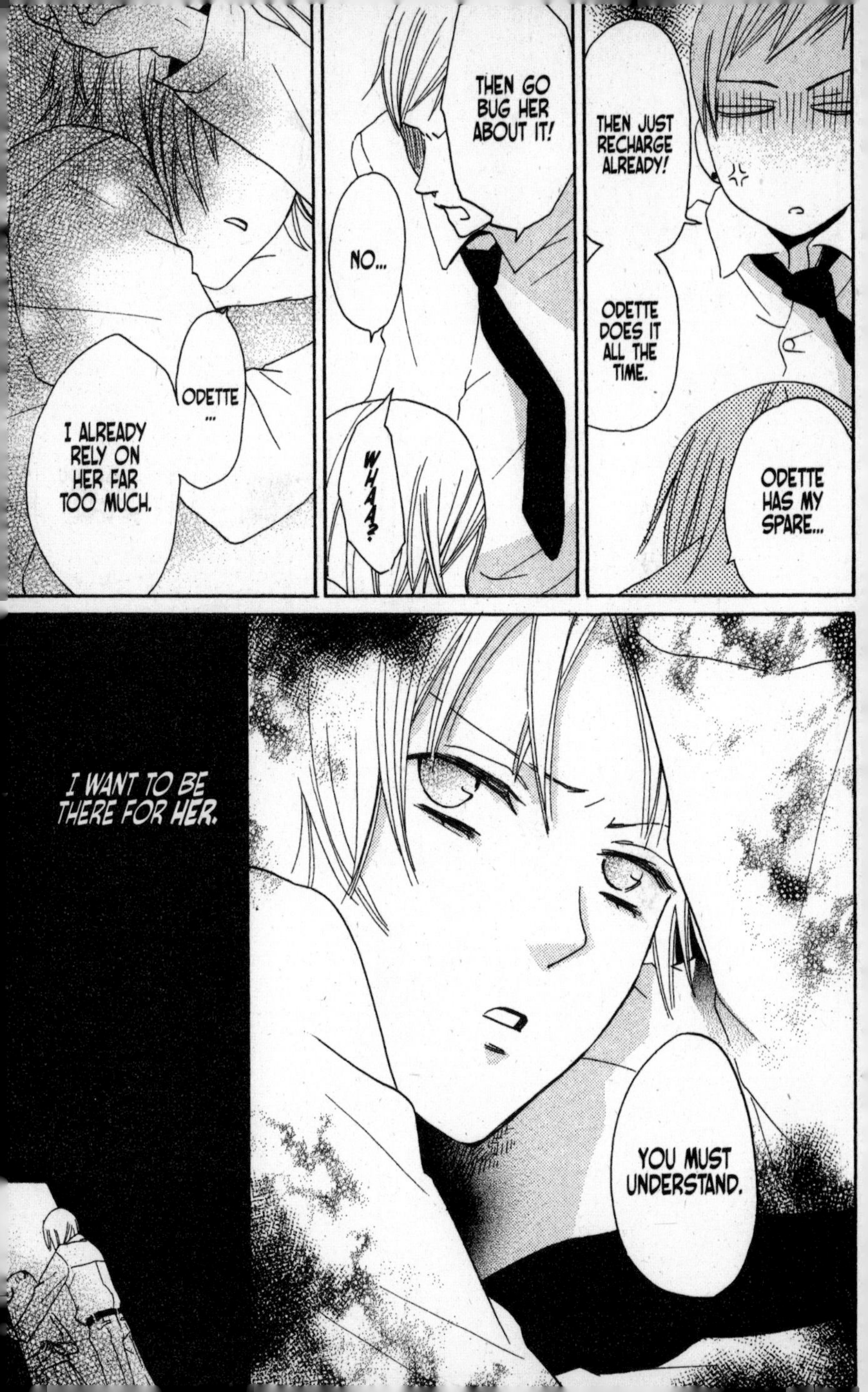
THEN JUST RECHARGE ALREADY!
ODETTE DOES IT ALL THE TIME.
ODETTE HAS MY SPARE...
THEN GO BUG HER ABOUT IT!
NO...
WHAA?
ODETTE ...
I ALREADY RELY ON HER FAR TOO MUCH.
YOU MUST UNDERSTAND.
I WANT TO BE THERE FOR HER.

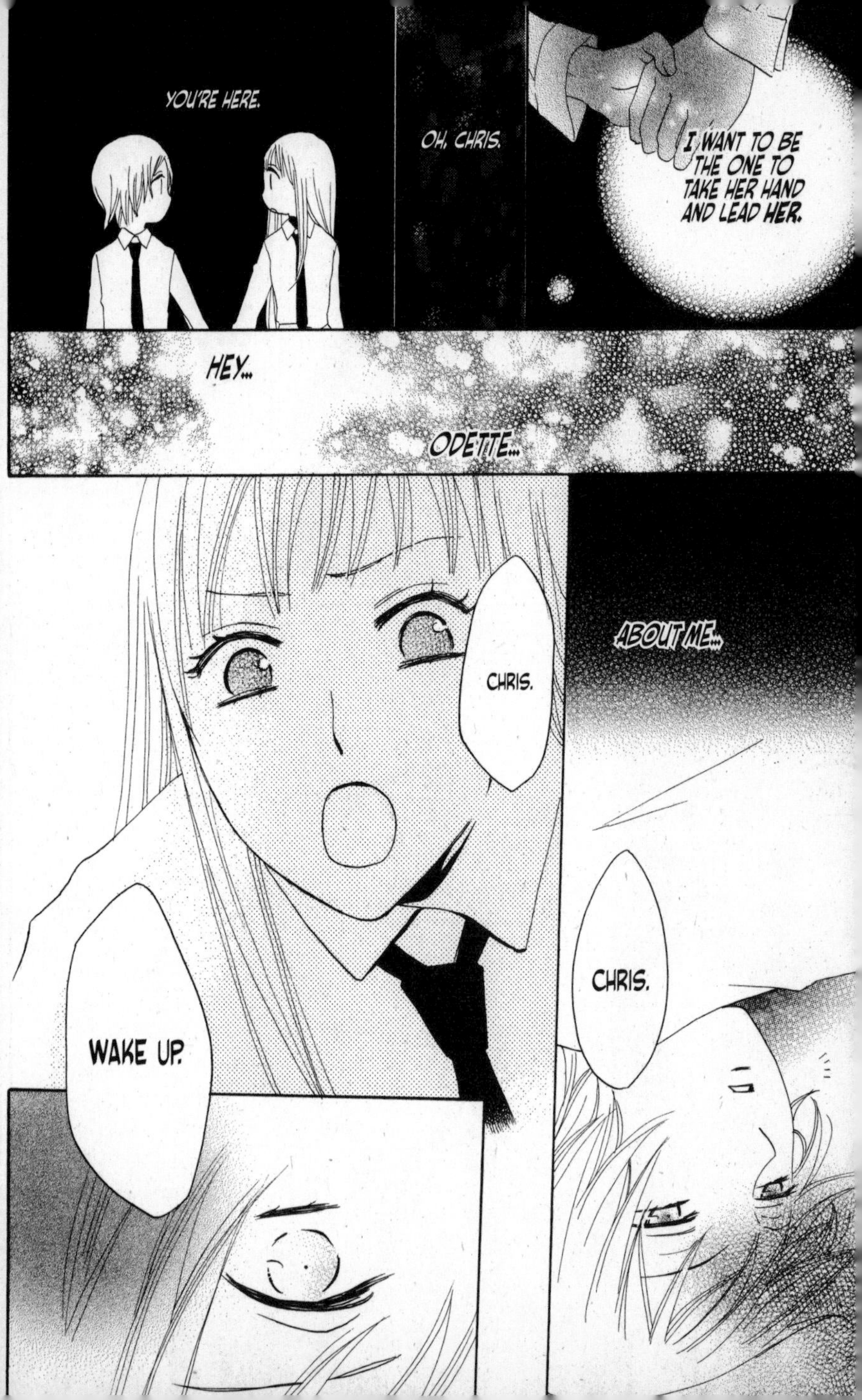
I WANT TO BE THE ONE TO TAKE HER HAND AND LEAD HER.
OH, CHRIS.
YOU'RE HERE.
HEY...
ODETTE...
ABOUT ME...
CHRIS.
CHRIS.
WAKE UP.

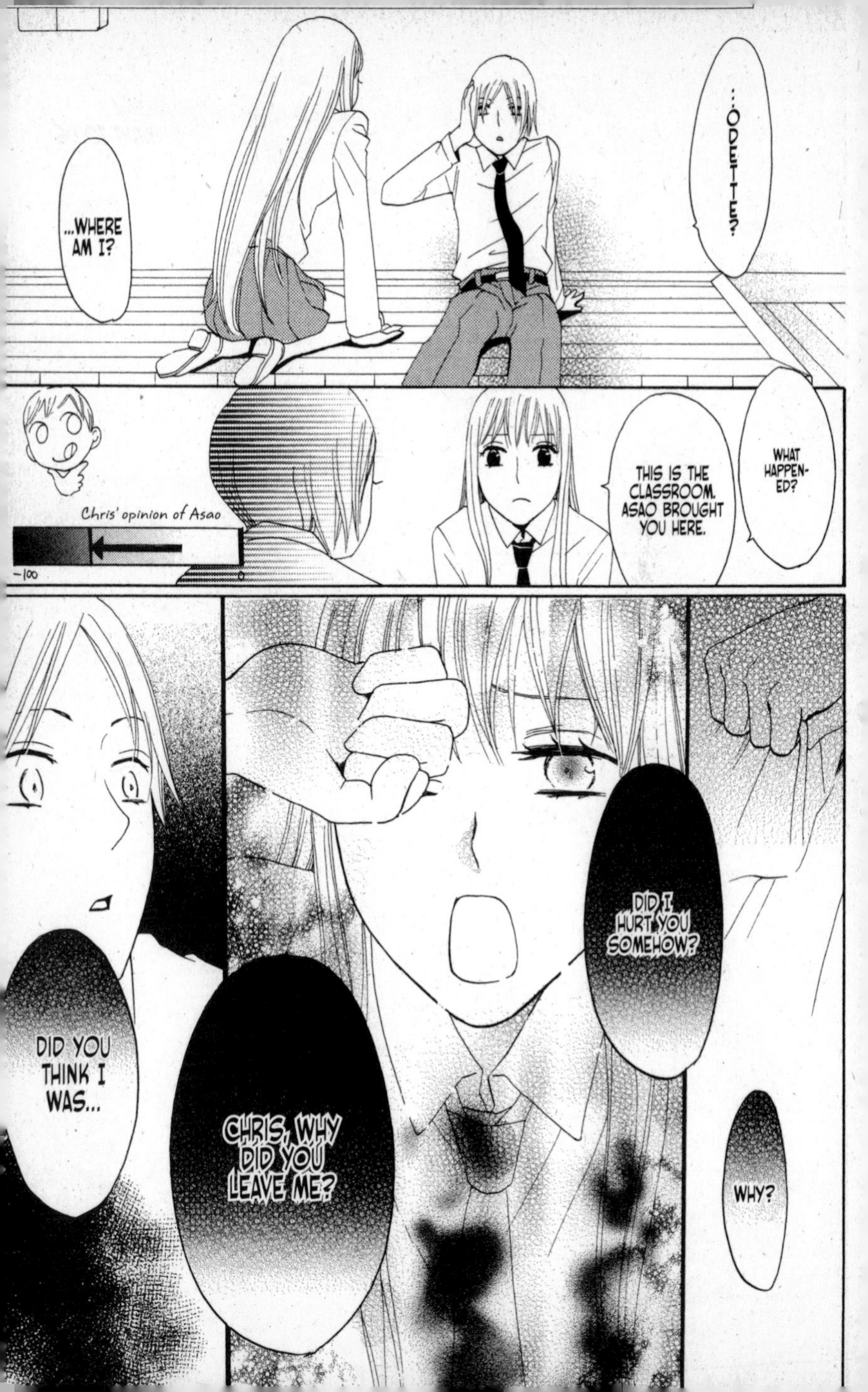
...ODETTE?
...WHERE AM I?
WHAT HAPPEN-ED?
THIS IS THE CLASSROOM. ASAO BROUGHT YOU HERE.
Chris' opinion of Asao
-100
0
WHY?
DID I HURT YOU SOMEHOW?
CHRIS, WHY DID YOU LEAVE ME?
DID YOU THINK I WAS...

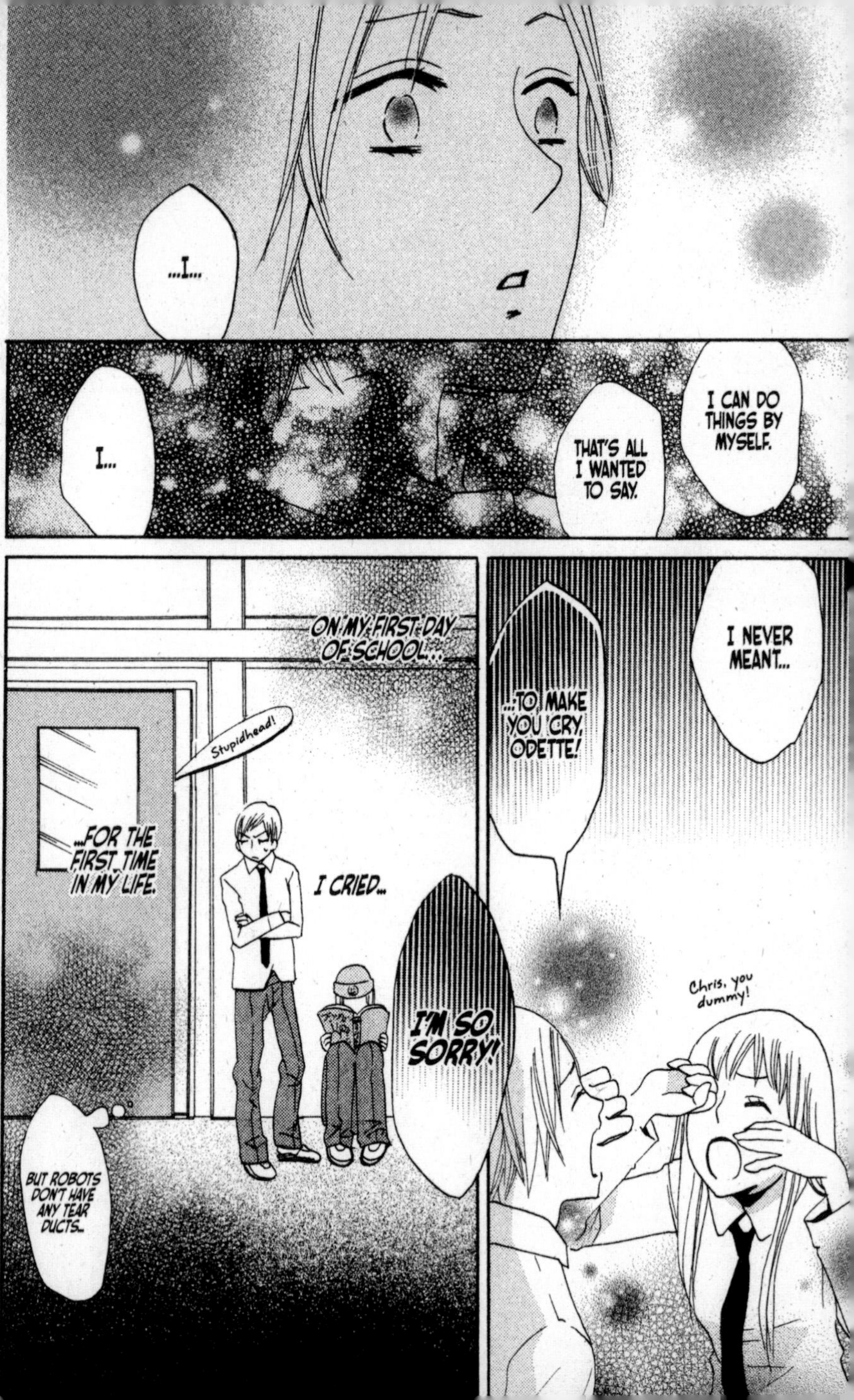
...I...
I CAN DO THINGS BY MYSELF.
THAT'S ALL I WANTED TO SAY.
I...
I NEVER MEANT...
...TO MAKE YOU CRY, ODETTE!
I'M SO SORRY!
Chris, you dummy!
ON MY FIRST DAY OF SCHOOL...
Stupidhead!
I CRIED...
...FOR THE FIRST TIME IN MY LIFE.
BUT ROBOTS DON'T HAVE ANY TEAR DUCTS...

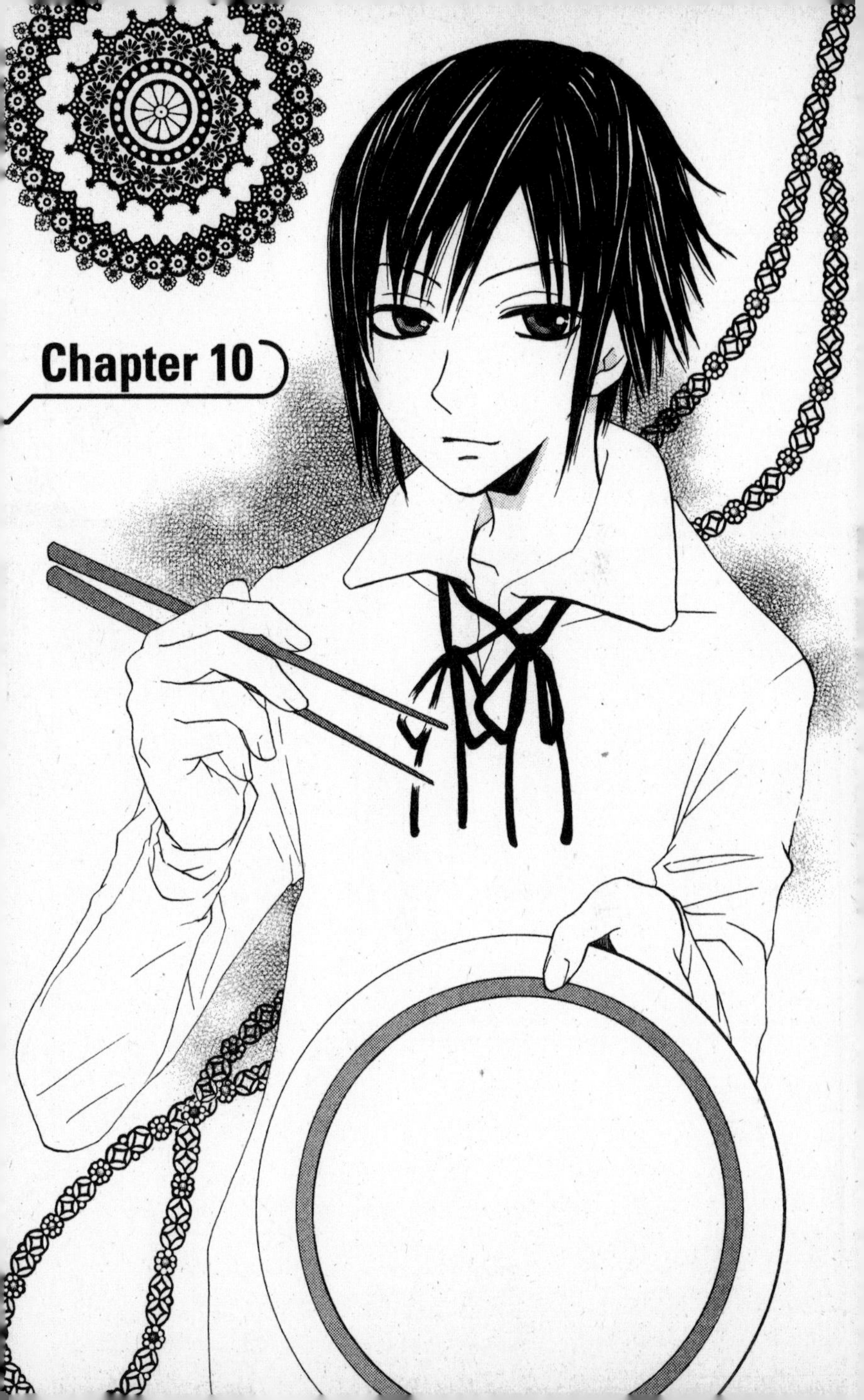
Chapter 10

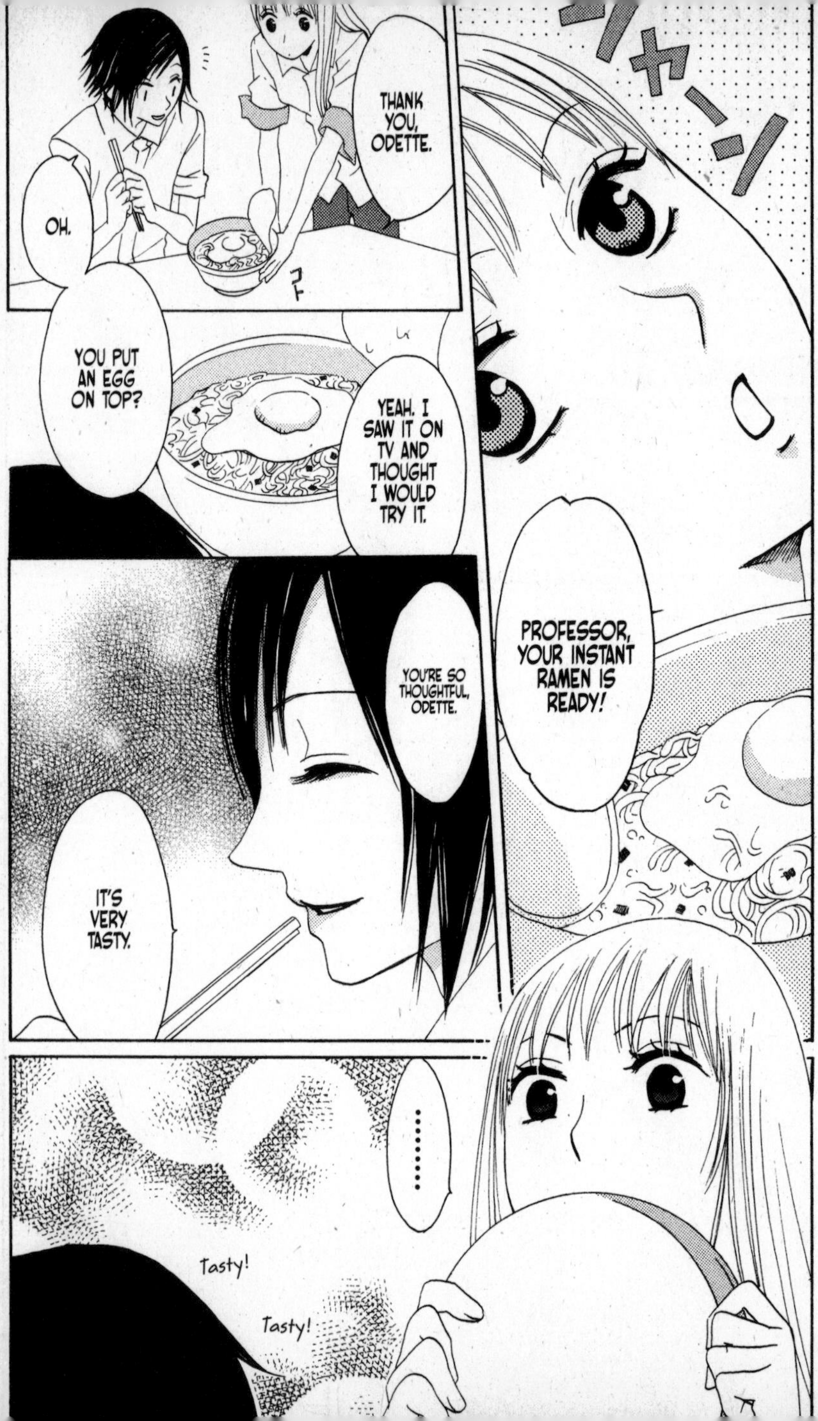
PROFESSOR, YOUR INSTANT RAMEN IS READY!
THANK YOU, ODETTE.
OH.
YOU PUT AN EGG ON TOP?
YEAH. I SAW IT ON TV AND THOUGHT I WOULD TRY IT.
YOU'RE SO THOUGHTFUL, ODETTE.
IT'S VERY TASTY.
......
Tasty!
Tasty!

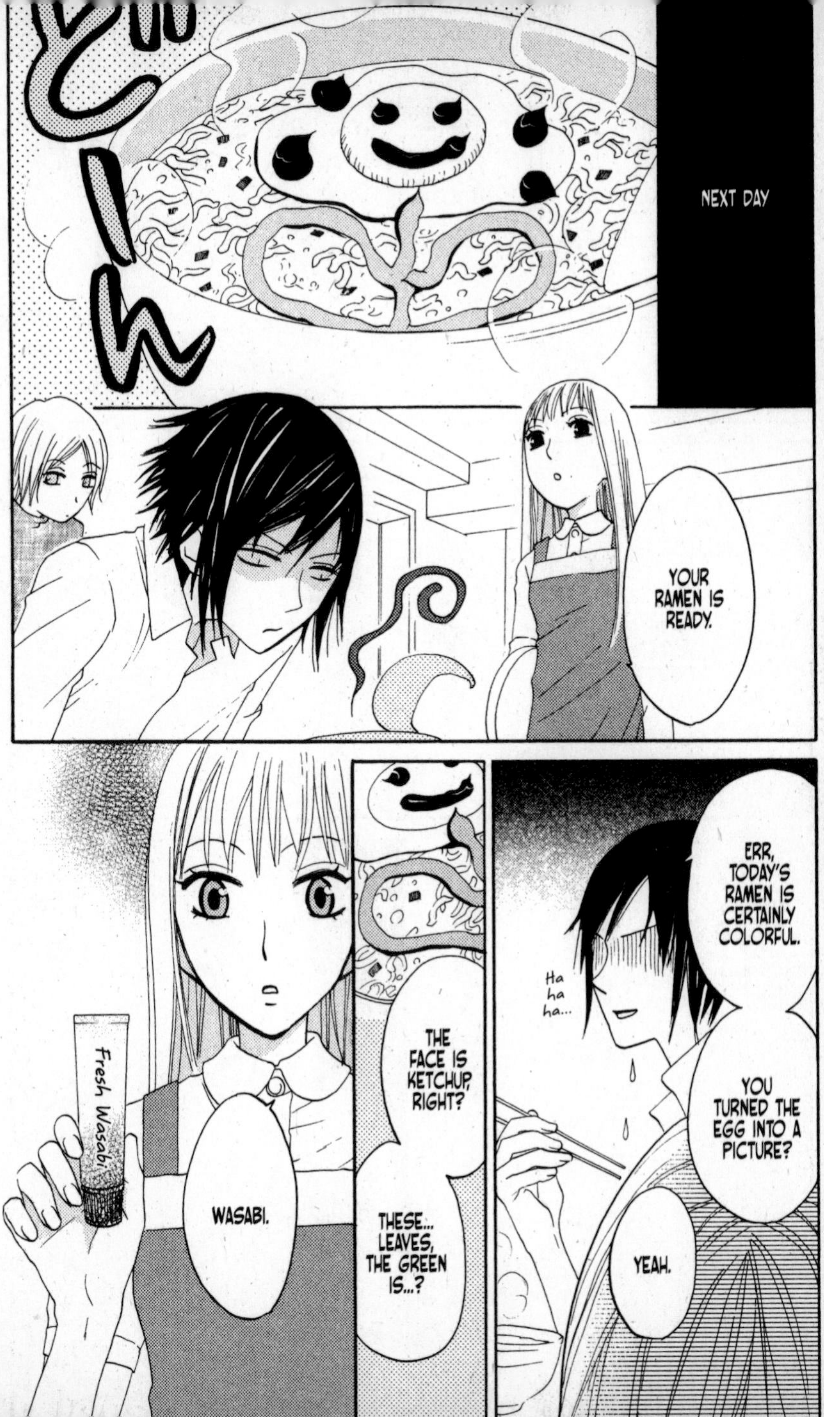
NEXT DAY
どーん
YOUR RAMEN IS READY.
ERR, TODAY'S RAMEN IS CERTAINLY COLORFUL.
Ha ha ha...
YOU TURNED THE EGG INTO A PICTURE?
YEAH.
THE FACE IS KETCHUP, RIGHT?
THESE... LEAVES, THE GREEN IS...?
Fresh Wasabi
WASABI.

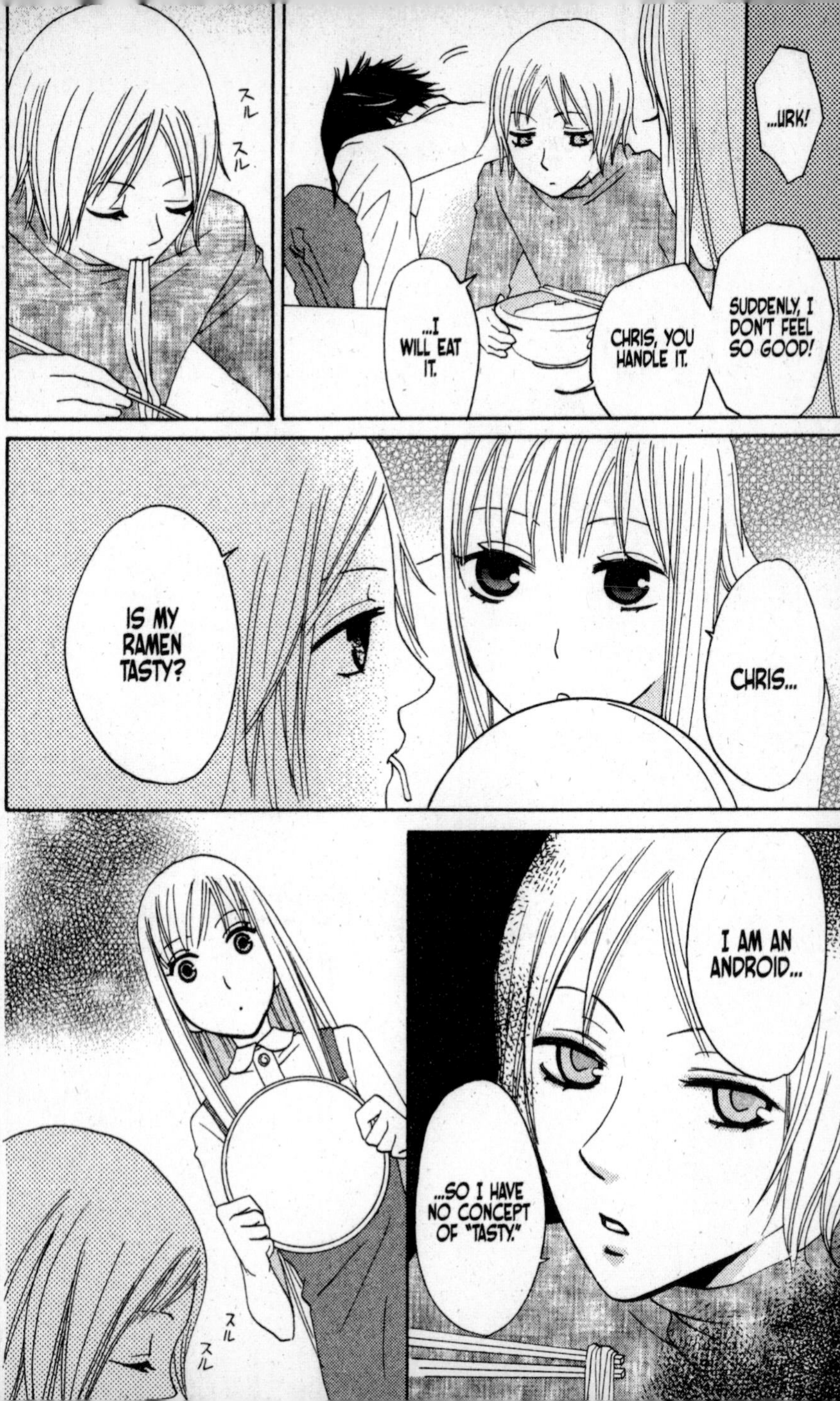
...URK!
SUDDENLY, I DON'T FEEL SO GOOD!
CHRIS, YOU HANDLE IT.
...I WILL EAT IT.
スル
スル
CHRIS...
IS MY RAMEN TASTY?
I AM AN ANDROID...
...SO I HAVE NO CONCEPT OF "TASTY."
スル
スル

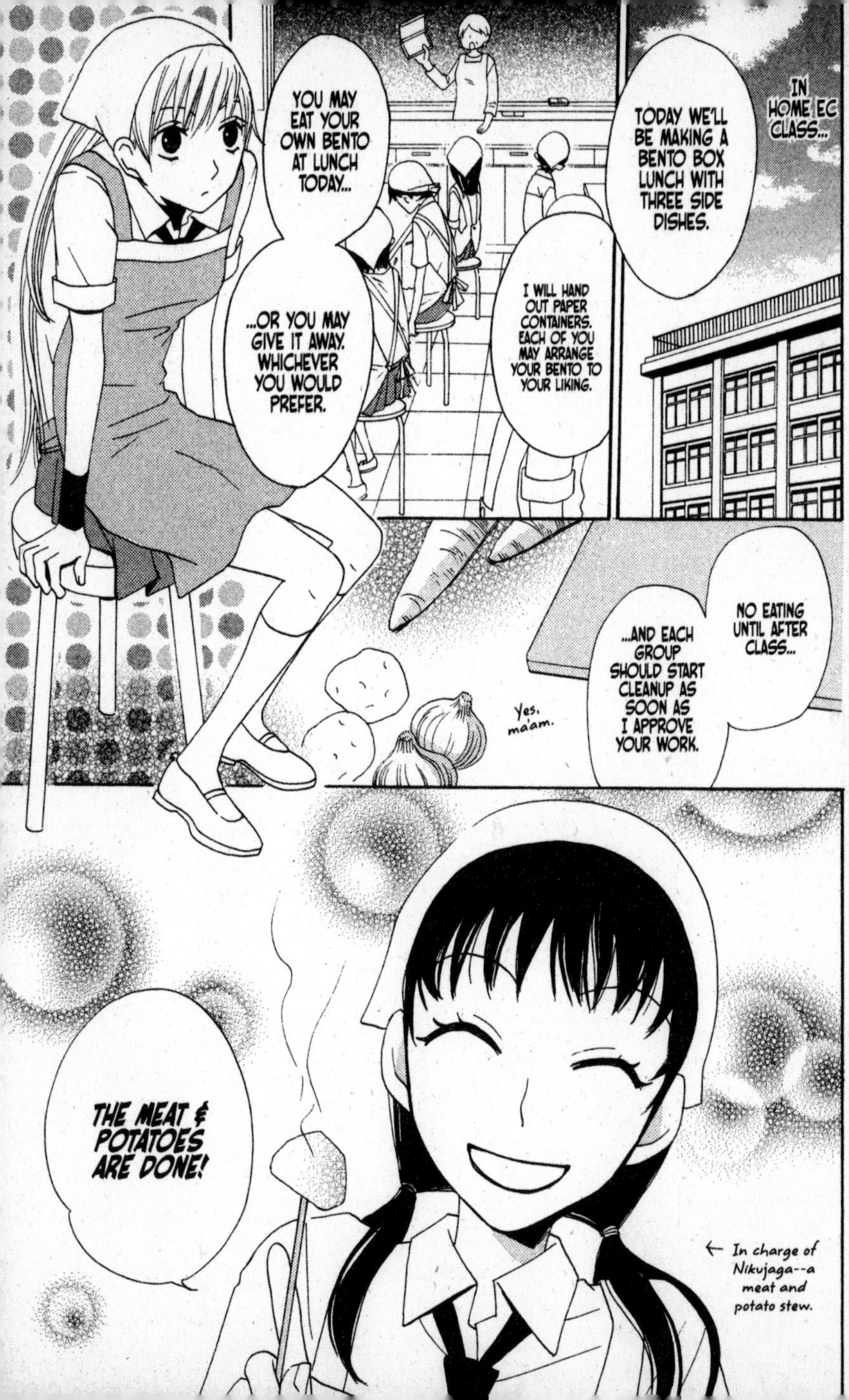
IN HOME EC CLASS...
TODAY WE'LL BE MAKING A BENTO BOX LUNCH WITH THREE SIDE DISHES.
I WILL HAND OUT PAPER CONTAINERS. EACH OF YOU MAY ARRANGE YOUR BENTO TO YOUR LIKING.
YOU MAY EAT YOUR OWN BENTO AT LUNCH TODAY...
...OR YOU MAY GIVE IT AWAY. WHICHEVER YOU WOULD PREFER.
NO EATING UNTIL AFTER CLASS...
...AND EACH GROUP SHOULD START CLEANUP AS SOON AS I APPROVE YOUR WORK.
Yes, ma'am.
THE MEAT & POTATOES ARE DONE!
← In charge of Nikujaga--a meat and potato stew.

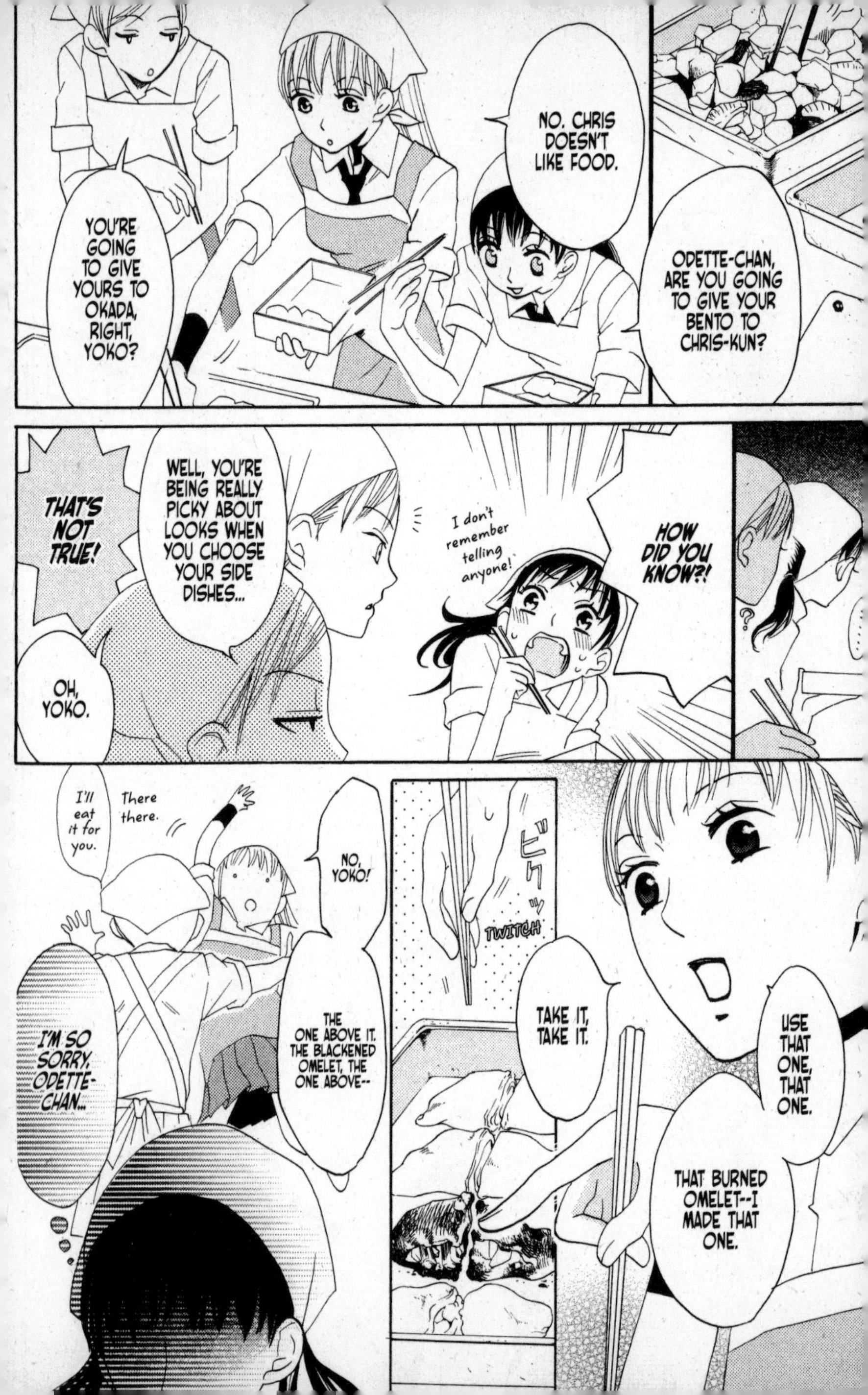
ODETTE-CHAN, ARE YOU GOING TO GIVE YOUR BENTO TO CHRIS-KUN?
NO. CHRIS DOESN'T LIKE FOOD.
YOU'RE GOING TO GIVE YOURS TO OKADA, RIGHT, YOKO?
HOW DID YOU KNOW?!
I don't remember telling anyone!
WELL, YOU'RE BEING REALLY PICKY ABOUT LOOKS WHEN YOU CHOOSE YOUR SIDE DISHES...
THAT'S NOT TRUE!
OH, YOKO.
USE THAT ONE, THAT ONE.
THAT BURNED OMELET--I MADE THAT ONE.
ビクッ
TWITCH
TAKE IT, TAKE IT.
NO, YOKO!
THE ONE ABOVE IT. THE BLACKENED OMELET, THE ONE ABOVE--
There there.
I'll eat it for you.
I'M SO SORRY, ODETTE-CHAN...

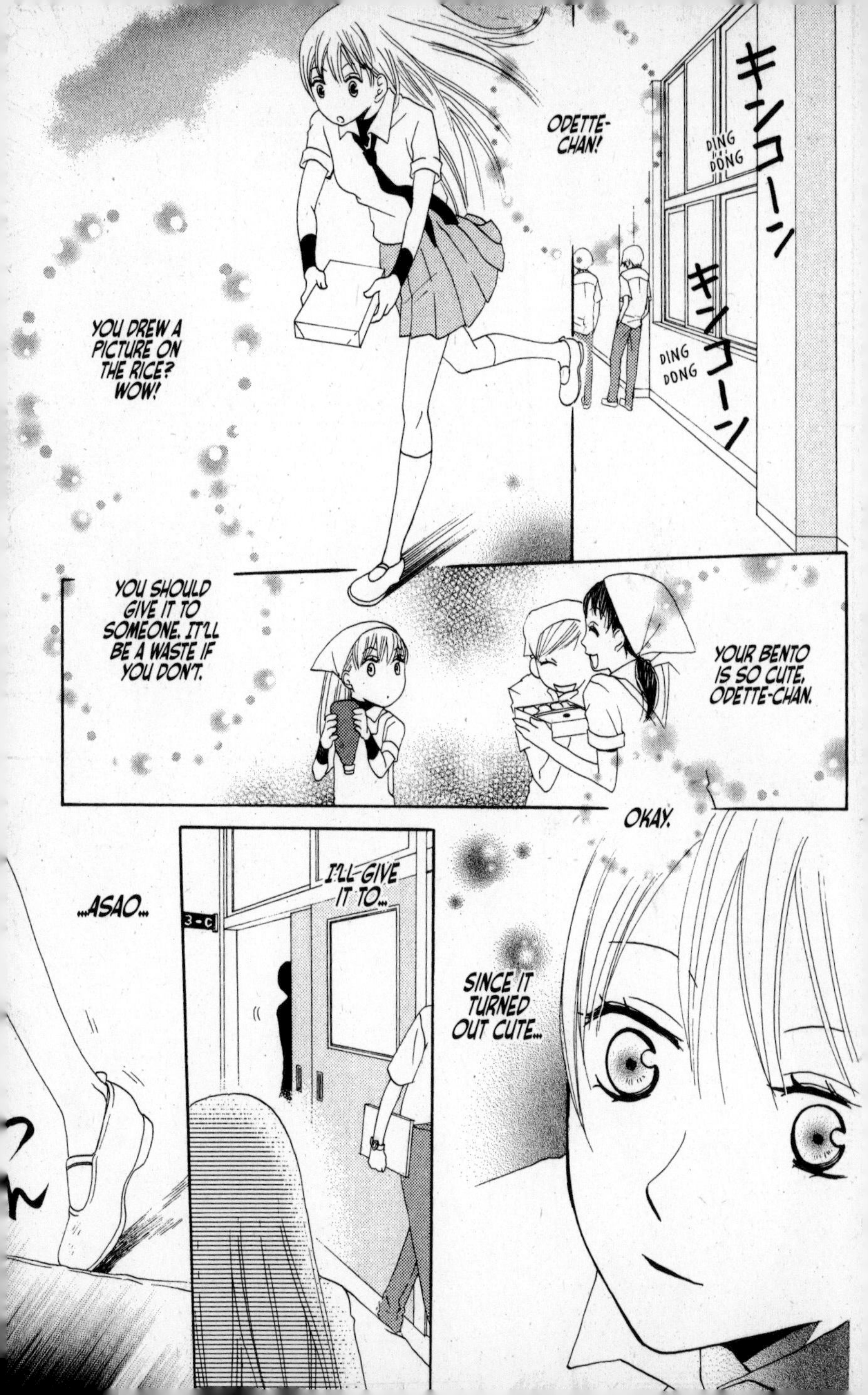
キンコーン
DING DONG
キンコーン
DING DONG
ODETTE-CHAN!
YOU DREW A PICTURE ON THE RICE? WOW!
YOUR BENTO IS SO CUTE, ODETTE-CHAN.
YOU SHOULD GIVE IT TO SOMEONE. IT'LL BE A WASTE IF YOU DON'T.
OKAY.
SINCE IT TURNED OUT CUTE...
I'LL GIVE IT TO...
...ASAO...
3-C

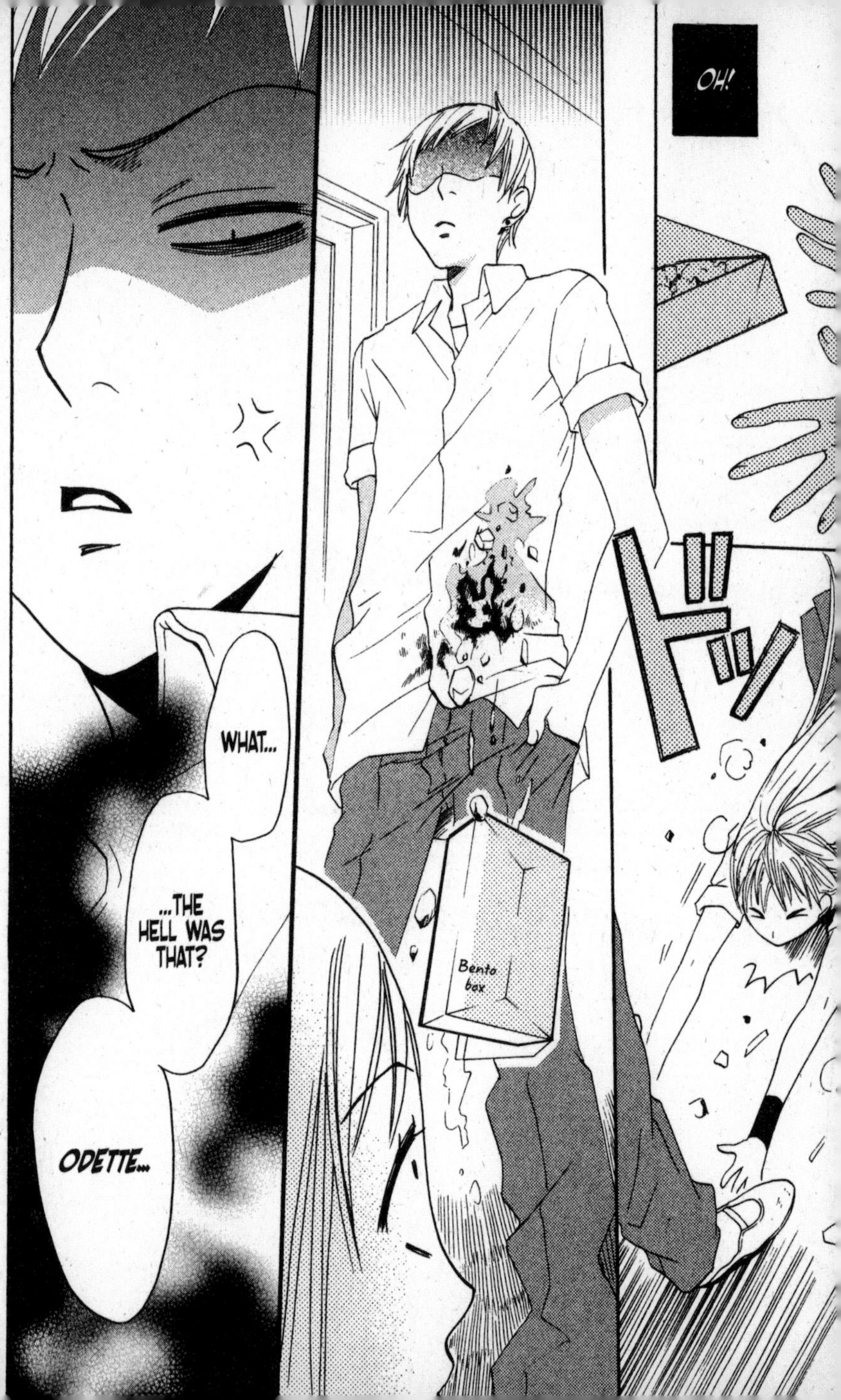
OH!
ドッ
Bento box
WHAT...
...THE HELL WAS THAT?
ODETTE...

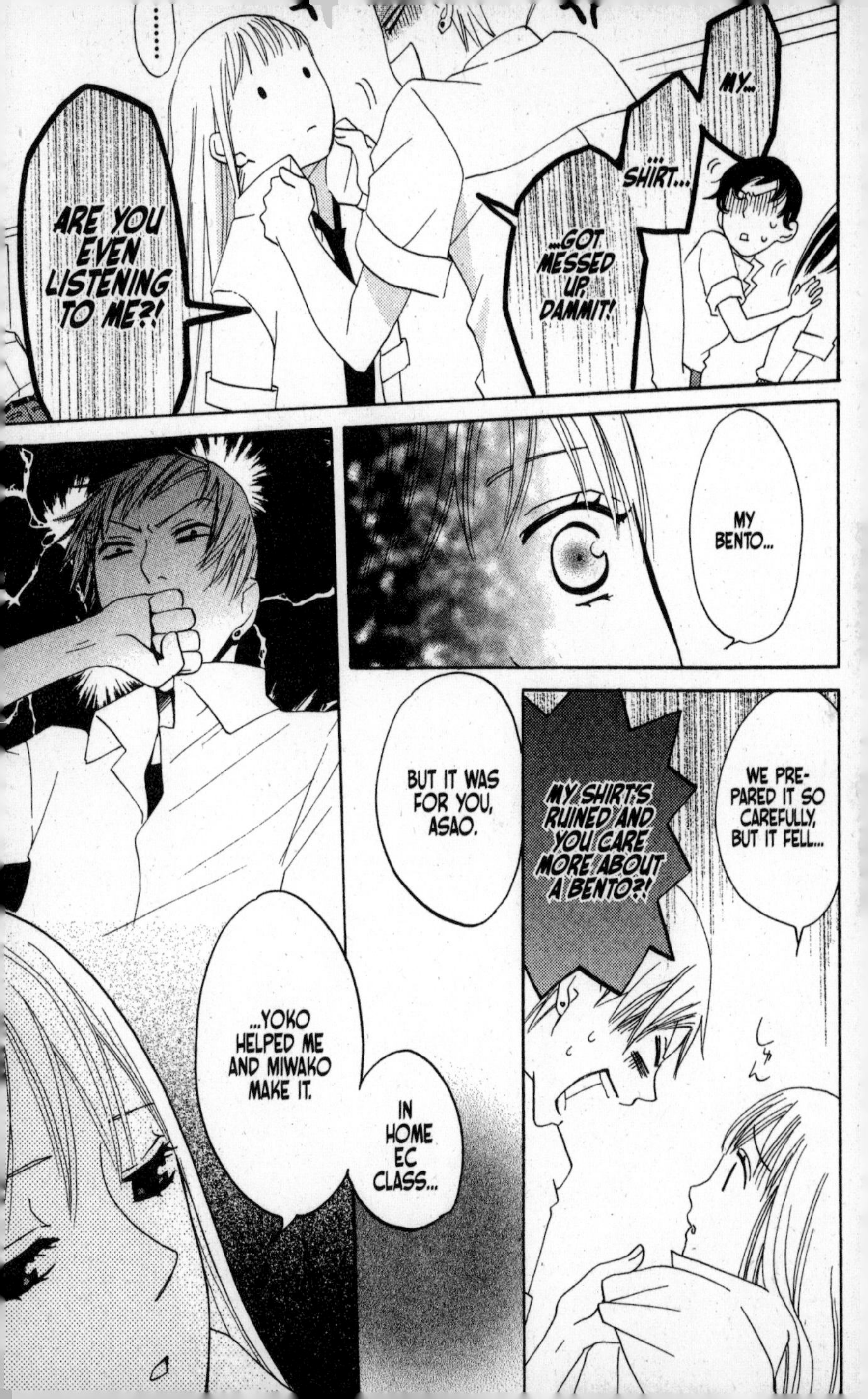
MY...
...SHIRT...
...GOT MESSED UP, DAMMIT!
......
ARE YOU EVEN LISTENING TO ME?!
MY BENTO...
WE PREPARED IT SO CAREFULLY, BUT IT FELL...
MY SHIRT'S RUINED AND YOU CARE MORE ABOUT A BENTO?!
BUT IT WAS FOR YOU, ASAO.
...YOKO HELPED ME AND MIWAKO MAKE IT.
IN HOME EC CLASS...

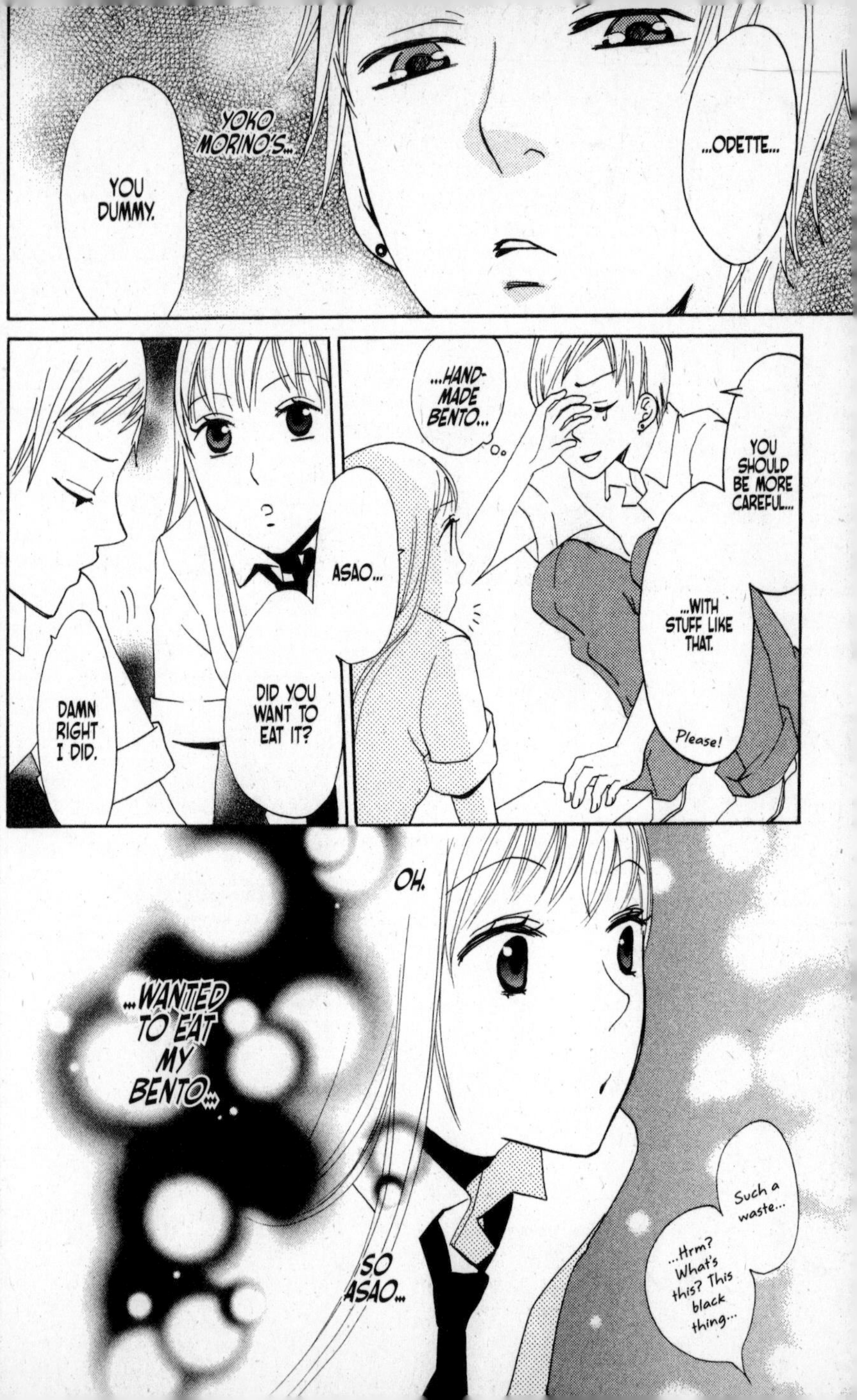
...ODETTE...
YOKO MORINO'S...
YOU DUMMY.
YOU SHOULD BE MORE CAREFUL...
...HAND-MADE BENTO...
...WITH STUFF LIKE THAT.
Please!
ASAO...
DID YOU WANT TO EAT IT?
DAMN RIGHT I DID.
OH.
Such a waste...
...Hrm? What's this? This black thing...
...WANTED TO EAT MY BENTO...
SO ASAO...

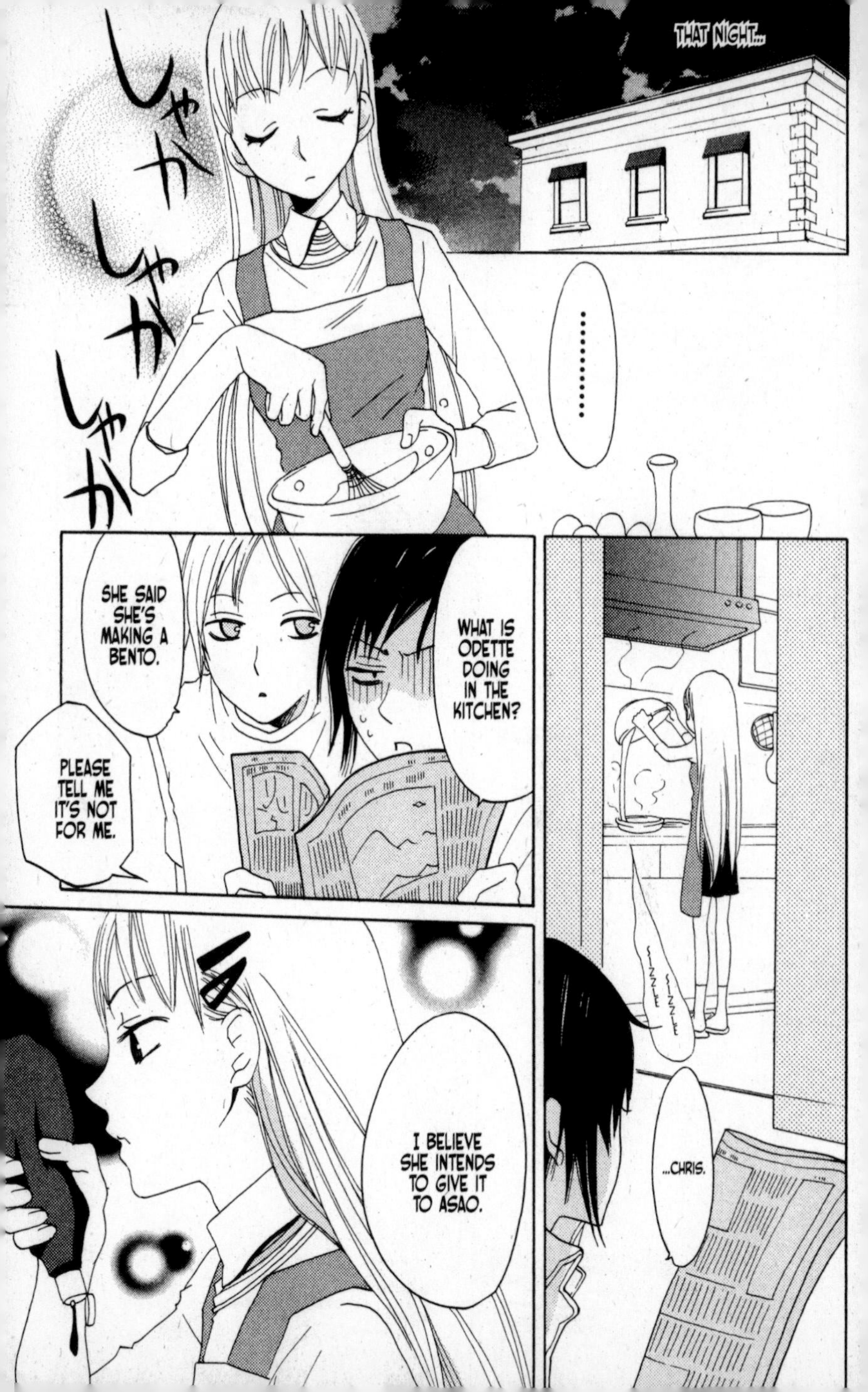
THAT NIGHT...
......
しゃかしゃかしゃか
SIZZLE
SIZZLE
...CHRIS.
WHAT IS ODETTE DOING IN THE KITCHEN?
SHE SAID SHE'S MAKING A BENTO.
PLEASE TELL ME IT'S NOT FOR ME.
I BELIEVE SHE INTENDS TO GIVE IT TO ASAO.

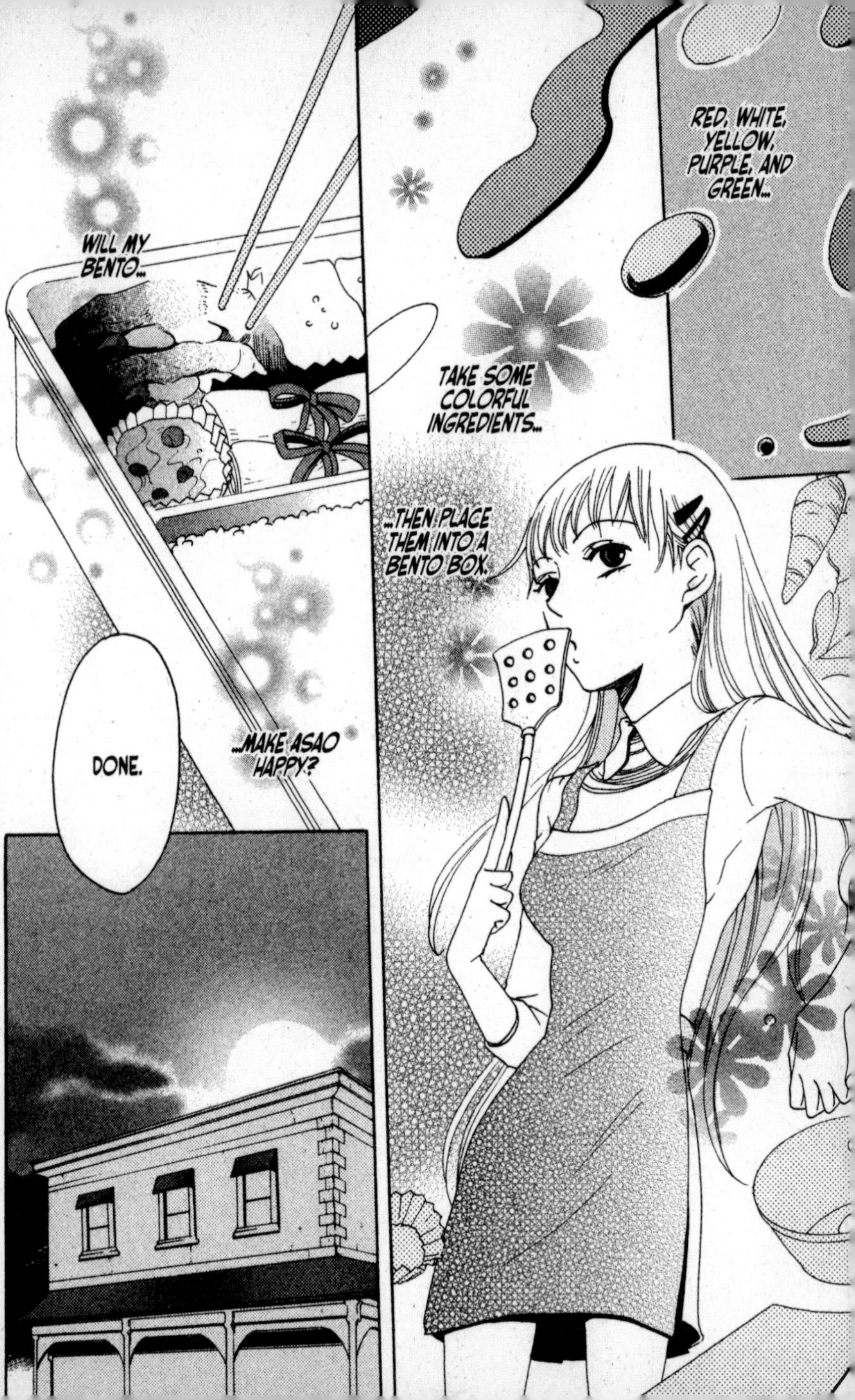
RED, WHITE, YELLOW, PURPLE, AND GREEN...
TAKE SOME COLORFUL INGREDIENTS...
...THEN PLACE THEM INTO A BENTO BOX.
WILL MY BENTO...
...MAKE ASAO HAPPY?
DONE.

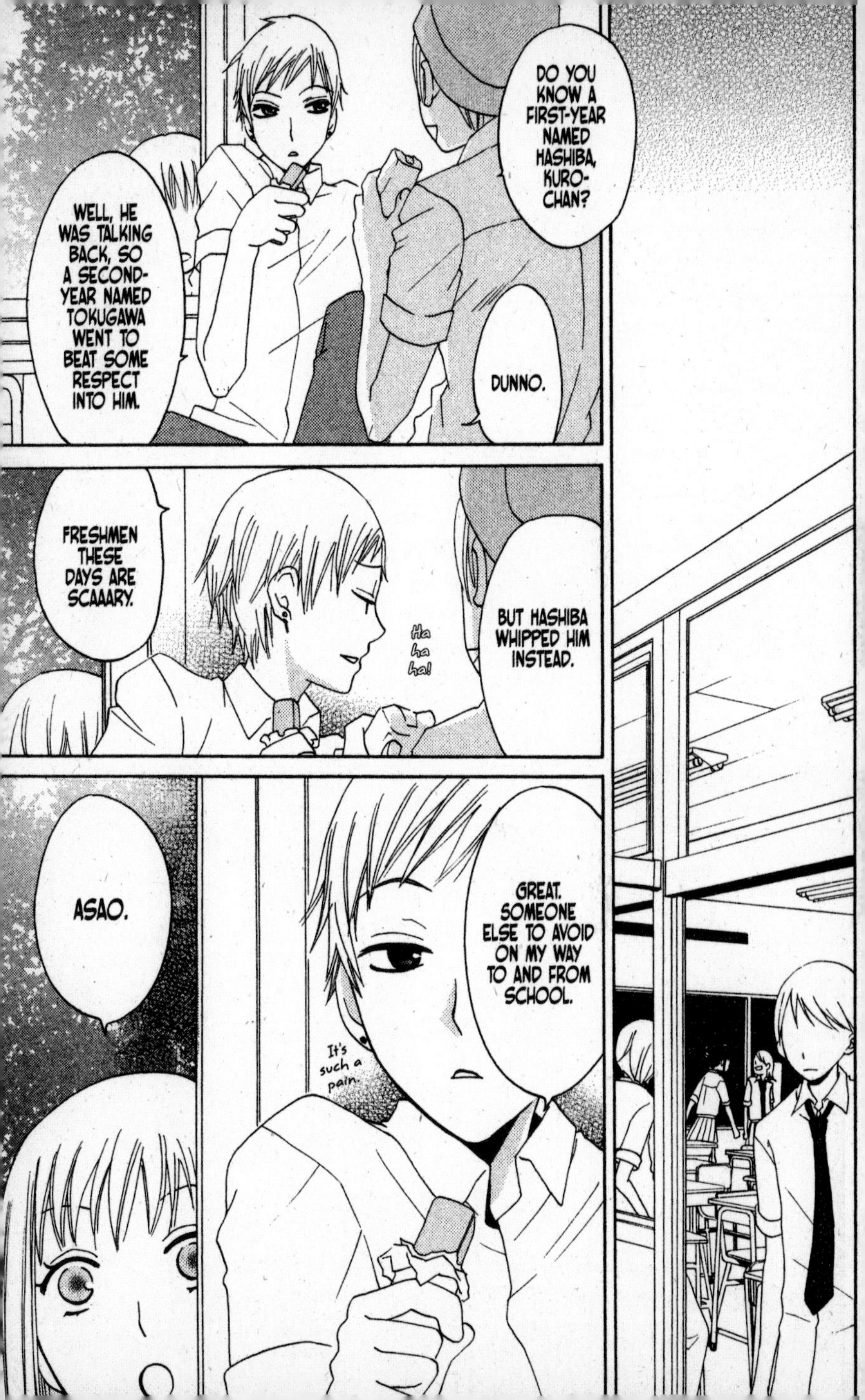
DO YOU KNOW A FIRST-YEAR NAMED HASHIBA, KURO-CHAN?
DUNNO.
WELL, HE WAS TALKING BACK, SO A SECOND-YEAR NAMED TOKUGAWA WENT TO BEAT SOME RESPECT INTO HIM.
BUT HASHIBA WHIPPED HIM INSTEAD.
Ha ha ha!
FRESHMEN THESE DAYS ARE SCAAARY.
GREAT. SOMEONE ELSE TO AVOID ON MY WAY TO AND FROM SCHOOL.
It's such a pain.
ASAO.

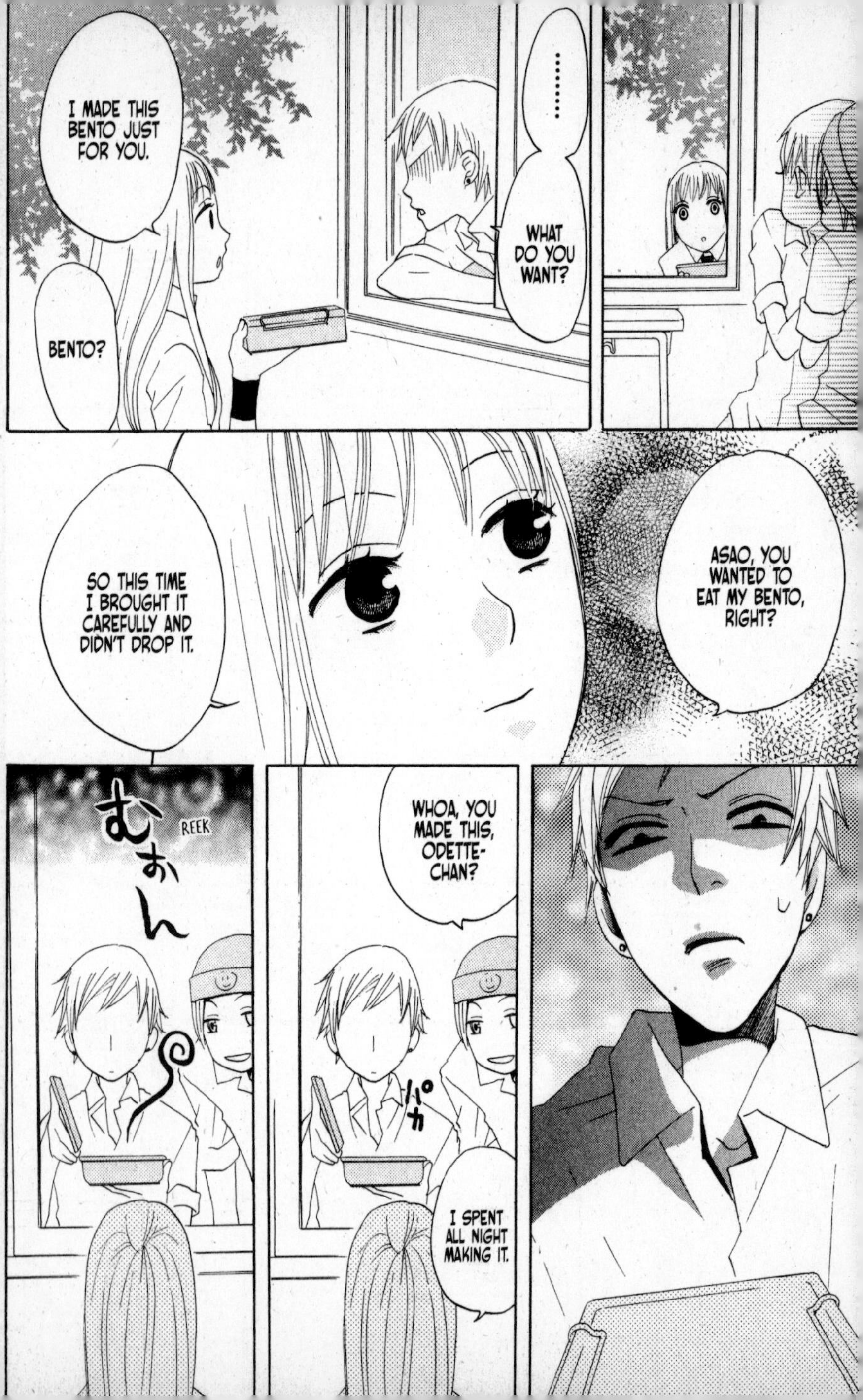
……
WHAT DO YOU WANT?
I MADE THIS BENTO JUST FOR YOU.
BENTO?
ASAO, YOU WANTED TO EAT MY BENTO, RIGHT?
SO THIS TIME I BROUGHT IT CAREFULLY AND DIDN'T DROP IT.
WHOA, YOU MADE THIS, ODETTE-CHAN?
パカ
I SPENT ALL NIGHT MAKING IT.
むおん
REEK

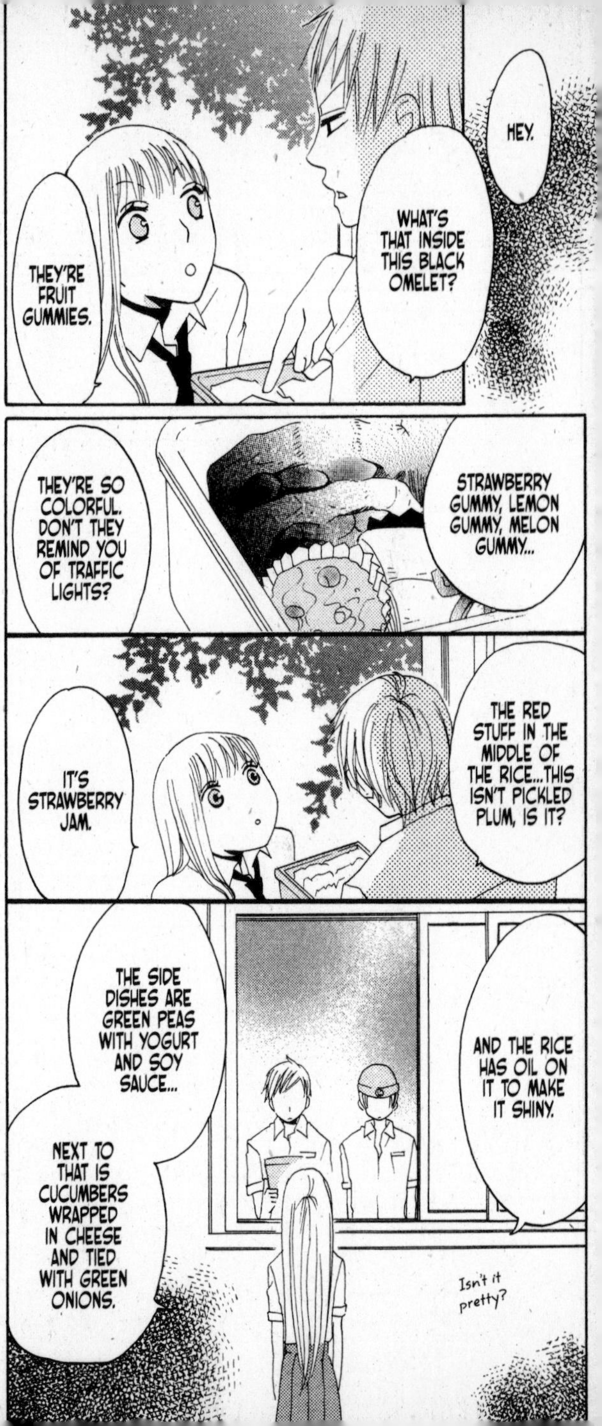
HEY.
WHAT'S THAT INSIDE THIS BLACK OMELET?
THEY'RE FRUIT GUMMIES.
STRAWBERRY GUMMY, LEMON GUMMY, MELON GUMMY...
THEY'RE SO COLORFUL. DON'T THEY REMIND YOU OF TRAFFIC LIGHTS?
THE RED STUFF IN THE MIDDLE OF THE RICE...THIS ISN'T PICKLED PLUM, IS IT?
IT'S STRAWBERRY JAM.
AND THE RICE HAS OIL ON IT TO MAKE IT SHINY.
THE SIDE DISHES ARE GREEN PEAS WITH YOGURT AND SOY SAUCE...
Isn't it pretty?
NEXT TO THAT IS CUCUMBERS WRAPPED IN CHEESE AND TIED WITH GREEN ONIONS.

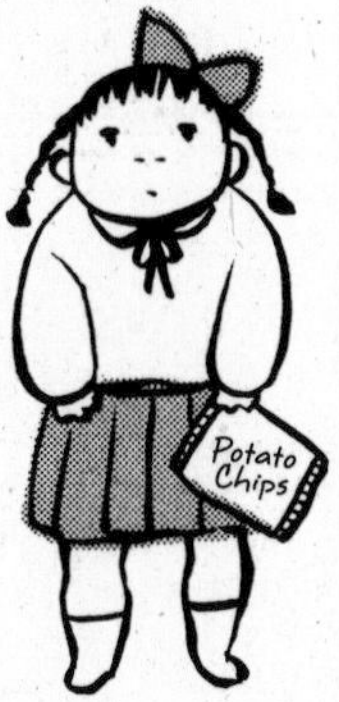
Potato Chips

Karin

Asao's younger sister. Grew up being doted on by both her parents (they always wanted a girl). Takes after her mother.

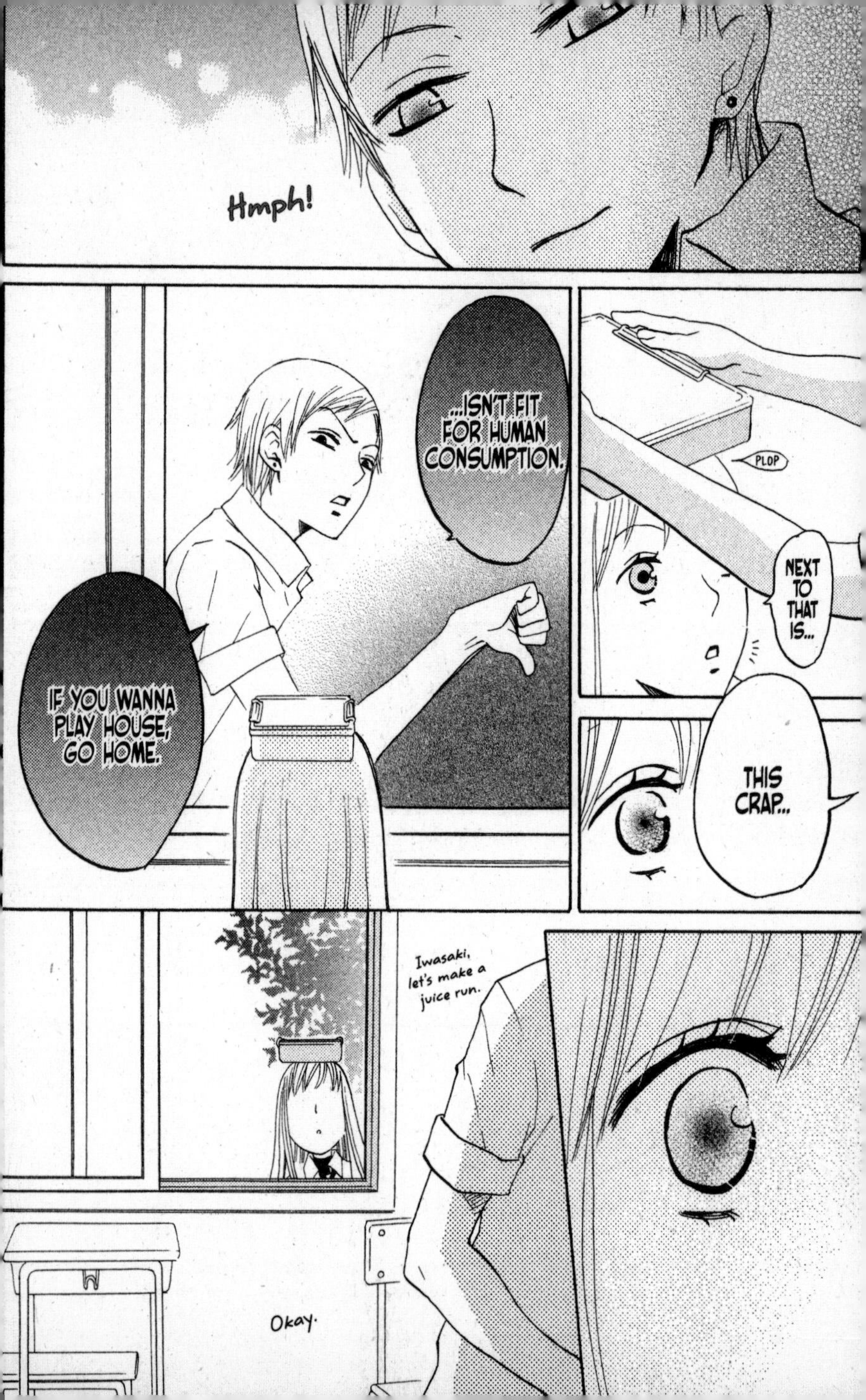
Hmph!
PLOP
NEXT TO THAT IS...
THIS CRAP...
...ISN'T FIT FOR HUMAN CONSUMPTION.
IF YOU WANNA PLAY HOUSE, GO HOME.
Iwasaki, let's make a juice run.
Okay.

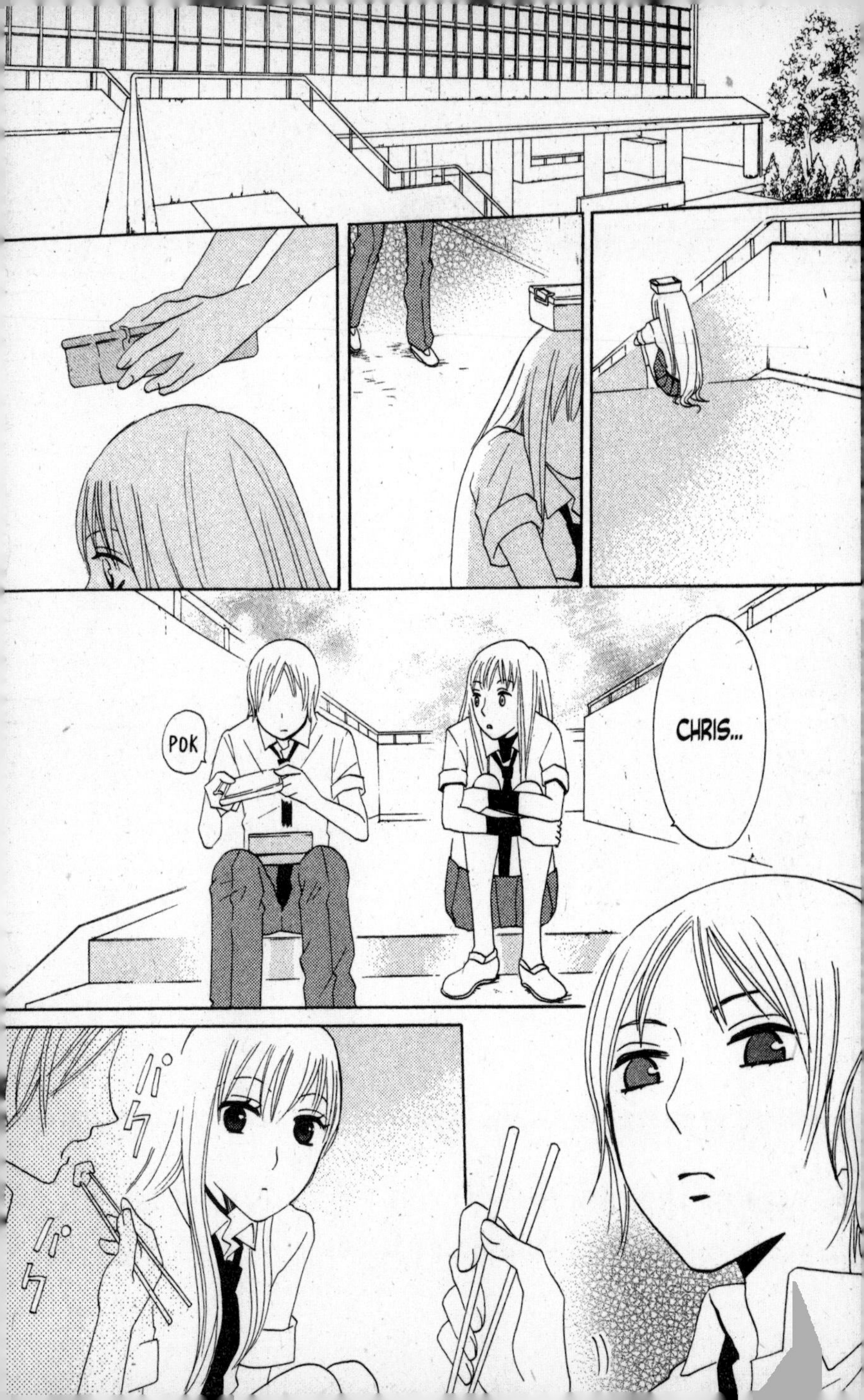
CHRIS...
POK
パク
パク

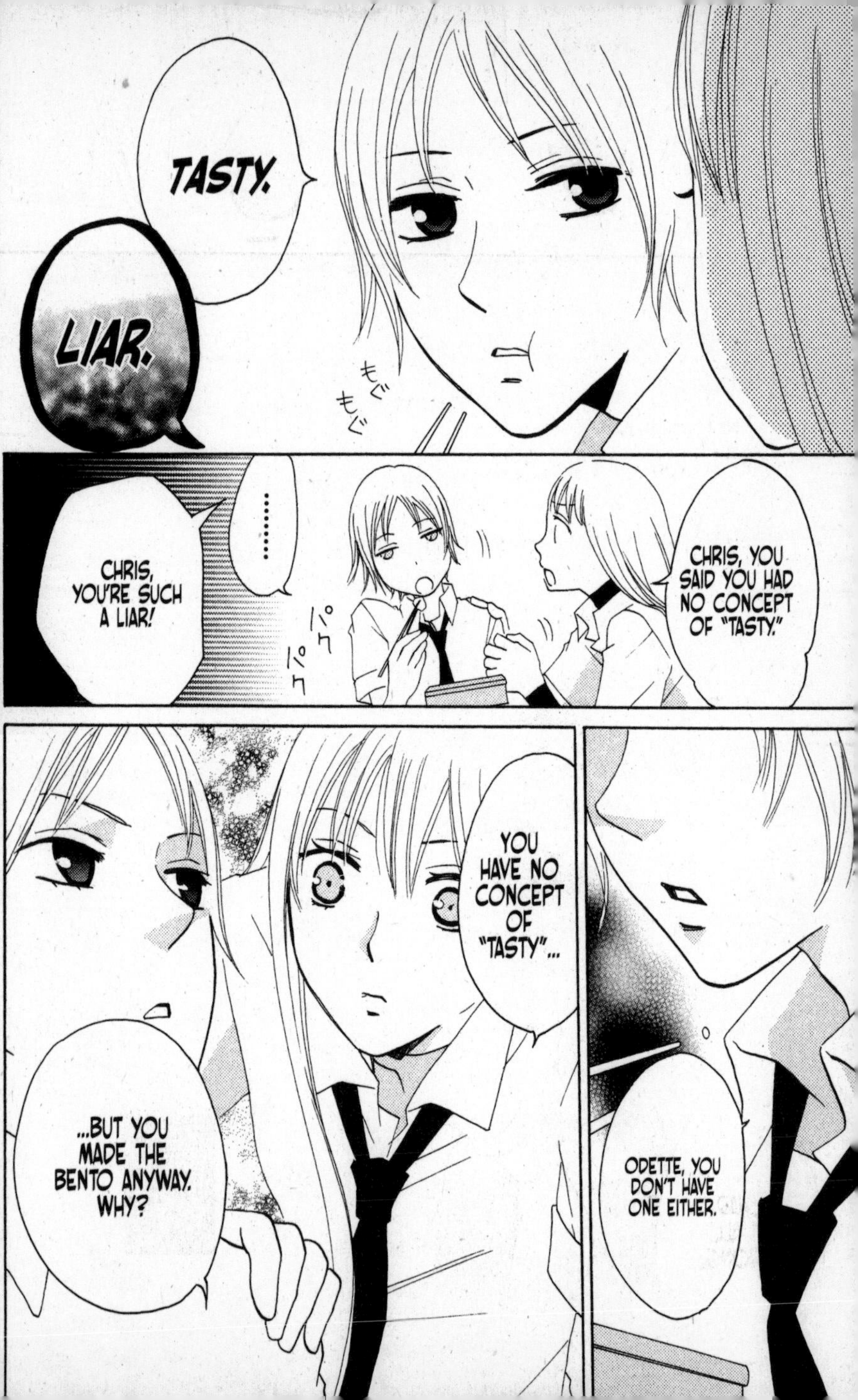
TASTY.
もぐもぐ
LIAR.
CHRIS, YOU SAID YOU HAD NO CONCEPT OF "TASTY."
......
パクパク
CHRIS, YOU'RE SUCH A LIAR!
ODETTE, YOU DON'T HAVE ONE EITHER.
YOU HAVE NO CONCEPT OF "TASTY"...
...BUT YOU MADE THE BENTO ANYWAY. WHY?

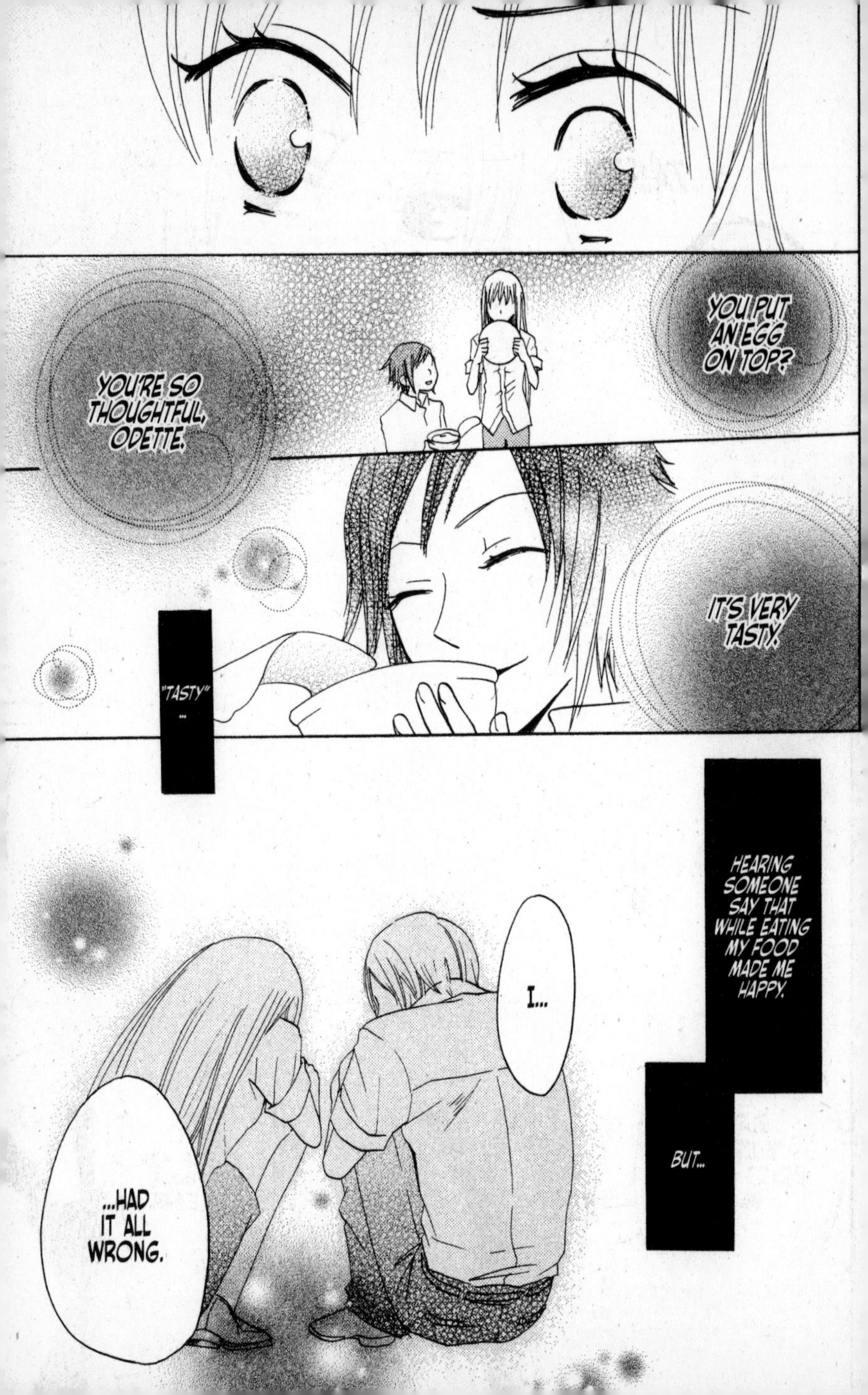
YOU PUT AN EGG ON TOP?
YOU'RE SO THOUGHTFUL, ODETTE.
IT'S VERY TASTY.
"TASTY" ...
HEARING SOMEONE SAY THAT WHILE EATING MY FOOD MADE ME HAPPY.
BUT...
I...
...HAD IT ALL WRONG.

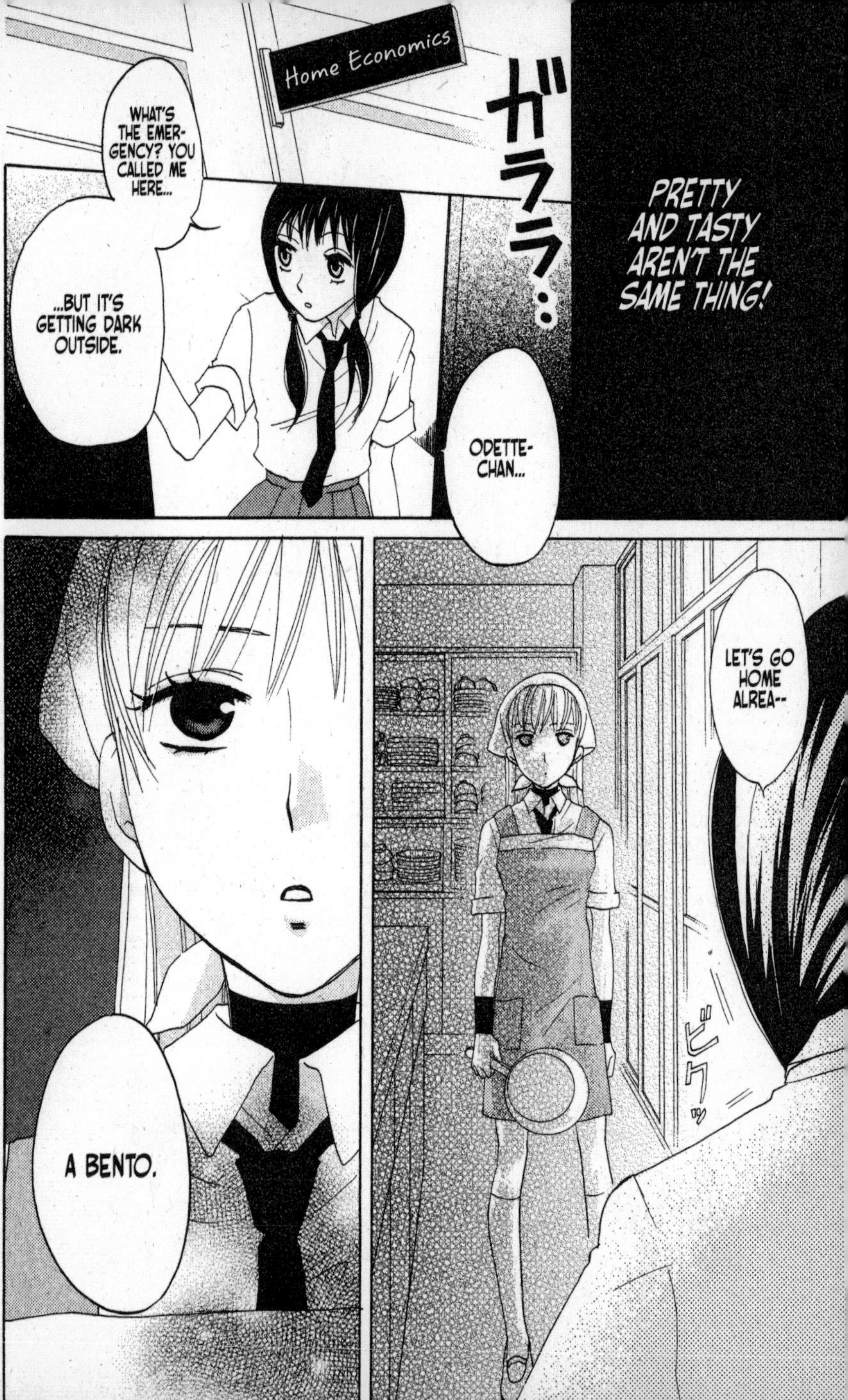
ガラ‥
PRETTY AND TASTY AREN'T THE SAME THING!
Home Economics
WHAT'S THE EMER-GENCY? YOU CALLED ME HERE...
...BUT IT'S GETTING DARK OUTSIDE.
ODETTE-CHAN...
LET'S GO HOME ALREA--
ビクッ
A BENTO.

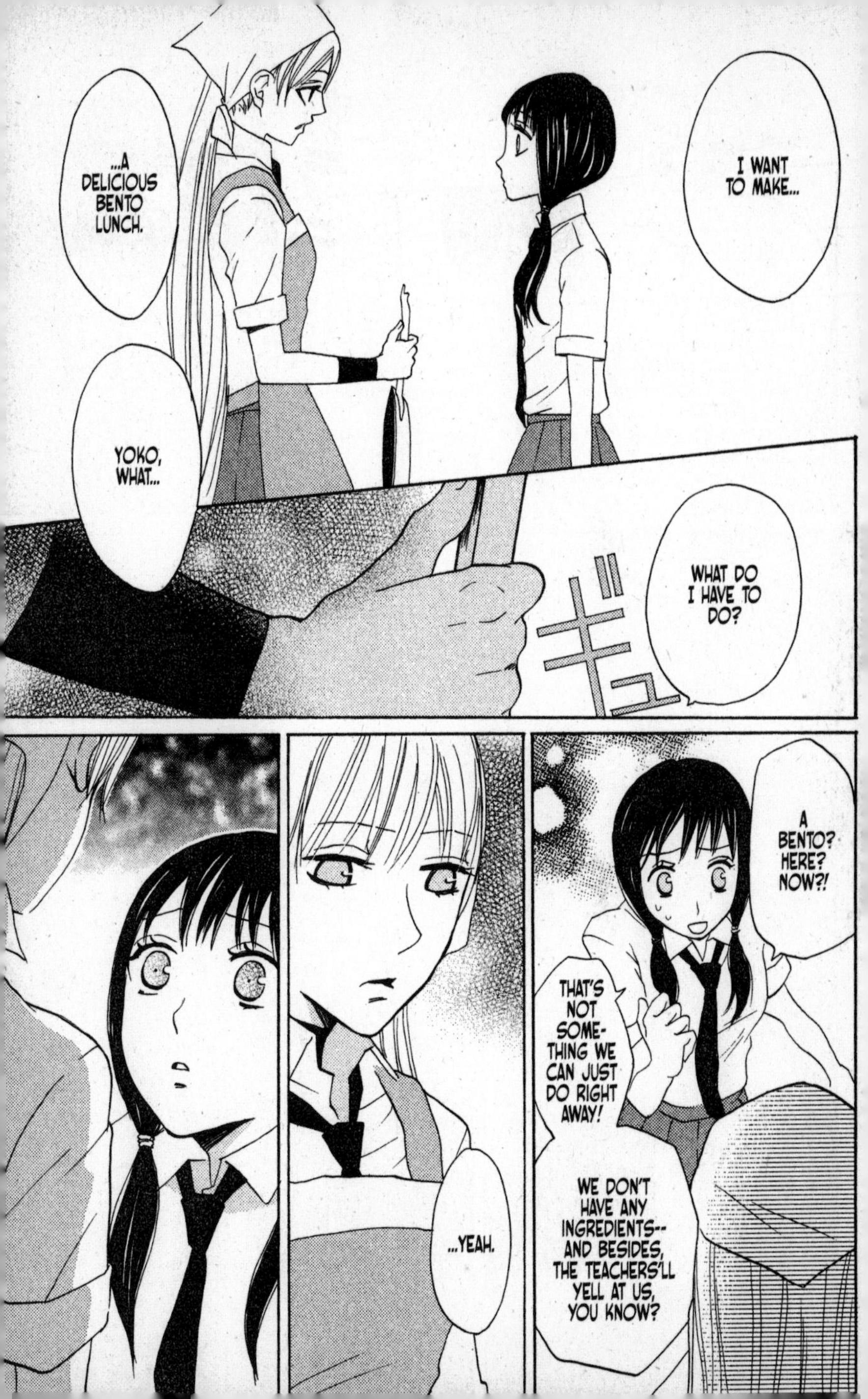
I WANT TO MAKE...
...A DELICIOUS BENTO LUNCH.
YOKO, WHAT...
WHAT DO I HAVE TO DO?
ギュ
A BENTO? HERE? NOW?!
THAT'S NOT SOME-THING WE CAN JUST DO RIGHT AWAY!
WE DON'T HAVE ANY INGREDIENTS--AND BESIDES, THE TEACHERS'LL YELL AT US, YOU KNOW?
...YEAH.

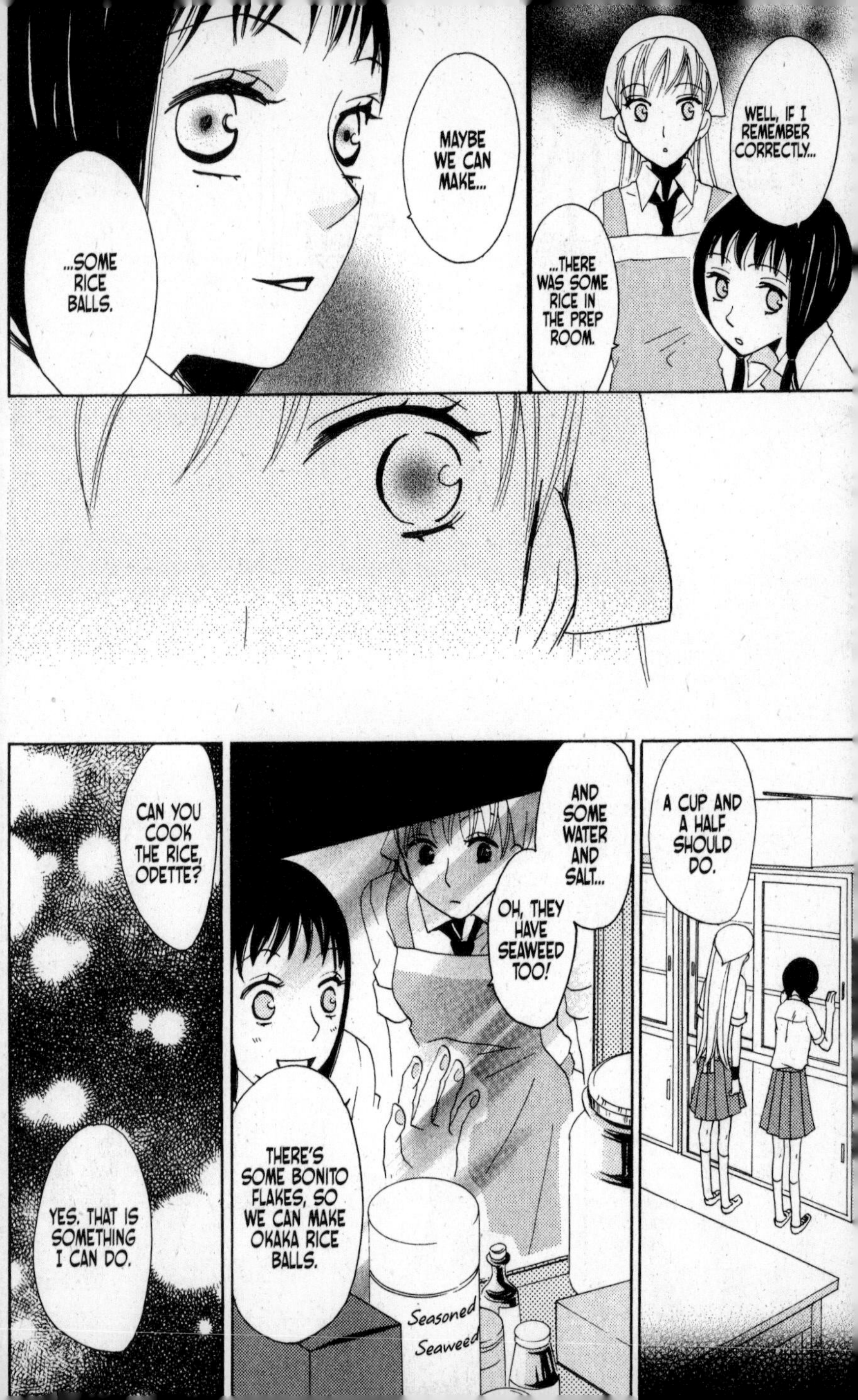
WELL, IF I REMEMBER CORRECTLY...
...THERE WAS SOME RICE IN THE PREP ROOM.
MAYBE WE CAN MAKE...
...SOME RICE BALLS.
A CUP AND A HALF SHOULD DO.
AND SOME WATER AND SALT...
OH, THEY HAVE SEAWEED TOO!
THERE'S SOME BONITO FLAKES, SO WE CAN MAKE OKAKA RICE BALLS.
Seasoned Seaweed
CAN YOU COOK THE RICE, ODETTE?
YES. THAT IS SOMETHING I CAN DO.

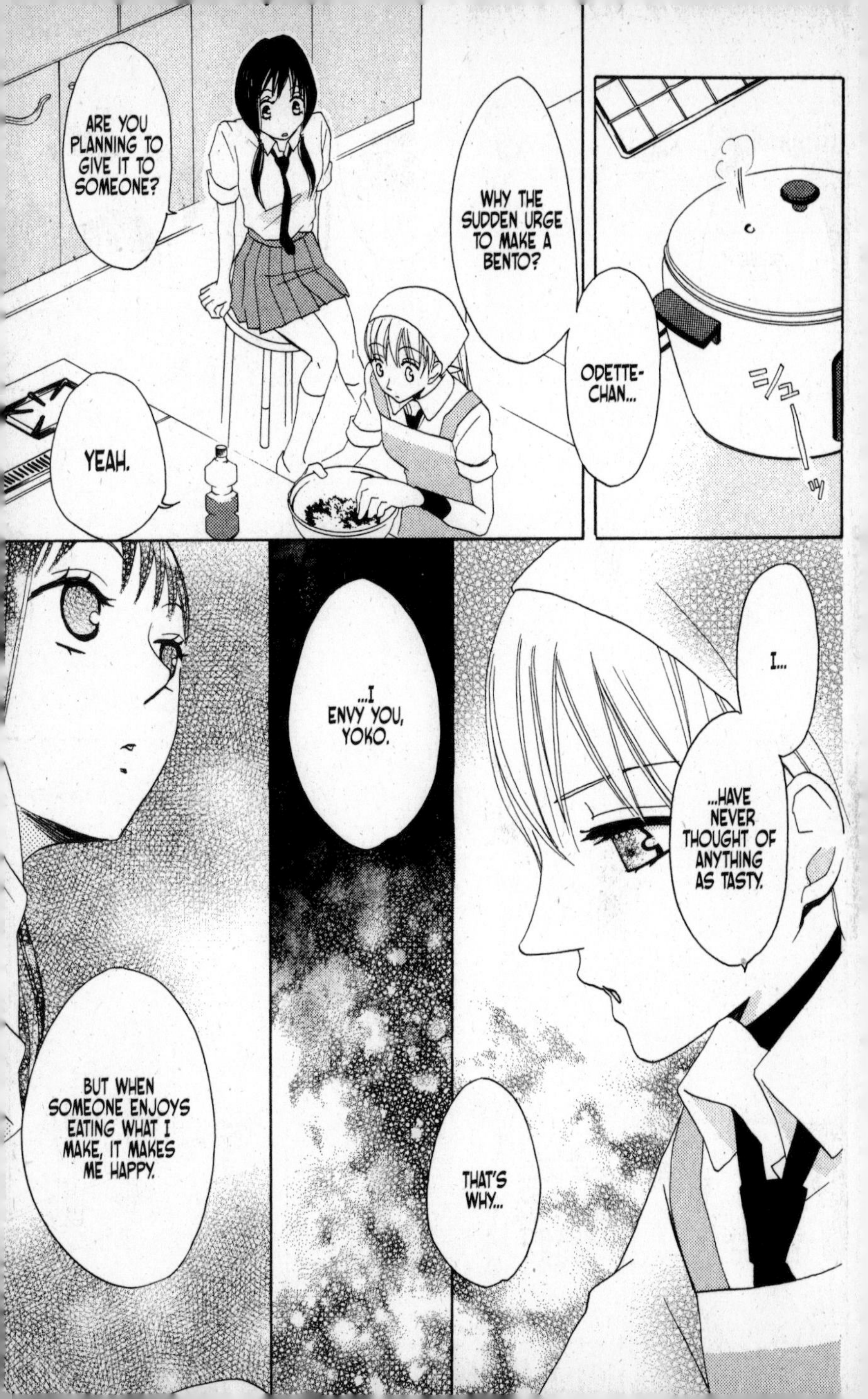
ODETTE-CHAN...
シューッ
WHY THE SUDDEN URGE TO MAKE A BENTO?
ARE YOU PLANNING TO GIVE IT TO SOMEONE?
YEAH.
I...
...HAVE NEVER THOUGHT OF ANYTHING AS TASTY.
THAT'S WHY...
...I ENVY YOU, YOKO.
BUT WHEN SOMEONE ENJOYS EATING WHAT I MAKE, IT MAKES ME HAPPY.

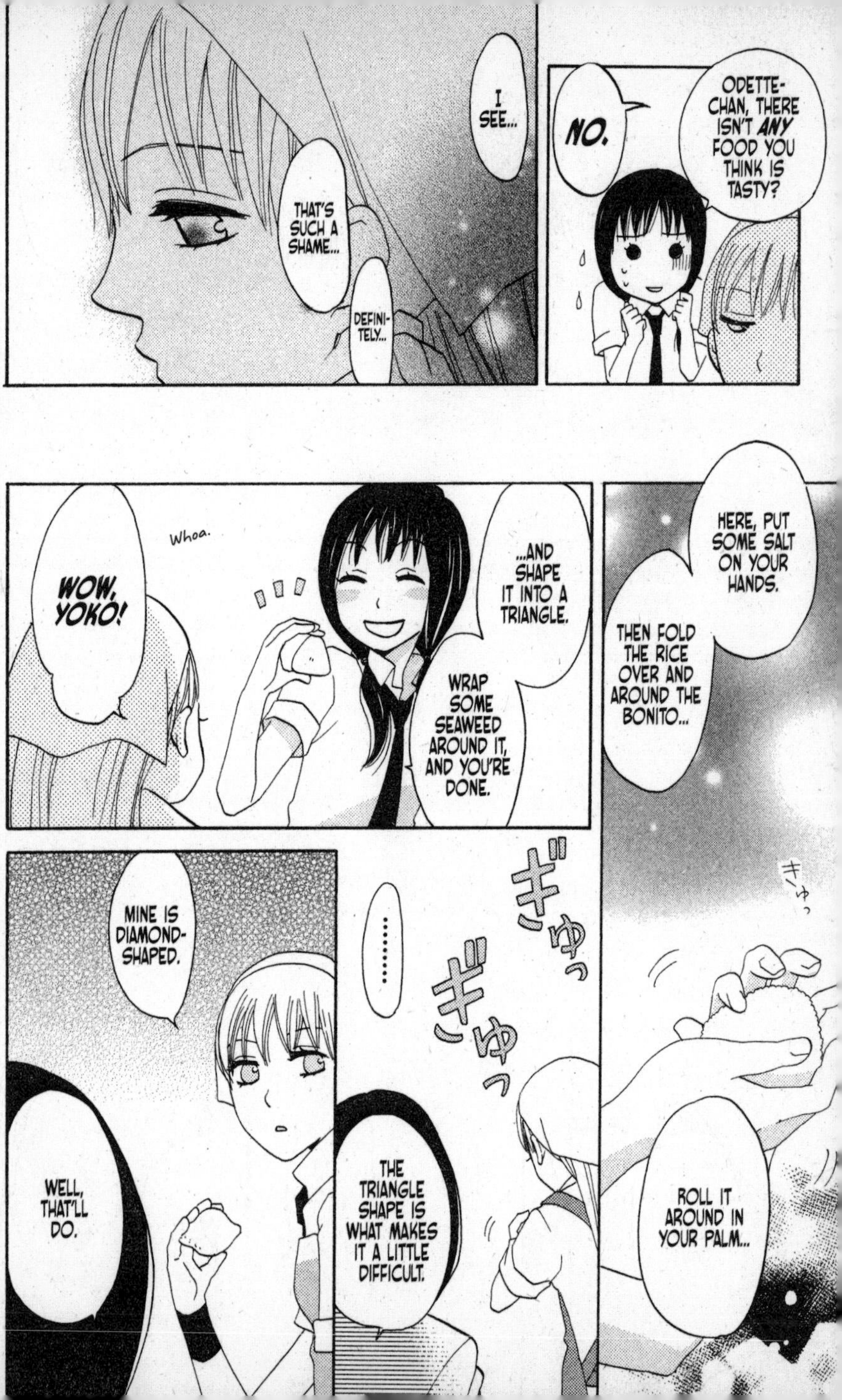
ODETTE-CHAN, THERE ISN'T ANY FOOD YOU THINK IS TASTY?
NO.
I SEE...
THAT'S SUCH A SHAME...
DEFINITELY...
HERE, PUT SOME SALT ON YOUR HANDS.
THEN FOLD THE RICE OVER AND AROUND THE BONITO...
きゅっ
ROLL IT AROUND IN YOUR PALM...
...AND SHAPE IT INTO A TRIANGLE.
WRAP SOME SEAWEED AROUND IT, AND YOU'RE DONE.
Whoa.
WOW, YOKO!
ぎゅっ
ぎゅっ
THE TRIANGLE SHAPE IS WHAT MAKES IT A LITTLE DIFFICULT.
......
MINE IS DIAMOND-SHAPED.
WELL, THAT'LL DO.

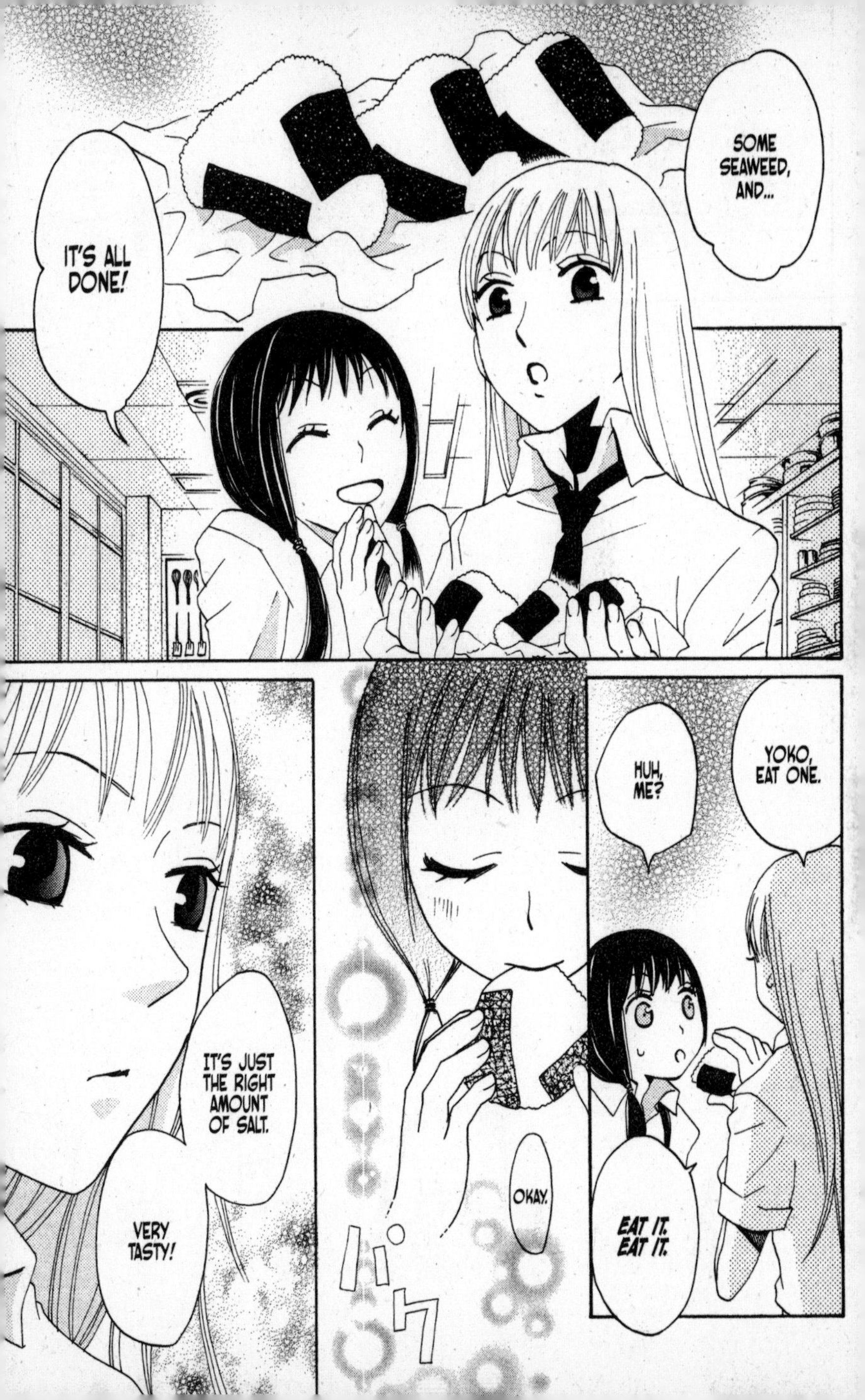
SOME SEAWEED, AND...
IT'S ALL DONE!
YOKO, EAT ONE.
HUH, ME?
EAT IT. EAT IT.
OKAY.
パク
IT'S JUST THE RIGHT AMOUNT OF SALT.
VERY TASTY!

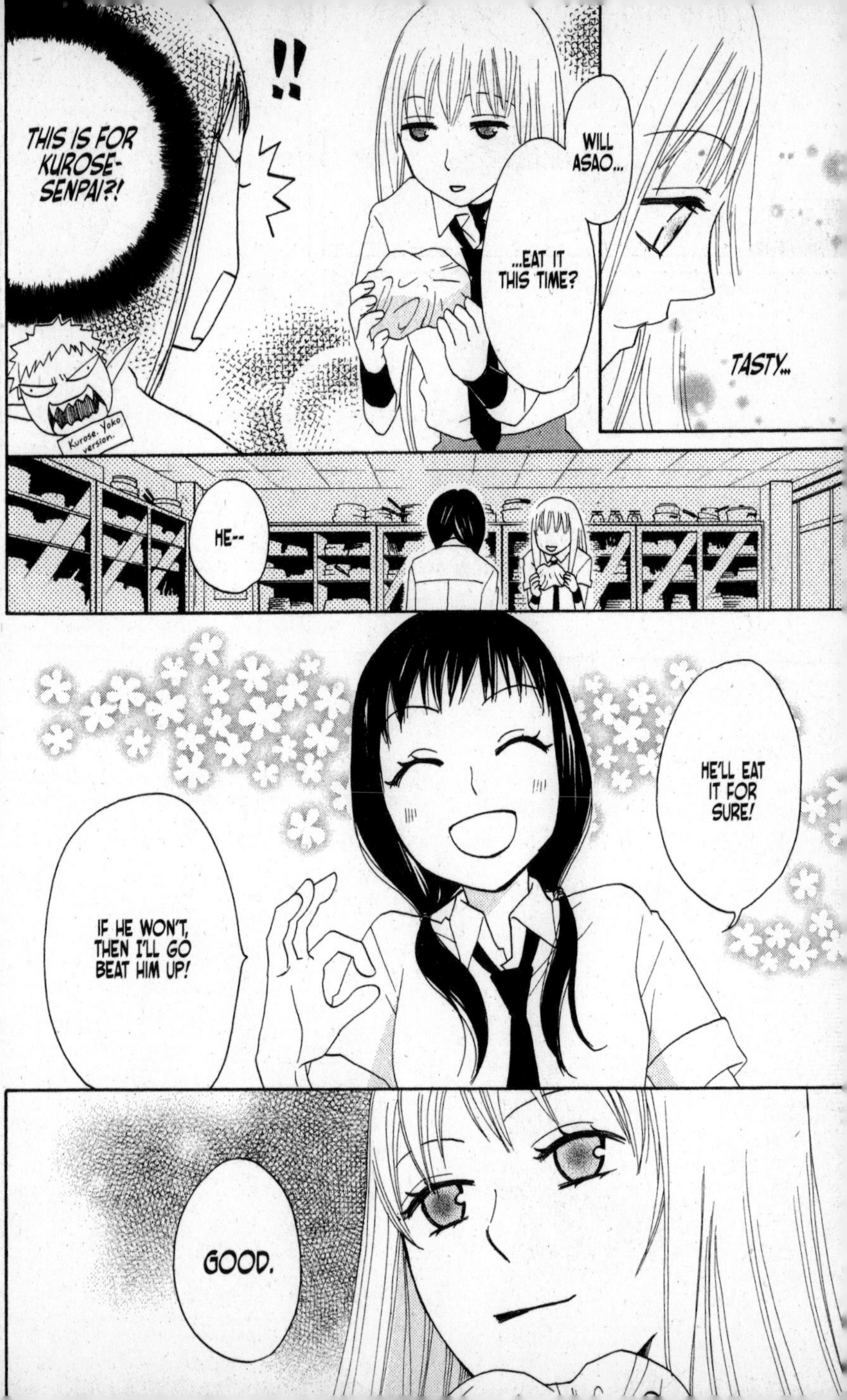
TASTY...
WILL ASAO...
...EAT IT THIS TIME?
!!
THIS IS FOR KUROSE-SENPAI?!
Kurose. Yoko version.
HE--
HE'LL EAT IT FOR SURE!
IF HE WON'T, THEN I'LL GO BEAT HIM UP!
GOOD.

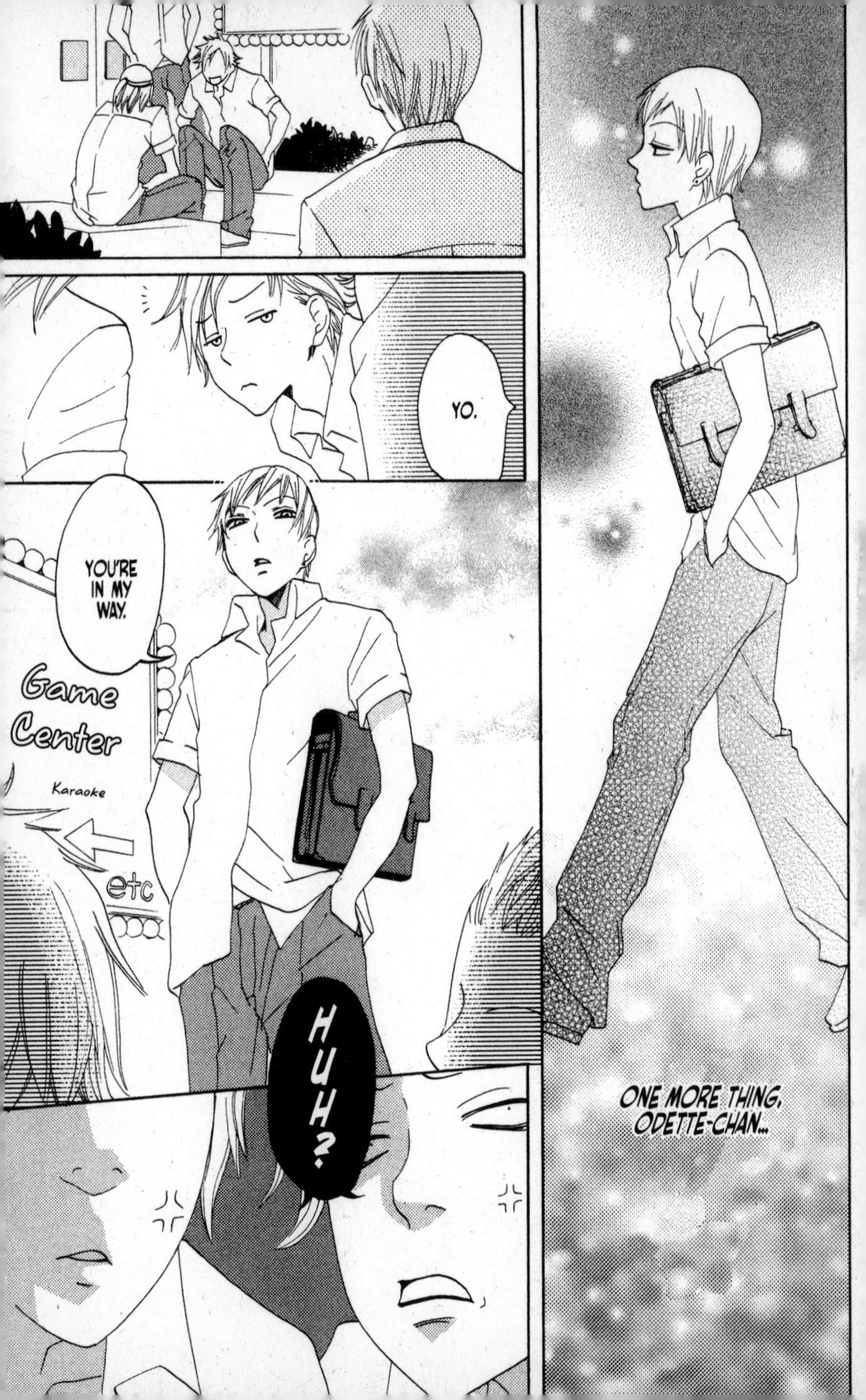
ONE MORE THING, ODETTE-CHAN...
YO.
YOU'RE IN MY WAY.
Game Center
Karaoke
etc
HUH?

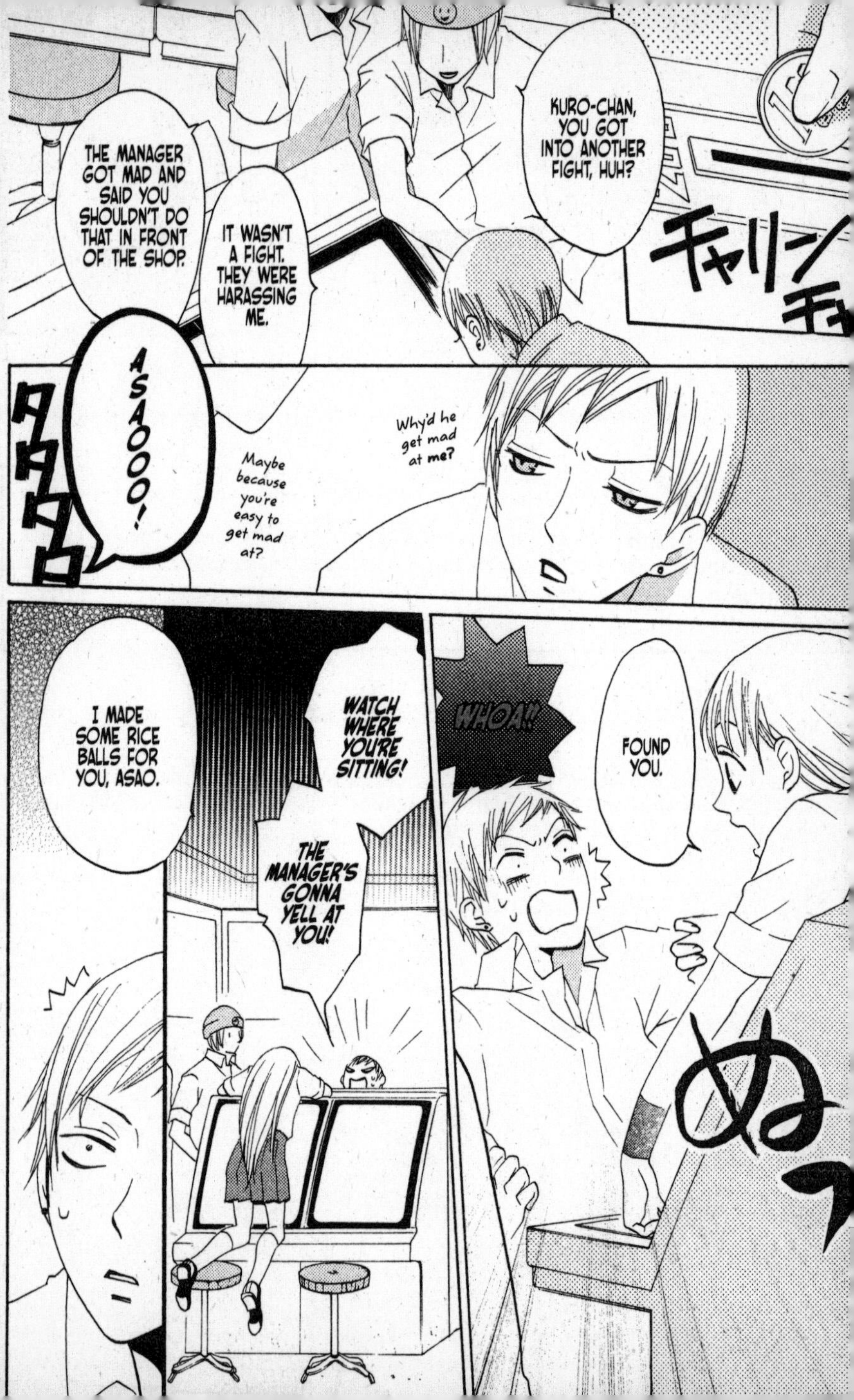
KURO-CHAN, YOU GOT INTO ANOTHER FIGHT, HUH?
チャリン
IT WASN'T A FIGHT. THEY WERE HARASSING ME.
THE MANAGER GOT MAD AND SAID YOU SHOULDN'T DO THAT IN FRONT OF THE SHOP.
Why'd he get mad at me?
Maybe because you're easy to get mad at?
ASAOOO!
FOUND YOU.
WHOA!!
ぬっ
WATCH WHERE YOU'RE SITTING!
THE MANAGER'S GONNA YELL AT YOU!
I MADE SOME RICE BALLS FOR YOU, ASAO.

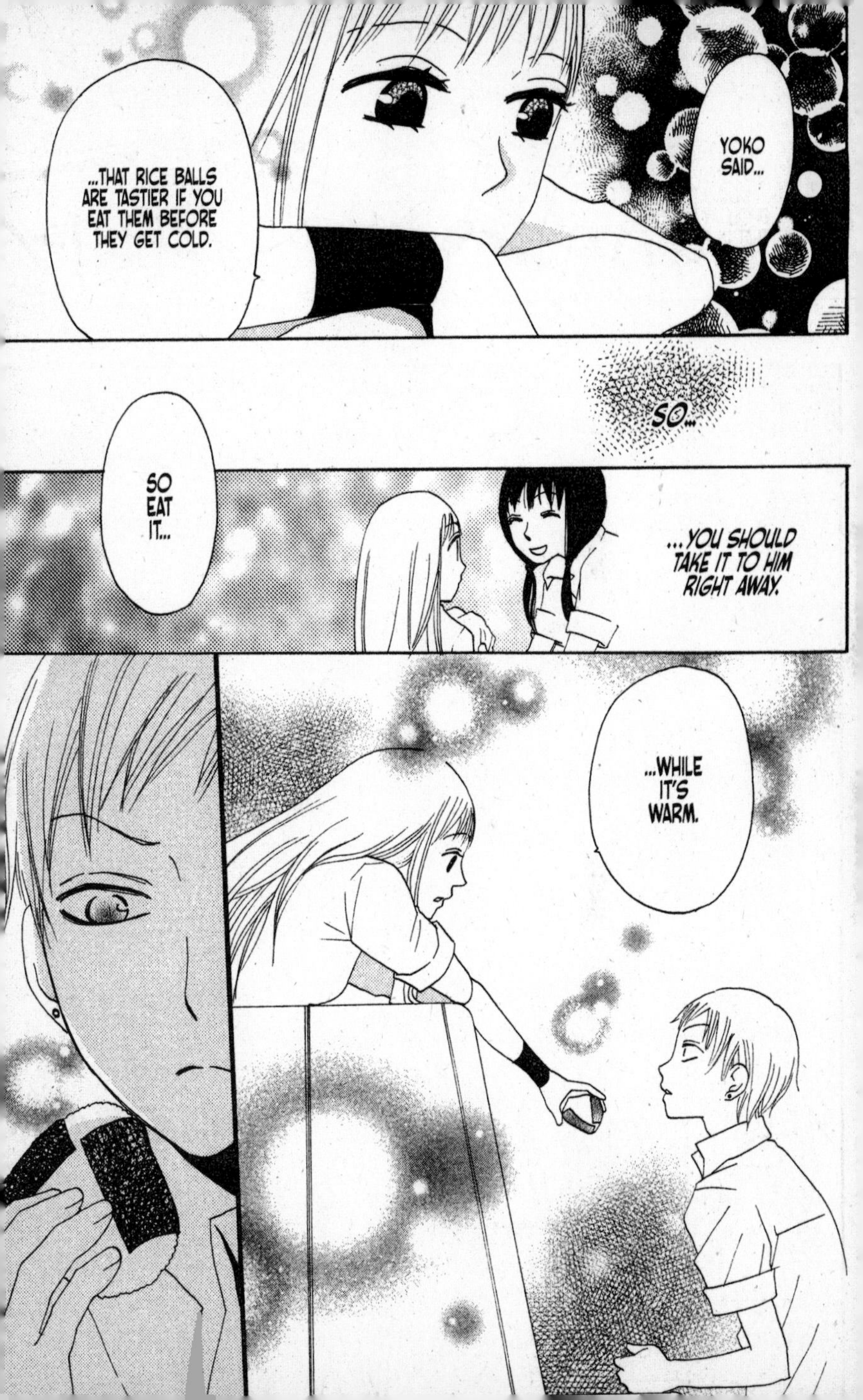
YOKO SAID...
...THAT RICE BALLS ARE TASTIER IF YOU EAT THEM BEFORE THEY GET COLD.
SO...
...YOU SHOULD TAKE IT TO HIM RIGHT AWAY.
SO EAT IT...
...WHILE IT'S WARM.

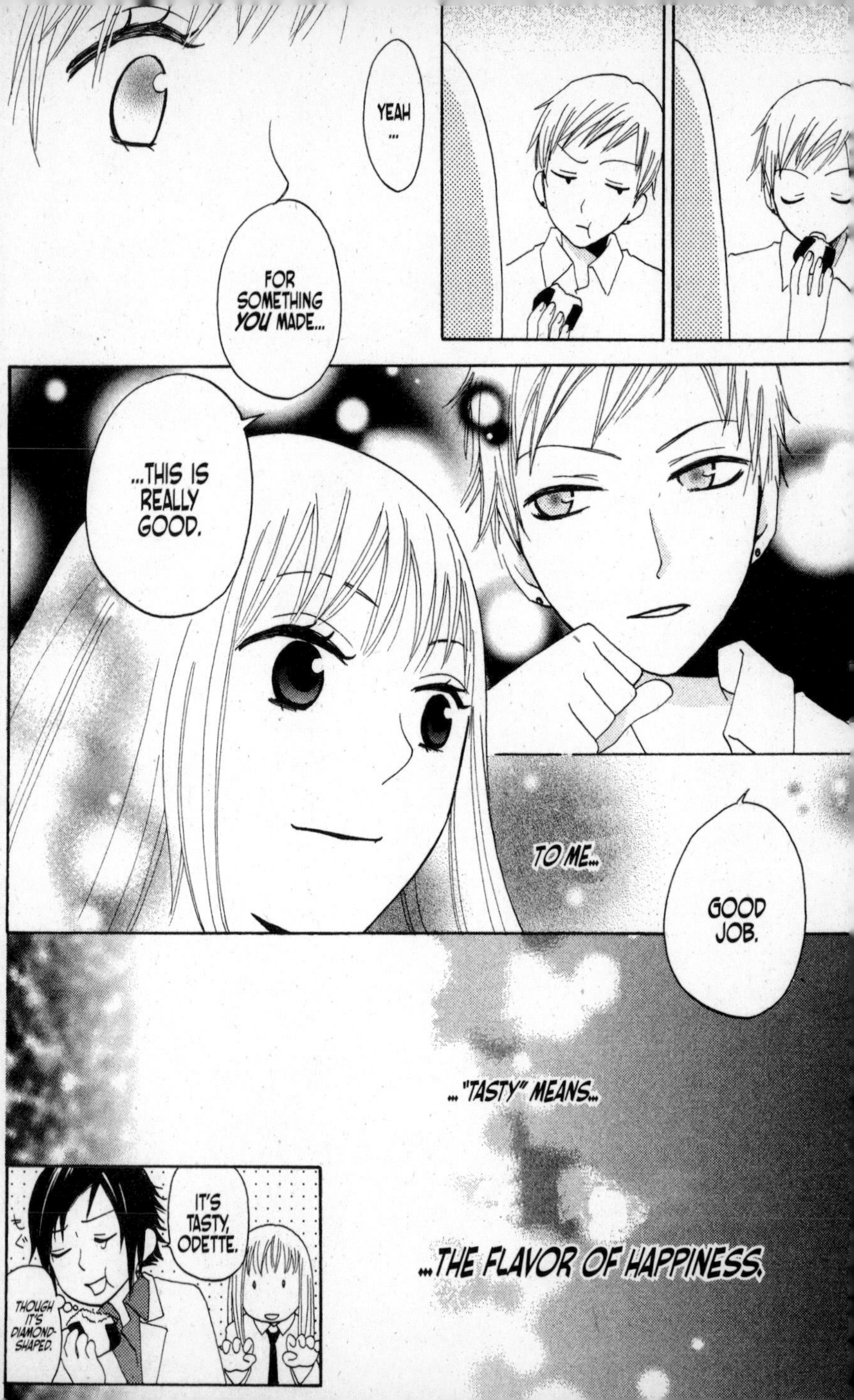
YEAH ...
FOR SOMETHING *YOU* MADE...
...THIS IS REALLY GOOD.
GOOD JOB.
TO ME...
..."TASTY" MEANS...
...THE FLAVOR OF HAPPINESS.
IT'S TASTY, ODETTE.
もぐ
THOUGH IT'S DIAMOND-SHAPED.

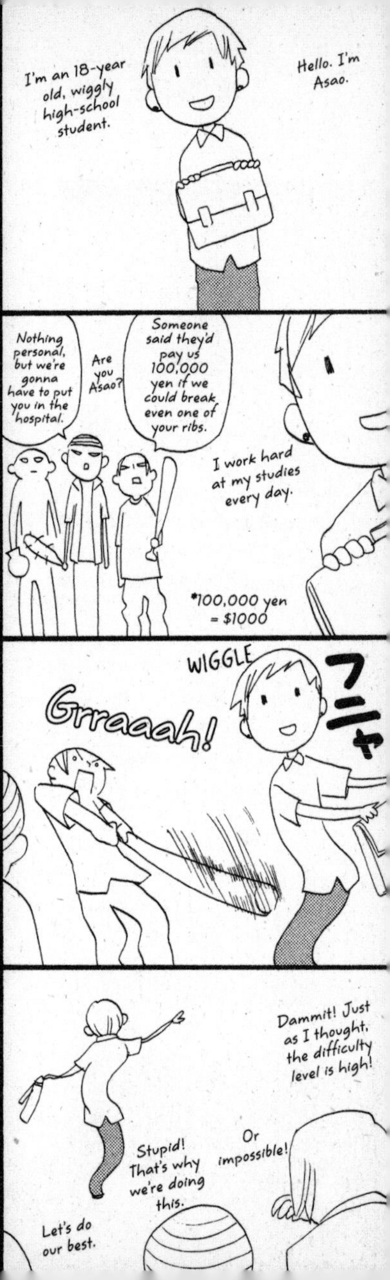
Hello. I'm Asao.
I'm an 18-year old, wiggly high-school student.
I work hard at my studies every day.
*100,000 yen = $1000
Someone said they'd pay us 100,000 yen if we could break even one of your ribs.
Are you Asao?
Nothing personal, but we're gonna have to put you in the hospital.
フニャ
WIGGLE
Grrraaah!
Dammit! Just as I thought, the difficulty level is high!
Or impossible!
Stupid! That's why we're doing this.
Let's do our best.
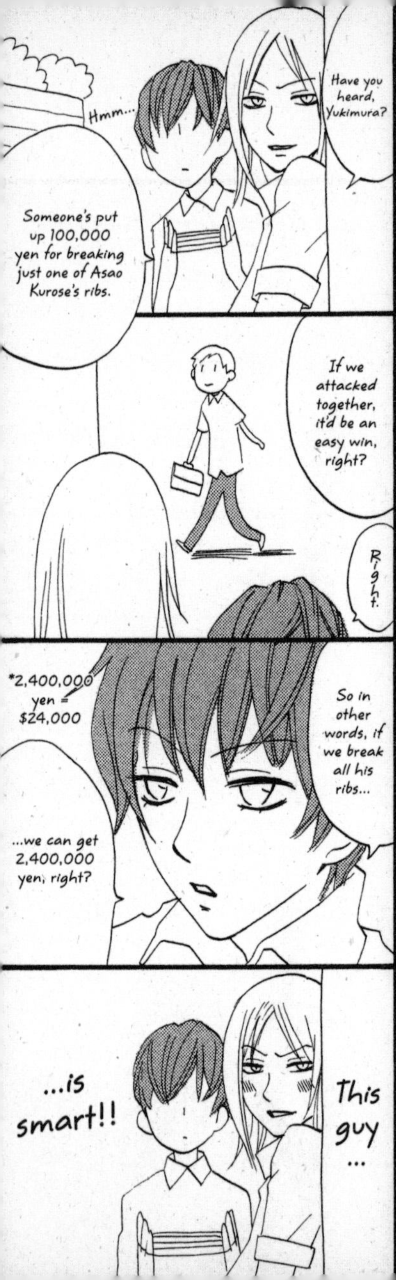
Have you heard, Yukimura?
Hmm...
Someone's put up 100,000 yen for breaking just one of Asao Kurose's ribs.
If we attacked together, it'd be an easy win, right?
Right.
So in other words, if we break all his ribs...
...we can get 2,400,000 yen, right?
*2,400,000 yen = $24,000
This guy...
...is smart!!

Chapter 11

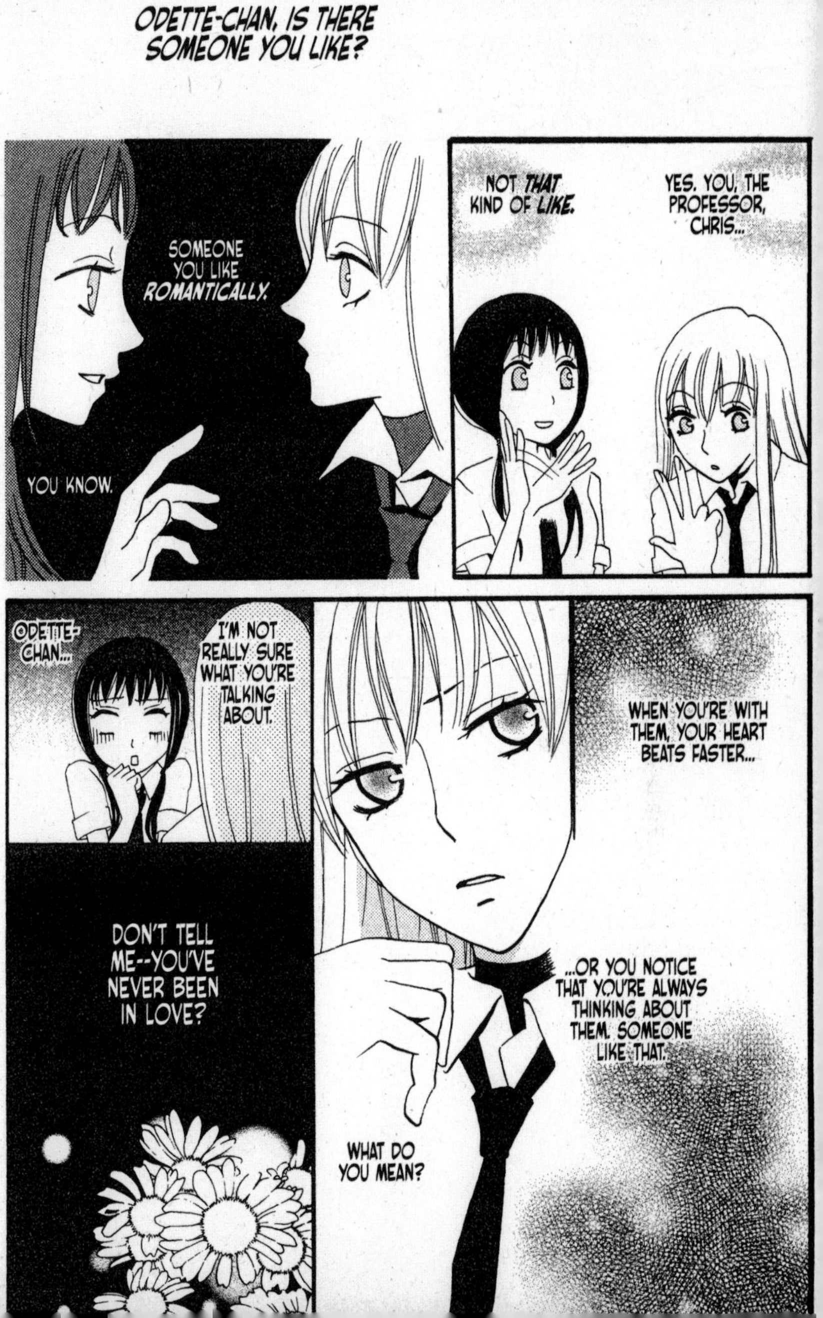
ODETTE-CHAN, IS THERE SOMEONE YOU LIKE?
YES. YOU, THE PROFESSOR, CHRIS...
NOT THAT KIND OF LIKE.
SOMEONE YOU LIKE ROMANTICALLY.
YOU KNOW.
WHEN YOU'RE WITH THEM, YOUR HEART BEATS FASTER...
...OR YOU NOTICE THAT YOU'RE ALWAYS THINKING ABOUT THEM. SOMEONE LIKE THAT.
WHAT DO YOU MEAN?
I'M NOT REALLY SURE WHAT YOU'RE TALKING ABOUT.
ODETTE-CHAN...
DON'T TELL ME--YOU'VE NEVER BEEN IN LOVE?

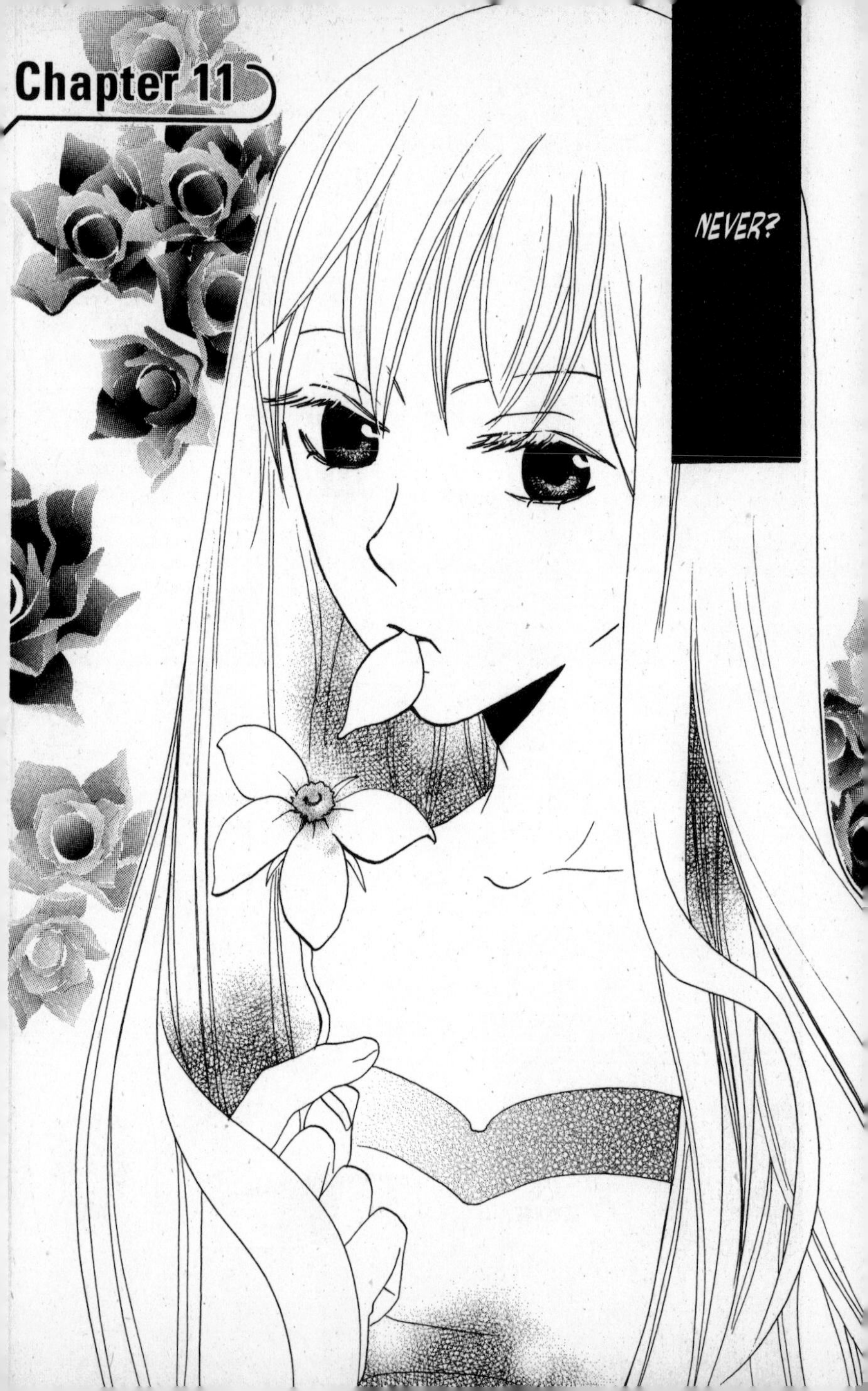

Chapter 11
NEVER?

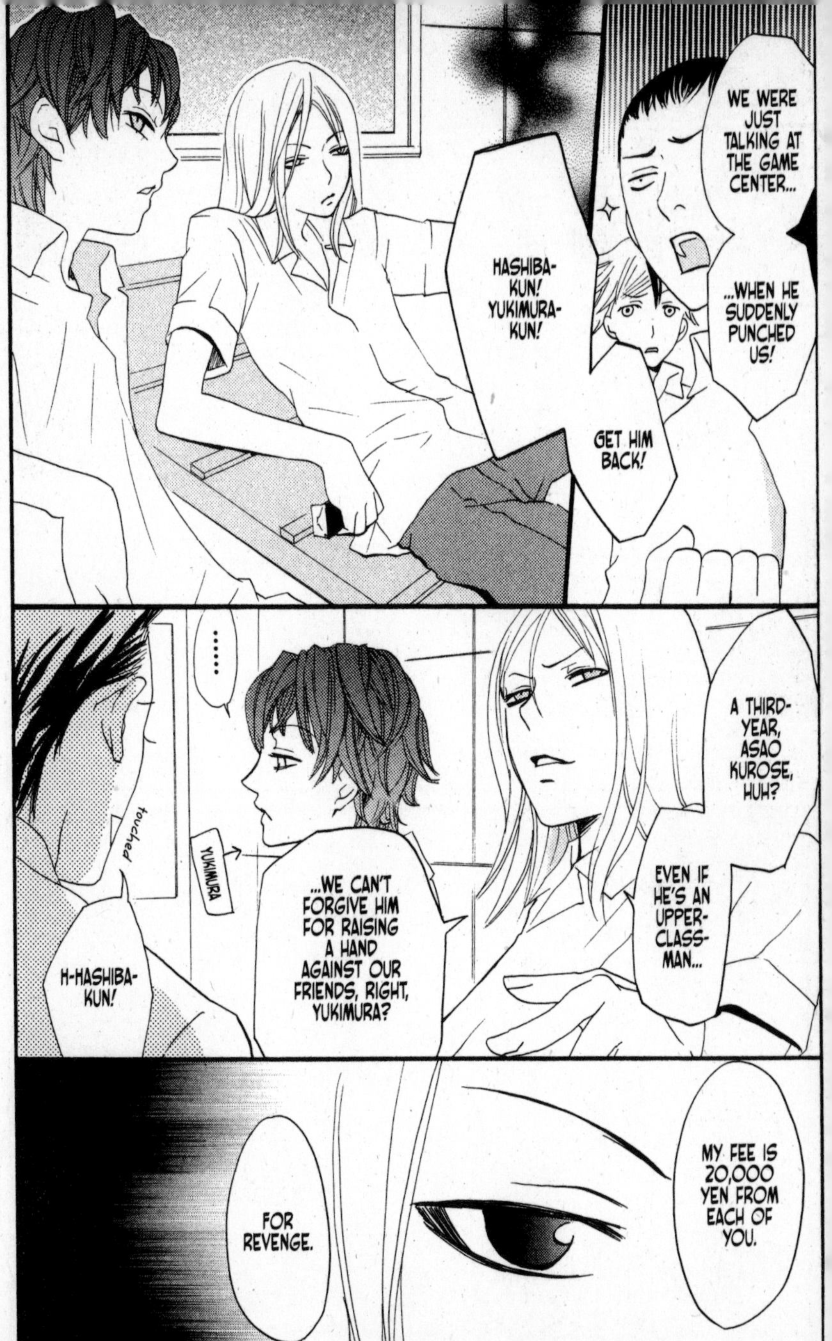
WE WERE JUST TALKING AT THE GAME CENTER...
...WHEN HE SUDDENLY PUNCHED US!
HASHIBA-KUN! YUKIMURA-KUN!
GET HIM BACK!
A THIRD-YEAR, ASAO KUROSE, HUH?
EVEN IF HE'S AN UPPER-CLASS-MAN...
...WE CAN'T FORGIVE HIM FOR RAISING A HAND AGAINST OUR FRIENDS, RIGHT, YUKIMURA?
YUKIMURA
......
touched
H-HASHIBA-KUN!
MY FEE IS 20,000 YEN FROM EACH OF YOU.
FOR REVENGE.

*20,000 yen = $200

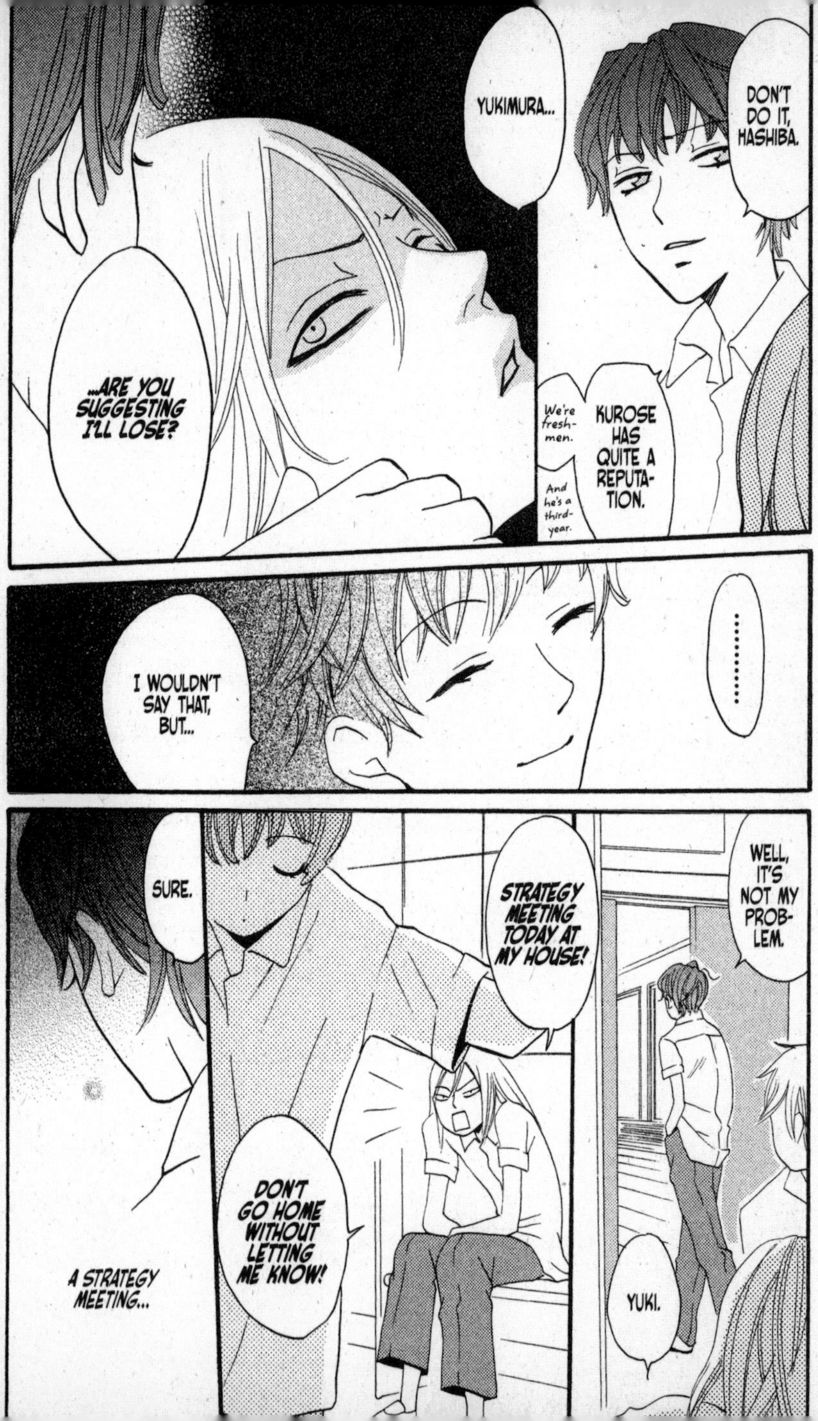
DON'T DO IT, HASHIBA.
KUROSE HAS QUITE A REPUTATION.
We're freshmen.
And he's a third-year.
YUKIMURA...
...ARE YOU SUGGESTING I'LL LOSE?
......
I WOULDN'T SAY THAT, BUT...
WELL, IT'S NOT MY PROBLEM.
YUKI.
STRATEGY MEETING TODAY AT MY HOUSE!
DON'T GO HOME WITHOUT LETTING ME KNOW!
SURE.
A STRATEGY MEETING...

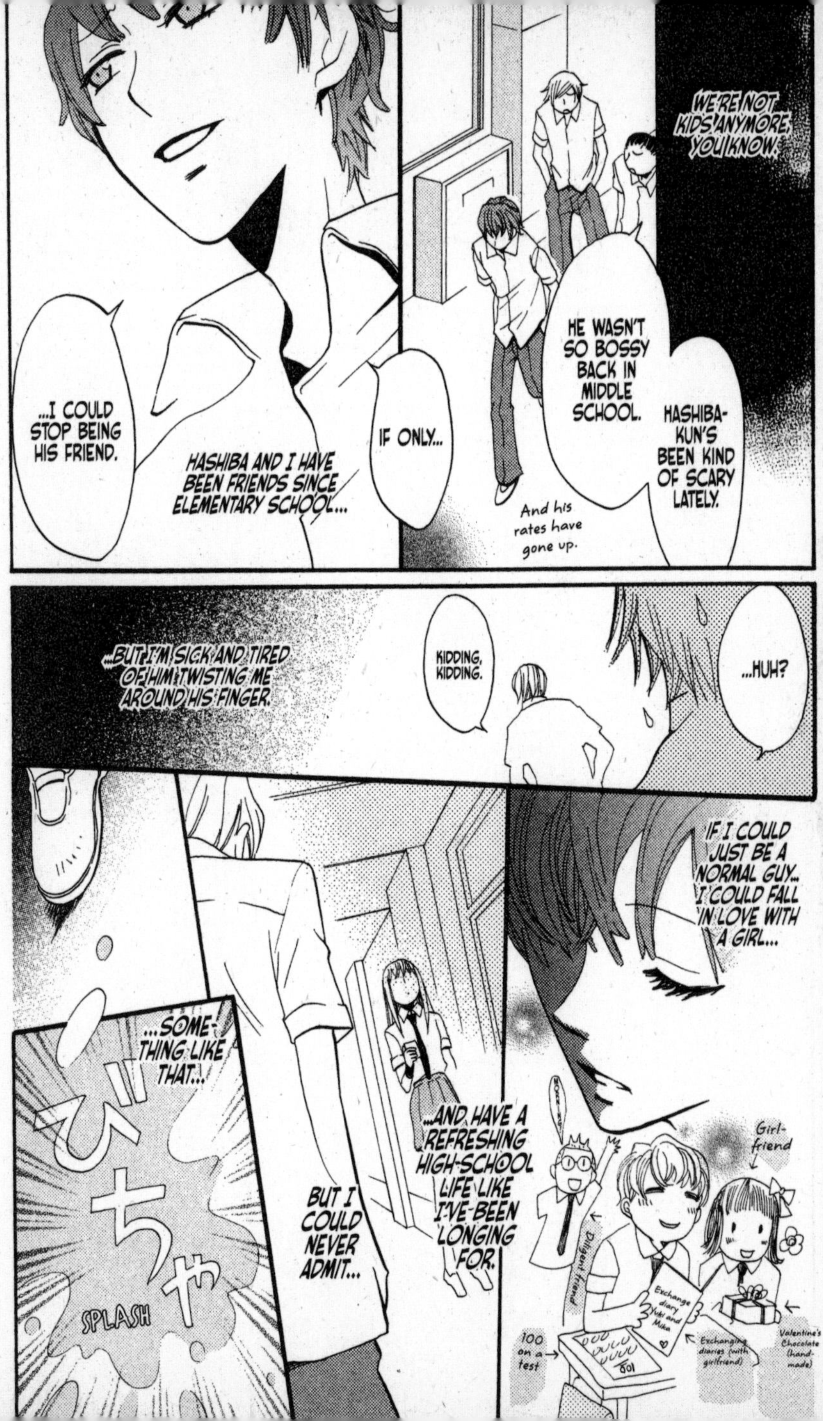
WE'RE NOT KIDS ANYMORE, YOU KNOW.
HASHIBA-KUN'S BEEN KIND OF SCARY LATELY.
HE WASN'T SO BOSSY BACK IN MIDDLE SCHOOL.
And his rates have gone up.
IF ONLY...
HASHIBA AND I HAVE BEEN FRIENDS SINCE ELEMENTARY SCHOOL...
...I COULD STOP BEING HIS FRIEND.
...HUH?
KIDDING, KIDDING.
...BUT I'M SICK AND TIRED OF HIM TWISTING ME AROUND HIS FINGER.
IF I COULD JUST BE A NORMAL GUY... I COULD FALL IN LOVE WITH A GIRL...
Girl-friend
Diligent friend
Exchange diary Yuki and Mika
Valentine's Chocolate (hand-made)
Exchanging diaries (with girlfriend)
100 on a test
...AND HAVE A REFRESHING HIGH-SCHOOL LIFE LIKE I'VE BEEN LONGING FOR.
BUT I COULD NEVER ADMIT...
...SOME-THING LIKE THAT...
びちゃ
SPLASH

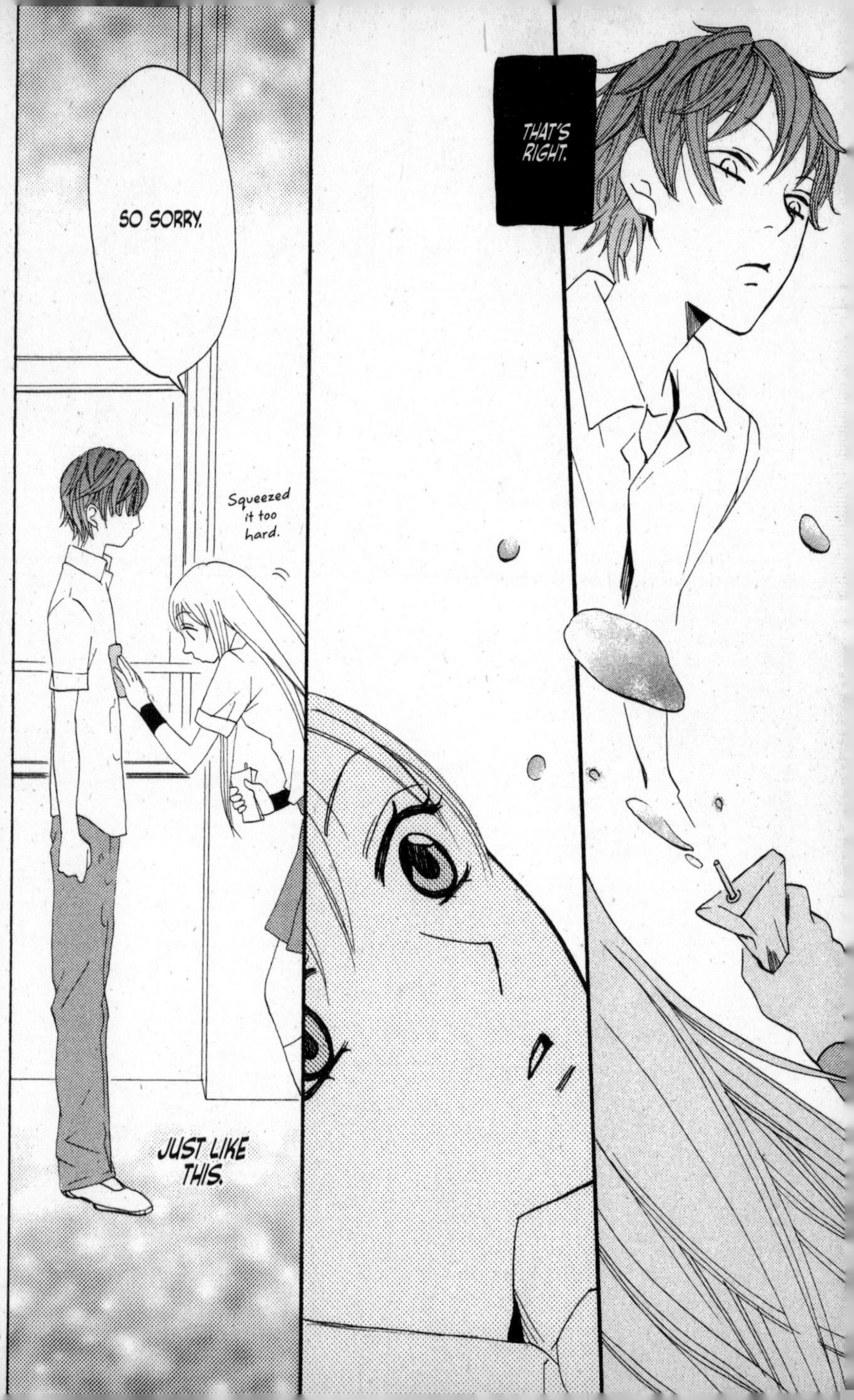
THAT'S RIGHT.
SO SORRY.
Squeezed it too hard.
JUST LIKE THIS.

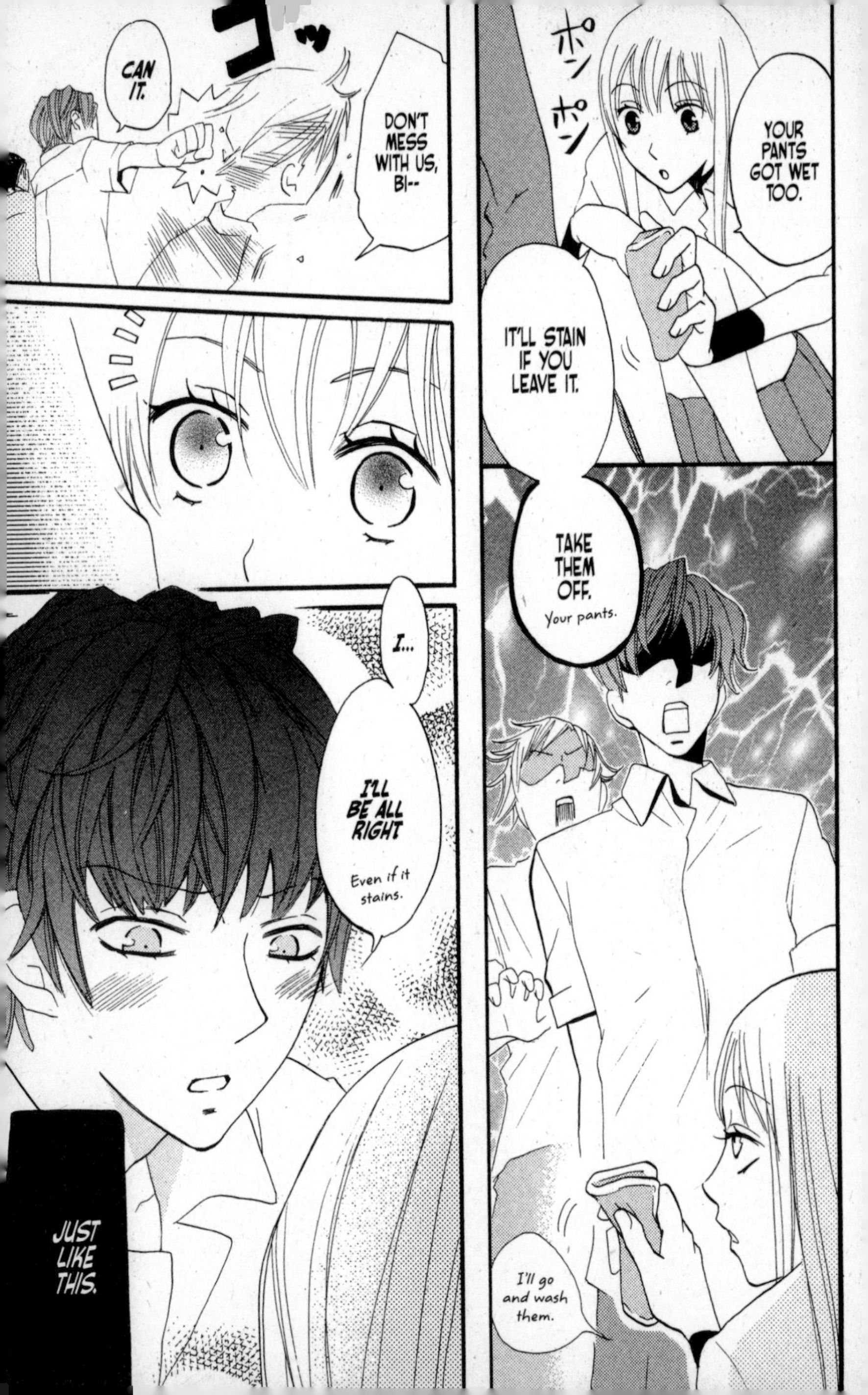
ポン
ポン
YOUR PANTS GOT WET TOO.
IT'LL STAIN IF YOU LEAVE IT.
TAKE THEM OFF.
Your pants.
I'll go and wash them.
ゴッ
DON'T MESS WITH US, BI--
CAN IT.
I...
I'LL BE ALL RIGHT
Even if it stains.
JUST LIKE THIS.

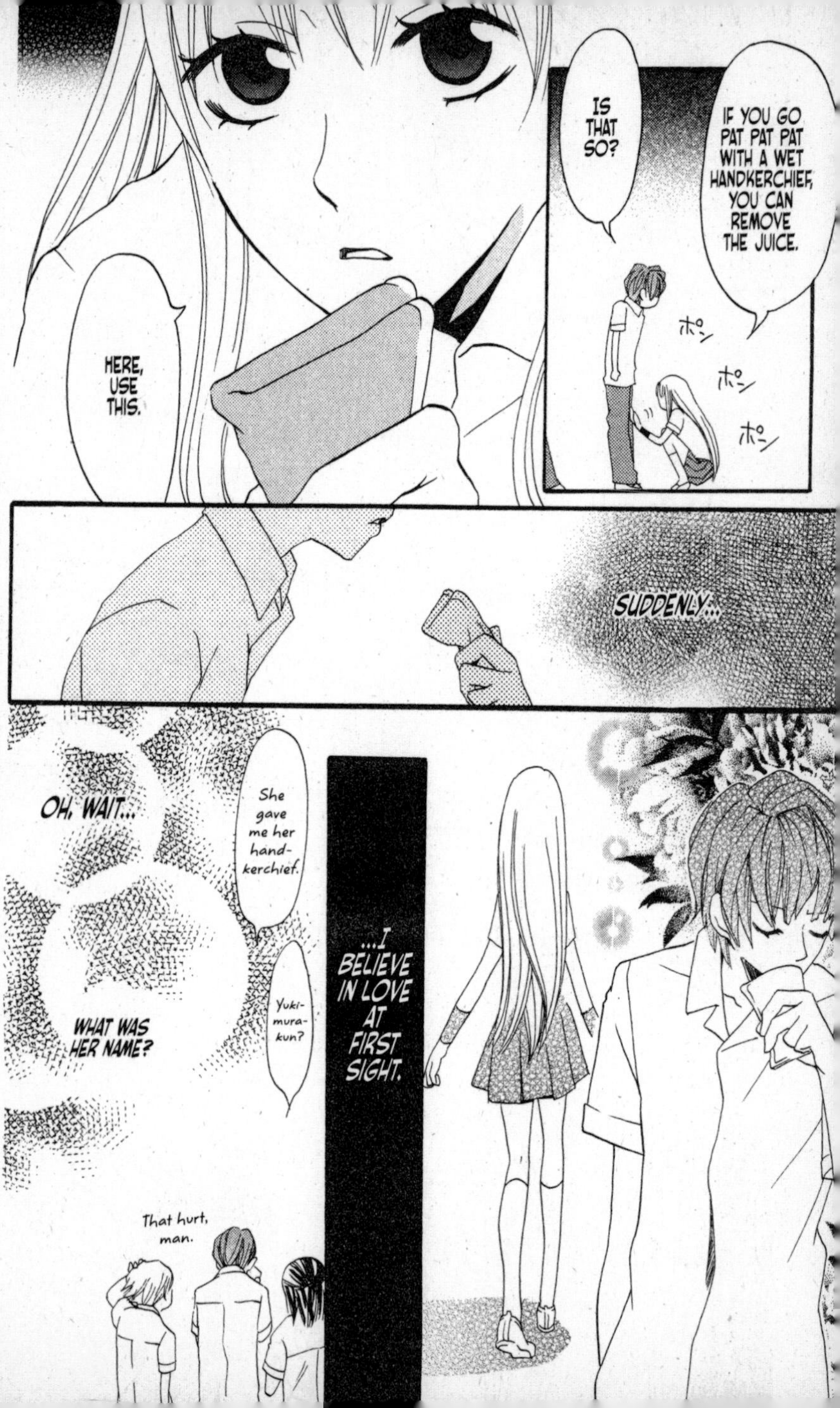
IF YOU GO PAT PAT PAT WITH A WET HANDKERCHIEF, YOU CAN REMOVE THE JUICE.
IS THAT SO?
ポン
ポン
ポン
HERE, USE THIS.
SUDDENLY...
...I BELIEVE IN LOVE AT FIRST SIGHT.
She gave me her hand-kerchief.
Yuki-mura-kun?
OH, WAIT...
WHAT WAS HER NAME?
That hurt, man.

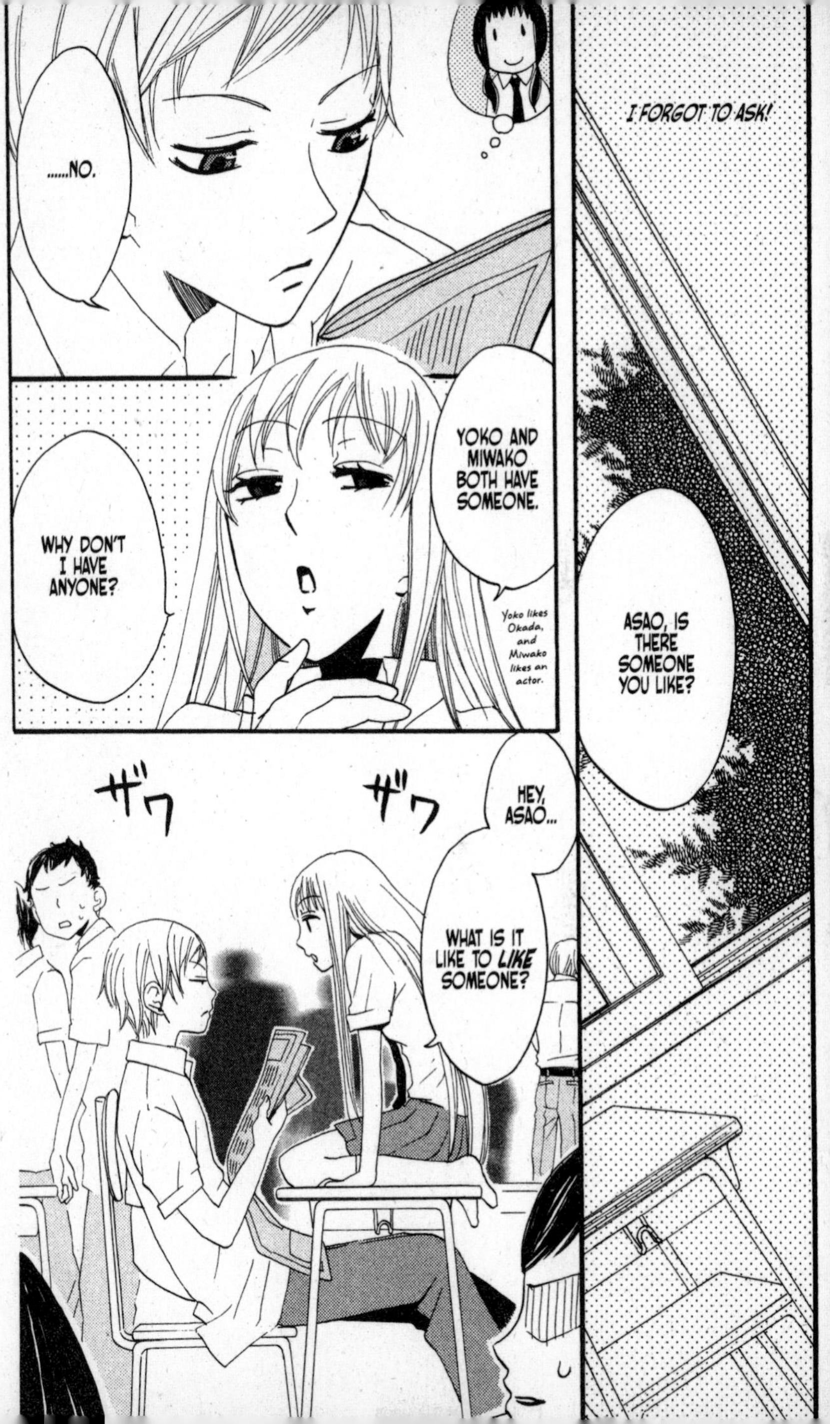
I FORGOT TO ASK!
ASAO, IS THERE SOMEONE YOU LIKE?
......NO.
YOKO AND MIWAKO BOTH HAVE SOMEONE.
Yoko likes Okada, and Miwako likes an actor.
WHY DON'T I HAVE ANYONE?
ザワ
ザワ
HEY, ASAO...
WHAT IS IT LIKE TO *LIKE* SOMEONE?

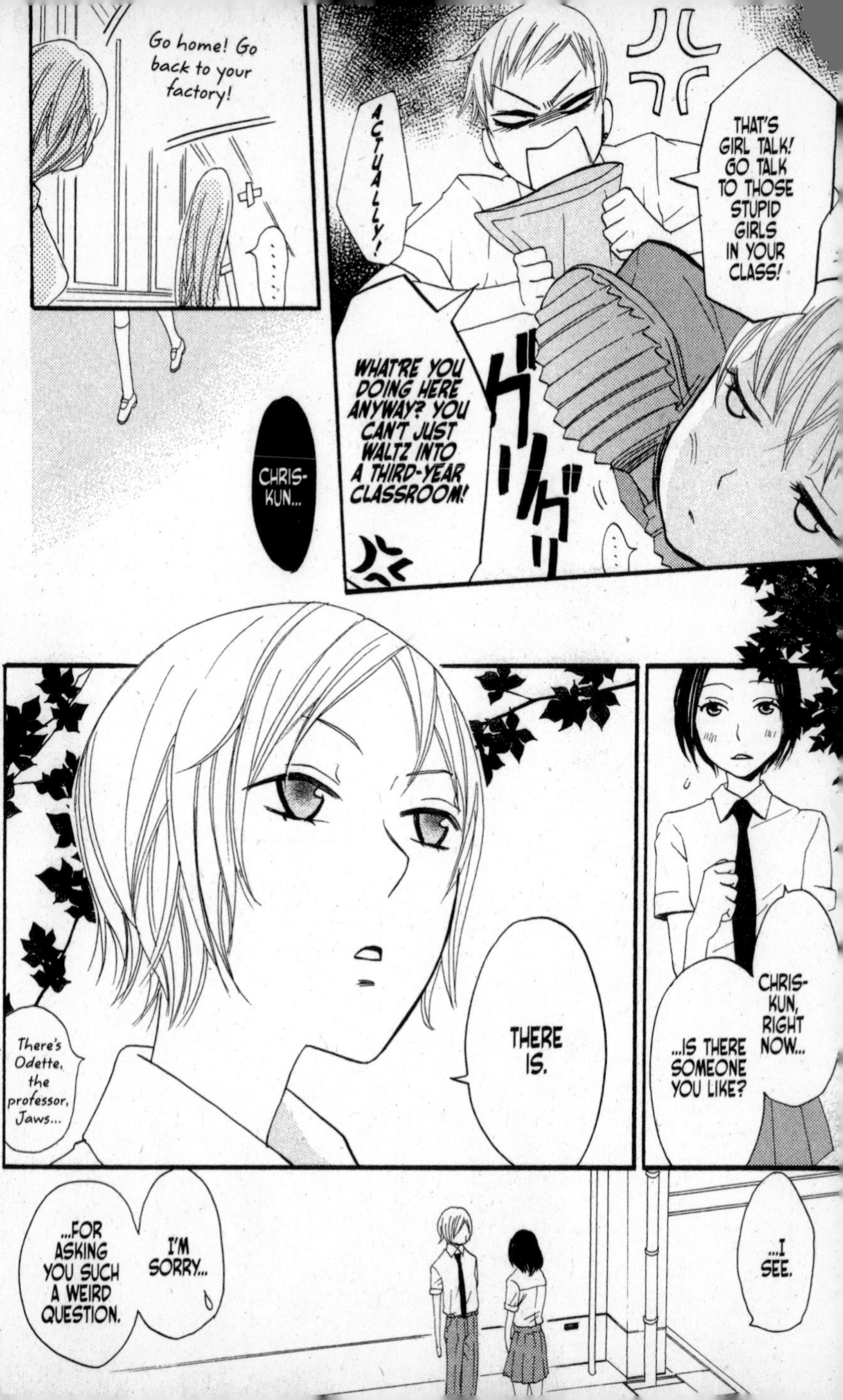
THAT'S GIRL TALK! GO TALK TO THOSE STUPID GIRLS IN YOUR CLASS!
ACTUALLY!
WHAT'RE YOU DOING HERE ANYWAY? YOU CAN'T JUST WALTZ INTO A THIRD-YEAR CLASSROOM!
Go home! Go back to your factory!
CHRIS-KUN...
CHRIS-KUN, RIGHT NOW...
...IS THERE SOMEONE YOU LIKE?
THERE IS.
There's Odette, the professor, Jaws...
...I SEE.
I'M SORRY...
...FOR ASKING YOU SUCH A WEIRD QUESTION.

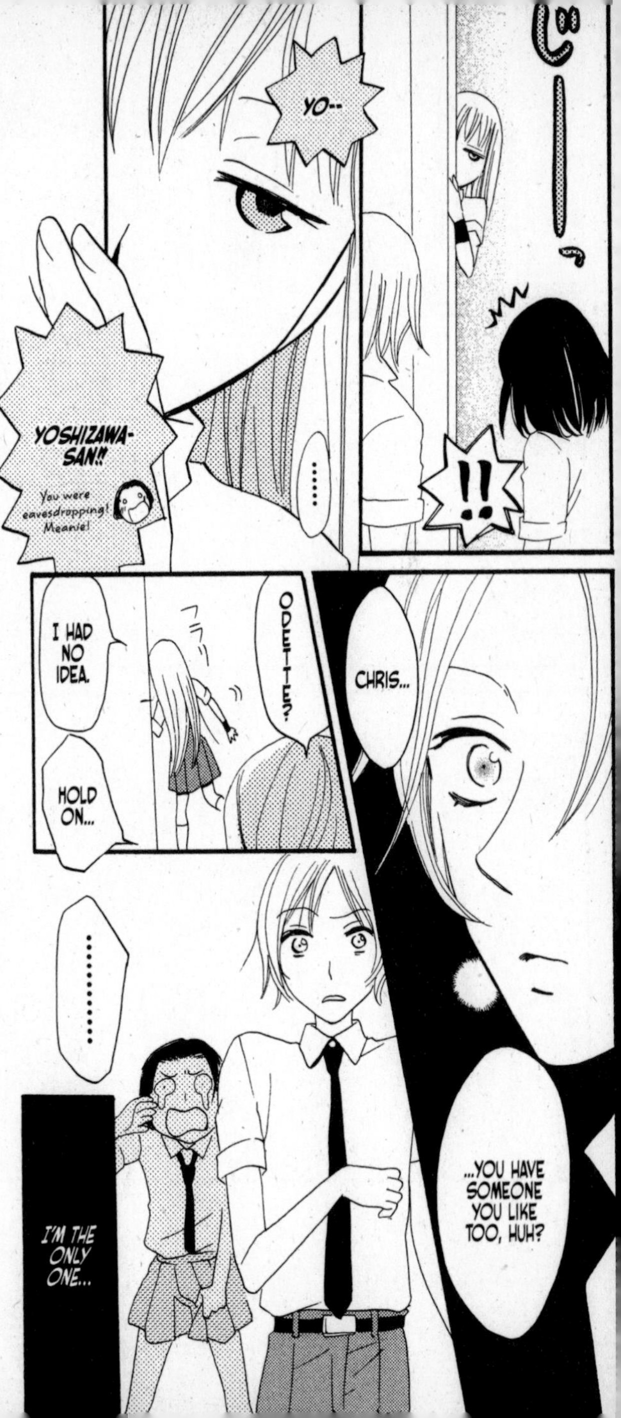
じー
!!
YO--
YOSHIZAWA-SAN!!
You were eavesdropping! Meanie!
......
CHRIS...
...YOU HAVE SOMEONE YOU LIKE TOO, HUH?
ODETTE?
フラ
I HAD NO IDEA.
HOLD ON...
....
I'M THE ONLY ONE...

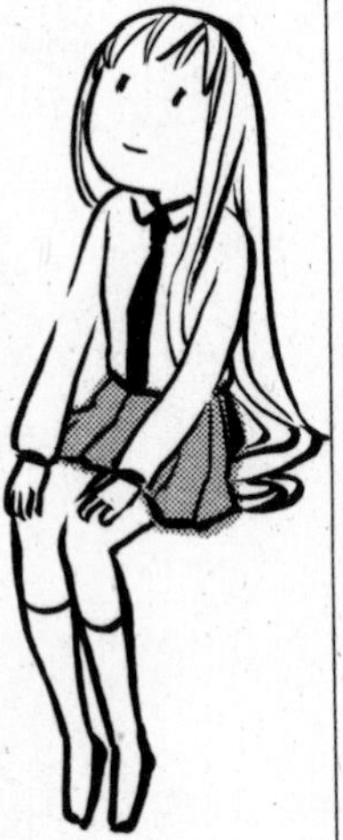

We have come to the last sidebar. After writing enough manga for these two volumes, I took a vacation to Kyoto. It was soooooo much fun. I hope I can go back someday! See you again in the next volume!

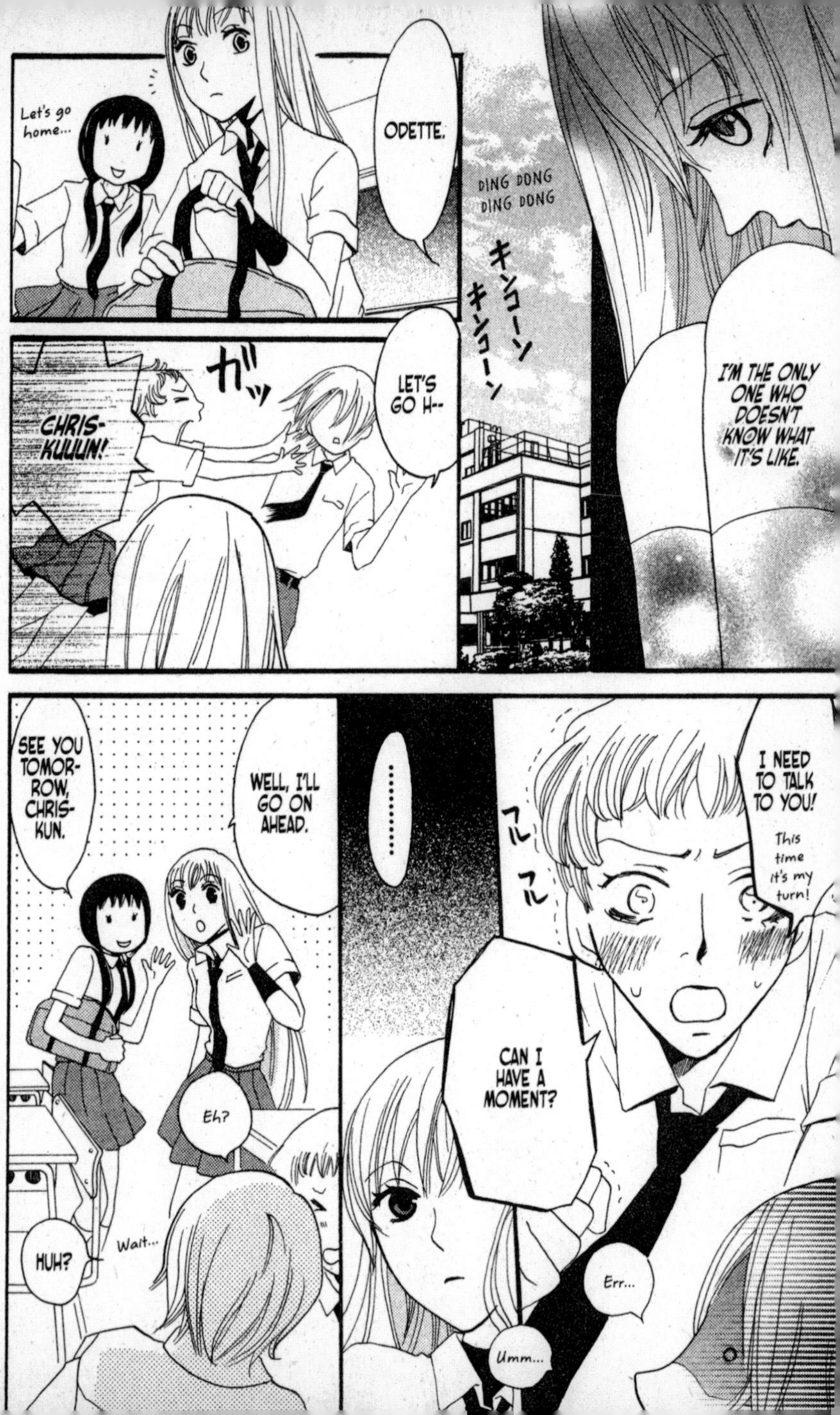

I'M THE ONLY ONE WHO DOESN'T KNOW WHAT IT'S LIKE.
DING DONG DING DONG
キンコーン
キンコーン
ODETTE.
Let's go home...
LET'S GO H--
ガッ
CHRIS-KUUUN!
I NEED TO TALK TO YOU!
This time it's my turn!
フル フル
CAN I HAVE A MOMENT?
Err...
Umm...
......
WELL, I'LL GO ON AHEAD.
SEE YOU TOMORROW, CHRIS-KUN.
Eh?
Wait...
HUH?

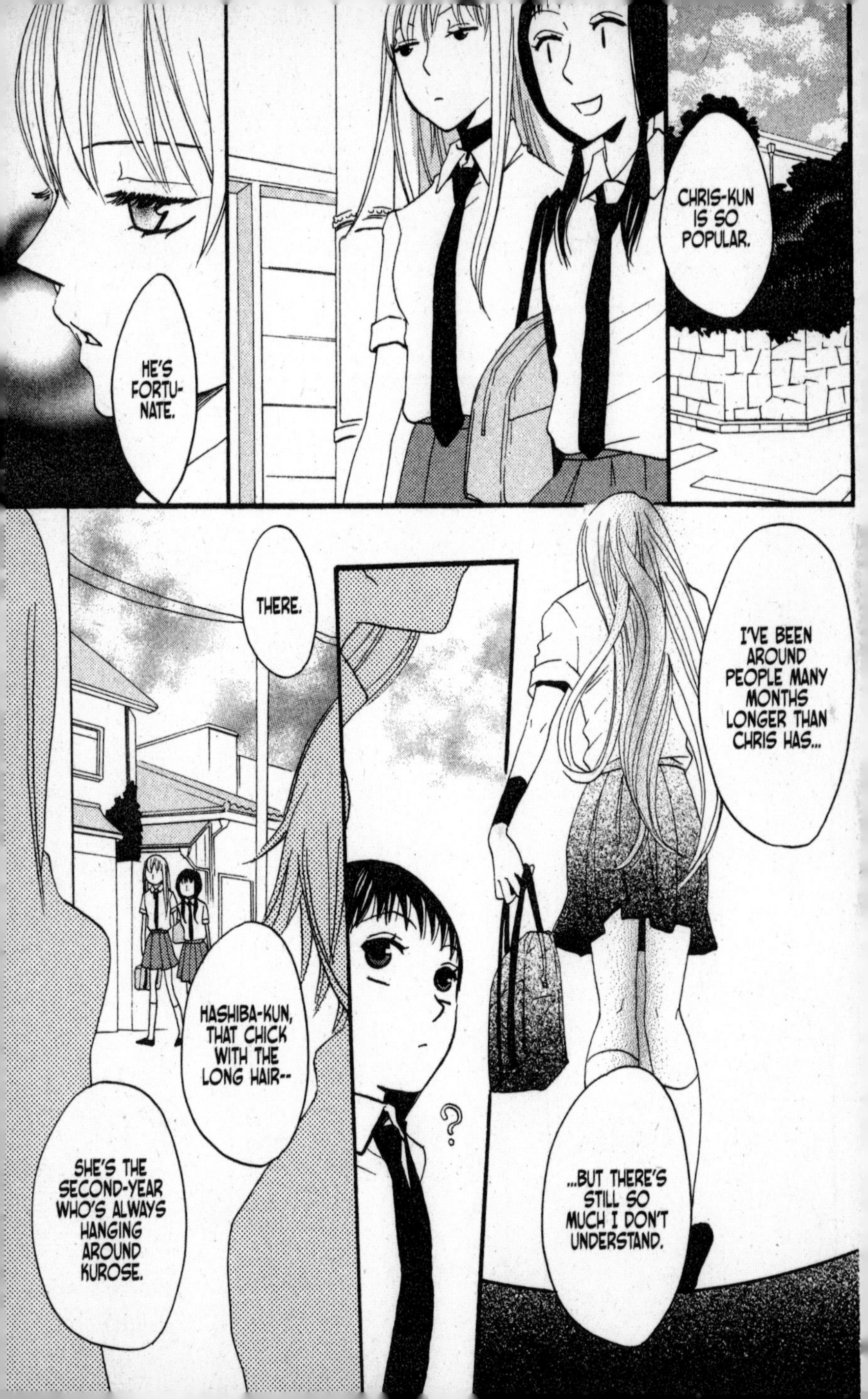
CHRIS-KUN IS SO POPULAR.
HE'S FORTU-NATE.
I'VE BEEN AROUND PEOPLE MANY MONTHS LONGER THAN CHRIS HAS...
...BUT THERE'S STILL SO MUCH I DON'T UNDERSTAND.
?
THERE.
HASHIBA-KUN, THAT CHICK WITH THE LONG HAIR--
SHE'S THE SECOND-YEAR WHO'S ALWAYS HANGING AROUND KUROSE.

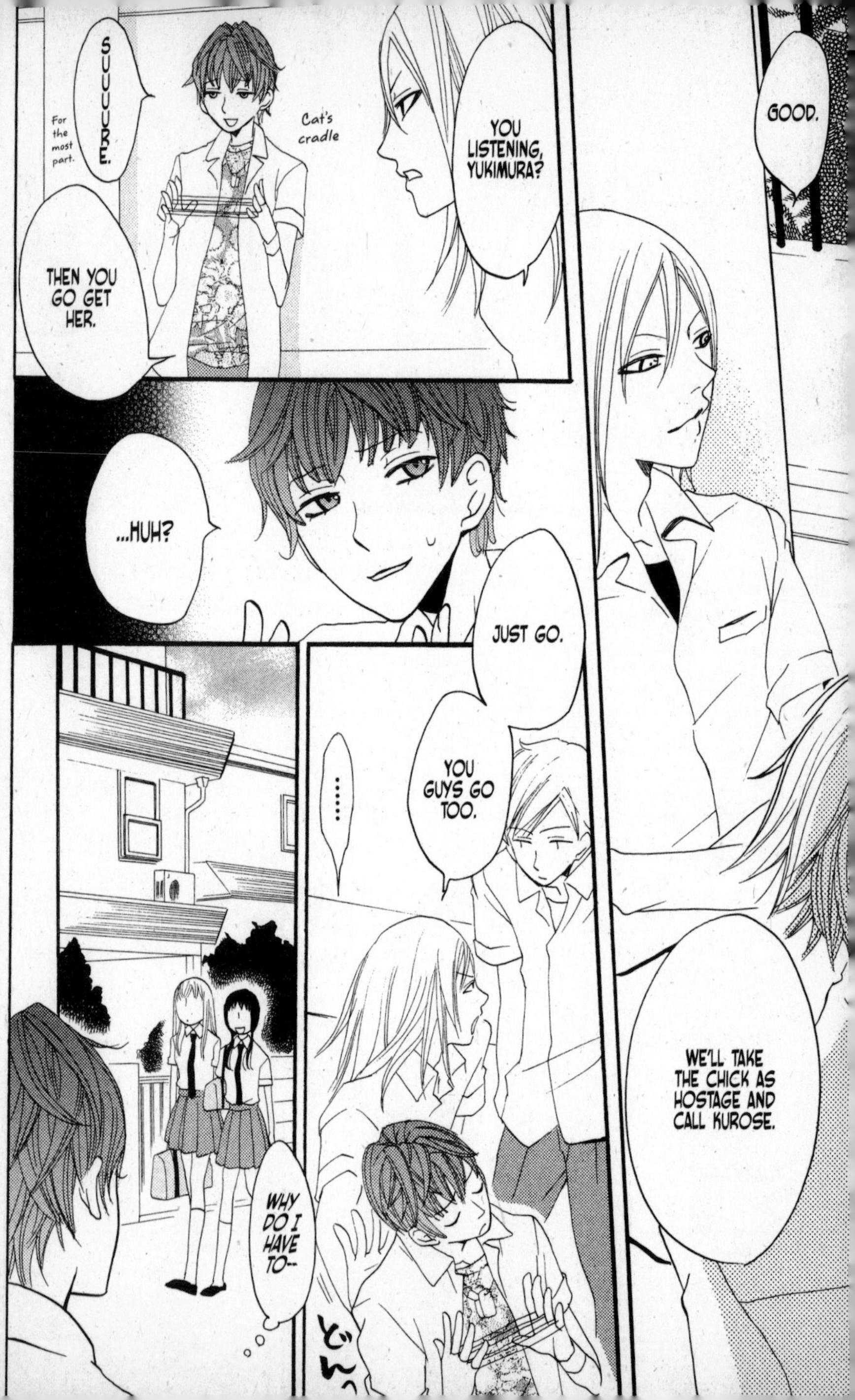
GOOD.
WE'LL TAKE THE CHICK AS HOSTAGE AND CALL KUROSE.
YOU LISTENING, YUKIMURA?
Cat's cradle
SUUUURE.
For the most part.
THEN YOU GO GET HER.
...HUH?
JUST GO.
YOU GUYS GO TOO.
......
WHY DO I HAVE TO--
どんっ

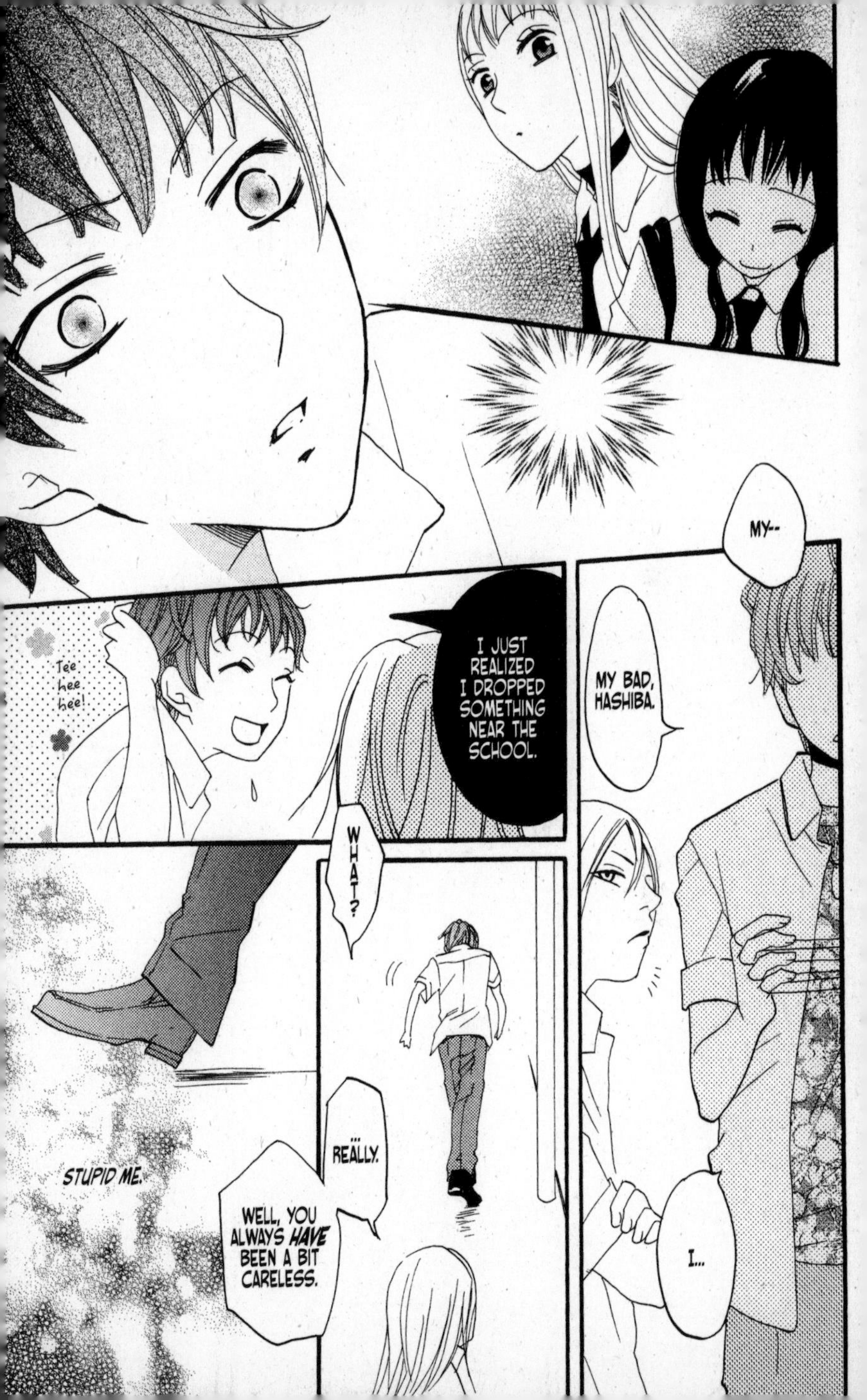
MY--
MY BAD, HASHIBA.
I...
I JUST REALIZED I DROPPED SOMETHING NEAR THE SCHOOL.
Tee hee hee!
WHAT?
...REALLY.
WELL, YOU ALWAYS *HAVE* BEEN A BIT CARELESS.
STUPID ME.

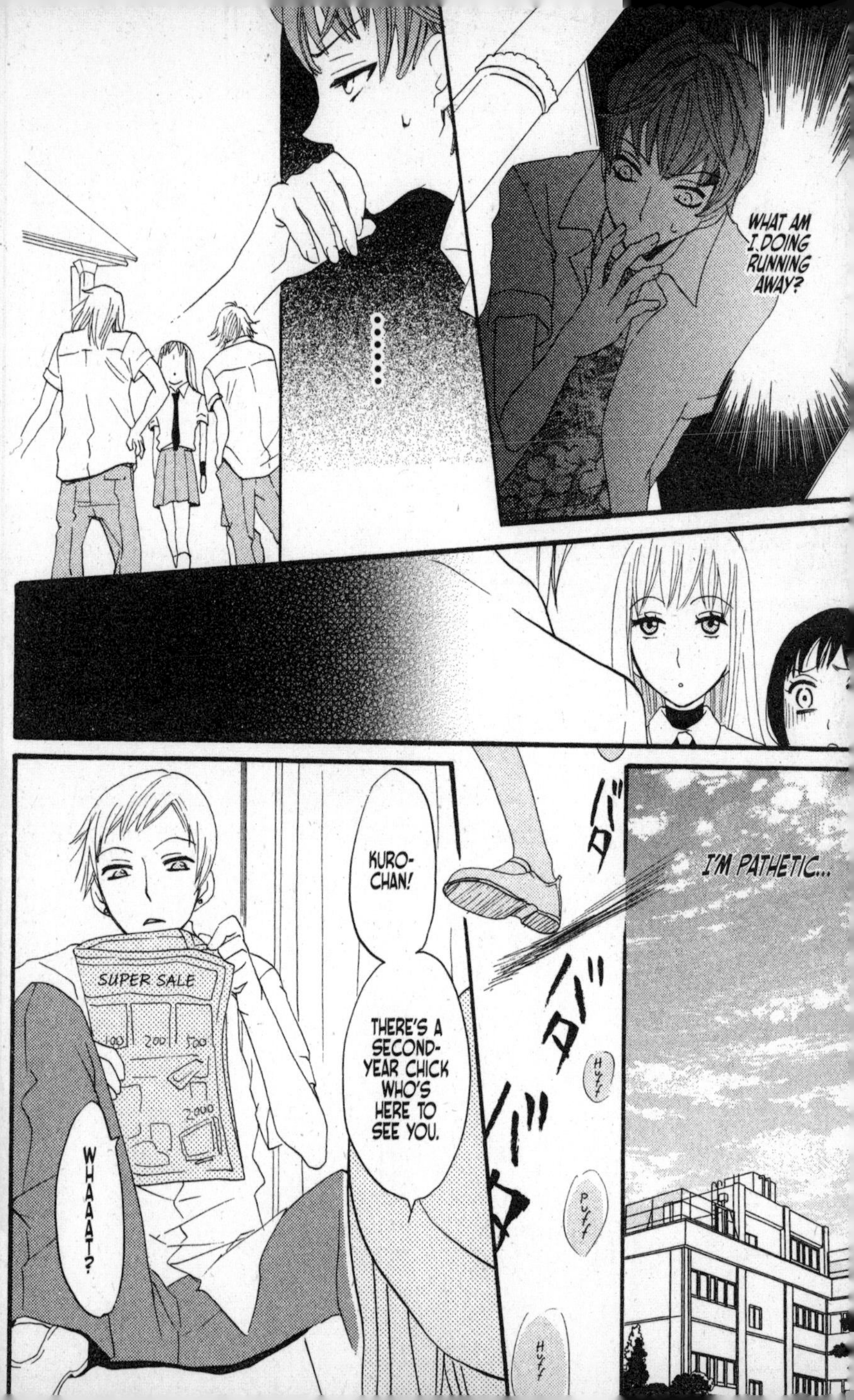
WHAT AM I DOING RUNNING AWAY?
......
I'M PATHETIC...
KURO-CHAN!
THERE'S A SECOND-YEAR CHICK WHO'S HERE TO SEE YOU.
Huff
Puff
Huff
SUPER SALE
WHAAAT?

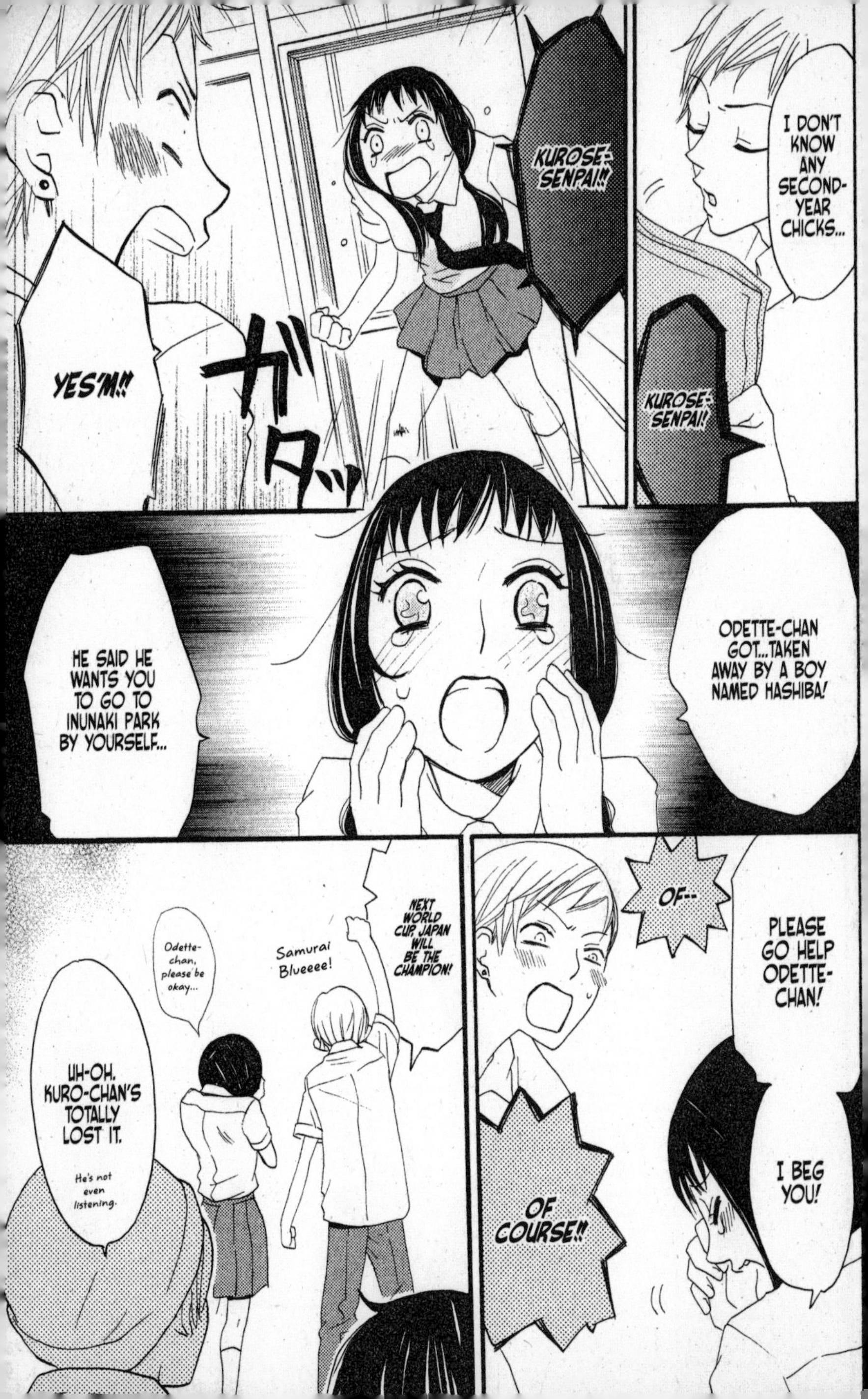
I DON'T KNOW ANY SECOND-YEAR CHICKS...
KUROSE-SENPAI!
KUROSE-SENPAI!!
ガタッ
YES'M!!
ODETTE-CHAN GOT...TAKEN AWAY BY A BOY NAMED HASHIBA!
HE SAID HE WANTS YOU TO GO TO INUNAKI PARK BY YOURSELF...
PLEASE GO HELP ODETTE-CHAN!
OF--
I BEG YOU!
OF COURSE!!
NEXT WORLD CUP, JAPAN WILL BE THE CHAMPION!
Samurai Blueeee!
Odette-chan, please be okay...
UH-OH. KURO-CHAN'S TOTALLY LOST IT.
He's not even listening.

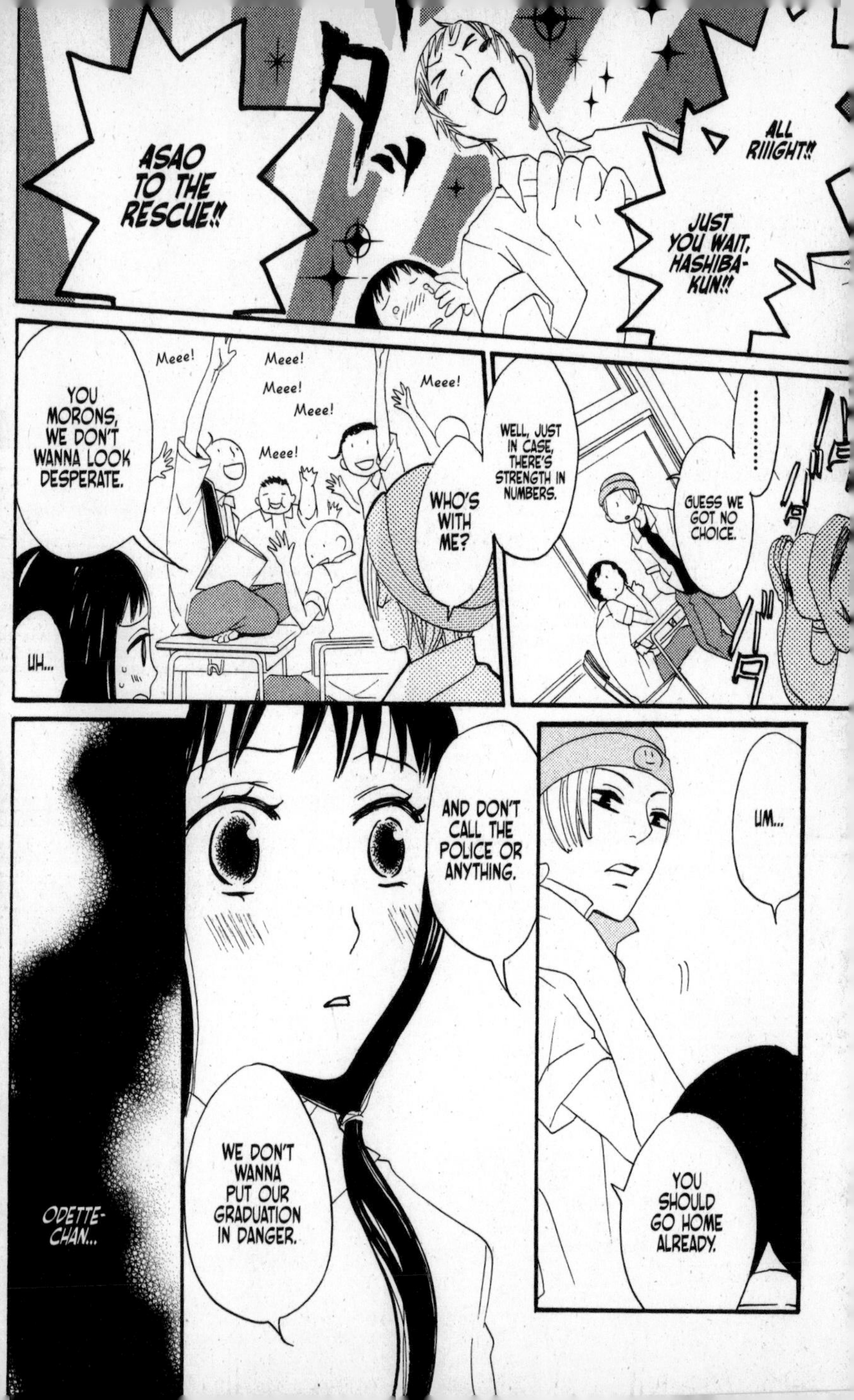
ALL RIIIGHT!!
JUST YOU WAIT, HASHIBA-KUN!!
ASAO TO THE RESCUE!!
......
GUESS WE GOT NO CHOICE.
WELL, JUST IN CASE, THERE'S STRENGTH IN NUMBERS.
WHO'S WITH ME?
Meee!
Meee!
Meee!
Meee!
Meee!
Meee!
YOU MORONS, WE DON'T WANNA LOOK DESPERATE.
UH...
UM...
YOU SHOULD GO HOME ALREADY.
AND DON'T CALL THE POLICE OR ANYTHING.
WE DON'T WANNA PUT OUR GRADUATION IN DANGER.
ODETTE-CHAN...

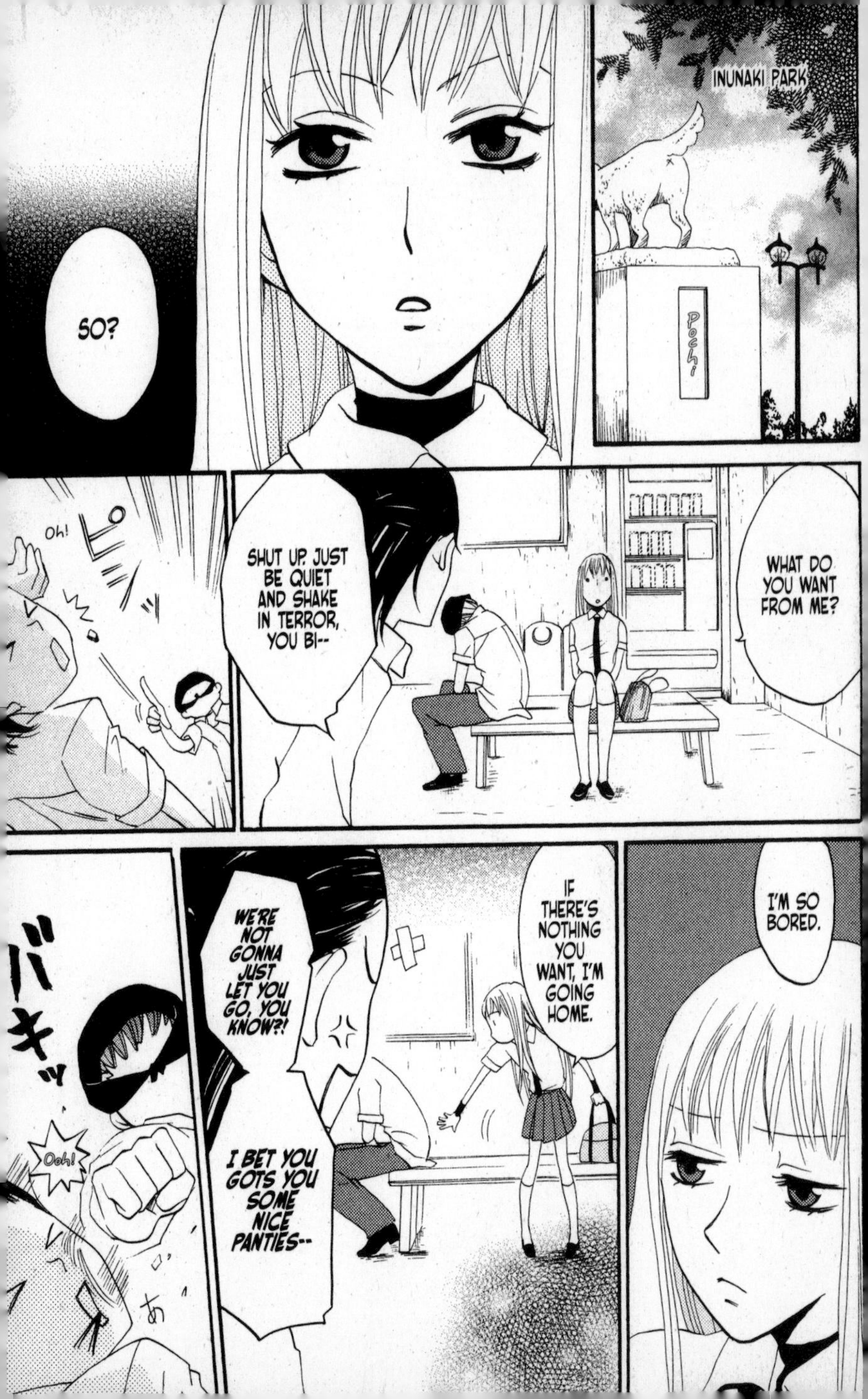
INUNAKI PARK
Pochi
SO?
WHAT DO YOU WANT FROM ME?
SHUT UP. JUST BE QUIET AND SHAKE IN TERROR, YOU BI--
Oh!
I'M SO BORED.
IF THERE'S NOTHING YOU WANT, I'M GOING HOME.
WE'RE NOT GONNA JUST LET YOU GO, YOU KNOW?!
I BET YOU GOTS YOU SOME NICE PANTIES--
バキッ
Ooh!

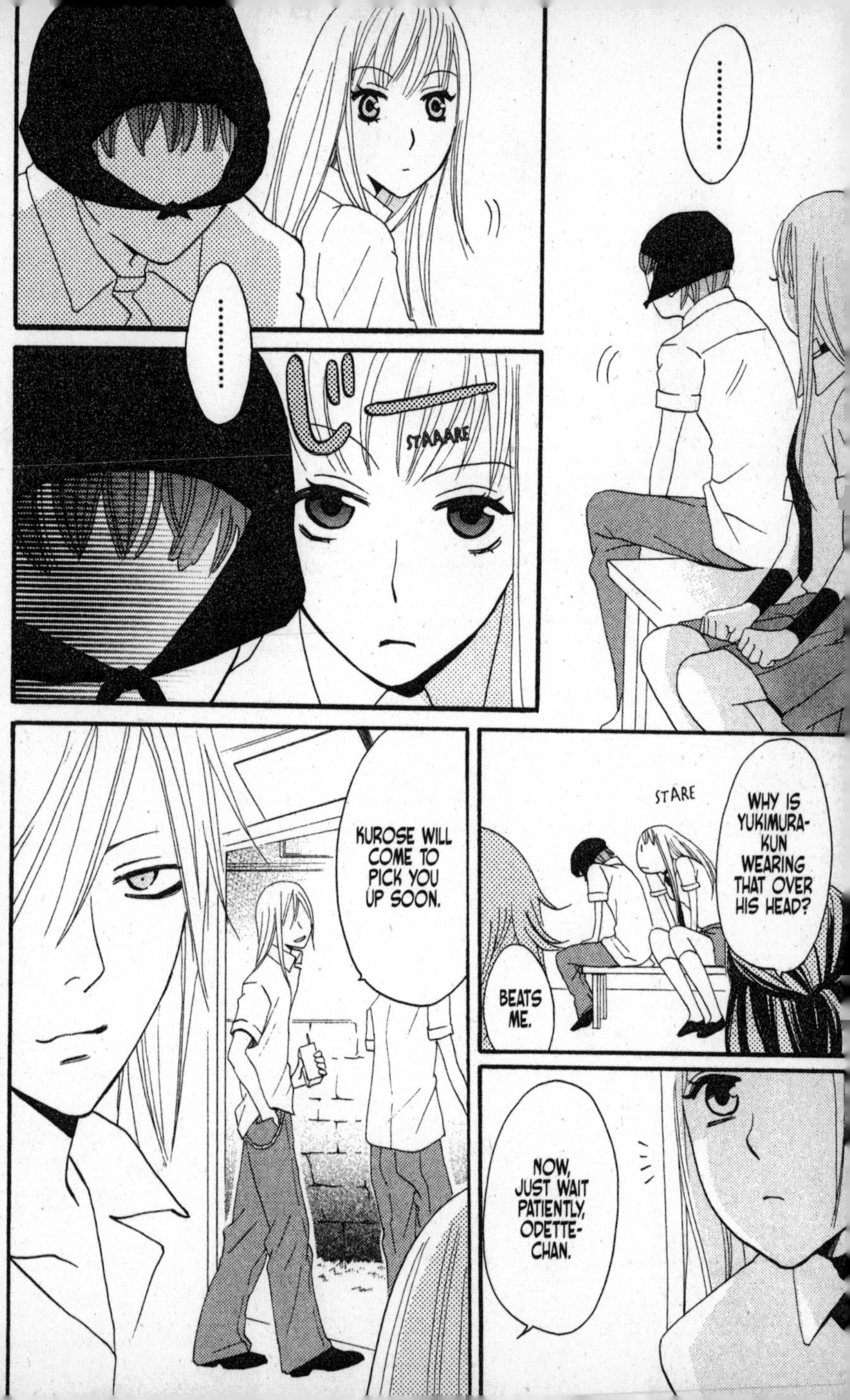
......
......
STAAARE
WHY IS YUKIMURA-KUN WEARING THAT OVER HIS HEAD?
STARE
BEATS ME.
NOW, JUST WAIT PATIENTLY, ODETTE-CHAN.
KUROSE WILL COME TO PICK YOU UP SOON.

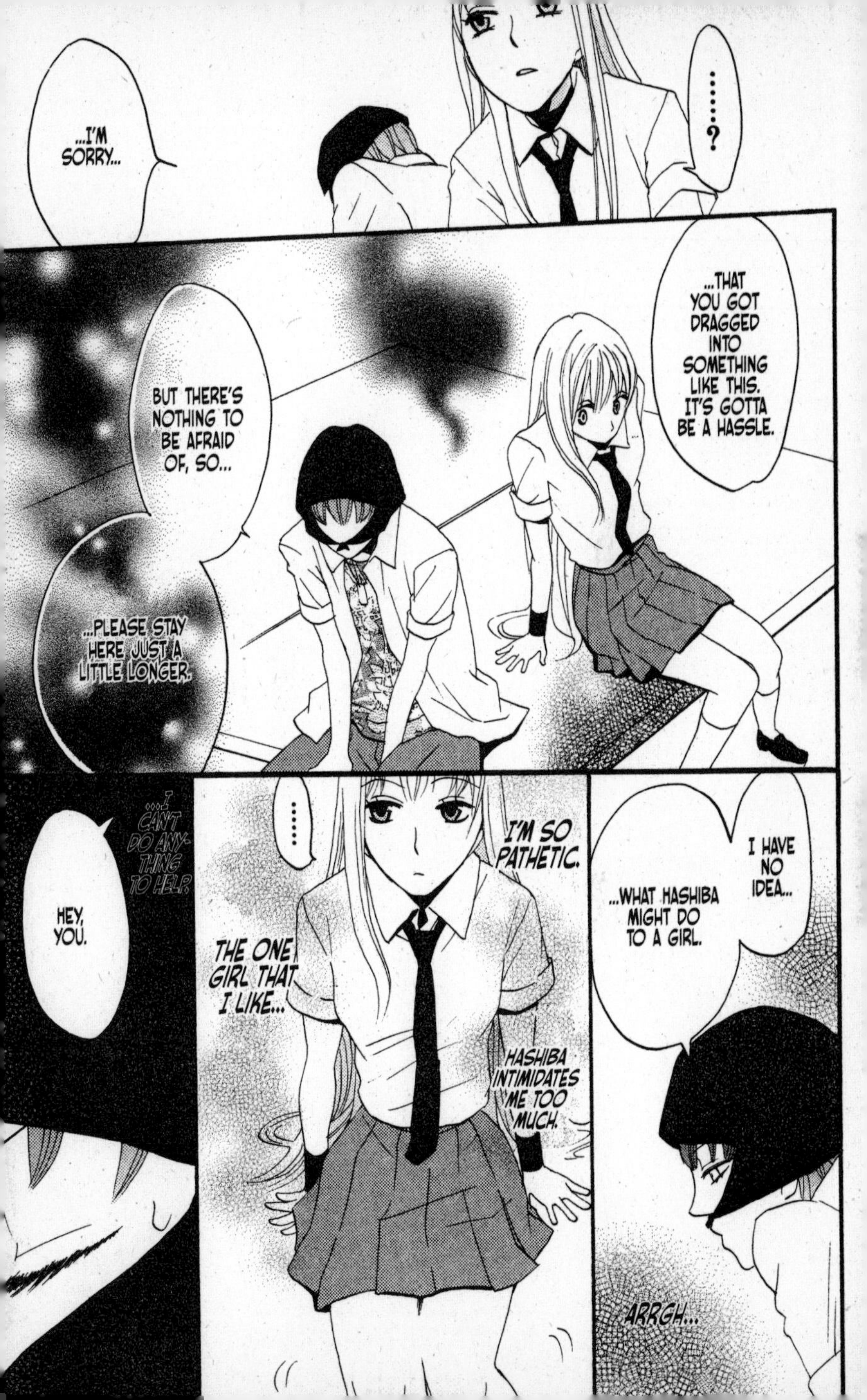
......?
...I'M SORRY...
...THAT YOU GOT DRAGGED INTO SOMETHING LIKE THIS. IT'S GOTTA BE A HASSLE.
BUT THERE'S NOTHING TO BE AFRAID OF, SO...
...PLEASE STAY HERE JUST A LITTLE LONGER.
I HAVE NO IDEA...
...WHAT HASHIBA MIGHT DO TO A GIRL.
ARRGH...
I'M SO PATHETIC.
......
THE ONE GIRL THAT I LIKE...
HASHIBA INTIMIDATES ME TOO MUCH.
...I CAN'T DO ANYTHING TO HELP.
HEY, YOU.

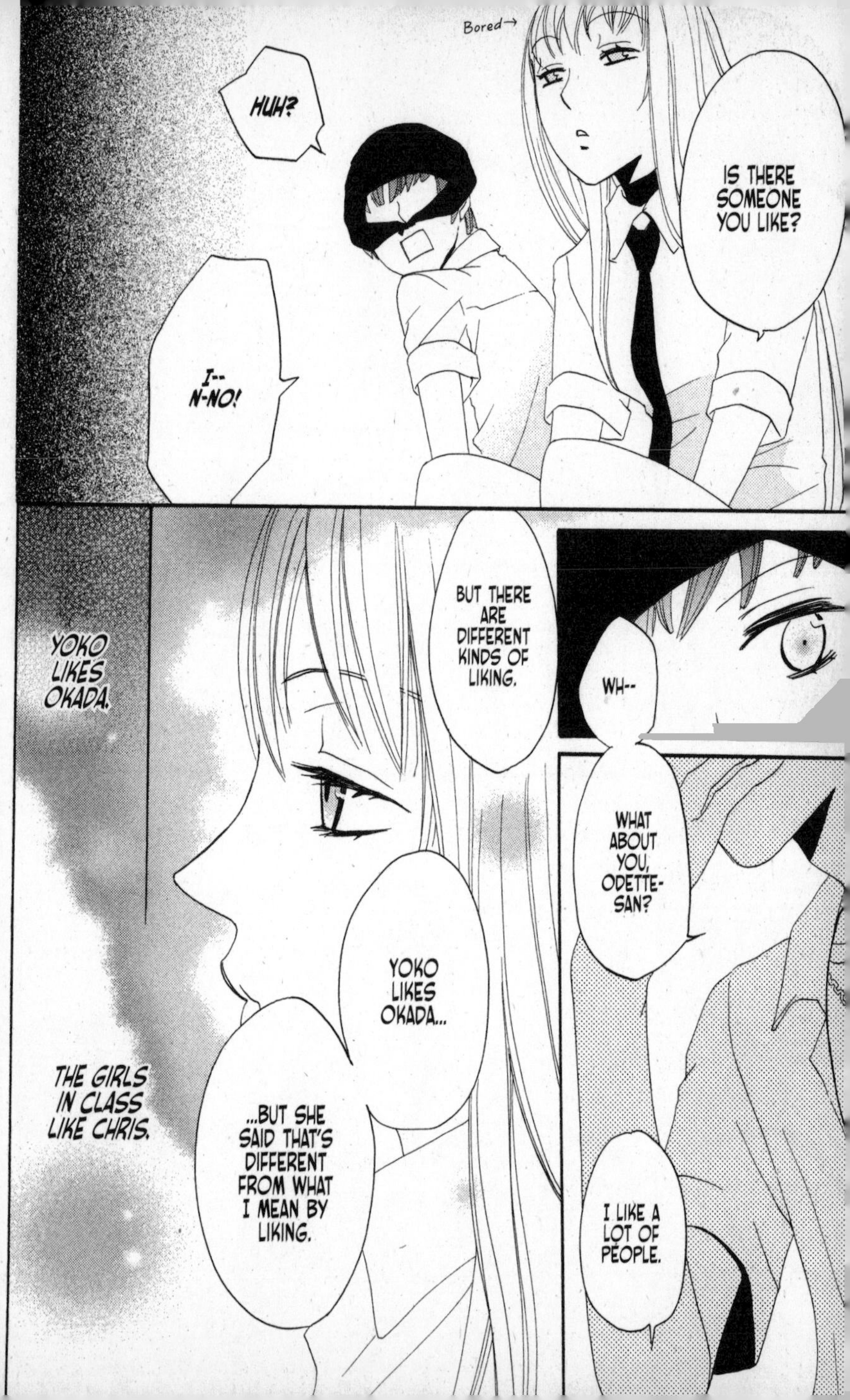
Bored→
IS THERE SOMEONE YOU LIKE?
HUH?
I-- N-NO!
WH--
WHAT ABOUT YOU, ODETTE-SAN?
I LIKE A LOT OF PEOPLE.
BUT THERE ARE DIFFERENT KINDS OF LIKING.
YOKO LIKES OKADA.
YOKO LIKES OKADA...
THE GIRLS IN CLASS LIKE CHRIS.
...BUT SHE SAID THAT'S DIFFERENT FROM WHAT I MEAN BY LIKING.

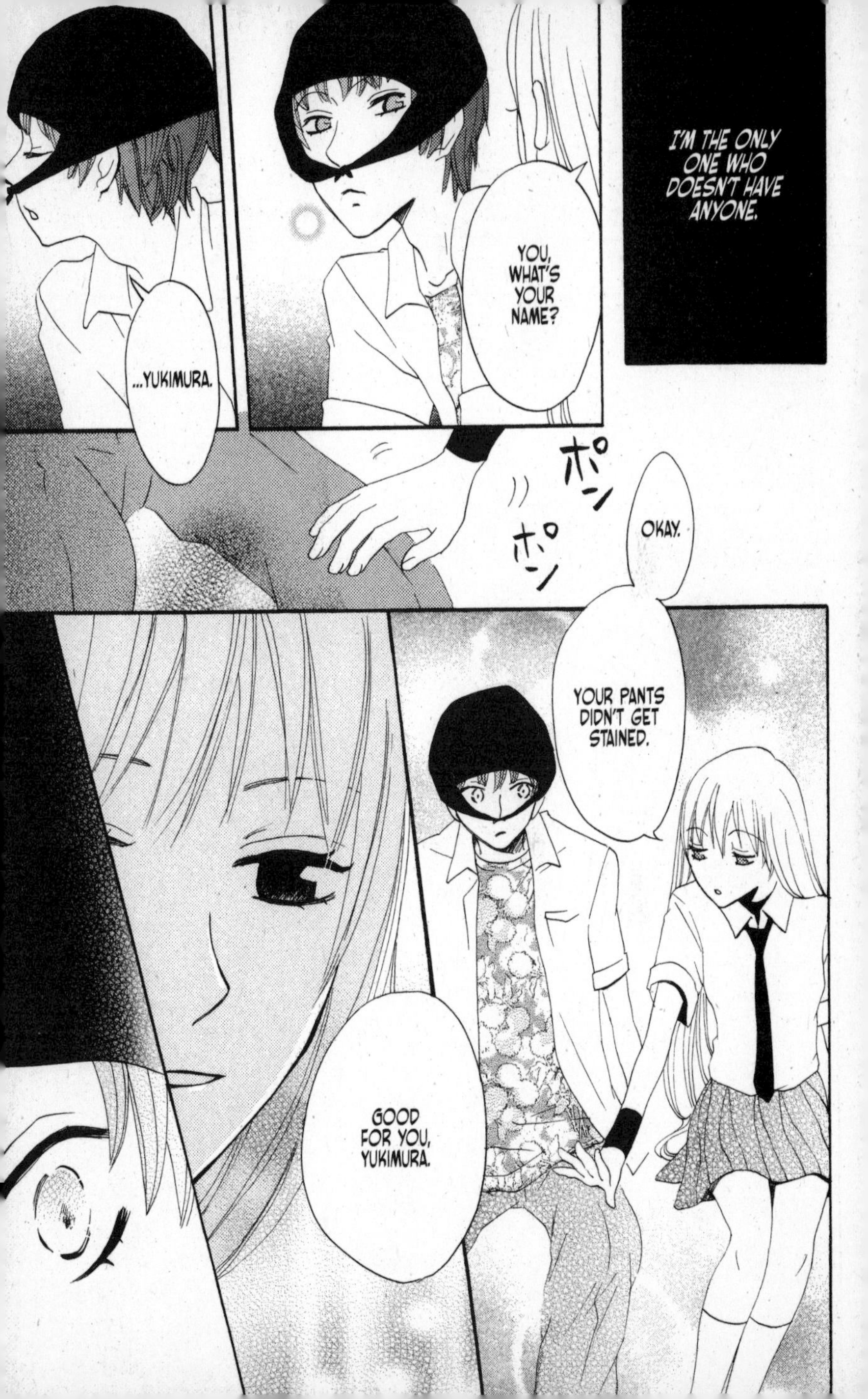
I'M THE ONLY ONE WHO DOESN'T HAVE ANYONE.
YOU, WHAT'S YOUR NAME?
...YUKIMURA.
OKAY.
ポン
ポン
YOUR PANTS DIDN'T GET STAINED.
GOOD FOR YOU, YUKIMURA.

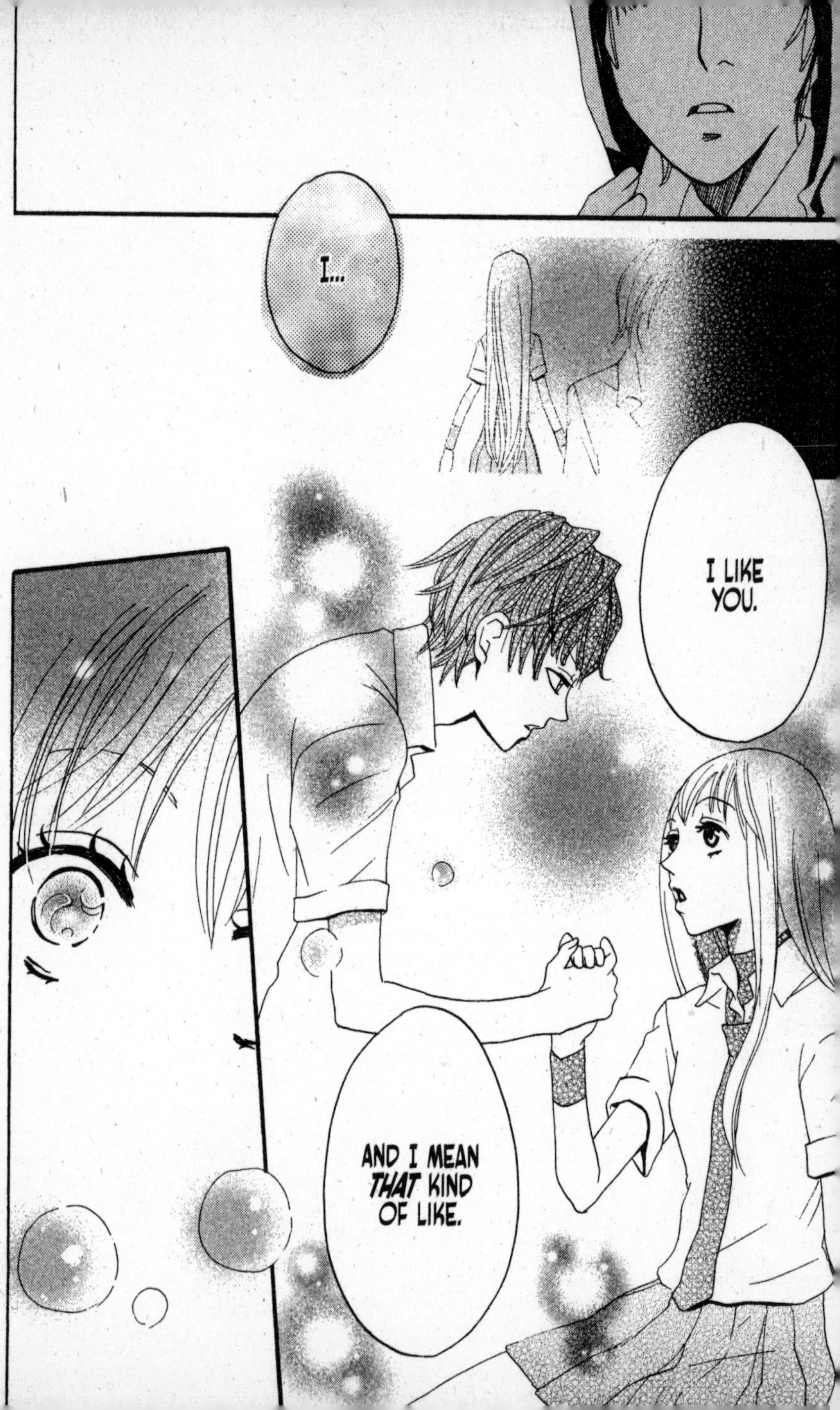
I...
I LIKE YOU.
AND I MEAN THAT KIND OF LIKE.

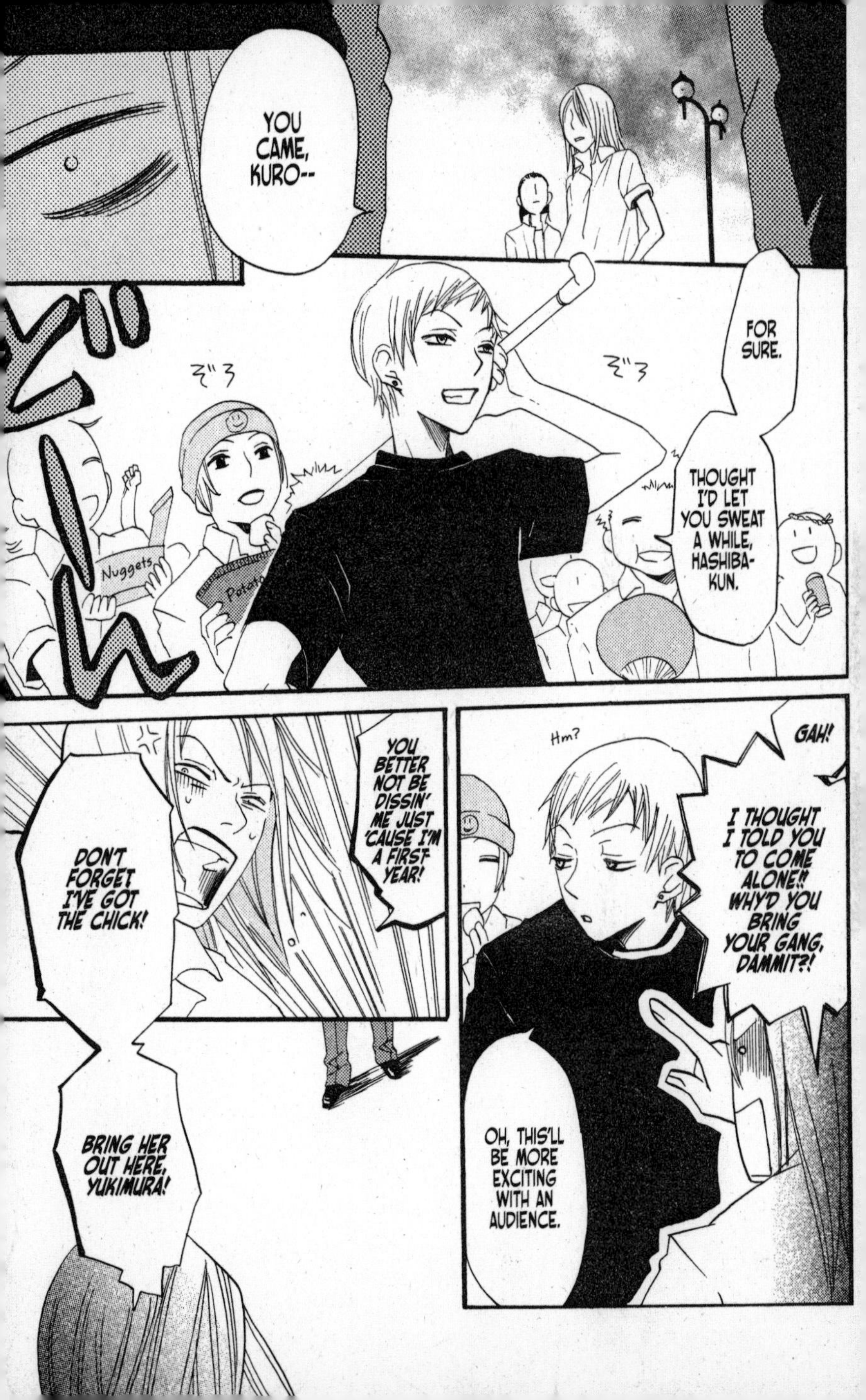
YOU CAME, KURO--
FOR SURE.
ぞろ
ぞろ
ドン
THOUGHT I'D LET YOU SWEAT A WHILE, HASHIBA-KUN.
Nuggets
GAH!
Hm?
I THOUGHT I TOLD YOU TO COME ALONE!! WHY'D YOU BRING YOUR GANG, DAMMIT?!
OH, THIS'LL BE MORE EXCITING WITH AN AUDIENCE.
YOU BETTER NOT BE DISSIN' ME JUST 'CAUSE I'M A FIRST-YEAR!
DON'T FORGET I'VE GOT THE CHICK!
BRING HER OUT HERE, YUKIMURA!

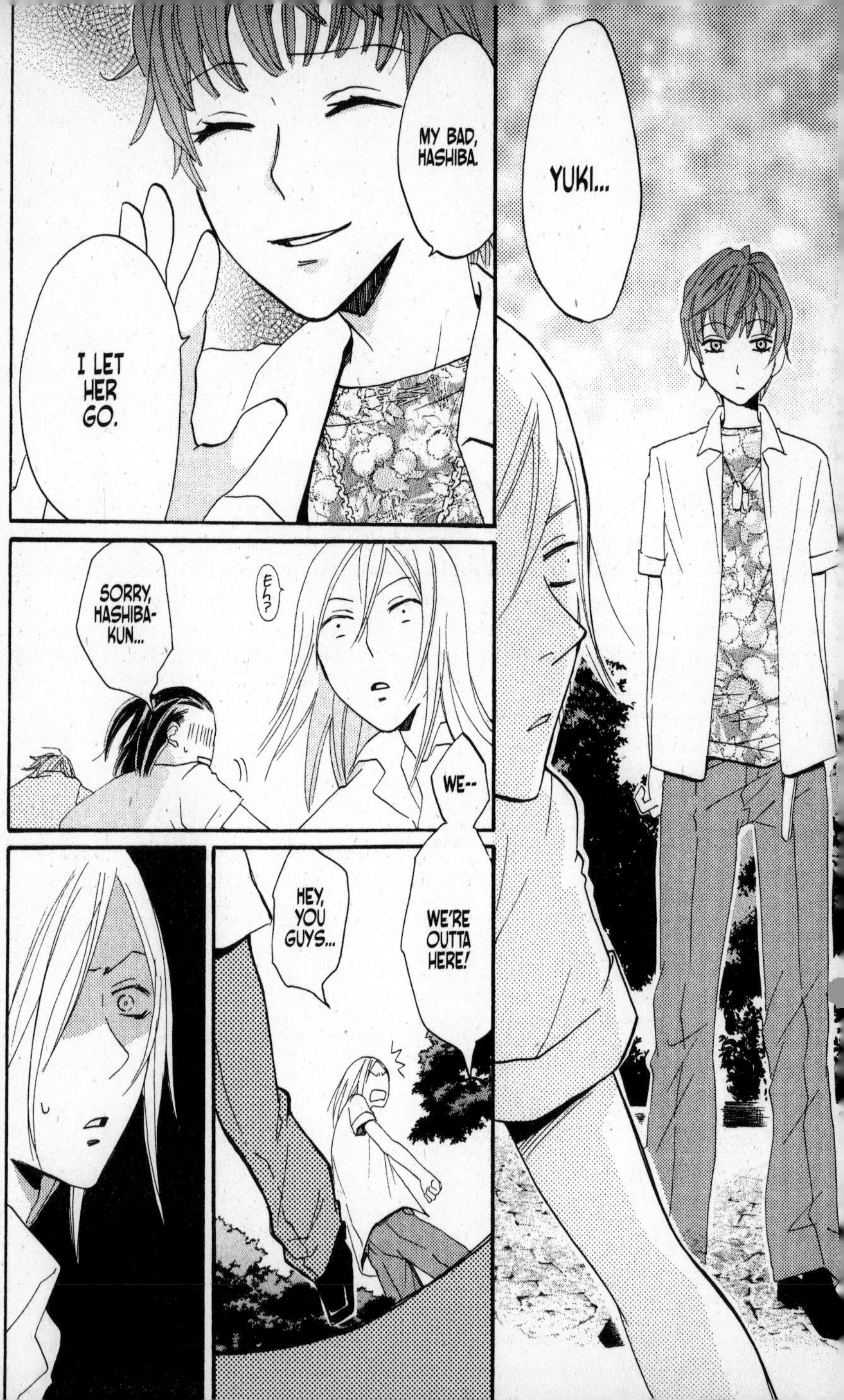
YUKI...
MY BAD, HASHIBA.
I LET HER GO.
SORRY, HASHIBA-KUN...
WE--
WE'RE OUTTA HERE!
HEY, YOU GUYS...

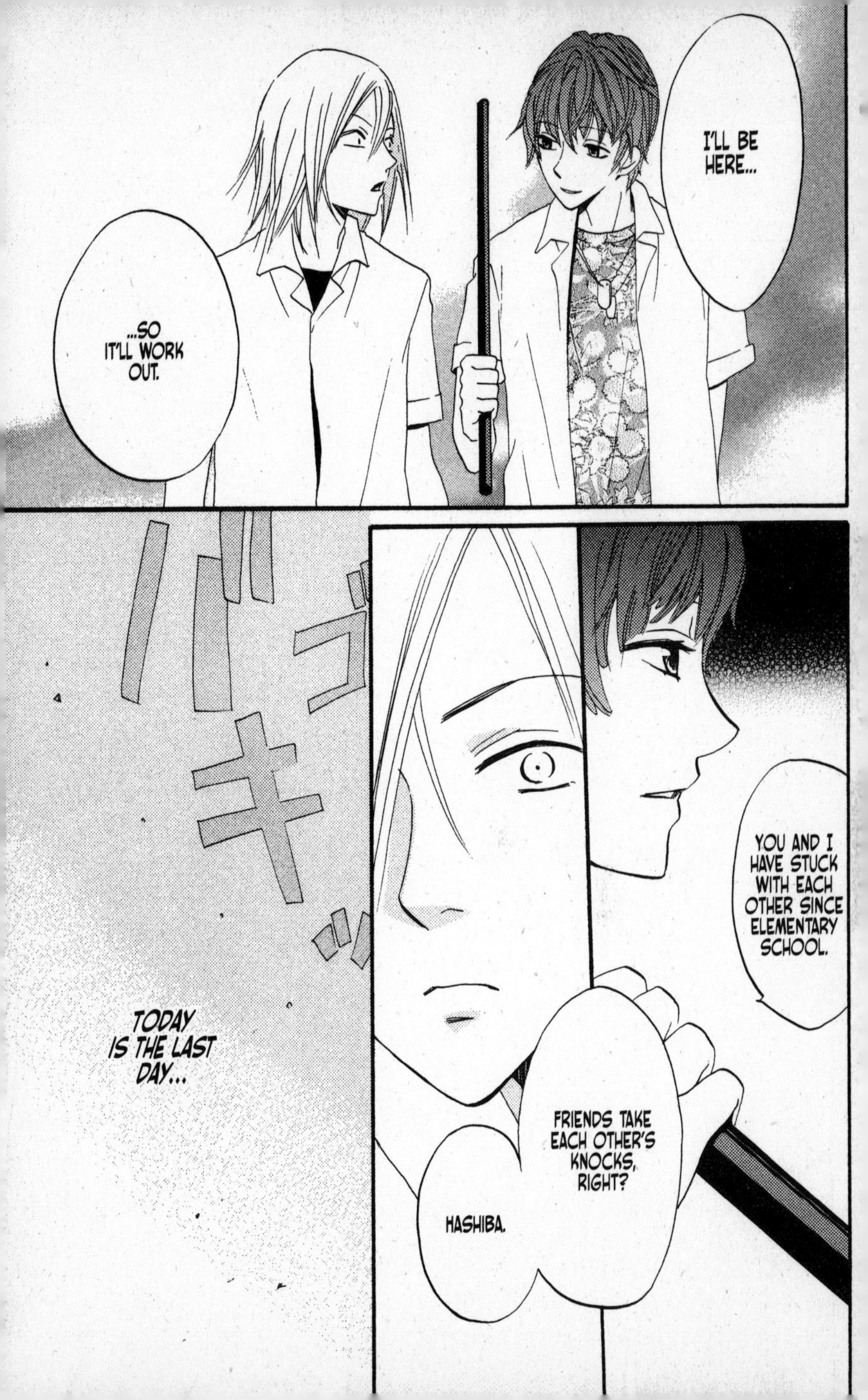
I'LL BE HERE...
...SO IT'LL WORK OUT.
YOU AND I HAVE STUCK WITH EACH OTHER SINCE ELEMENTARY SCHOOL.
FRIENDS TAKE EACH OTHER'S KNOCKS, RIGHT?
HASHIBA.
TODAY IS THE LAST DAY...

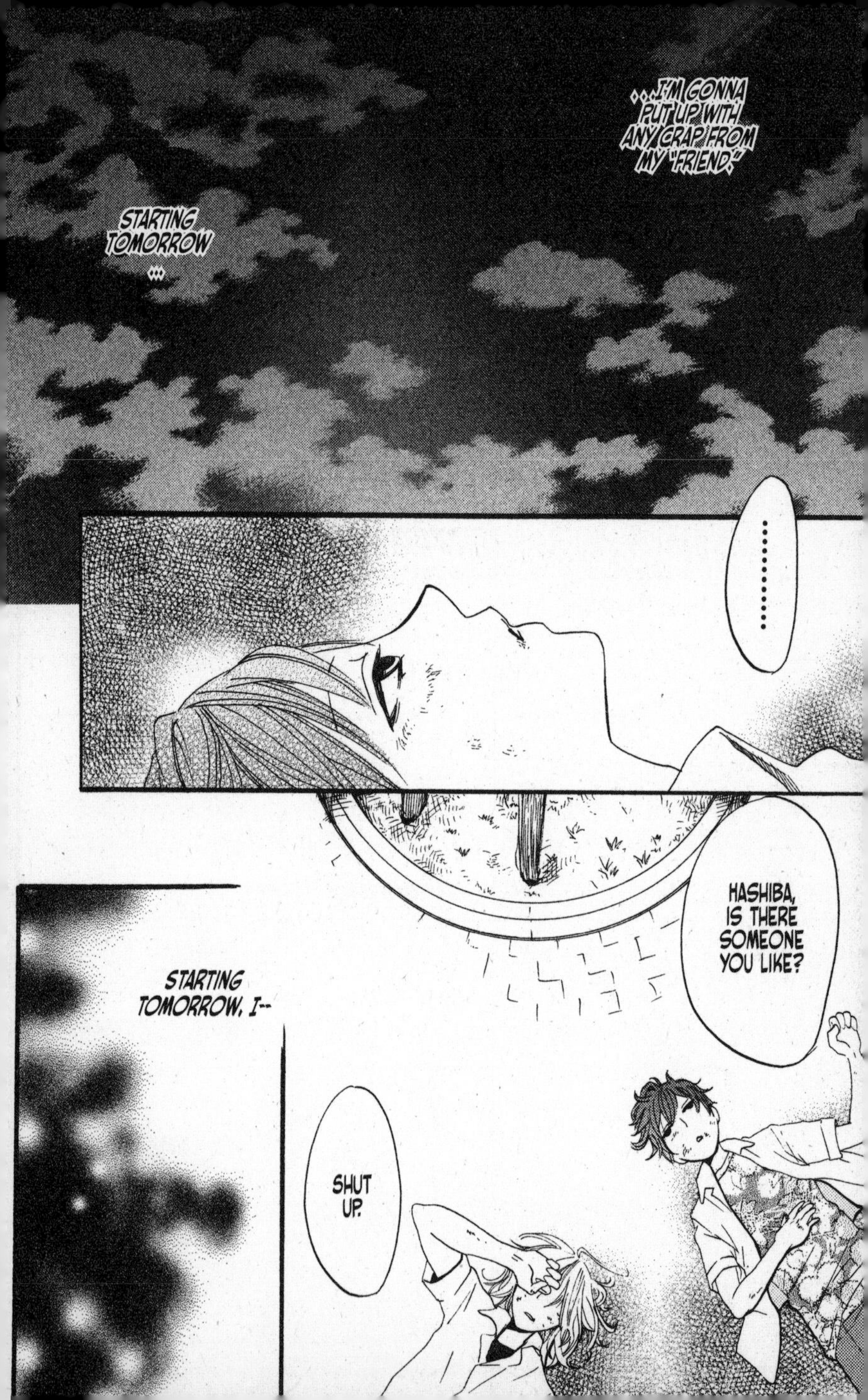
...I'M GONNA PUT UP WITH ANY CRAP FROM MY "FRIEND."
STARTING TOMORROW ...
......
HASHIBA, IS THERE SOMEONE YOU LIKE?
STARTING TOMORROW, I--
SHUT UP.

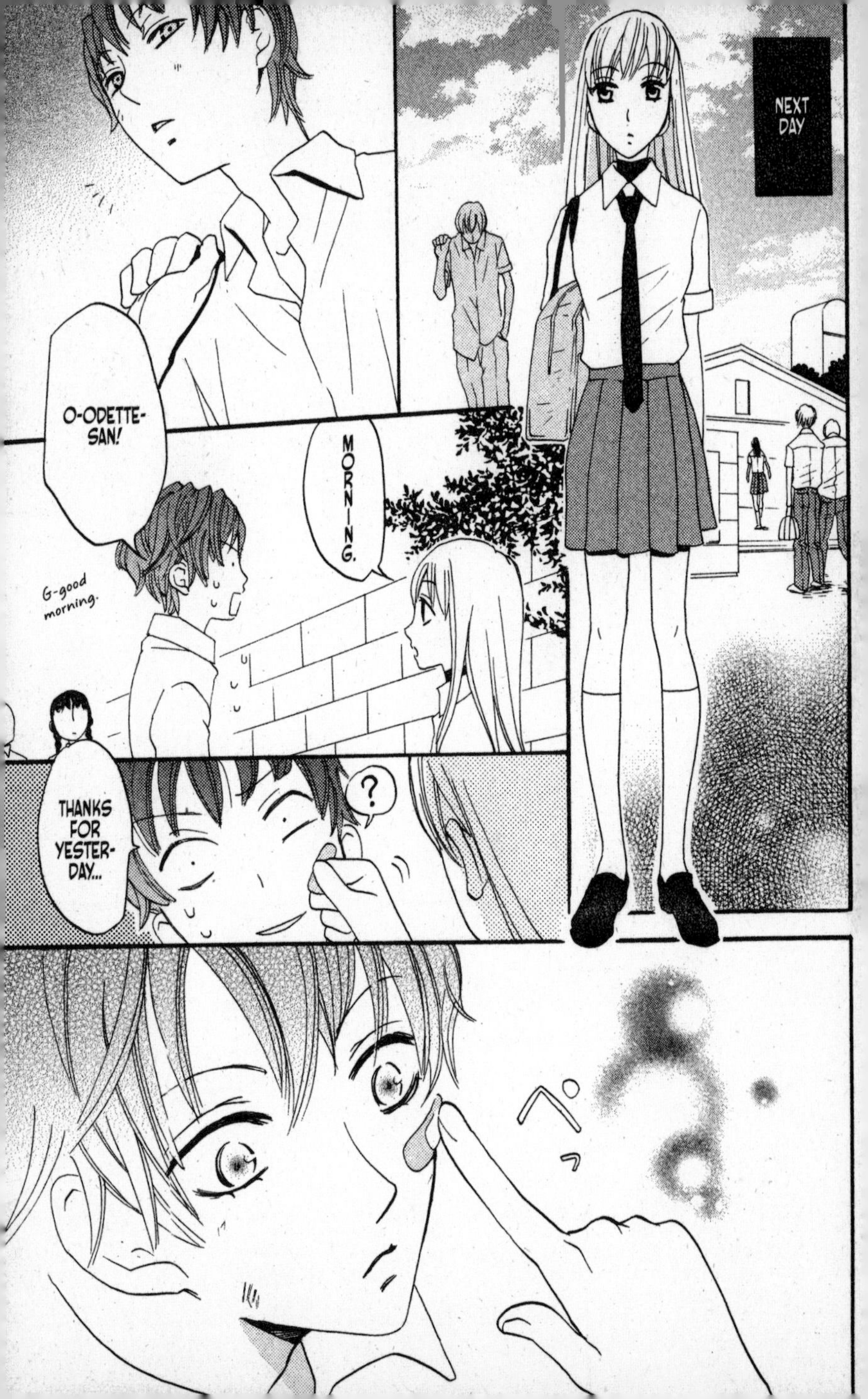
NEXT DAY
O-ODETTE-SAN!
MORNING.
G-good morning.
?
THANKS FOR YESTER-DAY...

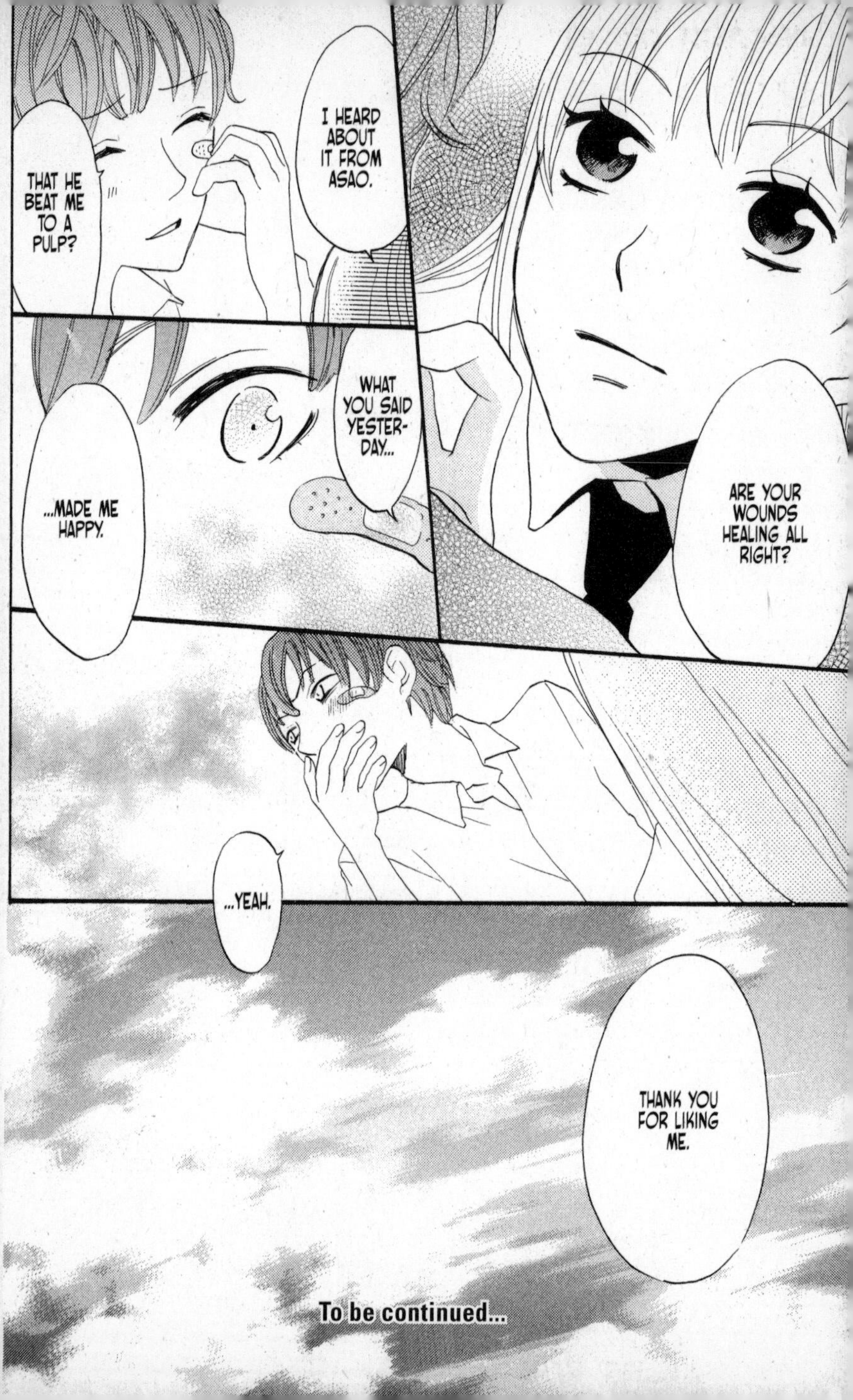
ARE YOUR WOUNDS HEALING ALL RIGHT?
I HEARD ABOUT IT FROM ASAO.
THAT HE BEAT ME TO A PULP?
WHAT YOU SAID YESTER-DAY...
...MADE ME HAPPY.
...YEAH.
THANK YOU FOR LIKING ME.
To be continued...

SPECIAL GUEST
Ryoko Fukuyama

Creator of Nosatsu Junkie

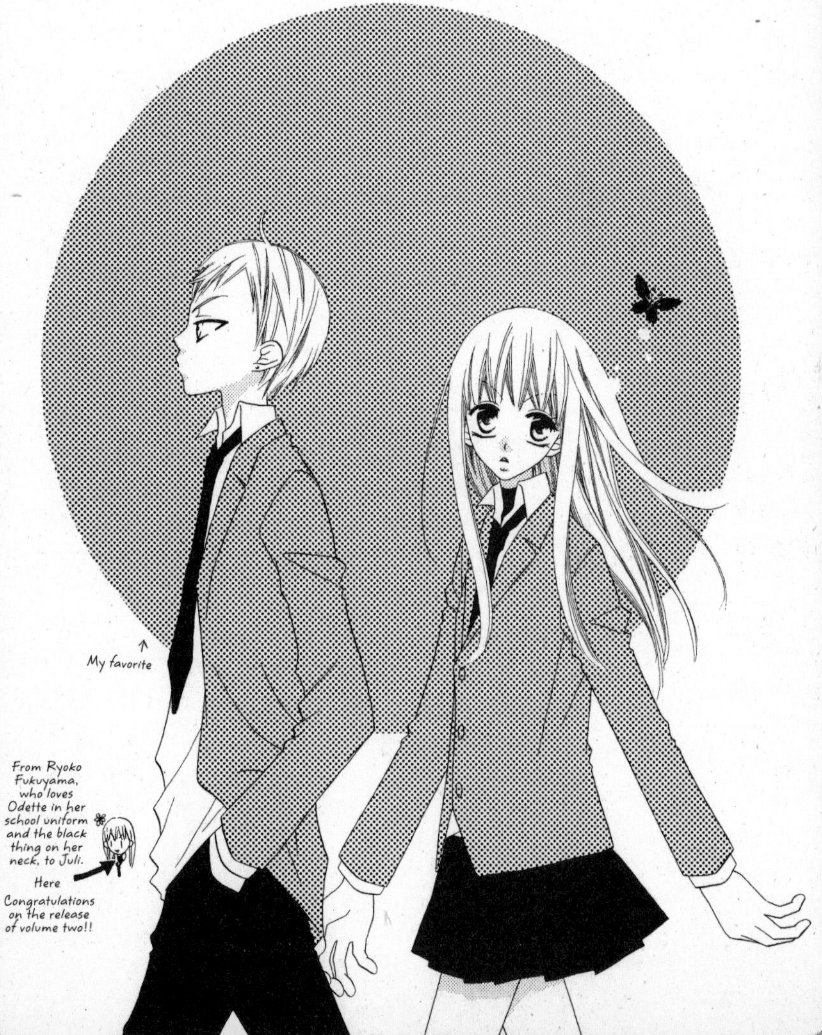
My favorite
From Ryoko Fukuyama, who loves Odette in her school uniform and the black thing on her neck, to Juli.
Here
Congratulations on the release of volume two!!

When I'm writing my manga I think of a lot of things to say, but when it comes time to fill a space like this, absolutely nothing comes out so I'm 30% less talkative.

Fukuyama-san, thank you for your lovely drawing! Both Odette and Asao are so cute that I could melt! (I'm so happy.) To my editor--I'm so sorry that I'm still causing trouble for you. Thank you so much. I wish you well!

And to this book's readers, thank you very much!! Let's meet again soon.✿

Julietta Suzuki

IN THE NEXT VOLUME OF...

KARAKURI ODETTE

カラクリ オデット

Yukimura confessed his feelings to Odette, but she's still struggling with the concept of "like" and romance. Not to mention she's struggling with the new auxiliary battery pack that she's forced to wear when her old one malfunctions. But she still finds time to rescue kitties, hang out with friends, make a few new ones, and even go to Pixy Land on a "double date" with Asao!

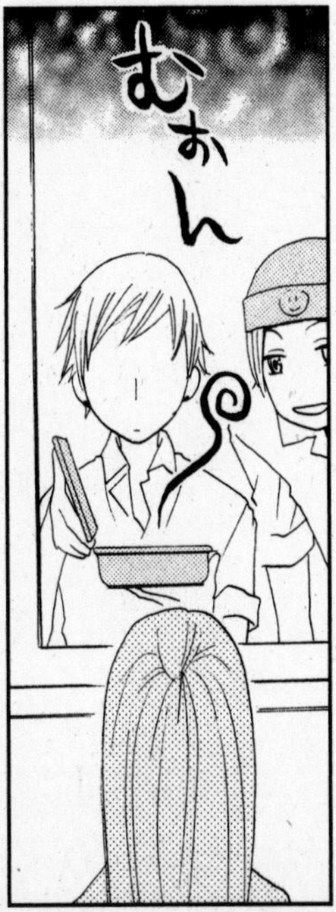
むぉん

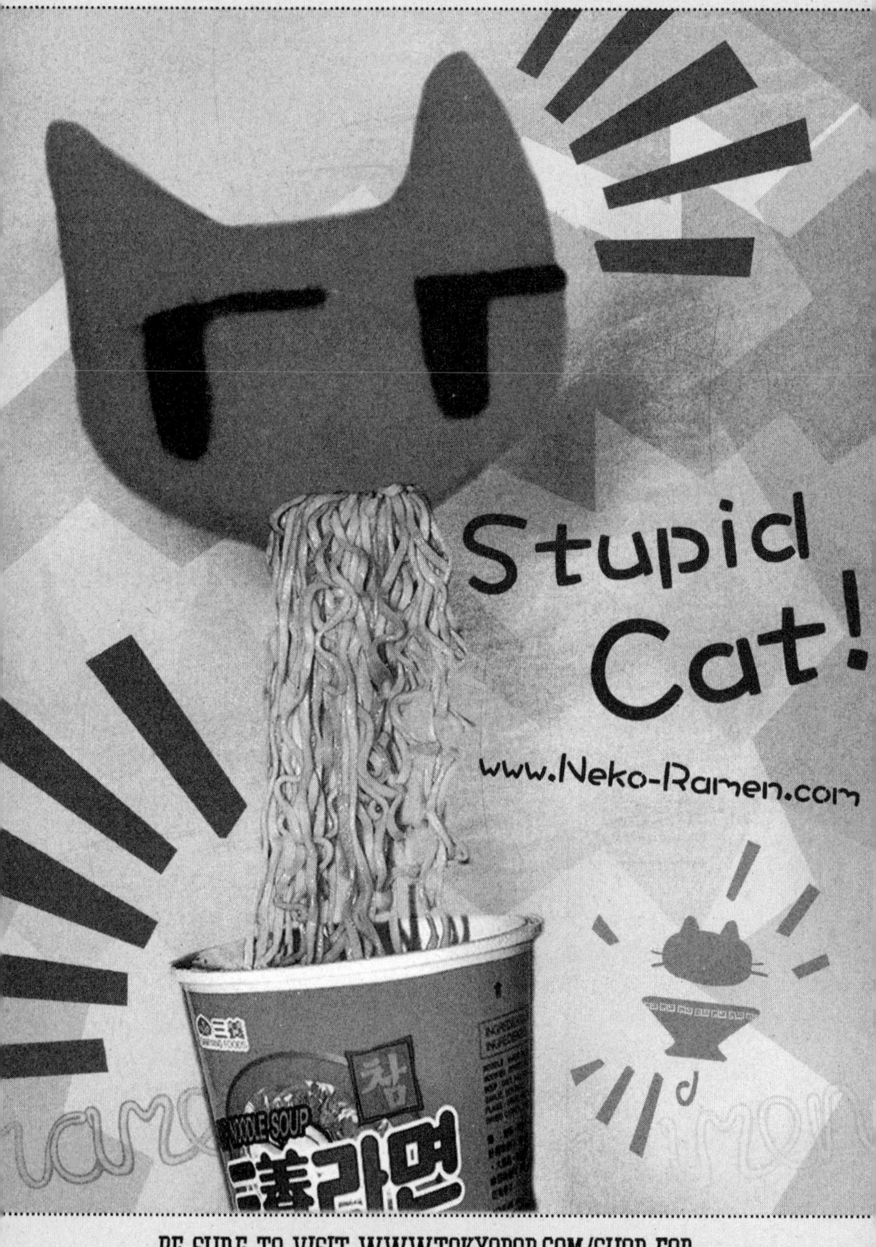
Stupid
Cat!
www.Neko-Ramen.com

The second epic trilogy continues!

Princess Ai: The Prism of Midnight Dawn

Ai fights to escape the clutches of her mysterious and malevolent captors, not knowing whether Kent, left behind on the Other Side, is even still alive. A frantic rescue mission commences, and in the end, even Ai's magical voice may not be enough to protect her from the trials of the Black Forest.

Dark secrets are revealed, and Ai must use all her strength and courage to face off against the new threat to Ai-Land. But will she ever see Kent again...?

"A very intriguing read that will satisfy old fans and create new fans, too."
— *Bookloons*

EVERY TEXT COULD BE YOUR LAST

FUTURE DIARY™

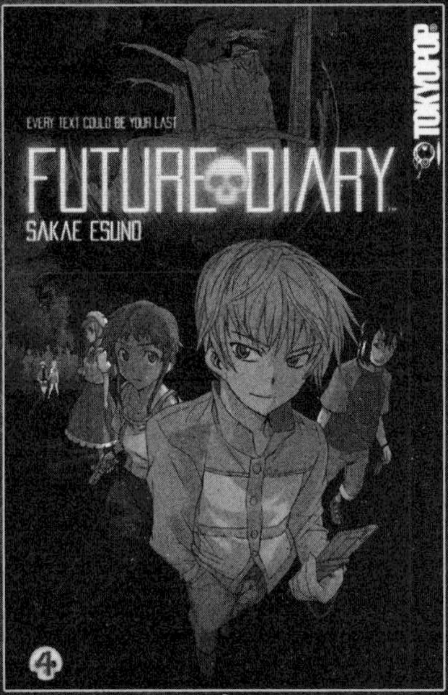
TOKYOPOP
EVERY TEXT COULD BE YOUR LAST
FUTURE DIARY
SAKAE ESUNO
4

Yukiteru is starting out fresh at a new school... or so he thought... Right along with his new classmates, Yukiteru finds himself ambushed by the mysterious Diary Holder Tenth!

"ESUNO'S ART IS SPRIGHTLY, SWEET AND DECEPTIVELY INNOCENT."
—*Publishers Weekly*

BE SURE TO VISIT WWW.TOKYOPOP.COM/SHOP FOR EVERYTHING YOU COULD EVER WANT!

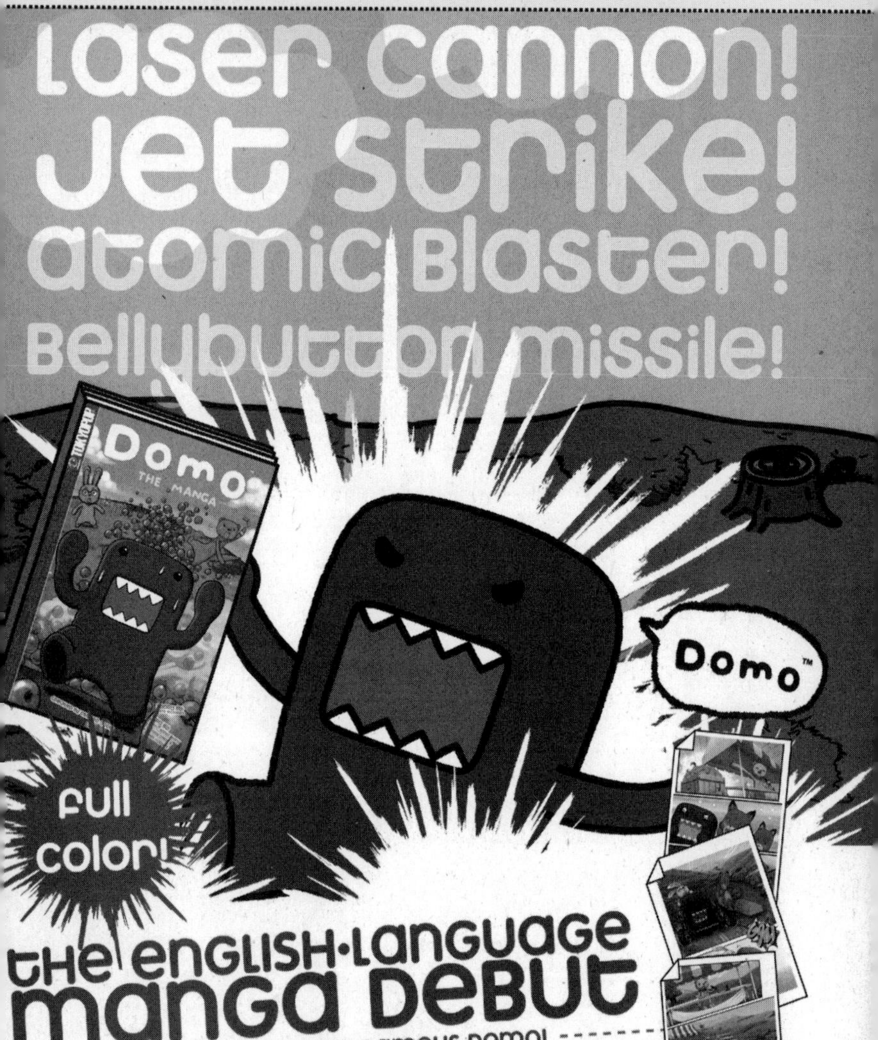
Laser Cannon!
Jet Strike!
atomic Blaster!
Bellybutton missile!
Domo THE MANGA
Domo™
full color!
THE ENGLISH-LANGUAGE MANGA DEBUT
OF THE WORLD-FAMOUS DOMO!
INVADING STORES EVERYWHERE!
PREVIEWS, CONTESTS, AND MORE AT WWW.TOKYOPOP.COM/DOMO_MANGA
DOMO © NHK-TYO 1998-2009. DOMO ANIMATION © DOMO PRODUCTION COMMITTEE. ALL RIGHTS RESERVED. WWW.DOMONATION.COM